Springer Studies in Alternative Economics

This book series offers an outlet for cutting-edge research in alternative, heterodox and pluralist economics. It features scholarly studies on various schools of thought beyond the neo-classical orthodoxy, including Austrian, Post Keynesian, Sraffian, Marxian, Georgist, Institutional-evolutionary, as well as feminist, radical, social, green, and ecological economics. It aims to promote pluralism of economic ideas, methodological approaches, and topics.

The series also welcomes works that seek to develop alternative visions of the economy, economic structures and new approaches that aim to serve society, for example by embedding the economy within the ecosystem, or to enrich economic thought by advancing diversity, gender, race, and social equality. All titles in this series are peer-reviewed.

Fritz Helmedag

Production of Commodities by Means of Labour

Rehabilitation of the Law of Value

Springer

Fritz Helmedag
Chemnitz University of Technology
Chemnitz, Germany

ISSN 2731-5908 ISSN 2731-5916 (electronic)
Springer Studies in Alternative Economics
ISBN 978-3-032-01456-6 ISBN 978-3-032-01457-3 (eBook)
https://doi.org/10.1007/978-3-032-01457-3

Previously published by Metropolis-Verlag

This Springer imprint is published by the registered company Springer Nature Switzerland AG
The registered company address is: Gewerbestrasse 11, 6330 Cham, Switzerland

Ridendo dicere verum.
Horace

Here is that great principle which is the corner-stone of all tenable Political Economy; which granted or denied, all Political Economy stands or falls. Grant me this one principle, with a few square feet on the sea-shore to draw my diagrams upon, and I will undertake to deduce every other truth in the science.

Thomas De Quincey

Preface

The first German edition of this book appeared in 1992. The present English version is a translation by the author of the fourth German edition published in 2024.[1] As alluded to by the subtitle, this monograph does not constitute another "refutation" of the labour theory of value. On the contrary, it will be demonstrated that *only* the distribution of profits according to sectoral labour payments establishes the equilibrium of "free" competition. This statement is likely to provoke a derisory reaction from individuals well-versed in contemporary economic theory; for some time now, even various avowed Marxists have admitted the failure of the labour theory of value as a theory of production prices.

Sraffa's book "Production of Commodities by Means of Commodities" (1960) provides the foundation for this verdict. If a surplus exists, prices determined in this system deviate from labour values. Sraffa's theory, though, is based on the hypothesis that profits are distributed as a markup on material costs. Still, whether this calculation meets the requirements of a competitive capitalist economy based on the societal division of labour has never been examined. According to the test carried out in the following, only the "value calculation" performs well. Since the problem is purely logical, i.e., it has neither an empirical nor a normative aspect, there is reason to hope that the "value question" accompanying economics from its very beginnings will finally find a convincing answer.

Nonetheless, it is probably unavoidable that the position advocated here will arouse emotions. The labour theory of value has long been regarded as an analytical underpinning for enforcing workers' interests in the class struggle. However, from the line of argument in this study, it would be more evident that the labour theory of value is a doctrine of *meritocracy*. Yet, such interpretations are irrelevant to the subsequent exposition. Primarily, sound reasoning is required to assess

[1] If German-language quotations have been rendered into English, this is indicated by adding [F. H.] in or at the end of the relevant footnote. Other translations or the respective dates of the first publication are enclosed in square brackets without initials.

competing concepts that diverge in their results within the same analytical framework. Therefore, the investigation employs straight thinking instead of deploying unproven hypotheses.

The first part of the book focuses on epistemology. If truth or (the degree of) verification indicates the quality of scientific statements, the respective considerations are the weakest deliberations in the present enquiry. Neither the "correct" subject matter nor the "adequate" method of economics can be definitively determined.

However, the standard method of outlining the object of knowledge by referencing a *formal* principle is futile. Substantiation of the typical economic action is necessary: the recommended criterion of economic exchange offers a firmer foothold. In this context, money has a high status. That is why its development and nature are discussed.

The content specification has both methodological and strategic consequences for research: the focus shifts to uncovering the structure of a society based on the division of labour and integrated through economic exchange, a topic that the classics dealt with under the heading "theory of value". The aim is to determine the *fundamental law* of modern economics.

The second part is about the history of economic thought. Piero Sraffa is regarded as one of the most astute thinkers in economics. His influence contributed to the fact that Wittgenstein, *the* logician of the twentieth century, eventually abandoned the position he had taken in his "Tractatus". Accordingly, the constructional error in Sraffa's system is not to be found in the higher storeys but in the foundations. The first pages of his "epoch-making" book contain the classical maxims of production price formation. From this perspective, exploring when and why the classics broke away from their original concept, the labour theory of value, is worthwhile.

It emerges that there was no reason for the change of course to the seemingly more effortless terrain of production price theory. In particular, Ricardo's wheat economy and the value-price transformation pioneered by v. Bortkiewicz are subjected to stricter scrutiny than usual. In both cases, the standard interpretations of their models cannot be confirmed. Even in the single-sector wheat economy, the profit rate by no means acquires the importance commonly attributed to it. The production prices conceptualised by v. Bortkiewicz also exhibit properties contradicting their derivation premises. In this arena, labour values demonstrate their explanatory power for the first time.

The third part is principally devoted to analysis. Initially, an examination of Sraffa's system is conducted, emphasising its "peculiarities". As a result, Sraffa's approach already founders in the case of a single production, which is regularly considered unproblematic. Subsequently, it becomes apparent that Sraffa's theory of joint production is also doomed to failure. This approach has caused a sensation because it was supposed to deal the final blow to the labour theory of value: allegedly, under such conditions, surplus value may become *negative* despite positive prices and a positive profit rate – a false doctrine since the labour theory of value is generally valid.

The rehabilitation of the labour theory of value has far-reaching effects on micro- and macroeconomics. It also results in divergent economic policy measures that contradict widely held beliefs. Against this backdrop, the dictum of Thomas De Quincey in the preliminaries of this investigation has proved to be true: a verified labour theory of value gives a fresh impetus to a political economy aiming to improve the living conditions of many people. In this regard, adhering to the second motto, in which Horace advocates performing the enlightenment mission with a cheerful countenance, may contribute to this undertaking.

May 2025

F. H.
Chemnitz University of Technology
Chemnitz, Germany

Contents

List of Symbols

Scalars

A	Private autonomous demand, including exports
a_{0j}, b_{0j}	Direct labour to produce one unit of product j using technique A or B
a_{ij}, b_{ij}	Input quantity of a product i per unit of product j using technique A or B
B	Quantity of the basic product or quantity of the wage commodity
C	Macroeconomic constant capital, commodity or cloth unit
ΔC	Cloth increment
c	Microeconomic constant capital or domestic consumption rate
c_i	Constant capital in sector i
D	Amount of public debt
ΔD	Change of government's debt
e	Profit factor $(1 + \varepsilon)$ within the labour value calculation
$f(N)$	Quantity of produced wheat (X) depending on labour input (N)
f_i	v/c_i
f_N	Marginal yield of labour in the wheat sector
f_{NN}, f_{NNN}	Higher derivatives of $f(N)$
GA	Total autonomous demand, including the change of government's debt ΔD
GPD	Gross domestic product
g	Growth rate
g_D	Growth rate of government debt
h	Real unit labour costs
h^*	Optimal real unit labour costs for $r^* = 1$
I	Iron
i	Integer, non-negative index or interest rate
j	Integer, non-negative index
K	Circulating Capital (wheat economy)
k	Capital intensity
L	Wage bill

L_S	English plus Portuguese wage bill (cloth units) for given total profits (wine units)
L_{EA}	English wage bill (cloth units) in autarky
L_{ES}	English wage bill (cloth units) for given total profits (wine units)
L_{PA}	Portuguese wage bill (cloth units) in autarky
L_{PS}	Portuguese wage bill (cloth units) for given total profits (wine units)
l_i	Quantity of labour to produce one unit of commodity i or Sraffa-Steedman labour value of one unit of commodity i
M	Money or quantity of money
ΔM	Change in the quantity of money
M'	$M + \Delta M$
m	Number of activities
N	Labour input, volume of work or employment
$N*$	Employment which maximises the sum of wages and profits
N_B	Employment in the basic sector
N_P	Profit-maximising employment
N_S	Employment in the steady state ($f_N = w_S$) or total employment for given profits
N_X	Employment in the luxury sector
N_{CE}	Labour input per cloth unit in England
N_{CP}	Labour input per cloth unit in Portugal
N_{EA}	Employment in England in autarky
N_{ES}	Employment in England for given total profits
N_{WE}	Labour input per wine unit in England
N_{WP}	Labour input per wine unit in Portugal
N_{PA}	Employment in Portugal in autarky
N_{PS}	Employment in Portugal for given total profits
n	Number of commodities or processes
P	Profit or pig(s)
P_B	Profit in the basic sector in wage goods
P_W	Profit at the maximum wage bill
P_X	Profit in the luxury sector in wage goods
P_i	Profit of sector i
$P^A_{1\max}$	Maximum profit of sector 1 with technique A
$P^B_{1\max}$	Maximum profit of sector 1 with technique B
p	Iron price in wheat units
p'	Profit rate (Marx)
p_B	Price of the basic commodity
p_X	Price of the luxury commodity
p_I, p_S, p_W	Price of iron, pig or wheat
p_i	Price of commodity i
p_{CW}	Cloth price in wine units
$p_{CW}*$	Performance-based price of cloth in wine units
$p_{CW\max}$	Maximum cloth price in wine units
$p_{CW\min}$	Minimum cloth price in wine units

p_{CWS}	Cloth price in wine units for stationary profits
Q	The sum of wages and profits or the macroeconomic organic composition of capital (C/V)
q	Microeconomic organic composition of capital (c/v)
q_j^A, q_j^B	Gross production of sector j with technique A or B
R	Rent or maximum profit rate
r	Profit rate (Sraffa)
$r*$	Profit-maximising profit rate of 100 %, determined in the primary or basic sector
r_P	Profit rate at the profit maximum
r_{maxA}	Maximum profit rate with technique A
r_{maxB}	Maximum profit rate with technique B
$r_{\max}^I$	Maximum profit rate of iron production
S	Macroeconomic surplus value
s	Microeconomic surplus value
s'	Rate of surplus value
T^A, T^B, T^C	Technique A, B or C
TP	Total profit
t	Tax rate
t_i	Production time of commodity i
t_{0j}	Direct labour in activity j
t_{SF}	Tax rate for self-financing public loans
u	Profit factor $(1 + r)$
V	Macroeconomic variable capital
v	Microeconomic variable capital
v_B	Labour value of the basic commodity
v_i	Variable capital in sector i
v_X	Labour value of the luxury good
w	Wage rate
$w^{(j)}$	Wage rate, measured in units of product j
w_E	English real wage in cloth
w_P	Portuguese real wage in cloth
$w_{\max}$	Maximum wage rate
$w_{\min}$	Minimum wage rate
$w_{\max B}$	Maximum wage rate with technique B
w_{nom}	Nominal wage rate
w_S	Subsistence wage
w_W	Wage rate which maximises the wage bill
W	Labour value of a commodity, quantity of wheat or wine
ΔW	Change of the quantitiy of Wine
W_B	Wage bill in the basic sector
W_X	Wage bill in the luxury sector
X	Wheat output or quantity of the luxury commodity
x	Price/value ratio in department I
y	Price/value ratio in department II

y_1	Net output of commodity 1 per period
z	Price-value ratio in department III or the Portuguese share of the surplus product
z^*	Portugal's fair share of surplus product
α	Expansion coefficient in the v. Neumann model
β	Interest factor in the v. Neumann model
γ	Export ratio of the additional cloth production
ε	Profit rate in the context of value calculation
λ	Eigenvalue of a matrix
$\lambda_{\max}$	Maximum eigenvalue of a matrix
Π	Price of a commodity unit (Marx)
π_i	Productivity index of labour in sector i
ρ	Profit rate (Bortkiewicz)
σ	Profit factor $(1 + \rho)$
ω	Export ratio of the additional wine production

Vectors and Matrices

$\mathbf{a}_0$	Row vector with the elements a_{0j} indicating the direct labour input per unit of a commodity j
$\mathbf{A}$	Coefficient matrix or direct requirements matrix with the elements a_{ij} indicating the input quantity of commodity i per unit of commodity j; $i, j = 1, 2, \ldots n$
$\mathbf{B}$	Output matrix in case of joint production
$\mathbf{d}$	Column vector of the real wage
$\mathbf{e}$	Summation vector whose elements are all ones
$\mathbf{e}_j$	Unit vector whose j-th element is one and the other elements are zeros
$\mathbf{H}$	Pasinetti-matrix $\mathbf{AL}$ containing all inputs to manufacture the means of production
$\mathbf{L}$	Total requirements matrix or Leontief-inverse $[\mathbf{I} - \mathbf{A}]^{-1}$
$\mathbf{l}$	Row vector of the Sraffa-Steedman values
$\mathbf{I}$	Unit matrix
$\mathbf{M}$	Direct requirements matrix enriched by the workers' consumption $\mathbf{A} + \mathbf{da}_0$
$\mathbf{p}$	Row vector of prices
$\mathbf{p}^*$	Row vector of labour commanded prices, i.e. the wage rate is the numéraire
$\mathbf{q}$	Column vector of gross production
$\mathbf{S}$	Sraffa-inverse $[\mathbf{I} - (1 + r)\ \mathbf{A}]^{-1}$
$\mathbf{t}_0$	Row vector of the labour inputs adjusted to the technology matrix
$\mathbf{T}$	$n \times m$ technology matrix with m available activities for the production of n commodities; $m \geqq n$

v Row vector of labour values

y Column vector of net output

$\mathbf{y}_1$ Column vector with zero elements apart from y_1, indicating the net output of the subsystem of commodity 1 per period

Part I
Value Theory as Basic Research in Economics

Chapter 1
The Economy and Economic Action: A Critical Appraisal

Epistemological reflections in economics are subject to business cycles: after a depression phase, attempts increase to gain guidance by returning to the basics. Tellingly, these efforts have mainly concentrated on *methodological* problems: how can reliable insights be extracted from a given object of knowledge called "the economy"? However, the preceding question about the essential characteristics of economics as a subfield of social sciences has received far less attention, let alone a convincing answer.

No logical or factual truth standards can be applied to defining a discipline's subject. It is a determination that must prove its *usefulness*. In our case, this is demonstrated above all by the strategic research perspective opened by a suitable concept of economics. In economic theory, such considerations do not constitute the beginning of scientific work but rather mark a (provisional) end.

For this reason, a dilemma regularly arises when undergraduates are to be familiarised with the philosophy of science: novices lack the material that can be organised and assessed using epistemological procedures. Therefore, the explanations sometimes encounter incomprehension, and students occasionally question the subject matter's relevance. In addition, principles to evaluate the progress of knowledge are rarely adduced during further study. In the current situation, this need not necessarily be a cause for complaint: certainly, here and there, it would be rather demotivating to put the lessons acquired with much diligence to strict epistemological tests.

The situation compares to the concepts of economics and economic activities. Initially, textbooks and lecturers usually present an idea of economics that supposedly delineates the terrain of economics. Later, whether the material presented fits within the established framework is mostly deliberately overlooked. This omission can be interpreted as a reflex of cognitive dissonance: the predominant description of economics neither matches the actual teaching and research practices nor is it suited to comprehend economic activity.

The discrepancy between aspiration and reality often manifests itself in an appeal to intuition: it is proposed to get the gist of economic aspects inductively based on

F. Helmedag, *Production of Commodities by Means of Labour*, Springer Studies in Alternative Economics, https://doi.org/10.1007/978-3-032-01457-3_1

processes and facts that one "feels" to be economic. This method is perhaps appropriate for didactic reasons, but it should not be left at that. Describing the nature of an object by listing its conceivable uses or manifestations remains inevitably superficial and incomplete. This insight will be confirmed in the upcoming discussion of money. Whenever certain phenomena can be assigned to an "archetype" of economies, it should be possible to grasp the object of economic theory, the economy, *abstractly,* through sufficiently intensive reflection.

> "If it becomes desirable to formulate any cognition as science," Immanuel Kant stated, "it will be necessary first to determine accurately those peculiar features which no other science has in common with it, constituting its characteristics; otherwise the boundaries of all sciences become confused, and none of them can be treated thoroughly according to its nature."[1]

An economist who wants to take this wise advice to heart cannot get around clarifying the concept of economics. The easiest way to put this plan into action is, seemingly, as it will become apparent soon, to consult the literature. To assess the expediency of the definitions, they are checked for their *practical* suitability, i.e., we apply life (and research) experience to examine their quality. The *differentia specifica* of economics will finally emerge from the gleaned inspection results, which—this is the thesis—enable us to grasp the subject more precisely than the usual characterisations.

To begin with, we try our luck by turning to a reference work entitled "Deutsches Universalwörterbuch" [German Universal Dictionary]. The entry "Wirtschaft" [economy] reads: "Entirety of institutions and measures relating to the production and consumption of economic goods ..."[2] This explanation hardly leads any further. However, the reader later learns that an economic good "... serves to satisfy human needs".[3] Accordingly, the economy is the *totality of all institutions and actions* related to producing and consuming goods *that satisfy human needs.*

This explanation may help the layperson to get a rough idea of what the term economy indicates. Experts, i.e., people who have (or should have) intensively dealt with the theoretical comprehension of economics *ex professo,* will (be forced to) place a question mark.

Let us first put consumption and production aside. After a brief pondering, the second part of the sentence seems perplexing: it claims the "economy" generally deals with satisfying human needs. However, the economy does not include producing and consuming all that provides utility.

Writing a scientific treatise, e.g., may increase well-being—even if only for the author—but it does not fall within the scope of economics when the manuscript finally goes into the oven. If a mother prepares a birthday cake for her son, this is also not an activity that can be assigned to the field of economics. Nevertheless, the standard definition covers both examples. Of course, it would be unreasonable

---

[1] Kant, I., Prolegomena to Any Future Metaphysics [1873], ed. by Carus, P., 3rd ed., Chicago 1912, Project Gutenberg 2016, p. 17, https://dn721802.ca.archive.org/0/items/rmcg0004/Kant-Prolegomena-a1.pdf.

[2] Duden, Deutsches Universalwörterbuch, 5th ed., Mannheim / Leipzig / Wien / Zürich 2003, p. 1821, no. 1 (in the original in italics and with abbreviations). [F. H.]

[3] Ibid., p. 1822. [F. H.]

to expect a dictionary to offer the strict accuracy that professional literature should provide.

Let us, therefore, turn to a textbook that has been widely used for a long time in German-speaking countries, Günther Wöhe's "Einführung in die Allgemeine Betriebswirtschaftslehre" [Introduction to General Business Administration]. "*Economics*," it says, "is the quintessence of all planned human activities that are carried out under the economic principle (rational principle) to reduce the scarcity of goods—measured by people's needs."[4] This description, which analogously appears in almost all textbooks, deserves closer scrutiny.

Economic activity manifests itself in those "rational" actions that proceed *according to plan* and obey the economic principle. This precept occurs in two manifestations. The *maximum principle* requires a suitable combination of given resources to guarantee the greatest possible yield. According to the *minimum principle*, the aim is to achieve a specific outcome with the least possible use of resources. Such an activity implies that rational action is worthwhile. If you take water from a river to clean a pair of glasses, you have little reason to pay attention to minimising liquid consumption. The "general principle of reason" or "rational principle", after which *every* expedient human action should be aimed at realising a fixed goal with the least effort,[5] applies at the utmost *subjectively* to all life situations. Nor do all who pay radio licence fees maximise the hours spent in front of the television.

An approach based on the economic principle *necessarily* presupposes scarcity of resources or the usability of the result. When the maxim is thought through to its logical conclusion, it states that the execution must be goal-oriented: if you want to climb a mountain, digging a hole does not help to promote the project. Of course, there may be various ways to climb clear heights, and perhaps the shortest and fastest route is chosen, but is this an "economic" decision?

Wöhe's definition of economics explicitly includes overcoming scarcity as a further constitutive feature, which is already inherent in the "economic principle". The importance of scarcity is emphasised by another, often copied, traditional characterisation of economics: "Economics is the science, which studies human behaviour as a relationship between ends and scarce means which have alternative uses."[6] This description dispenses with the assumption of any specific rationality in human behaviour—indeed, Robbins rejects such notions: "... our economic subjects can be pure egoists, pure altruists, pure ascetics, pure sensualists or—what is more like—mixed bundles of all these impulses."[7]

Remarkably, Robbins first published his characterisation of economics in 1932—during the Great Depression. If one follows his suggestion, the world economic crisis can be classified as an essentially non-economic problem: rarely have resources

---

4 Wöhe, G., Einführung in die Allgemeine Betriebswirtschaftslehre, 21st ed., München 2002, p. 2. [F. H.]

5 Cf. ibid., p. 1.

6 Robbins, L., An Essay on the Nature and Significance of Economic Science, 2nd ed., London 1952, p. 16.

7 Ibid., p. 95.

probably been less scarce; involuntary unemployment and idle capacity mark "the economy" of the time. According to Robbins' terminology, business cycles and crises are not at all an object of economic analysis—a conception that does not live up to many economists' teaching and research activities.

Against this background, it comes as no surprise that criticism of the common interpretation of the economy has been heard for quite some time[8] and is illustrated with striking examples:

> "The fact that the nursing mother disposes of scarce resources for the purpose of satisfying needs," Dieter Schneider remarks with apt sarcasm, "is just as undeniable as the cannibal chief's considerations as to whether he wants to impale the captured missionary and let him dry or boil him soft."[9]

Suppose economics wants to be "merely" the study of the economy. In that case, the discipline is inevitably overloaded if it only refers to a formal principle; unintentionally, it becomes a social all-science. Considering the great range of the rational principle, the whole (somewhat) conscious life attracts attention, which can always be interpreted as a "choice between alternatives" or as a "disposition of scarce means for the purpose of satisfying needs". The actual scope of economics remains obscure: Paul is not "economising" if he invites Paula instead of Paulina to look at his stamp collection. And the chosen one, in case she signals consent, does not (always) think in economic categories either. Essentially, there is no getting around a material identification of economic activity.

Symptoms of the lack of enclosure in research are "economic" theories of tooth brushing, marriage, childbearing, crime, etc.[10]

> "Meanwhile, there are also studies on the economics of church attendance, Scrabble, mental illness, assault, and the reduction of teaching loads in faculties; there is an economic theory of smuggling, highway robbery, and marital infidelity; and the demand for children in agricultural households has been explored, as has the question of why the American tourist is cheated abroad. The borderline to satire is sometimes touched upon ('The person who dies with a perfect liver may have forgone a number of drinks during the course of his life that could have contributed significantly to his own welfare: a liver in good order is useless if the heart goes first') ..."[11]

Of course, the borderline to satire is not merely *touched upon*; it is (unintentional) comedy.[12] Such "art for art's sake" results from the rigid application of a purely

---

[8] See, e.g., Albert, H., Ökonomische Ideologie und politische Theorie, Göttingen 1954, p. 25.

[9] Schneider, D., Geschichte betriebswirtschaftlicher Theorie, München / Wien 1981, p. 10. [F. H.] In the revised edition of this book with a changed title, the cannibal chief no longer appears. Cf. Schneider, D., Allgemeine Betriebswirtschaftslehre, München / Wien 1985, p. 18.

[10] The standard reference for this development is McKenzie, R. B., Tullock, G., The New World of Economics – Explorations Into Human Experience, 2nd ed., Homewood 1978.

[11] Stobbe, A., Volkswirtschaftslehre II, Mikroökonomik, Berlin et al. 1983, p. 9 n. [F. H.] The source of the quotation in the citation is McKenzie, R. B., Tullock, G., op. cit., p. 151.

[12] Cf. the brilliant persiflage on this set of issues by Lehner, H., Meran, G., Möller, J., De Statu Corruptionis, Entscheidungslogische Einübungen in die Höhere Amoralität, Konstanz / Litzelstetten 1980.

formal calculus to all human decision-making situations, which are thus lumped together regardless of their content. Although it is undeniable that the examples mentioned above *can* have an economic dimension, the would-be economists are searching on terrain where they have lost nothing and will, therefore, find nothing. The phenomenon of "economic imperialism"[13] will be rampant if economists do not know where their home territory is.

Wandering around in foreign domains would not be a cause for concern if economists did not bring about any lasting damage there: one could merely complain that academic resources—which include the space available in scholarly journals—are being wasted. To be sure, economists sometimes convey, or at least try to convey, the impression to their sister disciplines in the social sciences that they have, in principle, the more potent *method* at command. Even the most insidious difficulties can be successfully targeted and penetrated by their mathematical artillery. For a whole range of socio-scientific problems, long-awaited exact results are promised. Access is granted by "the" economic approach, which leads to an optimisation task under constraints.[14]

In some cases, however, the initial euphoria has given way to a more sober approach. All advances in optimisation methods—as welcome as they are—do not lead anywhere if puzzles are solved that do not arise. Moreover, the treatment often takes such a general form that any practical application is ruled out.[15] The intense use of mathematics has not at all created the increase in knowledge that most economic theorists mutually assure each other.

> "Contrary to the hopes of its practitioners," Joan Robinson wrote in her introduction to the (excellent) history of economic thought written by Vivian Walsh and Harvey Gram, "the apparent precision of mathematics has generated vagueness. Mathematical operations are performed upon entities that cannot be defined; calculations are made in terms of units that cannot be measured; accounting identities are mistaken for functional relationships; correlations are confused with causal laws; differences are identified with changes; and one-way movements in time are treated like movements to and fro in space. The complexity of models is elaborated merely for display, far and away beyond the possibility of application to reality."[16]

---

[13] Cf. the anthology Radwitzky, G., Bernholz, P. (eds.), Economic Imperialism, The Economic Approach Applied Outside the Field of Economics, New York 1987.

[14] The identification of economics with optimisation under constraints was propagated by Samuelson, P. A., Foundations of Economic Analysis [1947], Cambridge (Mass.) / London 1983. He emphasised this view in his Nobel Prize speech. Cf. Samuelson, P. A., Maximum Principles in Analytical Economics, in: The American Economic Review, vol 62 (1972), pp. 249–262.

[15] The examples *par excellence* of this are the utility functions to be maximised in decision theory, which are hardly specified if they can be specified at all. Critical comments on utility measurement can be found in Helmedag, F., Fortschrittsillusionen in der Ökonomik: Die Neue Handelstheorie, in: Enke, H., Wagner, A. (eds.), Zur Zukunft des Wettbewerbs, In memoriam Karl Brandt (1923–2010) und Alfred E. Ott (1929–1994), Marburg 2012, pp. 39–55. Incidentally, the rational principle tacitly supposes 'well-behaved' objective functions. Cf. the succint account by Bartels, H. G., Was ist dran am Rationalprinzip?, in: das wirtschaftsstudium (wisu), vol. 17 (1988), pp. 135–137.

[16] Robinson, J., Introduction, in: Walsh, V., Gram, H., Classical and Neoclassical Theories of General Equilibrium, New York / Oxford 1980, pp. xi–xvi, p. xi.

This quotation is not intended as a blind attack against the typical application of mathematics: it is undoubtedly an indispensable tool for the economic theorist striving for precision; also, in this book, its assistance cannot be renounced. Mathematics as a formal method—like the economic principle as such—is content-wise arbitrary. Similarly, in an initial encounter with a knife, it is perceived as a mere blade affixed to a handle. The critical factor in its application is the purpose for which it is used or misused.[17]

As mentioned at the start, attempts are sometimes made to concretise the content of economics through an intuitive-inductive collection of material. For example, Artur Woll tries in his widely used German textbook on general economics "… to clarify what the economist's scientific occupation is by describing economics …."[18] He then presents a canon of questions that goes back to the German neo-liberal Walter Eucken: what is produced, for what, when, how and where.[19]

Samuelson pursued a similar approach in his international bestselling textbook:

> "Every society – be it that of a collectivist state, that of a tribe of South Sea islanders, that of a capitalist industry nation, that of a Swiss Family Robinson, that of a Robinson Crusoe or even that of a bee colony – is confronted with three fundamental and interdependent problems."[20]

Samuelson's list of tasks is somewhat thinner than Eucken's programme; now it is "only" about what is produced, how and for whom.[21] However, both authors finally present the crux of their questionnaires. Eucken, e.g., identifies the most prominent attribute of economic activity in planning:

> "At all times and everywhere, human economic activity is carried out by developing and implementing economic plans. All economic activity is therefore based on plans."[22]

By contrast, Samuelson identifies in the "law of scarcity"—like Robbins—the all-embracing bracket of economics.[23] Finally, Woll also exposes the reader "… what the economist's scientific occupation consists of" because: "Economic action means to make choices according to certain criteria … Anyone who does business must decide what to forego."[24]

Obviously, all the authors quietly straighten out their "opening digression", i.e., emphasising *production* as an element of economics. This disregard is understandable; on closer inspection, people fabricate many things under many circumstances,

---

[17] Hans Peter has drawn a similar comparison with 'the' theory: "Theory is neutral. It acts like a magnifying glass that recognises what escapes the naked eye. It is like a knife, but it depends on the hand that wields it." Peter, H., Einführung in die politische Ökonomie, Stuttgart / Köln 1950, p. XVI. [F. H.]

[18] Woll, A., Volkswirtschaftslehre, 15th ed., München 2007, p. 4.

[19] Cf. Eucken, W., Die Grundlagen der Nationalökonomie, 5th ed., Godesberg 1947, p. 5 ff. [F. H.]

[20] Samuelson, P. A., Volkswirtschaftslehre, vol. I, 7th ed., Köln 1981, p. 33. [F. H.]

[21] Cf. ibid., p. 33 f. [F. H.]

[22] Eucken, W., op. cit., p. 127. [F. H.]

[23] Cf. Samuelson, P. A., Volkswirtschaftslehre, op. cit., p. 36.

[24] Woll, A., op. cit., p. 28. [F. H.]

including less fertile definitions of a science. These are not always the fruits of economic activity. Nevertheless, there is a lot of truth in the reference to production, but this is of little help without a more detailed indication of when the production achieves economic significance. The same applies to the explanation of economics as a theory of decision-making per se. Strictly speaking, the entire human life can be interpreted in the light of choices between alternatives, just as from the vantage point of scarcity.[25]

The usual descriptions of economics leave an even weaker impression if one considers that other sciences study the expediency of means for ends, too. Engineering, e.g., examines the practical suitability of findings from different disciplines, namely the natural sciences. Lionel Robbins already recognised the possibility of overlap in the general characterisation of economics and engineering. However, Robbins believed he had found a distinguishing feature: a technical problem exists when *one* goal can be reached by different means, and an economic problem arises whenever *several* goals and various means compete.[26]

As elegant as this resolution seems *prima facie*, dissatisfaction ensues as soon as one tries to apply it to practical cases. In a gravel pit, there are several options—from wheelbarrows to conveyor belts—for transporting the rock. Although the goal is clear, the choice between the technical alternatives is based on *economic* criteria.

Occasionally, the economic principle is even declared to be the maxim of sacred acts:

> "If the Roman peasant of the imperial era sacrificed to Saturnus, the god of crops, and the other gods, and otherwise adhered to the traditional primitive technique, he acted entirely according to the economic principle. He expected something in return from the gods; the sacrifice was part of the economic expenditures."[27]

Indeed, it is not entirely absurd to interpret the behaviour of some believers as an advance payment (in this world) in the expectation of a high interest rate (in the hereafter)—economic theories of heaven and hell send their best wishes. In principle, however, it would be too short-sighted to regard coping with existence in general, including the metaphysical moment of human life, as a source of normative rules throughout all of time, as a utilisation of the *economic* principle.[28]

---

[25] From a system theoretic perspective, it was argued that scarcity is not a relationship to things. Instead, this system-internal formula allows needs to be expressed and discussed without regard to a particular situation. Scarcity does not decrease but increases as a result of an increase in economic performance. Cf. Luhmann, N., Knappheit, Geld und die bürgerliche Gesellschaft, in: Jahrbuch für Sozialwissenschaft, vol. 23 (1972), pp. 186–210.

[26] Cf. Robbins, L., op. cit., p. 35.

[27] Eucken, W., op. cit., p. 329. [F. H.]

[28] Eucken's explanation of the economic principle refers to economic plans that are in turn characterised by the economic principle: "Always and everywhere," reads his formulation, which is in the original throughout letterspaced printed, "people seek in their economic plans and thus in their actions to achieve a certain purpose with the least possible expenditure of values." Eucken, W., op. cit., p. 328. [F. H.]

This reservation by no means denies the connections between economics and metaphysics.[29] Yet, this multifaceted relation cannot be understood solely in terms of the rational principle, narrowed down to the economic principle. The offerings of the Roman peasant defy a purely economic interpretation. They are part of a *gift transaction* whose guidelines differ from exchange rules. Even if the sacrifice is not construed as a tax, a tribute from man to the deity, but as a reciprocal relationship between man and God, it remains subject to a *rite*, a set of rules dictating which sacrifices are to be immolated when and how.—More on this later.

The usual explanations leave open the characteristics that distinguish the cognition object of economics from adjacent disciplines. Even "great" economists did not seem to be sensible of this.[30] This vagueness also affects disciplines that embellish their names with the addition "economic": *with a grain of salt*, economic history roves through bygone times without an economic clock; economic geography roams the vast world without an economic compass; and business informatics gravitates without an economic message to the numerous professorships established.

> "In this way," Landshut rightly observes, "economic history, e.g., with its concepts borrowed from theory, comes to locate a particular 'economic life' everywhere without any clarification of their specific meaning and finds, like Faust Helena in every woman, 'capital' and 'enterprises' ubiquitously."[31]

To avoid reproducing the vague idea that generally accompanies the word economy, its *concrete* meaning through the ages is subsequently portrayed. This clarification creates the basis for the *abstract* definition of the term economy.

---

[29] Cf. Zinn, K. G., Politische Ökonomie, Apologien und Kritiken des Kapitalismus, Opladen 1987, p. 34 ff.

[30] "Perhaps, however, one problem of rigorous economic science is caused by the fact that important economists were not clear about the limits of their theory's scope ..." Faber, M., Manstetten, R., Der Ursprung der Volkswirtschaftslehre als Bestimmung und Begrenzung ihrer Erkenntnisperspektive, in: Schweizerische Zeitschrift für Volkswirtschaft und Statistik, vol. 124 (1988), pp. 97–121, p. 115. [F. H.]

[31] Landshut, S., Historische Analyse des Begriffs des „Ökonomischen" [1969], in: Wehler, H.-U. (ed.), Geschichte und Ökonomie, Köln 1973, pp. 40–53, p. 51. [F. H.]

Chapter 2
The Semantic Change of the Term "Economy"

The history of economic thought usually gives the impression that the development of this science is a series of errors.[1] It is pretended that economic thinkers, from ancient times to the present day, have always worked on the same subject. Scientific progress is expressed in the fact that, during continued conceptual refinement and the use of more sophisticated formal procedures, ever better answers are obtained to problems that have existed since the beginning. This "absolutist"[2] attitude assumes a constancy and continuity of the cognition object, the economy, without ever revealing the criteria by which the progress of knowledge is judged.

The conception tempts one to separate partial "economic" statements by an author from their context and to label him a "forerunner" of modern economics, who "naturally" was not quite as advanced as we—supposedly—are today. Such a view assumes a cumulative increase in understanding; consequently, it would only be a matter of time and sweat until all economic "secrets" were deciphered. Yet, the term economy has undergone a profound change in meaning, which must be considered when appreciating the achievements of the precursors. It is not legitimate to confront their thinking unmodified with our current ideas of the economy. They lived in phases in which the connotation of the word economy differed from the modern association.

This shift in emphasis corresponds to the two radical alterations that have (so far) characterised the human mode of production: the Neolithic and the Industrial Revolution. In a society of hunters and gatherers, there can be no question of an economy that even remotely encompasses what we understand by this term today. The economic aspect of coping with existence only gained noticeable influence and

[1] Cf. Landshut, S., op. cit., p. 50.

[2] Cf. Winch, D., Das Aufkommen der Volkswirtschaftslehre als Wissenschaft 1750–1870, in: Cipolla, C. M., Borchardt, K. (eds.), Europäische Wirtschaftsgeschichte, vol. III, Die Industrielle Revolution, Stuttgart / New York 1985, pp. 335–377, p. 355.

F. Helmedag, *Production of Commodities by Means of Labour*, Springer Studies in Alternative Economics, https://doi.org/10.1007/978-3-032-01457-3_2

autonomy much later. This distinction does not mean that the study of hunter-gatherer societies is unrewarding for economists—on the contrary.[3]

The ensuing account does not aim to dissect around ten thousand years of economic and social history on just a few pages.[4] Instead, the following remarks intend to illuminate phenomena essential for exploring the coherences here. To this end, two significant epochs are distinguished: the period from the Neolithic to the Industrial Revolution, called the "traditional" era for brevity, and the "modern" period, i.e., the timespan from the Industrial Revolution to the present.

2.1 Economic Activity in the Traditional Sense

In Old High German, "Wirtschaft" [economy] meant "hospitality, banquet". Since the sixteenth century, it has been used for inns; around the seventeenth century, it also involved housekeeping in the broad sense.[5] "Wirtschaft" is derived from "Wirt", which initially signifies "keeper". This word refers to the housefather who instructs, cares for, and protects his family and the servants in husbandry: the *paterfamilias*.[6]

Xenophon (around 430–354 BC) addressed his work "Oikonomikos" to this group. In this manual, he suggests suitable measures for promoting the household. Xenophon assigns specific roles to men and women and advises on agriculture and animal farming.[7] Furthermore, Xenophon, as Marx remarks, "… with characteristic bourgeois instinct, approaches … to division of labour within the workshop."[8] The intention here is not to pay tribute to Xenophon's achievement and celebrate

[3] Cf. with numerous references Schaaff, H., Kritik der eindimensionalen Wirtschaftstheorie: Zur Begründung einer ökologischen Glücksökonomie, Thun / Frankfurt a. M. 1991, p. 122 ff.

[4] Such a *tour d'horizon* is offered by Helmedag, F., Weber, U., Entwicklungslinien und Schwankungen des Sozialprodukts im Überblick, in: Wirtschaftswissenschaftliches Studium (WiSt), vol. 33 (2004), pp. 80–87.

[5] Cf. Stoltenberg, H. L., Zur Geschichte des Wortes Wirtschaft, in: Jahrbücher für Nationalökonomie und Statistik, vol. 148 (1938), pp. 555–561.

[6] Cf. Brunner, O., Die alteuropäische „Ökonomik", in: Zeitschrift für Nationalökonomie, vol. 13 (1950), pp. 114–139, pp. 117 f.

[7] Cf. Xenophon, Die sokratischen Schriften, Stuttgart 1956, p. 238 ff. (Die Hauswirtschaftslehre); cf. in addition Vogel, G., Die Ökonomik des Xenophon, eine Vorarbeit für die Geschichte der griechischen Ökonomik, Erlangen 1895 and Singer, K., Oikonomia: An Inquiry into Beginnings of Economic Thought and Language, in: Kyklos, vol. 11 (1958), pp. 29–57. The oldest known economic author also wrote a memoir entitled "Mittel und Wege, dem Staat Geld zu verschaffen" [Ways and means to procure money for the state]. Cf. Xenophon, Ökonomische Schriften, Berlin 1992, p. 140 ff. To remedy Athens' financial difficulties, the former equestrian general in Sparta's service suggested socialising silver mining and thus the production of money. On the current discussion of public debt, see Helmedag, F., Mit der Schuldenbremse zum Systemcrash, in: Gesmann-Nuissl, D., Hartz, R., Dittrich, M. (eds.), Perspektiven der Wirtschaftswissenschaften, Wiesbaden 2014, pp. 123–137.

[8] Marx, K., Capital, vol. I, A Critical Analysis of Capitalist Production, [1867], Progress Publishers Moscow, p. 345, https://archive.org/details/capitalvol1.

him as the (perhaps first) herald of the productivity-enhancing division of labour.[9] Instead, the aim is to demonstrate that the precursors wanted to fulfil other tasks and that we are not entitled to apply to their accomplishments standards calibrated to contemporary problems.

The overall system of philosophy in the ancient, medieval, and early modern sense encompassed logic, metaphysics, physics, and ethics. Ethics culminated in a theory of the virtues of man, landlord and statesman; accordingly, it ramifies into doctrines for the individual—called monasticism by the scholastics—into economics as instructions in organising the *entire* house and finally into politics, the government of the polis.[10]

In economics, the focus is not only on the activities in the house and farm but also on interpersonal ties, the relation between husband and wife, parents and children, and master and servants.[11] Aristotle, in particular, emphasises the seigneurial element in the home administration; the head of the family is at the centre, and inequality prevails in the "oikos".[12] Despite all other fundamental differences, there is a similarity to modern firms, whose internal connections are also structured hierarchically.

In those days, economics was mainly concerned with the "good life" in the private world; only marginally does it include considerations of acquiring wealth through exchange: chrematistics. There, not in economics, explanations of price, the monetary system, interest, and rent occur. Yet the desire for wealth did not develop any autonomous dynamics at the time; it was tolerated and approved of solely as a means to an end, the good life in the home.[13] As soon as the pursuit of wealth no longer merely served to supplement the household's self-sufficiency but threatened to become a goal in itself, i.e., aimed at acquiring money through trade, it was considered reprehensible.[14] Chrematistics, therefore, discusses the permitted extent of trade within the boundaries of ethics and politics. In antiquity, a significant market exchange can be observed, but it does not exert any noticeable influence on the social structure.[15] As one would put it today, economic activity was ethically and morally

---

[9] However, as can be seen from n. 7 above, Schumpeter's remark that he did not discuss Xenophon because his work belongs exclusively to the treatises on household management does not do justice to the author. Cf. Schumpeter, J. A., History of Economic Analysis, ed. by Schumpeter, E. B., London 1954, p. 53 n., https://archive.org/details/dli.ernet.505700/page/n3/mode/2up.

[10] Brunner, O., Die alteuropäische ..., op. cit., p. 123.

[11] Cf. Brunner, O., Hausväterliteratur, in: Handwörterbuch der Staatswissenschaften, vol. V, Stuttgart / Tübingen / Göttingen 1956, p. 92 f.

[12] Cf. Hüther, M., Die „Sattelzeitgerechte" Entstehung der Nationalökonomie. Ein Beitrag zur Dogmengeschichte, in: Jahrbücher für Nationalökonomie und Statistik, vol. 205 (1988), pp. 150–162, p. 152 f.

[13] Cf. Faber, M., Manstetten, R., op. cit., p. 105.

[14] Cf. Brunner, O., Die alteuropäische ..., op. cit., p. 116.

[15] "Despite intensive commercial activity and a fairly developed use of money, Greek business life as a whole was still in the very early stages of market trade at the time of Aristotle." Polanyi, K., Ökonomie und Gesellschaft, Frankfurt a. M. 1979, p. 150. [F. H.] On the significance of markets in ancient times, see Belshaw, C. S., Traditional Exchange and Modern Markets, Englewood Cliffs 1965; Herskovits, M. J., Economic Anthropology—A Study in Comparative Economics, New York 1952; Polanyi, K., Arensberg, L. M., Pearson, H. W. (eds.), Trade and Market in the Early Empires,

limited. Likewise, Scholasticism later examined 'economic' problems, such as the "just" price, from a metaphysical perspective.

The ancient meaning of economy outlined above still lives on today: when farmers in rural areas talk about their "economy", they mean "… the entire complex of their domestic and agricultural activities, the oikos, which is inconceivable without the people living in it, the housewife, the working family members, the servants."[16] The term economy was used in this sense until the middle of the eighteenth century. Until then, the economy did not appear as an independent, autonomous area of human existence. However, around this time …

> "... a process is drawing to a conclusion and its effects are becoming recognisable all-round, although its roots go back much further. It is nothing less than the decay of the worldview and human image created by the Greeks, which had prevailed until this time, the disintegration of the 'cosmos idea' ..."[17]

An external sign of this evolution is the increasing significance of the division between household and economy:

> "The problem area that the household literature dealt with so extensively no longer existed; it was transferred to the latitude of society. Just as the Enlightenment generally describes the departure of the bourgeois intelligentsia from the private sphere, the question of satisfying economic needs was transferred from the personal life to society. The notion of economics lost its content because it no longer existed; it became superfluous and thus free for a new meaning."[18]

Along the way, the word "economic" acquired the connotation of thrifty and frugal; only later—around the beginning of the twentieth century—did it attain the purport of "profitable".[19] In between, a change in "economic" activity on an unprecedented scale has been taking place, recognisable by the fact that during the eighteenth century, real industrial production rose fourfold: "This growth and the increasingly bourgeois environment in which it took place constitute the essence of the Industrial Revolution."[20] This period saw the birth of political economy as an academic discipline. The new economy and the transformation of the concept of economy go hand in hand with the emergence of a *national economy*, i.e., the awareness of a network of individual economies. Let us take a closer look at this phase.

Glencoe 1957 and North, D. C., Structure and Change in Economic History, New York / London 1981.

[16] Brunner, O., Die alteuropäische …, op. cit., p. 117. [F. H.]

[17] Ibid., p. 127. [F. H.]

[18] Hüther, M., op. cit., p. 154. [F. H.]

[19] Brunner, O., Die alteuropäische …, op. cit., p. 118.

[20] Lilley, S., Technischer Fortschritt und die Industrielle Revolution 1700–1914, in: Cipolla, C. M., Borchardt, K. (eds.), op. cit., pp. 119–163, p. 137. [F. H.]

2.2 Economic Activity in the Modern Sense

Occasionally, the view is advocated that economics was established as a *spin-off* of the Industrial Revolution. "For beholders of the history of economics as different as Alfred Marshall and Karl Marx," Winch notes, "the development of economics was a by-product of the succession of agrarian and industrial revolutions that swept across Europe from 1750 onwards."[21] Such a far-reaching thesis—regardless of whether Marx and Marshall actually shared it[22]—deserves closer examination.

If this unambiguous cause-effect chain linked the Industrial Revolution and the emergence of economics, it would be possible to conclude that the Industrial Revolution was independent of intellectual currents. This opinion is indeed frequently enunciated. If the claim is correct, a simple equation ensues: population growth plus the steam engine equals the Industrial Revolution. In reality, the formula is more complicated.[23]

The term *Industrial* Revolution suggests that the radical change and expansion of production boosted the modern economy. Hence, the first wave of economic and social transformation fundamentally altered the industrial sector.

Such a statement obscures that an *agricultural* revolution preceded the industrial revolution.[24] At the beginning of the eighteenth century, 75–80% of the workforce was still employed in husbandry. Food at that time was mainly of vegetable origin. It took roughly eight plant calories to produce one animal calorie.

In Germany, the agricultural revolution accelerated from circa 1790–1800, some 100 years after England, which assumed the pioneering role.[25] On the one hand, England had a favourable starting position due to the lack of guild restrictions.[26] On the other hand, England possessed rich coal deposits, absent, e.g., in Holland, which was also considered a potential candidate at the turn of the century to blaze the trail for the industrial revolution.

The agrarian revolution, i.e., the clearing of additional land, the application of new equipment, the use of horses as draught animals and the abandonment of the two-year crop rotation in favour of the three-field system, was a *precondition* for the industrial revolution in several respects: the rapid upsurge in agricultural productivity not only provided the necessary food to feed a growing population but also made workers redundant who now offered their services the manufacturing sector. The

---

[21] Winch, D., op. cit., p. 333. [F. H.] Hüther also shares this view. Cf. Hüther, M., op. cit., p. 156.

[22] For instance, the passages cited by Hüther cannot be interpreted readily in the alleged spirit, cf. ibid.

[23] To what follows cf. also Helmedag, F., Industrielle Revolution(en): Transformationsprozesse des Kapitalismus, in: Wirtschaftsdienst, vol. 99 (2019), pp. 210–215.

[24] Cf. Bairoch, P., Die Landwirtschaft und die Industrielle Revolution 1700–1914, in: Cipolla, C. M., Borchardt, K. (eds.), op. cit., pp. 297–332.

[25] Cf. ibid., p. 302.

[26] Cf. Kromphardt, J., Analysen und Leitbilder des Kapitalismus von Adam Smith bis zum Finanzmarktkapitalismus, Marburg 2015, p. 59.

population explosion at that time justifies the label of a *demographic* revolution that accompanied the dramatic change in agriculture.

A large proportion of the entrepreneurs and the invested financial capital—initially considerably lower per capita in the industry than in agriculture—came from rural areas.[27] The alterations in agronomy were at least on a par with those in industry; in any case, they were an indispensable prerequisite for the latter. Moreover, the scale of the technical changes at the beginning of the Industrial Revolution is often exaggerated.

In fact, there was no such sudden and profound transition in technical processes as the name Industrial *Revolution* suggests. Instead, some relatively old methods were initially used, although continually refined. While it is true that other sources of energy began to replace human and animal muscle power, it would be wrong to think primarily of steam power: "The first factories had been operating for a generation before steam was harnessed on a large scale."[28] *Water power* rotated the axles, and the construction of such means of propulsion had reached a high level.[29]

Incidentally, Thomas Newcomen's "fire engine", patented in 1712 and redesigned by James Watt, could not produce a circular motion until 1784. The big question is when steam engines would have been fired to any significant extent if the fifth—"evil"—Lord Byron had not arbitrarily disrupted the water flow to a factory. That is why the owner—necessity is the mother of invention!—tried his luck with the steam engine in 1786.[30]

The career of the steam engine impressively illustrates the thesis that the Industrial Revolution was by no means initially set in motion by technical innovations alone. "It was an irregular and gradual process ... The steam-powered factory did not give us the capitalist; the capitalist gave us the steam-powered factory."[31] The innovations

---

[27] Cf. Bairoch, P., op. cit., p. 328.

[28] Lilley, S., op. cit., p. 121. [F. H.]

[29] In this context, it is instructive from a scientific history perspective to mention the achievement of John Smeaton, who, by experimentally determining the efficiency of alternative designs of waterwheels, succeeded in disproving the mathematicians' assertion that undershot waterwheels were superior to overshot ones. See Paulinyi, A., Die industrielle Revolution, in: Troitzsch, U., Weber, W. (eds.), Die Technik, Stuttgart 1987, pp. 232–281, p. 255 f.

[30] Cf. Lilley, S., op. cit., p. 121. Similarly, exemplary research into the technological genesis of other key products shows that the technical potential was not exhausted as quickly as is sometimes believed. Rather, e.g., the diesel engine and the typewriter had to assert themselves against conservative entrepreneurs, who occasionally acted almost as dampers, and against a slack demand. See Knie, A., Das Konservative des technischen Fortschritts – Zur Bedeutung von Konstruktionstraditionen, Forschungs- und Konstruktionsstilen in der Technikgenese, Wissenschaftszentrum Berlin 1989 (FS II 89–101). Moreover, Watt's extensive patent rights, which were in force until 1800, had a doubly obstructive effect on the rapid diffusion of the steam engine: firstly, the premiums to be paid were considerable; secondly, Watt had practically all other possible uses and applications included in his patent rights without realising them. See Paulinyi, A., op. cit., p. 263.

[31] Marglin, S., Was tun die Vorgesetzten? Ursprünge und Funktionen der Hierarchie in der kapitalistischen Produktion, in: Duve, F. (ed.), Technologie und Politik, vol. 8, Die Zukunft der Arbeit 1, Reinbeck bei Hamburg 1977, pp. 148–203, p. 186. [F. H.]

were tackled when they appeared promising against the background of existing *know-how*.[32] "It is no insult to Newcomen to say that the state of technical knowledge at the turn of the century was such that as soon as the need became urgent enough, as soon as people started trying to deploy steam for pumping, *someone* was bound to succeed."[33]

Some fundamental inventions lay dormant for centuries before they were brought out and improved on a larger scale. For example, Leonardo da Vinci's notebooks contain sketches of a lathe. The silk twisting machine had been employed in Italy for a hundred years before T. Lombe first used it in an English factory in 1709.[34]

Medieval technology, conversely, cannot be seen as a continuation of processes already known in principle: "The real break in the development of technology took place at the beginning of the Middle Ages, not in the 18th century."[35] Whipple-tree and horse collar, the ship's helm, the compass—medieval creations that, on a broader front, came into effect in output levels much later. Before the Industrial Revolution, the sometimes extraordinarily high level of technical skill was expressed in the construction of music boxes, automatic chess players and other amusing pastimes[36]—no one thought of overturning the prevailing mode of production.

The example of China also proves that highly developed technology is a necessary but insufficient prerequisite for an industrial revolution. Given the outstanding achievements of the Chinese in many areas, the question arises as to why the industrial revolution did not begin its triumphal march from eastern China in the late European Middle Ages. Trade and commerce flourished there; around 600 prints with movable type were introduced—around 900 years before Gutenberg's creative idea—and gunpowder was mixed shortly afterwards.[37] As early as the eleventh century, porcelain was baked in imperial manufactories, maritime navigation could rely on

---

32 Similarly, Marx summarises: "Mankind thus inevitably sets itself only such tasks as it is able to solve, since closer examination will always show that the problem itself arises only when the material conditions for its solution are already present or at least in the course of formation." Marx, K., A Contribution to the Critique of Political Economy [1859], ed. by Dobb, M., Progress Publishers Moscow, p. 21 (preface), https://archive.org/details/marxcontributioncritpolecon/page/2/mode/2up.

33 Lilley, S., op. cit., p. 135. [F. H.] As far as the steam engine was concerned, Denis Papin had provided laboratory proof that it worked in 1690, and he sailed on his first steamship from Kassel to Münden in 1707. A detailed history of the steam engine with numerous technical details can be found in Matschoss, C., Die Entwicklung der Dampfmaschine, 2 vols, Berlin 1908.

34 Cf. Mathias, P., Wer entfesselte Prometheus? Naturwissenschaft und technischer Wandel von 1600–1800, in: Braun, R. et al. (eds.), Industrielle Revolution, Köln 1972, pp. 121–138, p. 129.

35 Lilley, S., op. cit., p. 122. [F. H.] At the beginning of the modern era, firearms were developed in Europe, whereupon Europe's military superiority was based. In this respect, there is a close interaction between the perfection of war technology and the spread of capitalism. Cf. Zinn, K. G., Kanonen und Pest, Über die Ursprünge der Neuzeit im 14. und 15. Jahrhundert, Opladen 1989. This book also contains a wealth of material on the state of medieval technology.

36 Cf. Siegenthaler, H., Industrielle Revolution, in: Handwörterbuch der Wirtschaftswissenschaft, vol. IV, Stuttgart / Tübingen / Göttingen 1978, pp. 142–159, p. 158. A tabular overview of inventions is provided by Mathes, M. (ed.), Geschichte der Technik, Düsseldorf 1983.

37 The Arabs called the powder 'Chinese snow'; it should not be confused with black powder. Cf. Zinn, K. G., Kanonen ..., op. cit., p. 122 f.

the compass, and in 1290, the world's longest canal (1300 km) was dug from Beijing to Hangzhou—and the Middle Kingdom introduced the world's first paper currency before 1300.[38]

Nevertheless, the Chinese achievements in science and technology did not fundamentally modify the mode of production. The path to modernity lacked intellectual support:

> "The answer to the question as to why the seemingly imminent breakthrough to industrialisation in China failed to materialise seems less to be due to rigid monocultural land use for rice cultivation and the deficiency in long-distance domestic trade than in social and psychological conditions. Buddhism praised the worldly tranquillity, and the prevailing New Confucianism acted as an obstacle to progress through its emphasis on the family community."[39]

Improvements in human skills, the increasing control of nature and the deepening knowledge of its laws do not necessarily bring about an epochal social change. Anyone who wants to explain the Industrial Revolution conclusively cannot avoid referring to its *sufficient* condition: the far-reaching emancipation of people from traditional, metaphysical, and religious guiding principles. The Enlightenment, the triumph of Reformation and rationalism, and the change in people's minds now cast a rosy light on actions previously tainted with moral reprehensibility. This pervasion could thrive based on a new, ethically supported code of conduct.

The Enlightenment sensitised people to the injustice in this world and undermined its traditional vindication. Leibniz's theodicy lost credibility; God had bad press: "The merciless accusation against God had at the same time taken away the persuasive power of Christian dogma so that the commandment to love one's neighbour was no longer able to disavow self-interest morally."[40]

People seeking reassurance were offered an alternative that excused their economic ambition: utilitarianism. In the future, it was considered legitimate to trust in a mechanism that was supposed to have the attractive property of promoting prosperity—perhaps not for all, but for the greatest number—through everyone's greed for advantage.

Henceforth, the individual is allowed to cast off—with good reason!—the old, worn-out ethical and moral categories; from now on, he is no longer culpable if he indulges exclusively in his private, material pleasures and gives in to these inclinations. Instead of the medieval, naturally limited "idea of food",[41] the ownership of *money* takes centre stage in economic mentality:

---

[38] Cf. Zorn, W., Wirtschaftsgeschichte, in: Handwörterbuch der Wirtschaftswissenschaft, vol. IX, Stuttgart / Tübingen / Göttingen 1980, pp. 55–82, pp. 72 f. Cf. the authoritative work by Needham, J., Science and Civilization in China, 7 vols., Cambridge 1954 ff. (reprint 1972 ff.) on the nature and rank of Chinese science.

[39] Zorn, W., op. cit., p. 73. [F. H.]

[40] Hüther, M., op. cit., p. 159. [F. H.]

[41] See Sombart, W., Der moderne Kapitalismus [1902], vol. I, 2nd ed., München / Leipzig 1916, p. 34. [F. H.]

> "To conquer means to acquire in the field of material aspiration: to increase a sum of money. And nowhere does the striving for unboundedness, the conation for power, find a field of activity so much following its innermost nature as in the pursuit of money, this completely abstract value symbol, removed from all organic-natural limitations, the possession of which then appears more and more as a symbol of power."[42]

Economic activity gains a new quality. At last, the individual desire to accumulate property, which has always been latent but previously despised as immoral, fits into the design of the burgeoning economic society without causing a scandal:

> "The idea that our rationalist and capitalist present age possesses a stronger possessive urge than other epochs is a childish notion ... If the possessive urge is universal as such, the question is under what conditions it can be legitimised and rationally tempered in such a way that it creates rational entities such as capitalist enterprises."[43]

The traditional world was corporative: both the good life in the home in antiquity and the guild-based existence in the Middle Ages created a barrier to economic activity that was almost insurmountable for a single person. Now that the economy has developed its own dynamic, the process knows no end from the individual perspective: the pursuit of profit, the accumulation of abstract wealth, and economic integration increasingly displace socio-political interests from the first place in communal life.

Economic success in this world even becomes its guarantor in the hereafter.[44] Economic activity grows beyond the mere provision of the means to a given objective and moves into the centre of coping with existence; the economic agent sends the use value into the backdrop and calls the exchange value to the forestage:

> "On the one hand, the economic emancipates itself as something special from the process of production and elaboration, i.e., from everything 'technical' ... Whether the work was yielding, whether it was productive, is only decided on the market ... And secondly, the economic becomes free of all housekeeping ... the household as such, the private fulfilment of needs falls outside the realm of the economy."[45]

Economic activity takes on unprecedented importance; it becomes a motive in its own right and increasingly determines people's behaviour. Individuals who no longer feel metaphysically constrained are now commercially driven and oriented, doing so with a clear conscience. *This* source of energy fuelled the Industrial Revolution and gave it impetus.[46] The enumeration of apparently successive industrial revolutions—the first was followed by a second, and now we are supposedly experiencing the fourth ...—demonstrates the underestimation of this momentum. Those who seek to claim a front window seat on the train of time cannot discern the driving force of the Industrial

---

[42] Ibid., p. 328. [F. H.]

[43] Weber, M., Wirtschaftsgeschichte, München / Leipzig 1923, p. 303. [F. H.]

[44] Cf. the seminal work by Weber, M., The Protestant Ethic and the Spirit of Capitalism [1904/05], New York / London 1930, https://archive.org/details/protestantethics00webe/page/n17/mode/2up.

[45] Landshut, S., op. cit., p. 48. [F. H.]

[46] Polanyi calls the shift from 'integrated societies' with an embedded economy to separately existing capitalist market economies the "Great Transformation". Cf. Polanyi, K., The Great Transformation, New York / Toronto 1944.

Revolution. In reality, the locomotive remains unaltered; we find ourselves in the midst (or perhaps at the inception) of the Industrial Revolution!

The common feature of the attempts mentioned above to grasp the essence of the economy is that the two divergent historical meanings of economy, which still resonate in this term today, are mixed up and not separated from each other. As a result, the opportunity to develop a concept of economic activity appropriate for economics was squandered. Before we tackle this task, reflecting on the status that should be attached to research findings in economics seems worthwhile.

Chapter 3
The Character of Economic Laws

The combination of the two dimensions of economics, which this word has exhibited with varying degrees of importance throughout its history, is reflected in the original name of economics: political economy.[1] This label echoes the ancient conception of the discipline; however, the "principles of the good life in the home" are now extended to the organisation of social relations. Accordingly, the main works of Adam Smith and David Ricardo contain detailed discussions of state action. "For the classics and their critics, political economy is a *social theory*, i.e., it encompasses the totality of socio-economic relationships, right down to the mental (ideological) components of politics."[2]

With the decline of the classical school, the understanding of science shifted: one of the pioneers of the marginal utility revolution, William Stanley Jevons, energetically propagated the substitution of the outdated "political economy" with "economics" in the second edition of his *magnum opus*: "I cannot help thinking that it would be well to discard, as quickly as possible, the old troublesome double-worded name of our Science."[3] The new, precise and mathematically formulated science should be distinguished from the old one with its philosophical and political inclusions by its very name.[4]

Marshall was one of the first to attempt to implement the programme.[5] The motto of his "Principles", "*Natura non facit saltum*", indicates that the author planned

---

[1] On the roots of the term, see Stollberg, G., Zur Geschichte des Begriffs „Politische Ökonomie", in: Jahrbücher für Nationalökonomie und Statistik, vol. 192 (1977/78), pp. 1–35.

[2] Zinn, K. G., Politische ..., op. cit., p. 26. [F. H.] Zinn rightly points out that Stollberg's assertion, after which the adjective 'politisch' [political] in the classical name would be only an *epitheton ornans*, is due to a narrow concept of politics. Cf. ibid., p. 209 n.

[3] Jevons, W. St., The Theory of Political Economy, 2nd ed., London 1879, p. xiv.

[4] Cf. Winch, D., op. cit., p. 373.

[5] Cf. Marshall, A., Principles of Economics [1890], 8th ed., London 1952.

F. Helmedag, *Production of Commodities by Means of Labour*, Springer Studies in Alternative Economics, https://doi.org/10.1007/978-3-032-01457-3_3

an architecture of economics according to Spinoza's formula *more geometrico*.[6] Nevertheless, Marshall was ultimately interested in practical questions.[7] Although a studied mathematician, he did not get to work with the methodological rigour that such an approach would have required. Instead, he was sceptical about the possibility of constructing economic theory "scientifically":

> "Attempts have indeed been made to construct an abstract science with regard of an 'economic man' who is under no ethical influences and who pursues pecuniary gain warily and energetically, but mechanically and selfishly. But they have not been successful, nor even thoroughly carried out."[8]

Instead, economics is …

> "... a study of mankind in the ordinary business of life; it examines that part of individual and social action which is most closely connected with the attainment and with the use of the material requisites of well-being."[9]

There is no need to assess Marshall's explanation in detail; it shares the inadequate precision of the exemplarily cited definitions at the beginning. However, there is more than a grain of truth in Marshall's remark that economic theory, as part of the social sciences, aims to shed light on selected aspects of individual and social action. Yet, as already noted, concrete human action is always determined by a bundle of motives that cannot and should not all be attributed to economics—even if they are supposed to be "closely connected with the attainment and the use of the material requisites of well-being". This fundamental problem of the social sciences arises because the subject of "the individual and the society" is extraordinarily complex and intricate; indeed, the scientist is himself an element of society, and his efforts to gain knowledge rebound more or less on the object of investigation.[10] The tremendous and impressive

---

[6] For the specific nature of a 'science of economics' in the spectrum of disciples and the elucidation of research concepts with their cognition potential, see Helmedag, F., Wissenschaftstheoretische Aspekte der Ökonomik: Überblick und Positionsbestimmung, in: Chemnitz Economic Papers, No. 037, May 2020.

[7] The German edition of his "Principles" is entitled "Handbuch der Volkswirtschaftslehre" [manual of economics] and expresses this concern more aptly than the English name, which was probably based on traditional considerations. Cf. Marshall, A., Handbuch der Volkswirtschaftslehre, Stuttgart / Berlin 1905.

[8] Cf. Marshall, A., Principles …, op. cit., p. v.

[9] Ibid., p. 1.

[10] It is not for nothing that Keynes addresses the influence of economic theories on practice at the end of his most important work: "… the ideas of economists and political philosophers, both when they are right and when they are wrong, are more powerful than is commonly understood. Indeed the world is ruled by little else. Practical men, who believe themselves to be quite exempt from any intellectual influences, are usually the slave of some defunct economist. Madmen in authority, who hear voices in the air, are distilling their frenzy from some academic scribbler of a few years back. I am sure that the power of vested interests is vastly exaggerated compared with the gradual encroachment of ideas … But, soon or late, it is ideas, not vested interests, which are dangerous for good or evil." Keynes, J. M., The General Theory of Employment, Interest and Money [1936], in: The Collected Writings of John Maynard Keynes, vol. VII, Cambridge 1978, p. 383 f. On the immanence problem, see Zinn, K. G., Politische …, op. cit., p. 28 ff.

successes of the natural sciences bear on the fact that their object of cognition has allowed them (for a long time) to abstract from man.[11] The laws of natural phenomena are without history, at least within the scope humans are accustomed to reflecting on history.

Besides Jevons, another leading figure of the marginal utility school studied the research concept of the "new" science in depth. In a special methodological writing, Carl Menger made a strong case for the application of the "abstract method" in economics:

> "The aim of this orientation, which in the future we will call the exact one, an aim which research pursues in the same way in all realms of the world of phenomena, is the determination of strict laws of phenomena, of regularities in the succession of phenomena which do not present themselves to us as absolute, but which in respect to the approaches to cognition by which we attain to them simply bear within themselves the guarantee of absoluteness. It is the determination of laws of phenomena commonly called 'laws of nature,' but more correctly should be designated by the expression 'exact laws'."[12]

Menger advocates a methodical approach that has proved particularly fruitful in the 'hard' sciences, and he contradicts the identification of natural laws and exact laws:

> "There are natural sciences which are not exact ones (e.g., physiology, meteorology, etc.), and conversely, there are exact sciences which are not natural sciences (e.g., pure economics) ... It is just as wrong, finally, to speak of the natural science method in the social sciences in general and in theoretical economics in particular. The method of the latter can be either the empirical or the exact one, but in truth never that of 'natural science'."[13]

Furthermore, it is not the task of exact science to test reality for the regularity of certain phenomena: "It examines, rather, how more complicated phenomena develop from the simplest, in part even unempirical elements of the real world in their (likewise unempirical) isolation from all other influences ..."[14] The correct method is, therefore, axiomatic-deductive, where the starting propositions do not have to be "realistic"—indeed, they should not even be, but are *set*.[15]

---

[11] Today, e.g., physics has advanced into a borderland where the experimental results seem to depend on scientists and their cognitive abilities. A standard example is the corpuscle-wave duality, according to which elementary particles have both particle, that is to say corpuscle, and wave properties, to wit frequency and amplitude. Modern natural sciences generally face the phenomenon of classical confines between disciplines becoming shaky. In 1971, e.g., a Max Planck Institute for "Biophysical Chemistry" was established in Göttingen, a denomination that has become more frequent in the meantime.

[12] Menger, C., Investigations into the Method of the Social Sciences with Special Reference to Economics [1883], ed. by Schneider, L., New York University Press 1985, p. 59, https://mises.org/library/book/investigations-method-social-sciences.

[13] Ibid., p. 59 n.

[14] Ibid., p. 61. More recently, the same issue was raised in the context of the 'assumptions-controversy', in which Friedman, Machlup, and Samuelson participated. For a detailed account of the discussion, see Arni, J.-L., Die Kontroverse um die Realitätsnähe der Annahmen in der Oekonomie, Grüsch 1989.

[15] Even empirical surveys are not spared from the abstraction of moments of reality that are considered 'irrelevant': "Scientific cognition, however, never has the task of providing an image

This determination does not exclude the practical applicability of the results: the instrumentalisation of exact sciences, such as utilising mathematics to natural phenomena, was worthwhile in numerous areas. Land surveying, e.g., is based on a geometry that assumes 'false' axioms in the palpable sense, namely a point without extension and a straight line without width. The leaf that has become the sport of the autumn wind in no way disproves the validity of the laws of gravity, an example economists have used since De Quincey.[16]

In a suitably *construed* world, it is possible to uncover structures and reveal connections, i.e., causalities may be laid bare, which *can* otherwise only be identified inadequately due to the diversity, interdependence, and circularity of real processes. Faced with this complexity, Max Weber rightly asks …

> "… how in general is the attribution of a concrete effect to an individual 'cause' possible and realizable in principle in view of the fact that in truth an infinity of causal factors have conditioned the occurrence of the individual 'event' and that indeed absolutely all of those individual causal factors were indispensable for the occurrence of the effect in its concrete form. "[17]

The facts speak a coded language, and the rendition of what one thought to hear can be quite different, depending on the actual standpoint. The "empirical evidence" that economists like to bring into play covers a considerable range—think of the vastly divergent results of relevant studies published in the context of the monetarism-fiscalism debate. Exact laws cannot be extracted simply by looking at reality.

Menger, the marginal utility revolutionary, had a predecessor in the methodological field, none other than the person who gave the classical system its final touch, as is often said: half a century before Menger, John Stuart Mill had dealt with questions of definition and research in political economy in a collection of essays.[18] In this little volume, which, as Marx judges, contains in contrast to his "bulky compendium", all that is original,[19] Mill already recommends a method of "abstract

---

of reality; every empirical science must select the essentials from reality, thus leaving it in its immediacy …" Hartfield, G., Wissenschaftliche und soziale Rationalität, Stuttgart 1968, p. 35. [F. H.] Against this background, the debate between induction and deduction is only a question of weighting and amounts ultimately to shadow-boxing. Reducing the so-called first 'Methodenstreit' in economics [methodological debate in Germany and Austria between 1880 and 1890] to this alleged fundamental decision is in any case a bogus claim. Cf. on Menger's methodology Boos, M., Die Wissenschaftstheorie Carl Mengers, Graz / Wien 1986.

[16] Cf. De Quincey, Th., Dialogues of Three Templars on Political Economy [1824], in: De Quincey's Collected Writings, vol. IX, London 1897, pp. 37–112, p. 96.

[17] Weber, M., Critical Studies in the Logic of the Cultural Sciences, A Critique of Eduard Meyer's Methodological View [1906], in: Weber, M., On the Methodology of the Social Sciences, ed. by Shils, E. A., Finch, H. A., Illinois 1949, pp. 113–188, p. 169, https://archive.org/details/maxweberonmethod00webe.

[18] Mill completed his "Essays on Some Unsettled Questions of Political Economy" in 1830; however, only after the success of his book "System of Logic" did he find a publisher (London: John W. Parker) who put the essays into print in 1844, https://archive.org/details/in.ernet.dli.2015.275463.

[19] Cf. Marx, K., Theories of Surplus Value, Part III, Moscow 1971, p. 190, http://www.marx2mao.com/PDFs/TSV-Part%203.pdf. Cf. also Marx, K., Capital, vol. I, op. cit., p. 125 n.

speculation", which in consequence amounts to Menger's "exact" approach.[20] The extraordinary interconnectedness of relationships and contexts in social life also justifies this method:

> "Since, therefore, it is vain to hope that truth can be arrived at, either in Political Economy or in any other department of the social science, while we look at the facts in the concrete, clothed in all the complexity with which nature has surrounded them, and endeavour to elicit a general law by a process of induction from a comparison of details; there remains no other method than the *à priori* one, or that of 'abstract speculation'."[21]

In this spirit, Johann Heinrich von Thünen, in his 1842 preface to his "Isolated State", requested readers "... not to be deterred by the assumptions made at the beginning, which deviate from reality ..."[22]; indeed, he regarded this method of utmost importance, to "... present the influence of a certain power ... for itself and make it recognisable."[23] And Marshall, who has been mentioned above several times and whose impact on teaching economics can hardly be overestimated, confesses—although his emphasis on "realistic" assumptions seems to contradict this—that he is strictly speaking also a supporter of "exact speculation" by propagating the *ceteris paribus* clause:

> "It is true that we do treat variables *provisionally* as constants. But it is also true that this is the only method by which science has ever made any great progress in dealing with complex and changeful matter, whether in the physical or moral world."[24]

Obviously, there is no shortage of renowned economists advocating the analytical-deductive method[25]—despite all originality in detail. Here are two points of particular interest that deserve a closer examination. Firstly, what significance is conceded to empiricism in each case? Secondly, on which axioms rests the logical deduction?

Menger takes the extreme position when it comes to the importance of empiricism:

> "To want to look for the criterion of the guarantees of the exact laws of economy in their congruence with its empirical laws signifies a failure to recognize the most elementary principles of scientific methodology. Such a procedure would be comparable to that of a

---

[20] Although Menger criticises Mill's methodological position in his "System of Logic", he also quotes Mill's collection of essays published in 1844, without comparing the methodological viewpoint presented there with his own. Cf. Menger, C., Investigations ..., op. cit., p. 118 n. and p. 211 n.

[21] Mill, J. St., On the Definition of Political Economy; and on the Method of Investigation proper to it, in: Mill, J. St., Essays on ..., op. cit., pp. 120–164, p. 148 f. In this light, it must remain unclear how v. Wiese counts Mill as a logician among those who place induction before deduction and ranks him as a philosopher among the empiricists. Cf. Wiese, L. v., Mill, John Stuart, in: Handwörterbuch der Staatswissenschaften, vol. VII, Stuttgart / Tübingen / Göttingen 1961, pp. 343–346, p. 344.

[22] Thünen, J. H. v., Der isolierte Staat in Beziehung auf Landwirtschaft und Nationalökonomie [1842], 3rd ed., Berlin 1875, ed. by Breuer, W., Gerhardt, E., Darmstadt 1966, p. XVI. [F. H.]

[23] Ibid., p. XVI f. [F. H.]

[24] Marshall, A., Principles ..., op. cit., p. 315 n.

[25] This approach is also pursued in the classical line Ricardo—Marx—Sraffa. Cf. Kurz, H. D., Zur neoricardianischen Theorie des Allgemeinen Gleichgewichts der Produktion und Zirkulation, Berlin 1977, p. 21 ff.

natural scientist who wants to test and rectify the laws of physics, chemistry, and mechanics by the empirical laws of natural phenomena; or even that of one who wants to test and rectify the results of the exact research of a Newton, Lavoisier, or Helmholtz by rules for farmers, surely extremely useful in their own way ..."[26]

Even if the facts should contradict the logically derived a priori statements due to the influence of special circumstances, this has no consequences: "But what else does this prove than that the results of exact research do not happen to find their criterion in experience in the above sense?"[27] As hackneyed as it may be, the leaf drifting in the autumn wind does not invalidate the laws of gravity; logically correct propositions cannot be overturned empirically. However, empiricism tells us something about the *relevance* of the models, their axioms, and their abstractions—therein lies their significance.

Menger's purist stance and the formal analyses conducted in this vein have repeatedly been criticised as "model Platonism". Especially followers of Karl Raimund Popper and the "critical rationalism" he founded have always accused neoclassical theorists of merely performing sand table exercises without subjecting their results to any attempts at falsification—if that is possible at all.

For quite some time, this reproach has undoubtedly contributed to the fact that the "leading" economic journals increasingly publish plain vanilla papers with an appended empirical test, especially since the mass distribution of computer-aided statistical packages—if you like, a late revenge of the historical school in economics.

However, it is neither necessary to assess the pros and cons of Popper's preference for eliminating falsehood over the search for truth nor is it imperative to appraise falsificationism as such.[28] Instead, it seems appropriate to counter two quite popular prejudices.

On the one hand, the belief that mathematical deductions based on definitions are devoid of information content must be rejected. The only thing, it is said, that can be filtered out of such systems is what has previously been inserted: "One does not realise," Eucken states on behalf of many, "that deductions from definitions can only yield findings that have been put into the definition before."[29]

However, this view disregards all the insights that come from *linking* particular statements:

"From *one* proposition there cannot result more than what is already to be found therein, that is to say, more than it itself states for the exhaustive comprehension of its meaning. But from *two* propositions, if they are syllogistically connected to premisses, more can result than is to be found in each of them taken separately; just as a body that is a chemical compound

---

[26] Menger, C., Investigations ..., op. cit., p. 73.

[27] Ibid., p. 71 f.

[28] On weighing up the logical shortcomings of falsificationism (i.e., the 'verification of falsification') against its pragmatic advantages, see Zinn, K. G., Wirtschaft und Wissenschaftstheorie, Herne / Berlin 1976, p. 51 ff.

[29] Eucken, W., op. cit., p. 47. [F. H.]

> displays properties that do not belong to any of its constituent elements considered separately. On this rests the value of syllogisms."[30]

There is an essential difference between objective truth and subjective certainty for the individual. A consistent system of equations with several unknowns contains its solution; however, it is hidden, and a strictly regulated analysis is required to extract it.

On the other hand, albeit in close connection with this, there is a widespread opinion that "model Platonism" has no practical relevance and serves as a kind of occupational therapy for otherwise unemployed mathematicians. This view remains superficial. It fails to recognise the ideology-forming and action-guiding function of the promises that stem from formal systems.

General equilibrium theory, e.g., does not describe the real world. Still, by attempting to prove that the teamwork of supply and demand in a *model* of competition between (infinitely) many sellers and buyers produces positively rated stability and optimality characteristics, it acquires normative appeal: in "perfect" competition, the performance of the price mechanism is unbeatable, and its beneficial effects must not be hindered.[31] With such an ideal in mind, policy *is* justified—regardless of its logical or empirical substance:

> "Whether a theory is 'right' or 'wrong' does not play the decisive role, but what is *socially* significant is whether the doctrine is believed and becomes part of people's *reliable* knowledge: Ptolemy – not Aristarchus of Samos – represented the *correct* cosmology in the eyes of the ancient world and the Middle Ages."[32]

It is therefore necessary to critically scrutinise these seemingly empirically irrelevant models and point out their possible use as an apologia. Should it even be possible to prove that the models suffer from *logical* defects, this would engender the most serious damage to the thought structures that can now be labelled as definitively "false". Hence, such efforts are to be considered meritorious, not only from a scientific point of view.

An adherent of the exact method who intends to establish and test economic laws does not have to pass by reality with his eyes closed. There is room for factual validation alongside logical truth. Mill, as an advocate of the a priori method, emphatically pointed to this additional source of knowledge:

> "The discrepancy between our anticipations and the actual fact is often the only circumstance which would have drawn our attention to some important disturbing cause which we had overlooked. Nay, it often discloses to us errors in thought, still more serious than the omission of … a disturbing cause."[33]

---

[30] Schopenhauer, A., Parerga and Paralipomena [1851], Short Philosophical Essays, vol. II, Oxford 1974, p. 22 (§ 24).

[31] For a critical discussion of General Equilibrium Theory, see Helmedag, F., Ohne Werte und kreislaufschwach: Zum Status der Allgemeinen Gleichgewichtstheorie, in: Helmedag, F., Reuter, N. (eds.), Der Wohlstand der Personen, Festschrift zum 60. Geburtstag von Karl Georg Zinn, Marburg 1999, pp. 43–68.

[32] Zinn, K. G., Politische …, op. cit., p. 69. [F. H.]

[33] Mill, J. St., On the Definition …, op. cit., p. 154.

Pragmatic handling of falsificationism *has* its merits. This procedure makes it possible to examine whether the assumptions supporting the exact economic laws are "correctly" chosen, i.e., whether the premises carry a building that accommodates a relevant social totality. It will never be possible to achieve one hundred percent agreement between the predictions of the exact laws and the empirical findings. There is no way around a convention within the *scientific community* regarding the extent to which deviations are still tolerable.

Exact economic laws that must always be logically valid and may not fail in reality gain as rules of empirical reality a status of "pattern predictions" or "explanations of principle".[34] They instruct about the *tendency* of the economic process in practice; Mendel's laws also do not teach which genes a flower will develop in a singular instance. Likewise, natural laws, as in the case of a river, provide no information about the movement of each water particle; yet, the direction and perhaps even the strength of the current can be determined. Then—to use the same metaphor—it is possible to take measures against the risk of flooding.

The congruence between theoretical prediction and actual finding depends on the extent to which the economic driving forces—whose effects are studied analytically and deductively to condense them into economic laws—determine the observable actions of people. Economic theory as an exact science needs only empirical assistance as it is necessary to ascertain how much of the constructed, axiomatically erected economic system can be found in the real social world. Thus, the open question regards the significance of economic action at its finest, which is an integral part of "economic" events in ordinary life.

Yet the core of the discipline is still unknown. To conclude this chapter, we should not neglect to look at the proposals of the protagonists of the abstract method, Mill and Menger. Perhaps they can also help us with this problem.

Let us begin with Menger: "By economy we understand the precautionary activity of humans directed toward covering their material needs; by *national economy*, the social form of this activity."[35] With this definition of economics, Menger joins the group of economists who do not circumscribe the economy in terms of a general formal principle but rather content-wise. According to his idea of economics as the precautionary activity of people to cover their desired consumption, the doctrine of needs plays a prominent role in Menger's work. It forms the starting point and, simultaneously, the centre of his considerations.[36]

It has already been noted that this approach is too global and covers far more than is dealt with. For this reason, Menger's description of the economy hardly seems convincing, especially not if one strives for an exact science in the sense he intended. However, we will return to his suggestion of appropriate social organisation to meet the demand for goods.

---

[34] These formulations characterise Hayek's methodology. See Graf, H. G., „Muster-Voraussagen" und „Erklärungen des Prinzips" bei F. A. von Hayek, Tübingen 1978.

[35] Menger, C., Investigations ..., op. cit., p. 63.

[36] Cf. Menger, C., Principles of Economics [1871], Ludwig von Mises Institute, Auburn 2007, https://cdn.mises.org/principles_of_economics.pdf.

Let us first look at Mill. More consistently than Menger, Mill originates an ideal figure of economic activity corresponding to an "exact speculation". Since an abstract science is, in principle, to be understood as the *construction* of a world, its inhabitants are also artificial creatures:

> "Geometry presupposes an arbitrary definition of a line, 'that which has length but not breadth.' Just in the same manner does Political Economy presuppose an arbitrary definition of man, as a being who invariably does that by which he may obtain the greatest amount of necessaries, conveniences, and luxuries, with the smallest quantity of labour and physical self-denial with which they can be obtained in the existing state of knowledge."[37]

Mill thus combines a substantive specification, the satisfaction of needs, with an optimisation behaviour: maximisation of utility. The launched *homo oeconomicus* was henceforth to embody the character sketch of the economically active subject—often reviled but never driven into exile. Today, he even has a descendant, the *resourceful, evaluative, maximising man*: REMM.[38] However, little is gained materially with the introduction of this utility-maximising *homunculus*: as long as the economy is not differentiated from other social subsystems, every action can "somehow" be interpreted as maximising utility; it remains a sample without value.

> "Even the pure destruction of wealth does not correspond to the entire renunciation," Mauss' notes in his anthropological study, "that it apparently represents. These acts are not free of self-interest either. The lavish, almost always excessive, and often purely destructive form of consumption, especially in potlatch, where considerable and long accumulated goods are given away or destroyed in one fell swoop, gives this institution the appearance of pure wasteful spending and childish extravagance ... But the motive of these excessive gifts and this reckless consumption, these senseless losses and destruction of property is in no way altruistic ..."[39]

The arbitrariness of maximising utility in individual cases sometimes produces strange results. Woll, e.g., (rightly) states that the economic principle as information about consumer activities is an empty formula. Still, on the next page, we read: "The idea of homo oeconomicus has been the subject of much ridicule. However, the principle on which it is based is a sensible guideline for action."[40] Woll gives the readers credit for assessing the usefulness of an empty formula as a guideline for behaviour.

Behind all of this lies the failure of modern economic theory to sort out the *nature* of economic actions from the whole spectrum of human activity. It may seem quite appealing to constitute economics as an exact science based on an abstract a priori construction of a *homo oeconomicus* who performs as a typical representative economic activity; yet, this endeavour will not be successful until it is clarified what economic actions as such are. Next, we shall tackle this task.

---

[37] Mill, J. St., On the definition ..., op. cit., p. 144.

[38] Cf. Kaufmann, F.-X., Wirtschaftssoziologie I: Allgemeine, in: Handwörterbuch der Wirtschaftswissenschaft, vol. IX, Stuttgart / Tübingen / Göttingen 1982, pp. 239–267, p. 244.

[39] Mauss, M., Die Gabe [1923/24], 2nd ed., Frankfurt a. M. 1984, p. 170. [F. H.]

[40] Woll, A., op. cit., p. 31. [F. H.]

Chapter 4
The Core Element of Economic Activity: Economic Exchange

To the extent that the definitions of the economy presented so far have made any statements at all about the scope of this concept, they have always addressed—albeit with varying degrees of emphasis—the interconnectedness of production, distribution and consumption of social wealth. Some authors see this interplay as the common point of reference of economic theory or, more precisely, its subject matter. Yet, how production and distribution are socially regulated has varied historically. The economic anthropologist Karl Polanyi has identified three "pure" modes of distribution: reciprocity, redistribution and exchange.[1]

Reciprocity means "… taking turns to bear burdens and sharing with each other."[2] A social code of conduct prescribes certain mutual obligations to help and the compulsory presentation of gifts.[3]

Redistribution refers to circumstances in which a collecting institution (king, priest, planning authority) levies duties to either store them as stocks or distribute them to the needy. "Redistribution obtains within a group to the extent to which the allocation of goods is collected in one hand and takes place by virtue of custom, law or ad hoc central decision."[4]

In the case of *exchange*, distribution is based on supply and demand. Institutionally, this requires corresponding rights of property as well as disposition.

These three typical distribution methods cover the *permitted* possibilities for allocating goods: "Transfers and transactions that cannot be included in these categories are regarded in society … as illegitimate and unjust."[5]

---

[1] Cf. Polanyi, K., The Economy as Instituted Process, in: Polanyi, K., Arensberg, C. M., Pearson, H. W. (eds.), Trade …, op. cit., pp. 243–270, especially pp. 250–256, https://archive.org/details/in.gov.ignca.36501/page/n5/mode/2up.

[2] Polanyi, K., Ökonomie …, op. cit., p. 166. [F. H.]

[3] On the significance of the gift in archaic societies, see Mauss, M., op. cit.

[4] Polanyi, K., The Economy …, op. cit., p. 253.

[5] Codere, H., Verteilungsmodus und Gesellschaftsform, in: Schlicht, E. (ed.), Einführung in die Verteilungstheorie, Reinbek bei Hamburg 1976, pp. 73–84, p. 73 f. [F. H.]

F. Helmedag, *Production of Commodities by Means of Labour*, Springer Studies in Alternative Economics, https://doi.org/10.1007/978-3-032-01457-3_4

Depending on the time and place, the mentioned distribution modes have varying importance; alongside the dominant mode, which primarily shapes daily life, the others are either more or less pronounced. Every Christmas, we also experience the collective *compulsion to give gifts*, where there are often clear ideas of their appropriateness. "Even today, an unanswered present humiliates the person who has accepted it, especially if he accepts it without any thought of a return."[6]

According to Polanyi, the forms of integration, i.e., the way society is structured according to social, political and economic motives and models, correspond to the modes of distribution, namely reciprocity, redistribution and exchange. Still, they do not result from simply aggregating the respective personal behaviour.[7] Reciprocity presupposes corresponding symmetrical structures, such as large families. Redistribution requires the existence of an allocation centre, while the organisation of the distribution of goods in such societies does not necessarily rest on the use of money.[8] Barter as the predominant form of exchange presupposes the prevalence of corresponding ownership structures and some scope for individual decision-making: "Acts of exchange on the personal level produce prices only if they occur under a system of price-making markets, an institutional setup which is nowhere created by mere random acts of exchange."[9]

It is worth evaluating Polanyi's work for the definition of economic actions and, thus, the subject matter of economics. Indeed, the blanket discussion of production, distribution, and consumption of social wealth does not encompass the gist of economics closely enough. Neither do economists primarily study the nature and driving forces of reciprocity and redistribution, although these aspects should be considered complementary. Finally, several other sciences, from technical disciplines to psychology, address production, distribution and consumption aspects.

In contrast, *exchange* is at the forefront of the activities of modern economists. From this perspective, it seems reasonable to understand economics as the study of exchange per se: catallactics.[10] In this sense, Buchanan explains: "Economics, the

---

[6] Mauss, M., op. cit., p. 157. [F. H.]

[7] Polanyi, D., The Economy ..., op. cit., p. 251.

[8] Examples of such societies include the Jesuit state in Paraguay during the sixteenth and seventeenth centuries and the Inca Empire before the Spanish conquest. In this economy, all surplus goods had to be delivered to the state; occasionally, even the stocks deemed unnecessary were confiscated. The state redistributed the goods that came into its possession in line with needs. Cf. Baudin, L., Der sozialistische Staat der Inka, Reinbek bei Hamburg 1956.

[9] Polanyi, D., The Economy ..., op. cit., p. 251. Similarly, Andreae writes: "A meaningful price can result even less from a rare exchange with a random alternation of abundance and scarcity ... For with random abundance, superfluous, easily perishable goods have no value at all for the seller, while the buyer suffering from scarcity must acquire them at any price. How, then, is a price to be formed?" Andreae, W., Geld und Geldschöpfung, Stuttgart / Wien 1953, p. 17 f. [F. H.]

[10] The proposal goes back to Whately: "The name I should have preferred as the most descriptive, and on the whole least objectionable, is that of CATALLACTICS, or the 'Science of *Exchange*'." Whately, R., Introductory Lectures on Political Economy, London 1831, p. 6. Cf. also the critical comment of Schumpeter, J. A., History ..., op. cit., p. 536 n. Yet in his debut book, Schumpeter

science of market and exchange institutions ..."[11] However, markets and exchanges are quite old institutions, and the determinants of exchange relations were different in antiquity than in later times. This difference must not be ignored, despite all superficial similarities, if we want to identify economics in its modern meaning:

> "The concept of the economic, as it became constitutive for the national economy or economics, refers to a phenomenon that itself only began to appear at a particular time ... It is the all-round market economy, in which more and more all kinds of active life are included ... Every economic subject, in so far as it participates in the market, be it presenting (supply) or desiring (demand), has as a point of reference for its possibilities and decisions those figures which, as prices, indicate the relation of all commodities to one another. By orienting towards prices, market participants begin to act economically."[12]

With the emphasis on markets and price formation processes, a substantive concretisation of economics finally seems to be approaching; Dieter Schneider also believes that he has found the solution there: in his opinion, economic theory ...

> "... can be used as an abbreviation for the doctrine of the determinants of exchange relationships between goods and services and the possible applications of exchange relationships in the distribution of rights and obligations."[13]

On closer inspection, however, it becomes clear that the interpretation of economic theory as a science concerned with exchange needs to be supplemented. Even Polanyi's three forms of distribution may "somehow" all be understood as exchange. Reciprocity not only *demands* a gift but also *secures* a present in return; redistribution promises protection or a religious respective cultural service for payment: *all* social life can be interpreted in some way as an exchange. This view conforms, e.g., to Homans' sociological concept: "... interactions between persons is an exchange of goods, material or nonmaterial."[14] Belshaw takes a similar approach: "... all enduring social relations involve transactions, which have an exchange aspect."[15] It is even conceivable, if it must be, to impose the exchange paradigm on the definition of economic activity as a choice between alternatives: in a way, the individual exchanges with himself or with nature.

---

described the exchange as "... the bracket that holds the economic system together ..." Cf. Schumpeter, J. A., Wesen und Hauptinhalt der theoretischen Nationalökonomie [1908], Berlin 1970, p. 50. [F. H.]

[11] Buchanan, J. M., The Limits of Liberty, Between Anarchy and Leviathan, Chicago 1975, p. 19. In a footnote, Buchanan points out that his view of economics departs from the usual one. Cf. ibid., n. Hayek also suggests replacing the terms capitalism and market economy with "extended order" or catallactic. Cf. Hayek, F. A. v., The Fatal Conceit, The Errors of Socialism, in: Bartley III, W. W. (ed.), The Collected Works of F. A. Hayek, vol. I, London 1988, p. 6.

[12] Landshut, S., op. cit., p. 48. [F. H.]

[13] Schneider, D., Allgemeine ..., op. cit., p. 19.

[14] Homans, G. C., Social Behavior as Exchange, in: Homans, G. C., Sentiments and Activities, London 1962, pp. 278–293, p. 279. Cf. in addition Homans, G. C., Elementarformen sozialen Handelns, Köln / Opladen 1968. Several sociological schools place exchange at the centre. According to Lévi-Strauss, e.g., every society is divided into three levels of exchange: the exchange of women, of goods as well as services, and messages. For further references, see Morel, J. et al., Soziologische Theorie, Abriß der Ansätze ihrer Hauptvertreter, München / Wien 1989, p. 107 ff.

[15] Belshaw, C. S., op. cit., p. 4.

Although this does not mean that the battle has been won, it does indicate the direction in which we can look with hope of success: what characterises *economic* exchange? The obvious thing to do would be to consult the major dictionaries of the discipline, but neither the twelve-volume "Handwörterbuch der Sozialwissenschaften" [handbook of social sciences] nor the sequel "Handwörterbuch der Wirtschaftswissenschaften" [handbook of economics] contains a separate entry of the keyword "Tausch" [exchange]. Remarkably, the economic literature provides only scattered remarks about this topic.

Dieter Schneider has dwelt on this question with more extraordinary meticulousness and care than is customary. He specifies his portrayal of economics as the study of exchange relations and its determinants by defining the subject matter more precisely: " 'Economics' is equated here with the 'income aspect' of human activity."[16] There is a broad spectrum of very different operations that are related to the generation or use of income:

> "Making music and running races, praying and murdering can also be linked to the use of exchange relations, i.e., take on the character of a 'commodity', like building a power station, fattening pigs or collecting paintings."[17]

In this interpretation, the popular Robinsonades of marginal utility theory, in which the laws of the capitalist market economy are derived from the "psychology of hermitism",[18] provide an unsuitable experimental field for economic analyses. The self-sufficient economy of Robinson Crusoe is blind to the deliberations presented by marginal utility theory. There is no exchange and thus no price system on the island: "... Robinson Crusoe is in a situation of which Political Economy takes no cognizance ..."[19] Economic activity requires particular interactions between the members of societies where specialised commodity production prevails.

Even when Freitag joins Robinson, the two are not engaged in any "business"; they apply the rational principle (in whatever form) but do not conduct transactions characterised by the selfish pursuit of advantage.[20] Both presumably produce under the principle of job sharing—Robinson perhaps cooks better, and Freitag possibly catches fish more quickly—but they constitute a *household*, a community with non-economic internal relationships that do not rest on the laws of exchange.[21] Therefore, the two islanders' coexistence resembles a "cooperative"[22] rather than a market economy.

---

[16] Schneider, D., Allgemeine ..., op. cit., p. 19. [F. H.]

[17] Ibid., p. 20. [F. H.]

[18] Cf. Eckstein, G., Die vierfache Wurzel des Satzes vom unzureichenden Grunde der Grenznutzentheorie. Eine Robinsonade, in: Die neue Zeit, vol. 20 (1902), pp. 810–816, p. 810, https://www.marxists.org/deutsch/archiv/eckstein/1902/xx/wurzel.html. [F. H.]

[19] Whately, R., op. cit., p. 7.

[20] On the relationship between the two characters, see Hymer, S., Robinson Crusoe and the secret of primitive accumulation, in: Monthly Review, vol. 23 (1971), pp. 11–36.

[21] Cf. Schneider, D., Allgemeine ..., op. cit., p. 20.

[22] Cf. ibid., p. 22.

Let us take a closer look at Dieter Schneider's ideas. Does his proposal succeed in eliminating the shortcomings of the previously considered ones? Suppose the main elements of economic activity are seen in the income generation as a result of human action and in the use of income by human decision. In that case, the question arises about what "income" means. Schneider's answer is somewhat shallow: "... 'income' [is] understood in the everyday sense as an inflow of money or goods via markets ..., not in the sense of any sophisticated theoretical definition ...".[23]

This explanation merely shifts the problem; we now have to clarify what "markets" are—again, no easy task.[24] Although Paul's invitation to Paulina for dinner in a well-known gourmet restaurant falls under the heading of the use of income in markets, it can be assumed that economic calculation plays a subordinate role here. Schneider expressly *does not* think that the generation and use of income is "rational".[25] At the same time, he refrains from naming the "economic hallmark of the economy". Therefore, his definition of content ultimately remains vague. Schneider does not manoeuvre himself into the dead end of arguing purely formally. Nevertheless, he overstates the case by resorting to the empirical phenomenon of "income generation and use". Several activities are dedicated to income generation or use without being economically motivated. Thus, they are not the subject of economics.

Schneider's compelling emphasis on exchange processes as the characteristic feature of economic activities should have been better continued with an analysis of transactions. To be sure, people swap many different things: car tyres for suits, stamps for beer mats, places, rooms and addresses. Even the Germanic tribes' barter of weapons was undoubtedly an exchange, but not in the economic sense: "... it is rather a mutual guarantee, an outward symbol of a friendly relationship."[26] Even the following completed short novel revolves around exchange: they exchanged glances, caresses, and finally, the partner. Not all the listed acts of exchange are manifestations of economic activity. What characterises *economic* exchange?

Two factors give an exchange process an economic quality. Firstly, the economic exchange is *voluntary*; neither party uses any means of coercion. There is no threat of violence or its practice, with which one exchange partner tries to influence the other. "Money or life", accompanied by presenting a stiletto as a decision-making aid, is not an offer of economic exchange. However, the prevailing doctrine would have no difficulty understanding this situation as a maximisation task under constraints. Therefore, it is, in their opinion, an economic problem.

If one emphasises the mutual voluntary nature of the transaction as a distinguishing mark of an economic exchange, definitions such as "economic activity means the procurement of things that have value"[27] fall through the sieve; our knifeman wants to do precisely that, yet he does not engage in economic activity.

---

[23] Ibid., p. 18 f. [F. H.]

[24] Cf. ibid., p. 42 and passim.

[25] Cf. ibid., p. 19.

[26] Laum, B., Heiliges Geld, Eine historische Untersuchung über den sakralen Ursprung des Geldes, Tübingen 1924, p. 60. [F. H.]

[27] Ott, A. E., Wirtschaftstheorie, Eine erste Einführung, Göttingen 1989, p. 16. [F. H.]

An economic exchange favours *at least one* of the two partners, as he views his situation as more advantageous after the transaction than before the business opportunity arose. In the edge case, the other participant must not experience deterioration in his welfare state to agree to the trade. Therefore, the voluntary or autonomous exchange is not associated with the prospect of losing benefits due to the change of ownership. In contrast, the person faced with the alternative of "money or life" loses one or the other—perhaps even both—as soon as the blade tickles his throat.[28]

The touchstone for determining whether a trade was voluntary is the unwillingness to reverse the transaction. After bacon and the Bible have been handed over, no one will be eager to return what was acquired in exchange for what has been given—apart from deception or error about the quality of the goods obtained. On the other hand, the person threatened by the dagger prefers the *status quo ante*, which would mean keeping cash and life.

The welfare of participants, therefore, *inevitably* increases with the number of *economic* exchanges. A change of initial endowments by an increase or decrease in goods is irreversible; once an economic exchange between two people has occurred, it will not be observed in the opposite direction, as at least one has gained, and nobody is worse off. This weak "Pareto improvement" becomes strong if both parties benefit.

The voluntary nature of the exchange sometimes has cynical traits: the parents who sent their children to the factories and mines in the early phase of the Industrial Revolution were not forced to do so by direct physical violence but by iron economic constraints—it was the only way to eke out the family's living. Nevertheless, the labour contract came about voluntarily; the most meagre meal takes precedence over starvation: "... no one would, in the situation in which he actually finds himself, work for a pittance if he did not prefer the poverty wage to not working."[29]

The opposite is also true. The statement: "I don't want to trade places with anyone", signals that you are doing well and are satisfied with the state of things. This contentedness illustrates the importance of "initial endowments", which are relegated to neoclassical general equilibrium theory data. Although an economic exchange necessarily increases the quality of life of those directly involved, the resulting advantages may be distributed very unevenly. While for the poor, the most modest prospect of improving their miserable existence immediately brings about a willingness to conclude a deal, the rich can allow themselves the luxury of waiting for better opportunities.

Not all voluntary transactions can be classified as an economic occurrence. From the set of all autonomous processes of giving and taking, those significantly influenced by the specific counterpart must be separated. In an economic exchange, however, no importance is attached to personal preferences, as it is carried out on the same terms with *any* trading partner. For a toothpaste manufacturer, it is irrelevant

---

[28] On this complex, see Kirsch, G., Zwang, Tausch und Geschenk, in: das wirtschaftsstudium (wisu), vol. 17 (1988), pp. 221–226, where, however, Polanyi is not mentioned.

[29] Simmel, G., Philosophie des Geldes [1907], 5th ed., München / Leipzig 1930, p. 52. [F. H.] However, such coercive situations can be interpreted as forms of 'structural' violence. Cf. Galtung, J., Violence, Peace and Peace Research, in: Journal of Peace Research, vol. 6 (1969), pp. 167–191.

whether a Christian, a Mohammedan or an atheist buys his product. On the other hand, the father who buys his son a bicycle because of his regular oral hygiene would not strike this deal with just any decent tooth-brushing individual. Personal relationships play a considerable role in "economic life". Cultivating such relationships with "business friends" does not happen without purpose. Polite behaviour, shared meals and gifts are known to foster such relationships, potentially leading to new business opportunities or ensuring the continuity of existing partnerships. To a certain extent, individuals engage in trade due to such interactions, even if they would prefer a different offer from a purely economic perspective.

> "In my purchase of bread," Robbins informs us, "I may be interested solely in the comparison between the bread and the other things in the circle of exchange on which I might have spent the money. But I may be interested too in the happiness of my baker. There may exist between us certain liens which make it preferable for me to buy bread from him, rather than procure it from his competitor who is willing to sell it a little cheaper."[30]

The exchange, as such, is not a sufficient indication of an economic situation. If Friday joins Robinson, they will probably both receive and give, and each has certain rights and obligations; nevertheless, this relationship is not economic; the interpersonal relationship characterises it—it could not be otherwise on the island. From an economic vantage point, this is the substance of a *household*: the acts of exchange in the interior connection always focus on the other *individual*, whether voluntary or not. In the household, reciprocal services are based on reciprocity and redistribution, i.e., on a *do ut des*-thinking, which is not measured in monetary units.

It is different in an enterprise or plant, without wanting to descend into the abysses that open in the business literature on this topic. By signing a *labour contract*, a person sells his labour power with the obligation to integrate into a hierarchy. The boss acquires an *inwardly* directed right to issue instructions; he may exercise command limited by custom and law. In a manufacturing facility, connections based on reciprocity, redistribution, solidarity, affection, etc. can also develop; it is not for nothing that one occasionally speaks—in the past more than today—of a *family* relation between staff members. However, the purpose of the firm as a profit-maximising unit, i.e., as an enterprise in the sense meant here, is pursued *externally* through economic exchange so that, unlike in the household, this becomes the criterion for employee performance.—The reasons companies exist are discussed at the end of this book.

Economic exchange can be summarised as the non-violent, reciprocal transfer of goods, services, rights and obligations without regard to the business partner's personality. If one accepts the autonomous, anonymous exchange as specifically economic, the *economic subjects* are the people or institutions involved in such transactions. *Economic objects* are all the goods, services, rights and obligations that constitute the item of an economic exchange.

Economic interaction is not an isolated phenomenon that only affects the welfare of those directly involved. Third parties can also be affected by others' economic activity, which refers to positive or negative external effects. The problem of negative

---

[30] Robbins, L., op. cit., p. 95.

external costs is fundamental in welfare economics. According to the traditional view, which goes back to Pigou,[31] in such cases, it is up to the *state* to ensure the optimal allocation of resources for the economy as a whole. Maximum social welfare requires intervention by the authorities in the private economy. Compensation for damages, taxation or prohibitive rules are the appropriate instruments.[32]

Economic policy can only be justified normatively: reducing discrepancies between individual and collective rationality is crucial. In the parliamentary decision-making process of a democracy, most votes decide; the minority must comply *nolens volens.* In the private economic sphere, however, the principle of unanimity applies: the voluntary nature of economic exchange grants the individual quasi a veto power; no one clinches a deal against his will with an equal. In contrast, the taxable population is obliged to pay a compulsory levy to the revenue board: the "welfare state" also digs into the pockets of many citizens. Those who feel unduly burdened consider the state a benefactor at the taxpayer's expense. The concept of economic exchange increases the awareness of such coherences.

Against this background, economic theory essentially has two tasks, which are hierarchically related to each other. Firstly, efforts should be directed towards revealing the *structure* of an economy earmarked by economic exchange: it is a matter of uncovering the economic laws that govern the *division of labour* in commercial societies. The second step addresses the question of which factors determine the *level* of economic activity, i.e., the volume of economic exchange acts. Thus, economic theory must initially determine the operating principles of unregulated capitalism under "free" competition conditions. With this knowledge, the structure and features to which modern economies are moving can be described. Then, the wheels that need to be set in motion to realise welfare improvements are identified. This endeavour usually leads to conflicts of interest, as economic policy only exceptionally consists of strong Pareto improvements.

The topic of "economy and society" is not limited to the state's economic role. Significantly, the success of economic activity is rarely measured by an individual yardstick. Instead, a social criterion dominates: *money.* Before the basic economic research program is explained in more detail, it should first be demonstrated that

---

[31] Cf. Pigou, A. C., The Economics of Welfare [1920], 4th ed., London 1952.

[32] The need for economic policy measures in the presence of external effects is controversial among experts. The so-called Coase theorem claims that for clearly assigned property rights and without transaction costs, negative external effects would be internalised through negotiations. Then, the optimal allocation of resources is realised. Furthermore, the legal design does not influence this outcome. If transaction costs are positive, however, it depends on the individual case whether liability for damages brings better macroeconomic results or not. Coase, therefore, disagrees with the view that the physical perpetrator of an external effect should always be liable for damages. Cf. Coase, R., The Problem of Social Cost, in: The Journal of Law and Economics, vol. 3 (1960), pp. 1–44. A critical appraisal is provided by Helmedag, F., Zur Vermarktung des Rechts: Anmerkungen zum Coase-Theorem, in: Wolf, D., Reiner, S., Eicker-Wolf, K. (eds.), Auf der Suche nach dem Kompaß, Politische Ökonomie als Bahnsteigkarte fürs 21. Jahrhundert, Köln 1999, pp. 53–71.

money gives economic exchange a unique quality: it represents *the precondition and motive* for economic activity in competitive capitalist societies. In addition, the history of money reflects the dissemination of economic exchange and, thus, the career of the *homo oeconomicus*.

Chapter 5
The Development of the *Homo Oeconomicus* or the Evolution and Nature of Money

The decision favouring economic exchange as the distinctive feature of economic action implies rejecting the absolutist approach in economics. There is no such thing as "the economic" as an epoch-spanning moment of human coexistence.

Instead, *economic* exchange as an *essential* element of commercial relations is a relatively recent phenomenon—just like economics. This dissociation contrasts with the central anthropological premise of the discipline's founders. The classics believed people had a "natural" tendency "… to truck, barter, and exchange one thing for another."[1]

Trade was even elevated to the *differentia specifica* between humans and animals: "Nobody ever saw a dog made a fair and deliberate exchange of one bone for another with another dog."[2] And many economists still attribute the origins of money to the inefficiency of natural exchange.[3] Anthropological research has refuted this belief[4]; the transfer of goods *and* the use of money are older than exchange:

> "But ethnology has long since taught us, and economic history and social economics have been able to accept and confirm this doctrine, that although there have been unimaginable long periods in which man has lived without exchange, he has not lived without any transfer of goods. Wherever a circulation in goods develops – gifts, offerings, penance, sacrifices on the one hand, hospitality, and distribution on the other – the conditions for the emergence

---

[1] Smith, A., An Inquiry into the Nature and Causes of the Wealth of Nations [1776], vol. I, Indianapolis 1981, p. 25.

[2] Ibid., p. 26. Likewise, the already mentioned Whately writes: "Man might be defined, 'An animal that makes *Exchanges*:' no other, even of those animals which in other points make the nearest approach to rationality, having, to all appearance, the least notion of bartering, or in any way exchanging one thing for another. And it is in this view alone that Man is contemplated by Political Economy." Whately, R., op. cit., p. 6.

[3] Aristotle is regarded as the founder of the 'convention theory of money', according to which a general medium of exchange was introduced to facilitate barter. Cf. Aristotle, Politics I, Indianapolis / Cambridge 1998, p. 16.

[4] For an overview, see Hart, K., barter, in: The New Palgrave, vol. I, London / New York / Tokyo 1987, pp. 196–198. We shall soon deal with this point extensively.

F. Helmedag, *Production of Commodities by Means of Labour*, Springer Studies in Alternative Economics, https://doi.org/10.1007/978-3-032-01457-3_5

of money exist, i.e., a good that acquires the character of a generally esteemed and popular means of recompense."[5]

It is evident that the doctrine of the classics should be regarded in the context of their research strategy. They perhaps placed exchange so high because they sought to contradict the then prevailing view that the change of ownership was quasi a zero-sum game: one person's advantage was deemed to be necessarily the partner's disadvantage.

"The idea that exchange is beneficial for all parties involved only entered the general consciousness with the work of the classical economists. In the 18th century, writers and politicians influenced by mercantilism still believed that one could only gain what someone else lost by trade. From this conception, it was concluded with fatal logic that trade was just another form of war."[6]

Johann Joachim Becher formulated this persuasion as the third of his "mercantilist rules and axiomata", namely, "… that it is always better to sell goods to others than to buy goods from others, for the former brings a certain benefit and the latter an infallible harm."[7] The mercantilists located the source of wealth, which in their eyes was equated with stocks of precious metals, in circulation. With the total quantity of gold and silver taken as given, an increase here inevitably meant a decrease there.[8] This opinion did not change noticeably until the sixteenth century, when considerable inflows of precious metals, mainly silver, set in from the New World to Spain. At that time, Spain devoted around 70% of its public revenue to military spending,[9] and these riches came into circulation and provided the material basis for the spread of merchant capitalism. Insofar as measures were taken to increase economic performance, they aimed to achieve the highest possible surplus in the balance of trade to fill the treasure room of the absolutist ruler.[10] In addition to financing luxury consumption, the discretionary power over precious metals was primarily used to maintain a standing army and for warfare.

The mercantilist dogma of exchange as a zero-sum game was countered by the classics with their theory of free trade. Ricardo tried to show with his later called "theorem of comparative cost advantages" that every involved nation can benefit from foreign commerce, even if it manufactures all commodities more expensively than the trade partner.[11] Voluntariness as a constitutive element of economic exchange

[5] Gerloff, W., Die Entstehung des Geldes und die Anfänge des Geldwesens, 3rd ed., Frankfurt a. M. 1947, p. 26. [F. H.]

[6] Neumann, M., Theoretische Volkswirtschaftslehre II, Produktion, Nachfrage und Allokation, München 1982, p. 155. [F. H.]

[7] Quoted from Heckscher, E. F., Der Merkantilismus, vol. II, Jena 1932, p. 102. [F. H.]

[8] Cf. Blaich, F., Die Epoche des Merkantilismus, Wiesbaden 1973, p. 80.

[9] Cf. Weber, M., Wirtschaftsgeschichte, op. cit., p. 265.

[10] On the interlocking of economics, science and technology in mercantilism, see Troitzsch, U., Ansätze technologischen Denkens bei den Kameralisten des 17. und 18. Jahrhunderts, Berlin 1966.

[11] Ricardo assumes both full employment and unsatisfied demand. Yet, absolute cost differences are decisive with stagnating sales and idle capacities. An ensuing race to the bottom can cause trade wars and welfare losses. See Helmedag, F., Komparative Kostenvorteile, fairer Handel und

results from improving at least one party without disadvantaging any other; on that condition, business is a positive-sum game.

Along with economic activity, economic exchange has altered its appearance over time. Historical and analytical differences that are relevant to economic theory can be observed. These modifications are reflected in the functions of money, which—at least in modern everyday consciousness—is inextricably inherent in "economic" facts. Just as an exchange per se is not a characteristic of an economic situation in the contemporary sense, the essence of money cannot be understood solely by looking at the present. In truth, the development of the means of payment and its functions reflects the alterations that have paved the way to *economic society*:

> "... these mental and spiritual changes are particularly linked to the shift in the function of money, indeed nowhere can they be traced as clearly as in the use of money and the variations in the functions of money, with which they interact closely."[12]

Along with the history of economic activity, the career of money emphasises that only the increasing economisation of all living conditions has given the corresponding categories their modern meaning. From today's perspective, it is often pretended that these terms have had their present connotation since immemorial.

Contemporary accounts pay little attention to the origins of money and its nature. In this respect, a textbook first published in 1988 states succinctly:

> "In economics, the causes of the validity and value of money are no longer a matter of concern. Money is there, and one is more interested in its amount of value and its changes."[13]

This negligence was not always a common practice. The question of the nature of money has often been raised, particularly in German-language literature. However, it seems such a complicated matter that, despite all efforts, presenting a generally accepted definition of the universal return gift has been impossible. Even an author as profound as Polanyi considers the many attempts to define the nature of money to be fruitless.[14] Instead, it is usually typified solely by its functions:

> "Whereas different interpretations of the monetary system characterised the older theory, the modern theory of the function of money is unified: money is spoken of when a thing is a unit of account, a medium of exchange and a store of value."[15]

Thus, as far as this point is concerned, the doctrine of money has reverted to where it was some two and a half thousand years ago. Plato and Aristotle believed that the origin of money could be traced back to barter. As mentioned, Aristotle ascribes

---

Beschäftigung, in: Die Krise der europäischen Integration aus keynesianischer Sicht, Hagemann, H., Kromphardt, J. (eds.), Schriften der Keynes-Gesellschaft, vol. 10, Marburg 2017, pp. 167–183. Analytically, Ricardo's example can be transformed into a 'canonical' two-sector model, apt to illustrate the traits of capitalist competitive economies. Details are offered in Sect. 2.3.4, "Comparative cost advantages and employment" (p. 146 ff.).

[12] Schmölders, G., Geldpolitik, 2nd ed., Tübingen / Zürich 1968, p. 30. [F. H.]

[13] Wagner, A., Mikroökonomik, 5th ed., Marburg 2009, p. 178. [F. H.]

[14] Cf. Polanyi, K., Ökonomie …, op. cit., p. 317.

[15] Woll, A., op. cit., p. 481. [F. H.]

in his work "Politics" the introduction of money to the inconvenience of natural exchange; in the "Nicomachean Ethics", money is also recognised as a measure of value.[16] According to Schumpeter, Aristotle was even aware of its use as a store of value.[17]

Were so many authors' efforts to get closer to the gist of money, therefore, wholly in vain? This supposedly superfluous "detour of production" would be easier to cope with from today's perspective if, after careful examination, the prevailing theory of monetary functions could be classified as apposite. However, this is not the case.

A nearer review of the literature reveals that the three dimensions of money that dominate the textbooks—unit of account, medium of exchange and store of value—are not unreservedly accepted. Schilcher lists *thirteen* possible functions of money "with the omission of unusual formulations by individual authors".[18]

But it is not worth reproducing this catalogue—which can certainly be extended with some diligence—because no matter how lavishly an object is described in terms of its concrete uses, that must not be the last word; the list will always remain fragmentary. Like economics, which was intended to be explained by certain phenomena perceived as "economic", the definition of money based on its functions presupposes that the person addressed has at least an intuitive knowledge of what money is. Thus, it must be possible to detect the *differentia specifica* so that the hitherto vague idea can be conceptualised.

That said, it is unsurprising that the dominant "three-functions theory of money" fails the qualifying examination. As will soon be shown in more detail, the three aspects mentioned are neither equally important nor isolated from one another. The older authors had rightly endeavoured to discover the *essence* of money.

Of course, the definition fails if one merely begins to enumerate what can be done with money. Before the introduction of the euro, small-denominated coins were almost completely withdrawn from circulation in Italy because they were processed into button blanks. A functional theory of money that included the button alternative would certainly not have met with widespread approval. And the stray skier who, according to a newspaper report, burned a bundle of dollar bills to warm his numb fingers could hardly be cited as an indication that the heating value of the currency is another essential function of money.

It may be argued against the examples that they are not relevant because such uses of cash are not "economic". However, precisely with this argument, the usual doctrine would have its difficulties: there is no doubt that the possible applications of money mentioned in the examples illustrate dispositions of scarce resources for satisfying needs. The other escape route from the dilemma is also blocked: the Italian lira was and the US dollar is money.

However, the anticipated protest incorporates a kernel of truth: coins which are further processed to button blanks and the burnt banknotes are detached from a context constitutive of their monetary character. In both cases, the material use value

[16] Cf. Gerloff, W., Geld und Gesellschaft, Frankfurt a. M. 1952, p. 31 f.

[17] Cf. Schumpeter, J. A., History ..., op. cit., p. 62.

[18] Cf. Schilcher, R., Geldfunktionen und Buchgeldschöpfung, 2nd ed., Berlin 1973, p. 44 f. [F. H.]

exceeds their respective use value as exchange value. For the lost skier, the purchasing power of his dollar notes is even zero: he has left the social network that must be assumed for any monetary function. Robinson Crusoe, on his desert island, doesn't need money either.

The social conditions under which money acquires validity must be revealed to conceptualise the "general equivalent" and understand its functions. This project ought not to be erected on the premise that the emergence of money is a rationalist, constructive act:

> "The demonstration of the advantages of the use of money, or, to give another example, of the usefulness of the division of labour, which is based on the common execution of the process, can never be adduced to explain the origin of these institutions; for these, like most social institutions, have arisen independently of that purpose and its adaptation to which they have finally been directed."[19]

Money was no more created because of an agreement than society, language, and the state emerged from a convention between people. Wieser's assertion that the origins of money can be traced back to an innovation by "findige Wirte" [clever businessmen],[20] disregards the real course of events.

The answer as to when money saw the light of day naturally hinges on its definition: depending on what is referred to as money, its first use can be dated earlier or later. In the history of money, as generally in history, there is no zero hour.

It would, therefore, be inappropriate to start from a modern, systematic idea and try to uncover the roots in the past.[21] Such an approach presupposes a misguided belief in the continuity of certain phenomena despite long periods of change. "One cannot extend concepts that are abstracted from phenomena of a later stage of development to phenomena of an earlier one."[22]

This methodological ban does not have to end in assigning specific properties of money to the respective epochs of monetary history.[23] For our purposes, a working hypothesis is sufficient to follow the tracks of money in history. It initially includes "everything valid". Money is the name given to *generally* appreciated objects that structure the prevailing value hierarchy. In line with the procedure for determining the substance of the notions of "economy" and "economic activity", we first compile the

---

[19] Gerloff, W., Geld …, op. cit., p. 33 f. [F. H.]

[20] Cf. Wieser, F. v., Geld (Theorie des Geldes), in: Handwörterbuch der Staatswissenschaften, vol. IV, 4th ed., Jena 1927, pp. 681–717, p. 683. In the third edition of the handbook, Menger had (prematurely) noticed: "The obvious error, which has become dominant since *Plato* and *Aristotle*, that money is the product of a general agreement or positive legislation … can be described as overcome …". Menger, C., Geld, in: Handwörterbuch der Staatswissenschaften, vol. IV, 3rd ed., Jena 1909, pp. 555–610, p. 562 n. [F. H.], reprinted in: Collected Works (in German), vol. IV, London / Bradford 1936, p. 1–116, p. 16 n., https://mises.org/library/book/collected-works-carl-menger-german-four-volumes.

[21] Forstmann is of a different opinion: "*Money in the economic sense* can only ever be regarded as that which fulfils economic and indeed *all* economically relevant functions of money." Forstmann, A., Geld und Kredit, I. Teil, Göttingen 1952, p. 31. [F. H.]

[22] Laum, B., op. cit., p. 3 f. [F. H.] See also Andreae, W., op. cit., p. 10.

[23] This is the approach of Gerloff, W., Geld …, op. cit., p. 99.

concrete meaning of "money" over time. Then, we turn our attention to the analytical and systematic content of the study object.

5.1 Origins and Manifestations of Money

The development of money is not a continuous, straightforward process whose beginning can be recognised in a specific event: the emergence of a general standard differs in individual cultures both in terms of the items to which money status was attributed and in the motives from which a need for money arises. However, commonly respected symbols of value existed long before the social division of labour, the formation of states and the creation of a legal system.[24]

Much of the literature conveys the impression that the career of money started with the first minting of coins. In reality, it is necessary to go back much further to approach the origins of money. It is inappropriate to give an overview of the numerous variants of early and foreign means of payment here. There is a reliable body of literature on this subject.[25] Rare, however, are publications that go beyond the descriptive stage intending to *explain* why pecuniary institutions emerged.

Two researchers have made particularly noteworthy contributions to the *theory* of the unfolding of a monetary system. The more far-reaching concept comes from Wilhelm Gerloff, who derives the beginnings of money from human instincts as the cause of particular needs. Bernhard Laum presented the older and more specific study. For the culture of Homeric Greece, he shows that money is of holy origin, arising from a sacrifice offered to the deity.—Let us begin with Gerloff's more general concept.

Gerloff itemises the herd or sociability instinct, the distinction or prestige predisposition and the compulsive desire for new acquisitions or hoarding as the central motives that lead to the dissemination of money.[26] While the herd instinct leads *to* a society in the first place, the distinction instinct is the most substantial aspiration at work *in* society. Typically, this drive, which dominates social life, is satisfied by the *hoarding* of extraordinary things:

> "The origin of money is detected in the dedication of certain goods for such purposes. The original money is to be found in the hoarded goods with which mankind established its possession of material cultural goods."[27]

---

[24] Cf. Schmölders, G., op. cit., p. 14.

[25] Einzig, P., Primitive Money, Its Ethnological, Historical and Economic Aspects, 2nd ed., Oxford et al. 1966, is exceptionally comprehensive and systematic. See also Quiggin, A. H., A Survey of Primitive Money, The Beginning of Currency [1949], New York / London 1970.

[26] Cf. Gerloff, W., Geld …, op. cit., p. 23 ff.

[27] Gerloff, W., Die Entstehung …, op. cit., p. 29 (cursive in the original). [F. H.]

Which specific objects these are depends on the respective cultural context in the community; usually, they are generally wanted ornamental things, e.g., rings.[28] The honorary name of the generous Germanic prince is 'ring distributor'[29]: the delivery of the present is availed to transfer the friendship of the former owner. Even articles of "conspicuous consumption" such as kettledrums, gongs, jugs, bowls, plates and shields[30] are money, provided they are needed to *satisfy social obligations*.

Hoard money, be it in the form of pomp or trinket money, primarily serves to *display* value. According to Thorstein Veblen, it allows the "invidious comparison", the original ground of private property.[31] "The display, distribution and destruction of money, these original uses of money, are expressions of social conditions and social facts and thus statements about social circumstances."[32] Valuables of this kind acquire the quality of money as soon as they are lavishly distributed on prominent occasions.[33]

In many cases, hoard money was used to conclude unique business; it was used to buy women and allies or to pay fines and tributes. The acquisition of a wife could entail considerable liabilities in such cultural circles, as the bride's price was often related to her labour power. The first beginnings of bookkeeping can be found in the payment by instalments over many years: the redemptions already made over time are carved in wooden tablets to document the debt position in case of doubt.[34]

A monetary system beyond our imagination—and therefore ideal for broadening our horizons—was once established on the South Sea Island of Yap. The money, called "fei" or "rai", consists of perforated limestone or aragonite slices, ranging in size from a few decimetres to several meters. The big stones come from the island of Palau, some 400 nautical miles away, where glass beads were circulating for payment. Such pearls are also found on Yap but are not used as money there.[35] Remarkably,

[28] The Vienna Mint has supplied silver Maria Theresa thalers to Africa, where they are mainly in demand for hoarding. Especially Abyssinian women covet the thalers as jewellery. Cf. Veit, O., Reale Theorie des Geldes, Tübingen 1966, p. 26.

[29] Cf. Gerloff, W., Geld …, op. cit., p. 52.

[30] Cf. in detail Gerloff, W., Die Entstehung …, op. cit., p. 35 ff.

[31] Cf. Veblen, Th., The Theory of the Leisure Class, New York / London 1899, https://oll.libertyfund.org/titles/veblen-the-theory-of-the-leisure-class-an-economic-study-of-institutions.

[32] Gerloff, W., Die Entstehung …, op. cit., p. 274. [F. H.]

[33] Cf. Gerloff, W., Die Entstehung …, op. cit., p. 53.

[34] Cf. ibid., p. 30 ff.

[35] Cf. Polanyi, Ökonomie …, op. cit., p. 341. Because of the stone's heavy weight, a tree trunk was inserted through the hole so several porters could take hold of it. Sometimes, the fei had two holes. The more than head-high pieces date from the period after 1872, when the Irishman Dean O'Keefe became the absolute ruler of Yap because his steamboats were able to transport stones with a diameter of two to three meters, which was impossible with the traditional Yap rafts. This led to a veritable inflation. About half of the stone slabs during the Pacific War were devoted to building fortifications. Cf. Köhler, M., Akkulturation in der Südsee, Die Kolonialgeschichte der Karolinen-Inseln im pazifischen Ozean und der Wandel ihrer sozialen Organisation, Frankfurt a. M. / Bern 1982, p. 243 and p. 434.

the serfs on Yap were not allowed to possess stone money with a diameter of more than four spans,[36] an indication of the class-specific use of archaic money.

The passage to Palau and the arduous work in the quarry were considerable achievements. As a result, the young men, who often returned after a year, and their families were held in high esteem by those who stayed home.[37] The village received the stones and exhibited the best examples in public. During large celebrations known as "mitmits", e.g., on a marriage or birth occasion, two groups exchanged gifts in a competition. The winner was the one who could endow the other team with a more opulent gift.[38] Even when the proprietor changed, the large stones were not moved; knowing who owned the stone was crucial. The physical availability of the money could actually be missing. The attribution to a person alone conferred solvency:

> "When a large stone once fell overboard on the voyage from Palau to Yap, and it was impossible to heave it," Schmölders writes, "this did not in the least affect the wealth of its possessor; generations later, ownership of this stone could still be acquired and transferred as if it were gold bars in a bank vault."[39]

Early money was not only limited to certain social circles; there was also gender-differentiated money; men used a different currency than women. Moreover, certain forms of "intellectual property" were considered transferable. Among the Eskimos, for whom private ownership of property is alien, magic spells are traded that promise good luck in hunting. However, the incantation should only be effective if payment has been made beforehand.[40]

Furthermore, certain goods require special money; nowhere could one buy a woman for shells while they circulated as a means of payment for everyday transactions.[41] Bartering was usually only conducted to supplement consumption, as in older cultures, "basic needs" are covered by self-subsistence. These nearly autarkic groups mainly practised the division of labour only inside the community, so supply in the early markets depended, above all, on the climatically regulated surplus. In

---

[36] Cf. Gerloff, W., Geld …, op. cit., p. 90 ff.

[37] If one wishes, the value of the fei can be explained in terms of the labour theory of value. It is based "… solely on the difficulties that its extraction causes; it is therefore based on the labour power, time and danger required to break, hew and ship it. As soon as the transportation was made easier, the value sank." Helmreich, Th., Das Geldwesen in den deutschen Schutzgebieten, 2. Teil, Mikronesien, Fürth 1913, p. 104. [F. H.]

[38] See Köhler, M., op. cit., p. 93.

[39] Schmölders, G., op. cit., p. 32. [F. H.] This incident was first reported by Furness, W. H., The Island of Stone Money: Uap of the Carolines, Philadelphia / London 1910, p. 97. See also Robertson, D. H., Money, London / Cambridge 1922, p. 130 f., https://archive.org/details/cu31924013818145/page/n7/mode/2up?q=Uap. When the people of Yap refused to expand the land roads on their island as the German colonial masters had ordered, the island population was punished by having the letters B. A. (abbreviation for 'Bezirksamt' [district authority]) painted on their fei in black colour. To redeem their confiscated money, the rebels obeyed and built the roads. The 'bailiff's seal' was then crossed out. Cf. Helmreich, Th., Das Geldwesen …, 2. Teil, op. cit., p. 105 f.

[40] Cf. Gerloff, W., Geld …, op. cit., p. 82. The Catholic Church's sale of indulgences in the late Middle Ages was based on the same principle.

[41] Cf. Weber, M., Wirtschaftsgeschichte, op. cit., p. 209.

good times, an abundant supply meets a meagre demand; in bad times, this relationship is reversed. The market volume must, therefore, remain modest, even if prices fluctuate wildly. As a rule, trade was limited to vending goods acquired during wars, mainly enslaved people, who were usually sold to dispose of a spoil that was otherwise difficult to exploit because of their recalcitrant nature.[42]

Initially, the exchange of gifts between members of populations integrated by reciprocity is an essentially sentimental process in which the counter-donations gradually become obligatory. Step by step, the idea that the dedications had to correspond with each other gained currency. "Divergent opinions about the equivalence of the gifts exchanged often lead to bitter disputes among these peoples."[43]

Since the mutual presents naturally differ in quality, a quantitative standard of comparison is needed to estimate their equivalence. This appraisal does not imply that the unit of the good that predominantly plays the mediating role in barter trade, such as grain, becomes the measure of obligations in gift transactions. Nevertheless, the weight system, which also served to quantify precious metals, was often based on corn. In Africa, the dried seed of the carob tree was the counterpoise to gold, while in the East Indies, it was balanced against diamonds. The unit "carat", still used today, goes back to this. Despite all the peculiarities in the respective cultures, a swelling inclination to calculability spreads, which increasingly supports the scaling of the social value order.[44]

It would be rash, however, to conclude that the counting unit "automatically" becomes the medium of exchange. The physical equivalent is often created independently[45]; for practical reasons alone, hoard- and pomp-money is generally unsuitable to this effect. Selecting a good as a general standard is an incremental process, and it is not certain that a single medium of exchange will be established. As different as the processes may be in each case, initially, the good is not consciously selected to fulfil this function exclusively, and for all time, instead, it was at first only occasionally employed to transfer values:

> "Initially, there are only a few acts of exchange, often occurring at long intervals. In the meantime, however, the exchange good does not lie idle, waiting to be utilised as money; rather, it serves other purposes (such as jewellery needs) so that it can be reused as an exchange good if it has not been consumed in the meantime."[46]

The universal consideration is often a commodity that can be studied well in the colonies, as "... they have gone through significant stages of monetary development for around 300 years."[47] In many instances, the predominantly produced commodity became the currency, e.g., tobacco in Virginia or mahogany wood in British Honduras. Of course, unlike tobacco, timber did not circulate as a medium

---

[42] Cf. Laum, B., op. cit., p. 13.

[43] Ibid., p. 54. [F. H.]

[44] See, e.g., the relative prices compiled by Forstmann, which can be found among Indians in the Missouri region. Cf. Forstmann, op. cit., p. 51.

[45] Cf. Gerloff, W., Die Entstehung ..., op. cit., p. 63.

[46] Gerloff, W., Geld ..., op. cit., p. 79. [F. H.]

[47] Gerloff, W., Die Entstehung ..., op. cit., p. 57. [F. H.]

of exchange, but it did function as a measure of value in trade. Duties and fines were fixed in a quantity of wood, which related accounting and contract details to a common denominator.[48]

The events described above testify that money was subject to a shift of emphasis in which the emotional, social component was progressively replaced by a calculative, economic one. Money has always been "a means of communication like language",[49] "… a social good … that only obtains validity in society and through society."[50] Communities *organise* themselves using money; this applies both to civilisations characterised by economic exchange and to those in which the exchange of gifts predominates. In this process, the nature of money changes with social relationships, and these change with it.

> "Instinct, habit and reason," Gerloff summarises, "the original forces of all cultural creations have worked together in the creation of money. They determined the conformation of money in this sequence and thus indicate three different levels or stages of monetary development. The primal instincts, the drive for distinction and the collecting instinct lead to hoard money. The habit of using it as hoard money turns this money into payment money (fine money, feud money, bride money). Rationalisation turns it (without claiming a continuous advance) into barter money and further into general money for transactions of every kind."[51]

The more specific research work by Laum mentioned above, which is geographically and culturally limited to ancient Greece, also refutes the view that a convention between people inaugurated the general equivalent to make exchanges as smooth as possible. The progress of money in Homeric Greece also exhibits a phenomenon to be addressed below: the measure of value can appear in different value units.

One—if not the—ultimate ground of every religion is fear:

> "Primitive man lacks insight into the nature surrounding him; he does not yet recognise the causal connection of its forces. He only sees the effects, and those effects that threaten his existence make the strongest impression on him. He observes how a hailstorm or sunburn destroys the growing seed, how a disease strikes his flocks, and how he is seized by disease and perishes. Everywhere and always, man feels surrounded by danger. He lives in constant fear, which is the 'inception and reason for all worship of God'."[52]

First, humans try to avert harm; spells and magic appear to be suitable methods for this. At a later stage, man hopes to gain influence over the originator of the forces threatening his existence: The deity is to be appeased.

> "Man shapes the deity according to his self-image ... It is a simple consequence of this anthropomorphism that man applies the same device towards the deity that he employs in dealing with his fellow human beings to appease their anger or gain their favour: he offers them gifts. So, the sacrifice arises."[53]

---

[48] Cf. ibid., p. 58 ff.

[49] Gerloff, W., Geld …, op. cit., p. 273. [F. H.]

[50] Ibid., p. 108. [F. H.]

[51] Ibid., p. 258. [F. H.]

[52] Laum, B., op. cit., p. 19. [F. H.]

[53] Ibid., p. 20. [F. H.]

Etymologically, in German, "money" [Geld] derives from the verb "gelten", whose basic meaning is "to recompense, to pay" and was mainly related to religious sacrifices. The guilds of the Middle Ages derive their name from the same root; the original meaning is "sacrificial community".[54] The English word "guilt" also has this source.

> "The sacrifice is called 'gelt' [in Old High German]. The sacrifice is a good of a certain kind and quality. This good, set apart from the other goods, serves as a means of payment if the relationship between God and man is understood as a debt relationship; it serves as a means of exchange if the sacrifice is an act of swap."[55]

In his study, Laum shows that the sacred ox, as the most noble sacrificial animal, became a measure of value in ancient Greece. The steer was regarded as the incarnation of the supreme deities; its sacrifice could be offered to all the gods worshipped in the state cult. Laum sees selecting a suitable sacrificial animal as "the first act of economic thinking". Livestock had to meet a standard to be ideal as a sacrifice: "*... the valuation of goods began in the cult, not in trade, which knows no typification, but is purely individual.*"[56]

The Achaeans refer to this "standard bovine" when estimating other goods with this yardstick. The sources tell about a "twelve-cattle" tripod or a "four-cattle" female.[57] This valuation does not mean that the cattle were exchanged for a tripod; instead, the buyer handed over items *worth* twelve cattle. In this respect, Laum's study confirms Gerloff's previously reported finding: the medium of exchange presupposes a measure of value. This outcome is substantiated from a systematic perspective in the following section.

Laum's work contains plenty of material that illustrates the previous description of the semantic drift regarding the word "economy". The sacrifice creates not only a measure of value but also, in the changing customs and traditions of its execution, traces of certain "economic" phenomena are discernible.

First, a division of labour can be portrayed in the wake of the worship service. While the execution of the sacrifice was initially a private matter, some members of society gradually acquired a unique competence in the conduct of the sacrificial process: a priesthood became established. Eventually, no sacrifice could be performed without a priest "... because only he knew the rite as it was necessary to ensure its

---

[54] Cf. ibid., p. 39.

[55] Ibid., p. 40. [F. H.]

[56] Ibid, p. 27. [F. H.] In other cultures, magically and ritually significant goods also serve as money. The inhabitants of New Britain, e.g., spend their entire lives trying to accumulate as much as possible of their 'tambu' currency made from a sea snail. It not only circulates as a means of payment for everyday goods and as atonement money but also fulfils essential social and religious functions. Social advancement always requires a corresponding amount of tambu. After the owner's death, his entire tambu is bequeathed to the mourning community. If the deceased did not accumulate enough tambu during his lifetime for the funeral ceremony, his soul could find no peace and would be condemned to wander in the woods. Cf. Schneider, O., Muschelgeld-Studien, Dresden 1905, p. 13 ff. See also Helmreich, Th., Das Geldwesen in den deutschen Schutzgebieten, 1. Teil, Neu-Guinea, Fürth 1912, p. 37 f.

[57] Cf. Laum, B., op. cit., p. 10 and p. 15. [F. H.]

success. The priest is indispensable for human intercourse with the deity."[58] It is not far-fetched to identify the means of payment for the priest's activities: the bovine. "The ox is a *sacrificial reward for the priests because it was an offering to the gods*."[59] But this 'currency' was not reserved solely for the sacred sphere:

> "The important result for us," Laum concludes, "is that ... the norm created for cultic intercourse is transferred to private relationships. The good that serves as a means of payment in the cult is also recognised and used as such in private transactions."[60]

Although a bovine is an accepted value unit, neither payment nor calculation is performed in multiples of one animal. The relatively large item "ox" in relation to the economic potential is split to grade the payment according to the appropriate compensation.[61] In sacrifices, only specific, usually inferior pieces are dedicated to the god; the priest obtains certain parts, and others are either offered as "prize money" in competitions[62] or are eaten together as remuneration for service to the state.[63]

The priest's needs are not limited to the meat of the sacrificial animal assigned to him. Instead, he endeavours to convert the surplus into other goods that fall within his circle of wants. An exchange of goods *must* arise at the temple: "The sanctuary naturally becomes a nucleus of barter and the priesthood the first trading college."[64] Even if relatively self-sufficient households characterise society, the existence of a temple always points to barter. Because its income is always similar, the variety of provisions required can only be obtained through trade. This passing on explains why money as a medium of exchange first appears in the temple economy.[65]

The classic medium of exchange is the coin. However, like money altogether, it did not emerge from economic considerations. Its appearance stems from a change in man's attitude towards the deity. God is now interpreted as an *eternal*, *spiritual* being whose grace can no longer be won through short-lived, material gifts: "The sacrifice given in kind is replaced by a replica made of precious metal."[66]

The transition from content to form commences, and the substance of money evaporates; it becomes a mere token. The coin symbolises the sacrificial animal itself; the head henceforth stands as *pars pro toto*. But the "purchasing power" is transferred:

---

[58] Ibid., p. 41. [F. H.] The reasons for the prevalence of this division of labour are, therefore, completely different from those that operate in modern societies. We shall take up this topic later.

[59] Ibid., p. 43. [F. H.]

[60] Ibid. [F. H.]

[61] Cf. ibid., p. 50.

[62] Cf. ibid., p. 57.

[63] Cf. ibid., p. 49.

[64] Ibid., p. 101. [F. H.]

[65] Cf. ibid. p. 103. At later times, the church was also a place where a lot of bartering took place. "Today we refer to the large organisations for the sale of goods as fairs; the name comes from the religious and ecclesiastical activity. The fair and the market took place at the same time and in the same place." Ibid., p. 99. [F. H.]

[66] Ibid., p. 91. [F. H.]

> "As long as the belief is alive that the debt to the gods can be redeemed by ceding this image, goods are given in return ... The temple receives other goods for these idols, so they are means of exchange for it ..."[67]

The very significance of the coin stamp comes from *this* sphere. Its initial purpose is not to make counterfeiting more difficult, but it is a magical mark of ownership. As the temple lends the metal, it must be ensured that what belongs to the deity is repaid in the same quantity and quality. Therefore, the image of the god is imprinted.[68] The stamp is a holy signature; counterfeiting a coin is hence considered sacrilege, punishable by death. The associated faith in the authenticity transforms the stamp into a kind of quality seal. Its recognition is based on respect for the divine emblem. The Spartans' hardly valuable iron money also owed its validity to this reverence. When this awe waned, the state had to resort to coercion.[69]

In the age of the unbroken religious authority of the coin, every piece counted, regardless of size and weight. Herodotus reports on the forced temple prostitution in Babylon, where the silver coin could not be rejected, no matter how large it was, because it was considered sacred.[70]

There is only rudimentary evidence of the sacred origin of Roman coins; they are much more a creation of the state legal system.[71] As a result, the comparability of the individual coins' value is paramount. Nevertheless, the ratio of gold to silver remained mystical for a long time. Until the modern era, it was around 1:131/3. However, the swap rate between the two precious metals was not based on supply and demand, as one might think, but on the stars' orbital periods: the sun represented gold, and the moon symbolised silver.[72]

The sketch of the history of money shows, without being a purposeful process from the outset, that its development is marked by dwindling emotionality, diminishing magic, increasing secularisation, democratisation, and, finally, (today nearly perfect) dematerialisation. But pure token money dates earlier than modern bank money. In the Congo, some people use straw mats or grass cloths as universal considerations, which are originally square but later consist only of a tangle of hay. In parts of western Sudan, strips of blue cloth circulate, although they gradually become mere shreds.[73] Yet, money is always a social institution, a tool for organising relationships between humans and (their) things, and a means of communicating about valuables. For the individual, money always receives its value from the *outside* through an ascription by the community.

---

[67] Ibid., p. 95. [F. H.]

[68] Cf. ibid., p. 142.

[69] Cf. ibid., p. 155. One argument for the continuance of iron money in Sparta was that it prevented corruption by hampering the secret accumulation of treasures.

[70] Cf. Polanyi, K., Ökonomie ..., op. cit., p. 318.

[71] Cf. Laum, B., op. cit., p. 155. This aspect is emphasised by Knapp, G. F., Staatliche Theorie des Geldes (1905), 3rd ed., München / Leipzig 1921.

[72] Cf. Laum, B., op. cit., p. 128 f.

[73] Cf. Polanyi, K., Ökonomie ..., op. cit., p. 318.

The excursion into the past was worthwhile because it allowed us to correct frequently encountered prejudices. The tour also aroused curiosity about the extent to which money functions as a medium of communication in the modern economy, distinguished by economic exchange. The following section provides information to this effect.

5.2 Function and Gist of Money

For a systematic and analytical study to get the essence of money, starting with economic exchange and its history is expedient. The simplest manifestation of trade is barter, where one commodity is swapped directly for another, according to Karl Marx's notation: $C - C$. Such an exchange, say, of beavers for deer, is determined by the participant's concrete *use value* of the *goods*. Once their needs are satisfied, the process comes to an end. This allocation method does not require a social division of labour. If Jack gives John a Bible for a piece of bacon, this alone reveals nothing about the social mode of production.

Barter dominates within traditional cultures, where self-sufficient communities only exchange occasionally. Then, production is not yet systematically designed to satisfy an anonymous market demand.[74] For this reason, it would be more appropriate to speak in such cases of *goods* instead of *commodities*. This clarification should be reflected in an apposite symbolism. However, the conceptual vagueness is widespread and probably cannot be eradicated. We shall reencounter it in a moment.

In the case of barter, the terms buyer and seller make no sense. Neither a purchaser nor a vendor can be labelled accordingly. So, the distinction between acquisition and disposal always takes a general medium of exchange for granted.

In "simple circulation" $C - M - C$,[75] the bargain is separated into two halves of the whole exchange: the *sale* of "commodity for money" ($C - M$) and the *purchase* of "money for commodity" ($M - C$). This transaction also does not necessarily require a division of labour. Again, it should be differentiated between a somewhat random deal to supplement the self-produced range of goods and the social specialisation of producers in particular commodities. In the usual explanations of the functions of money, this—as will be shown later, decisive—distinction does not appear. According to the prevailing doctrine, the advantage of payment with currency stems from its ability to reduce the intricateness of a direct swap of use values. The following simple example, deliberately not founded on commodity production,

[74] One of the most interesting trading systems is the ring exchange known as Kula in the Massim archipelago of Papua New Guinea. Here, necklaces are passed clockwise from island to island between steady partners, while arm rings circulate in the opposite direction. Cf. Malinowski, B., Argonauts of the Western Pacific, An Account of Native Enterprise and Adventure in the Archipelagoes of Melanesian New Guinea, London 1922. More recent research results can be found in the collection Leach, J. W., Leach, E. (eds.), The Kula, New Perspectives on Massim Exchange, Cambridge et al. 1983.

[75] Cf. Marx, K., Capital, vol. I, op. cit., p. 145 ff.

Table 5.1 Supply and demand at a playground

	Alex	Bob	Charles
Supply	Gummy bears	Tin soldiers	Pebbles
Demand	Pebbles	Gummy bears	Tin soldiers

serves as a basis for comparison to illustrate the qualitative leap between barter and allocations mediated by money.

Let us imagine ourselves in a playground. Alex, Bob and Charles aim to enhance their welfare. To achieve this, they are willing to give up their endowments. Alex holds gummy bears and wishes to receive pebbles. In exchange for gummy bears, Bob is ready to part with his tin soldiers. Charles possesses pebbles and desires tin soldiers. Table 5.1 provides information on the "supply and demand of economic agents".

What happens?—Initially, nothing. Although every supply meets demand in the aggregate, no trade occurs at the first attempt. It is not possible to find a duo with two exchange partners who, at the same time, mutually want to have what the other is exactly willing to give; the so-called double coincidence is missing. Only through a triangular barter can supply and demand be balanced.[76] Alex, e.g., swaps his gummy bears with Bob's tin soldiers and then passes them for Charles' pebbles. After all, everyone has what they aspire.

However, the risk in the two-stage trade is unevenly distributed. Alex must transact twice before he gets what he desires, while the other two can satisfy their wishes in the first round. Still, without double coincidence, there is no a priori guarantee—especially with many suppliers and demanders—that the unpreferred goods acquired in the intermediate phase can ultimately always be traded for the favourite item.

A general equivalent protects against this precariousness. It reduces uncertainty during long exchange chains in a barter economy. Therefore, it must be (reasonably) sure that the medium of exchange allows the holder to acquire goods or services in the future. This peril is relatively low if the medium of exchange itself has a use value that is not based on its purchasing power. Early forms of money, such as grain, salt, furs, or cigarettes in Germany after the Second World War, were suitable for this

[76] Cf. Schneider, E., Einführung in die Wirtschaftstheorie, I. Teil, Theorie des Wirtschaftskreislaufs, 14th ed., Tübingen 1969, p. 20 f. In this context, Menger quotes a striking example from the report of a trip to Africa by Cameron and Barth: "My next thought was to obtain boats. As the owners of two boats I had been promised were absent, I tried to hire one belonging to Syde ibn Habib from his agent. Syde's agent, however, wanted to be paid in ivory, which I did not possess; but I learned that Mohamed ben Salib had ivory and needed cotton cloth. But as I had no cotton cloth, this was of little use to me until I heard that Mohamed ibn Gharib had cotton cloth and needed wire. Fortunately, I had it. So, I gave Mohamed ibn Gharib the appropriate amount of wire, whereupon he gave Mohamed ben Salib cotton cloth, who in turn gave Syde ibn Habib's agent the desired ivory. He then allowed me to take the boat." Menger, C., Geld, op. cit., p. 6. [F.H.] According to Erich Schneider, Walras deserves credit for recognising the importance of indirect exchange in the case of three or more goods: "Neither Menger nor Jevons pointed this out", he continues – as the quotation shows, not quite correctly. Cf. Schneider, E., Einführung in die Wirtschaftstheorie, IV. Teil, Ausgewählte Kapitel der Geschichte der Wirtschaftstheorie, vol. 1, Tübingen 1962, p. 252 n. [F. H.]

immediate consumption. In contrast, precious metal pieces are hardly applicable for such individual purposes.[77]

Thus, a steady decline in money's material value characterises its development history. During this time, its suitability for direct consumption naturally diminished; in the case of pure book money, even the button and heating functions, as usages of cash have disappeared.

Introducing a general means of payment proves sensible beyond a certain level of bartering and is *practically* necessary. This implementation reduces the transaction costs of allocating goods, which can otherwise be prohibitively high. Yet, the question of how a sufficiently documented payment medium is put into circulation turns out to be by no means trivial; in particular, the necessary amount of money and its location often play a neglected role.[78]

The distinction between barter and simple circulation consists not only of introducing a value unit to reduce the inconvenience of a direct transfer of ownership. The difference in quality between barter and simple circulation expands if simple circulation is, in fact, *commodity* production. Then, a social division of labour exists. Manufacturers specialise in producing particular objects and must procure externally produced inputs from markets to ensure their existence.

Now, one of the functions listed in the three-function theory of money, which is usually placed on an equal footing with the other two, becomes an indispensable prerequisite for the division of labour. It is the unit of account. A simple example illustrates the assertion.

Let us assume that only three homogeneous goods are produced in an economy: wheat (W), iron (I), and pigs (P).[79] The equation-like expressions represent manufacturing processes, with the arrow ($\rightarrow$) indicating that an input to the left is transformed into an output to the right of the arrow. The workers' food is included among the inputs. Because physically heterogeneous quantities cannot be added, the ampersand (&) symbolises the input in the sense of "take ..." as said in cooking recipes.[80]

$$\begin{array}{rcrcrcr}
240\,W & \& & 12\,I & \& & 18\,P & \rightarrow & 450\,W \\
90\,W & \& & 6\,I & \& & 12\,P & \rightarrow & 21\,I \\
120\,W & \& & 3\,I & \& & 30\,P & \rightarrow & 60\,P \\
\hline
450\,W & & 21\,I & & 60\,P & &
\end{array}$$

In this simple model, the entire output flows back into production; there is (yet) no social surplus. Consequently, such an economy cannot grow; economic activity

[77] "Even with full-value money, it was and is not the precious metal that gives value to the money – but the other way round: it is the money that makes the metal valuable ... Gold and silver would have been worth much less without this demand." Veit, O., op. cit., p. 10 f. [F. H.]

[78] Cf. Krause, U., Geld und abstrakte Arbeit, Über die analytischen Grundlagen der Politischen Ökonomie, Frankfurt a. M. / New York 1979, p. 62 ff.

[79] The example is taken from Sraffa, P., Production of Commodities by Means of Commodities, Prelude to a Critique of Economic Theory, Cambridge 1960, p. 4, http://pombo.free.fr/sraffa60.pdf.

[80] Sraffa uses the plus sign.

stagnates at the same level year after year—if this “agrarian” harvesting rotation is considered the unitary production and consumption timespan.[81]

At the end of the interval under consideration, goods are exchanged on the market. The yield of each process must suffice to acquire the necessary inputs for the next production cycle directly or indirectly. Of course, the wheat cultivation's grain consumption is not on sale; *mutatis mutandis,* the other two industries behave. We, therefore, have the following “budget constraints” in kind:

$$12\ I\ \&18\ P \leftarrow 210\ W$$
$$90\ W\&12\ P \leftarrow \quad 15\ I$$
$$120\ W\ \&\ 3\ I \quad \leftarrow \quad 30\ P$$

To the left of the arrow are the goods that, in each case, must be obtained for the net output listed to the right of the arrow. The wheat sector, e.g., offers 210 W to receive 12 I and 18 P.

How are the relative prices in this economy calculated? As a first step, let us try to confront the physical supply with the material demand. The wheat sector exchanges 12 I for 90 W with the iron industry and 18 P for 120 W with the pig farms. If we express the equalisation in trade by using the equivalence sign (⇔), we get:

$$12\ I \Leftrightarrow 90\ W \tag{5.1a}$$

$$18\ P \Leftrightarrow 120\ W \tag{5.2a}$$

The same applies to the iron industry:

$$90\ W \Leftrightarrow 12\ I \tag{5.1b}$$

$$12\ P \Leftrightarrow 3\ I \tag{5.3a}$$

And for the pig farming:

$$120\ W \Leftrightarrow 18\ P \tag{5.2b}$$

$$3\ I \Leftrightarrow 12\ P \tag{5.3b}$$

---

[81] “A year is assumed in political economy as the period which includes a revolving circle of production and consumption.” Mill, J., Elements of Political Economy, London 1821, p. 185. It will be shown, however, that this ‘successive’ approach elicits a misinterpretation of a fundamentally simultaneous (industrial) production.

We obtain three expressions, namely (5.1), (5.2) and (5.3), each of which appears twice (a, b)—only written the other way round. Let us try to solve the system. From (5.1a), we compute straightaway:

$$1\,W \Leftrightarrow \frac{12}{90} I \tag{5.1c}$$

(5.1c) in (5.2a) gives:

$$18\,P \Leftrightarrow 120\frac{12}{90} I \Leftrightarrow 16\,I \tag{5.4a}$$

The 'iron price of a pig' therefore amounts to:

$$1\,P \Leftrightarrow \frac{16}{18} I \Leftrightarrow 0,88889\,I \tag{5.4b}$$

From (5.3a), however, one gains:

$$1\,P \Leftrightarrow \frac{3}{12} I \Leftrightarrow 0,25\,I \tag{5.3c}$$

There is a discrepancy between (5.4b) and (5.3c); in this way, the determination of a consistent exchange system fails in the present case. As a rule, the bilateral material fulfilment of demands does not guarantee the implementation of the reproduction condition. This misperformance is one reason for the regular failure of pure quantity planning, as was attempted in the countries of actually existing socialism.[82]

How do we ascertain a price system without infringing the laws of logic? Of course, expenditure should always be equal to revenue, albeit one must not calculate "naturally" but only in *values*, weighing the individual goods—with prices!—is indispensable for reckoning exchange ratios free of contradiction.[83] It is now permissible to use the plus and the equal sign. Hence, the budget restrictions of our model economy are as follows:

[82] Sraffa was seemingly unaware of the possible incompatibility between prices derived in such a 'physical' manner. In his notes from winter 1927/28, available on the Internet, he comments on a production model without surplus for three goods *A*, *B* and *C*: "These are homogeneous linear equations. They have infinite sets of solutions, but the solutions of each set are proportional ... These proportions we call ratios of Absolute values. They are purely numerical relations between the things *A*, *B* ...". Cf. Sraffa, P., Notes on "looms", in: Papers of Piero Sraffa, Trinity College, Cambridge, SRAF/D/3/12/5, https://archives.trin.cam.ac.uk/index.php/notes-on-looms, p. 2.

[83] Erich Schneider refers to prices expressed in "DM [Deutschmark] as the unit of account" from the outset when analysing the exchange between three economic subjects with given initial endowments. Cf. Schneider, E., Einführung in die Wirtschaftstheorie, II. Teil, Wirtschaftspläne und wirtschaftliches Gleichgewicht in der Verkehrswirtschaft, 13th ed., Tübingen 1972, p. 408. [F. H.]

$$210p_W = 12p_I + 18p_P \tag{5.5}$$

$$15p_I = 90p_W + 12p_P \tag{5.6}$$

$$30p_P = 120p_W + 3p_I \tag{5.7}$$

In these equations, p_i ($i = W, I, P$) symbolises the respective price of a unit of the corresponding good. From (5.5) results:

$$p_I = \frac{1}{12}(210p_W - 18p_P) \tag{5.5a}$$

(5.5a) in (5.6) yields:

$$15\frac{1}{12}(210p_W - 18p_P) = 90p_W + 12p_P$$

Rearranging leads to:

$$p_P = 5p_W \tag{5.8}$$

The insertion of (5.8) in (5.5a) gives in the first step:

$$p_I = \frac{1}{12}(210p_W - 90p_W)$$

From the above expression follows:

$$p_I = 10p_W \tag{5.9}$$

The consideration of (5.9) and (5.8) in (5.7) boils down to:

$$150p_W = 150p_W$$

Obviously, a positive number for the price of wheat can be chosen at will. In addition, its physical unit becomes the price measure. Since the price system has one degree of freedom, only *relative* exchange ratios are determined. If we select a certain quantity of wheat (a quintal) as the counting unit and set its price equal to unity, we obtain the *absolute* prices $p_I = 10$ (quintals of wheat) and $p_P = 5$ (quintals of wheat).

The essential insight of the previous analysis is that a division of labour, coordinated via markets, *cannot function* without a standard unit of account. The relative values complying with the budget restrictions can only be established when *all* actors use the *same* yardstick for their dispositions. The choice of a numéraire is, therefore, by no means qualitatively restricted to the elimination of a degree of freedom, as the phraseology in general equilibrium analyses since Walras suggests. Moreover, as we will see later, not just any good can be the standard; only certain goods are eligible. Random exchange can dispense with such a reference point. Hence, an exchange out of stocks, which is (tacitly) the focus in textbooks, proves inappropriate to demonstrate the deeper meaning of the unit of account.

In the above example, we were concerned with determining the exchange ratios of an economy subject to simple reproduction conditions. In those models, the *flows* of manufactured goods *must* be valued so that an allocation comes about, allowing production to be carried out at the same level as in the previous period. In commodity production based on the division of labour, transforming heterogeneous quantities into homogeneous value magnitudes is essential for meeting the conditions the economy is subjected to: the revenue from specialised production must suffice to cover the accruing costs. This can only be achieved if inputs and outputs exhibit identical dimensions.

For a decentralised division of labour, all involved parties must think in terms of *values* revolving around the same numéraire. This intellectual, abstract phenomenon must have permeated the entire economic society. This precondition does not hold for exchanging surpluses between self-sufficient manufacturers who do not depend on acquiring inputs from outside their own production.

The unit of account establishes a ratio scale, a ranking in which the value zero is meaningful and information is preserved as a result of a similarity transformation, i.e., the multiplication of the numéraire by a positive factor. It is also irrelevant whether body sizes are compared in millimetres or centimetres: the giant is always taller than the dwarf. Accordingly, a currency cut does not change anything if nothing else occurs. The chosen calculation scale has no intrinsic value, like grams, meters or watts.

The benefits of a numéraire are commonly illustrated using examples that relate to *stocks*. If n goods are available in an economy, $\frac{n(n-1)}{2}$ independent, relative exchange ratios can be reckoned. If the price of an arbitrarily designated good serves as the general denominator, the number of absolute prices is reduced to $(n - 1)$. The agreement on a unit of account is associated with a significant reduction in information costs because for $n > 2$, the number of relative prices is greater than that of absolute prices, and their growth rate is twice as high.[84] A counting unit facilitates the overview of the relative prices resulting from exchanges out of stock, thus reducing transaction costs.

However, the existence of a numéraire in no way indicates the prevalence of a general medium of exchange. Nor do the two monetary functions necessarily merge. For centuries, the silver pound of the Carolingian coinage reform, e.g., was utilised as a *tertium comparationis* when different currencies were exchanged, even though

[84] The derivation can be found in Helmedag, F., Geldfunktionen, in: das wirtschaftsstudium (wisu), vol. 24 (1995), pp. 711–717 and p. 729, p. 714.

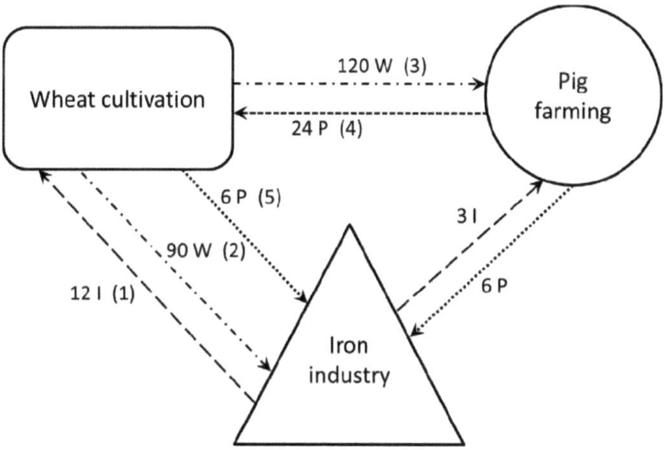

Fig. 5.1 The exchange structure of the wheat-iron-pig economy

it was never minted.[85] Throughout history, several goods have functioned as units of account without ever serving as a medium of exchange.

> "The Romans are said to have had nothing but copper money till within five years before the first Punic war," Adam Smith reports with Pliny as his source, "when they first began to coin silver. Copper, therefore, appears to have continued always the measure of value in that republick ... Though the *Sestertius*, therefore, was originally a silver coin, its value was estimated in copper."[86]

Eucken also mentions the chaos of monies in Hellenistic times in the Eastern Mediterranean, so that the medium of exchange and the unit of account had to fall apart.[87] Yet introducing a *general* equivalent has advantages when production rests on the division of labour. This statement is illustrated by Fig. 5.1, which shows the delivery relationships of the model.

The wheat industry obtains 12 I (1)[88] from the iron sector, for which 120 p_W must be paid. This sum cannot be directly covered by the sale of wheat to the iron industry to the tune of 90 p_W (2). How does the wheat sector finance the outstanding iron bill? To answer this question, look at the supply links between wheat cultivation and pig farming. The 18 pigs needed in the wheat sector cost 90 p_W. However, wheat worth 120 p_W (3) is delivered to pig farming. The wheat sector makes a surplus of 30 p_W or 6 pigs (4) from this transaction. The wheat cultivation transfers these 6 animals to the iron industry (5) in addition to its wheat delivery. Thus, the rest of the iron bill is settled.

---

[85] Cf. Schmölders, G., op. cit., p. 27.

[86] Smith, A., op. cit., p. 56. Further examples are provided by Gerloff, W., Die Entstehung ..., op. cit.

[87] Cf. Eucken, W., op. cit., p. 181.

[88] Numbers in brackets refer to the corresponding transaction in the diagram.

Suppose there is neither credit in kind nor transferable documentation of purchasing power. In that case, the wheat and pig sectors must *first* exchange goods before the wheat cultivation can enter business relations with the iron industry—just like before on the playground. The consistent price system is known, yet a triangular exchange occurs without an accepted means of payment. Only if the physical flows of goods between all sectors do not show any account balance will the direct quantity deliveries lead to relative prices free of contradiction.

The medium of exchange and the unit of account fulfil two independent functions.[89] But they differ in qualitative terms: "… a market is conceivable without a general means of payment, but not without a generally recognised unit of account."[90]

However, the mere existence of a general medium of exchange can increase the welfare of two traders who possess several objects that cannot be (reasonably) divided. An (almost) continuously divisible, universally accepted exchange medium of any kind whatsoever makes it possible to dissolve blockades in trading and generate prices that equalise benefits and are "fair" in this sense.[91]

Since every medium of exchange must be scalable to reduce transaction costs and increase allocation advantages, the counting unit also constitutes a *systematic* prerequisite for a universal manifestation of purchasing power. Furthermore, the market-coordinated social division of labour requires a general denominator in the budget restrictions, generating a price system consistent with reproduction. The essence of the numéraire's abstract function is the disposition with *values*; only then can production and exchange be *organised*. Regardless of how people agree on which standard, the procedure is always a vital precondition for commodity production.

The more economic exchange integrates society, the greater the importance of the division of labour: people increasingly produce something to offer for sale on the market; outputs become commodities. The proceeds are used to buy other goods. Initially, events are certainly still oriented towards the acquisition of use values. The first and last elements of the chain are different goods. Economic activity is merely a means to an end: the income guaranteeing a "standard of living" sets an upper limit to demand-driven production.

It is different in capitalist commodity production. *Money* is now the *alpha* and *omega* of the process. It is thrown into circulation to generate additional *earning* potential—abstract wealth:

> "The exact form of this process is therefore M – C – M'," Marx wrote, "where M' = M + ΔM = the original sum advanced, plus an increment. This increment or excess over the original value I call 'surplus-value.' The value originally advanced, therefore, not only remains intact

89 Koopmans already pointed this out in the 1930s. Cf. Koopmans, J. G., Zum Problem des „neutralen " Geldes, in: Hayek, F. A. v. (ed.), Beiträge zur Geldtheorie, Wien 1933, pp. 211–359, p. 247.

90 Veit, O., op. cit., p. 19. [F. H.]

91 The statement refers to the (long forgotten) example by Nash, J., The bargaining problem, in: Econometrica, vol. 18 (1950), pp. 155–162. In the example, Bill and Jack exchange their chattel (also on a playground?), whereby, according to Nash, Bill hands over a ball that he values higher than Jack. For an analysis and avoidance of this irrational process, see Helmedag, F., Barter, efficiency, and money prices: dissecting Nash's bargaining example, in: International Journal of Pluralism and Economics Education, vol. 9 (2018), pp. 292–299.

> while in circulation, but adds to itself a surplus-value or expands itself. It is this movement that converts it into capital."[92]

Now, the process is no longer dominated and limited by use values; instead, economic success is crystallised in money:

> "The simple circulation of commodities – selling in order to buy – is a means of carrying out a purpose unconnected with circulation, namely, the appropriation of use-values, the satisfaction of wants. The circulation of money as capital is, on the contrary, an end in itself, for the expansion of value takes place only within this constantly renewed movement. The circulation of capital has therefore no limits."[93]

The striving for more money that characterises capitalist commodity production is not materialised in a notional unit of account but in the tangible manifestation of money, the *object of universal desire*. Money acquires the status of the "general commodity", as it embodies the power to act as a buyer in *all* economic exchanges. The super commodity always finds a "demander" who voluntarily and without regard to the person, i.e., without further solvency checks, accepts it in return for relinquishing his unique commodity.

In economic exchange, money represents the all-purpose means of payment if all *other* sellers honour it equally. Money is not accepted because of its value; conversely, it has value because it is accepted. This respect is where the exceptional intrinsic value of money comes from, which is necessary to guarantee its function as a medium of exchange; the units in which people calculate are irrelevant.

The reason why the counting unit and the general medium of exchange are amalgamated in an advanced monetary economy is apparent: the information costs of exchange decrease, and there is no longer any need to transform units of the medium of exchange into those of the numéraire. Thus, it is advantageous to elevate the general medium of exchange to the universal denominator. Now, money unfolds its entire energy to structure economic life through and through:

> "The advance of rationalism in the area of commercial thinking and action and thus ultimately the complete rationalisation of the entire commercial economy with its unrestricted expansion of the pursuit of profit is based on money as a means of accounting, which is the means of expression of all economic transactions as they are recorded in the accounts of the private and public economy."[94]

If the basis of the disposition does not correspond to the unit of the medium of exchange, e.g., in times of inflation, it can still circulate—at least for a while. In some countries, national currencies are used for payment, but prices are, e.g., calculated in US dollars or euros.

However, the role of money as an exchange medium is inconceivable without a certain capability to store value. If this property were completely absent, it would never be the accepted universal means of payment.

---

[92] Marx, K., Capital, vol. I, op. cit., p. 149.

[93] Ibid., p. 150.

[94] Gerloff, W., Geld ..., op. cit., p. 155. [F. H.]

> "Only when money devalues so quickly," Schmölders explains, "that it is no longer able to bridge the technically determined time difference between receipt and expenditure, it also becomes useless as a medium of exchange; a certain minimal degree of stability in value is, therefore, indispensable for the exchange function of money."[95]

While initially hoarded goods were money, modern money has become predestined for hoarding as it allows potential demand to be shifted into the future.[96]

What about the orthodox three-function doctrine of money? The first feature to call into question is the allegedly stand-alone qualification as a store of purchasing power. If the medium of exchange were incapable of conserving value temporarily, no one would respect it as a customer's remuneration in economic exchange. And nothing but money can be considered best suited for accumulating value in the most liquid form, as it has the highest marketability.

Accordingly, the older literature only distinguished between the abstract "unit of account" and the concrete "medium of exchange". In the abstract dimension, money expresses value with which other values are compared. The material aspect of money is money as a means of exchange, debt repayment and preservation of value.[97] Patinkin, therefore, differentiates in his highly regarded study of monetary theory between "money as the abstract unit of account" and money as a "physical medium of exchange and store of value". These two categories of money correspond to two types of prices, "accounting prices" and "money prices".[98]

Some authors emphasise the medium of exchange, while others consider the unit of account to be the main attribute of money.[99] Sometimes, it is claimed that "real" money must integrate both qualities. Forstmann, e.g., who also differentiates between the two qualities mentioned, believes that one can speak of money in the economic sense only if "… these two functions of money, simultaneously united in one object, are fulfilled by it."[100] A short time later, he presents a 'monolithic' characterisation of money:

> "Money in the economic sense is an anonymous legitimation of claims to the national volume of goods and services that are generally recognised in a payment community and can be

---

[95] Schmölders, G., op. cit., p. 27. [F. H.]

[96] Cf. Gerloff, W., Die Entstehung …, op. cit., p. 56. The suspension of purchasing power harbours the risk of a crisis: "The difficulty of converting the commodity into money, of selling it, only arises from the fact that the commodity must be turned into money but the money need not be immediately turned into commodity, and therefore *sale* and *purchase* can be separated." Marx, K., Theories of Surplus Value, Part II, London 1969, p. 509, https://archive.org/details/marxtsvpart2. Marx's explanations correspond to what J. St. Mill remarked on Say's Law. This is even more astonishing as Marx—as mentioned above—was not exactly full of praise for Mill. See Balassa, B. A., Karl Marx and John Stuart Mill, in: Weltwirtschaftliches Archiv, vol. 83 (1959), pp. 147–165.

[97] See Veit, O., op. cit., p. 51.

[98] Cf. Patinkin, D., Money, Interest and Prices, 2nd ed., New York et al. 1965, p. 15 f.

[99] See in more detail Schilcher, R., op. cit., p. 39 ff. Cf. also Wilken, F., Die Phänomenologie des Geldwertbewußtseins, in: Archiv für Sozialwissenschaft und Sozialpolitik, vol. 56 (1926), pp. 417–469.

[100] Forstmann, A., op. cit., p. 71. [F. H.]

> activated at any time, the production and distribution of which it guarantees quantitatively and qualitatively as a unit of account and medium of exchange."[101]

Apart from the unclear conclusion—to what extent does money "guarantee" the production and distribution of the social product?—the reference to a "payment community" misses the point. Payment is to be understood as a money transfer to redeem debts, including, e.g., taxes. This compulsory disbursement without a specified reward is regularly made in a *currency* that was launched by the state as a "creature of the legal system".[102]

Let us also examine Schmölders' description of the nature of money. He sees it as "... any sufficiently documented promise of value of more or less general validity ..."[103] On closer inspection, Schmölders' definition appears blurred, too. His specification of money—as helpful as it seems at first glance—is more like a description than a concept of money that succeeds in indicating the *differentia specifica* of this general remuneration.

In light of the considerations above, the root of the dissatisfaction with the sundry definitions of money is easy to discover: the ambiguity that pervades the literature as to (from) when to speak of money in an economic sense is reflected in the nebulous notion of the typical economic action.

In a modern society dominated by economic exchange, *money* is a *metrically scaled expression of value*—if one wants to append: a sufficiently documented promise of value, an anonymous claim—whose authority is based on being recognised by *every seller as the buyer's remuneration in an economic exchange*. "Metrically scaled" in this context means that the denomination of the value expression is related to a *logically* prior numéraire—although both units should (expediently) coincide.

Money valued in this way makes its possession worthwhile for everyone in the economic community; therefore, it possesses the reputation required to fulfil the tasks of a medium of exchange and a store of value. This exceptional quality is not inherent in the substance of the general medium of exchange but is the result of a social process. The concrete value of money reflects its power over the commodity cosmos, measured by the prices formulated in it.

From a systematic perspective, the development of economic exchange via a unit of account leads to the division of labour, culminating in the spread of a universal equivalent in the monetary capitalist market economy. In it, the universal payment represents abstract wealth, as it confers the *potential* power of control over the entire

---

[101] Ibid., p. 72. [F. H.]

[102] The formula can be found on page 1 of the book by Knapp, G. F., Staatliche Theorie ..., op. cit. [F. H.] With his doctrine, Knapp became the forefather of the 'Chartalists', who regard money as a pure token. In contrast, the 'Metallists' emphasise the material value of money, where, as already explained, not only gold and silver functioned as a general equivalent. The transition from metallism to chartalism can be studied particularly well in the history of English money. See Helmedag, F., Monetäre (Un-)Ordnung als Ursache von Finanzmarktkrisen, in: Busch, U., Krause, G. (eds.), Theorieentwicklung im Kontext der Krise, Abhandlungen der Leibniz-Sozietät der Wissenschaften, vol. 35, Berlin 2013, pp. 179–193.

[103] Schmölders, G., op. cit., p. 22. [F. H.]

spectrum of all specific goods. If money is removed from this social context, it *does not* embody *any* wealth—besides the use value of the medium of exchange. In a society integrated through economic exchange, on the other hand, the owner of money is wealthy: his purchasing power makes him strong.

At the end of this treatise, we return to the question of whereupon the value of money in the contemporary economy rests. However, a critical comment on prevailing explanations seems appropriate at this point. The preceding historical and analytical remarks on the nature of money should have opened the eyes to the fact that the standard dichotomy of the subject matter into the supply and demand of money is of little help. This separation, whose relationship to the market paradigm of neoclassical theory is apparent, suggests that money is traded on the market like potatoes or fridges. But nobody demands money and offers money in return: What should be used to pay? With (more or less?) money? The 'price' of a euro could only be a euro; the general money consideration would only be exchanged for the general money consideration in the ratio 1:1. The supply and demand curves coincide in a "price-quantity diagram of the money market" with the angle bisector; this is the purest form of the exchange of equivalents, which we shall soon consider in more detail.

In reality, it is a *temporary transfer of purchasing power*, deposits, and loans for which a fee, the interest, must be paid.[104] The lender agrees for an emolument to be a payer without becoming a buyer, where the pure "production costs" of a loan are negligible nowadays.[105] Accordingly, in textbooks under the heading "money supply", one encounters explanations of money creation and money extinction techniques. More sophisticated accounts extend this to include bank behaviour in the course of their profit maximisation: the optimal credit volume is wanted. In the same way, under the heading "demand for money", there is no discussion of the demand for money but rather the determinants of cash holdings or the velocity of money circulation.

Given what we have experienced so far, the rejection of the established monetary theory should be no surprise: there is no *individual* money producer. Currency is a social means of communication; its (economically relevant) fabrication is nowadays a live broadcast, not a recording. Modern money is received at the moment of its emergence; it comes into the world *pari passu* with its making out of thin air. This insight can even be encountered occasionally in traditional textbooks: "If the *supply of money* is understood to mean the respective *quantity of money*, 'money supply' always presupposes a corresponding willingness on the part of non-banks to hold

[104] In the institutional sense, the 'money market' brings about horizontal and vertical liquidity balancing in the banking system: commercial papers are traded for central bank deposits at conditions whose upper and lower limits are set by the central bank. See Helmedag, F., 330 Ultra posse nemo obligatur: Grenzen und Möglichkeiten der Geldpolitik, in: Berliner Debatte Initial, 33 Jg. (2022), pp. 48–65.

[105] Contemporary credit money is a claim against a commercial or central bank and comes into being as a *creatio ex nihilo*. See for a schematic depiction of this mechanism Helmedag, F., Monetäre (Un-)Ordnung …, op. cit., p. 187 ff.

cash, i.e., a corresponding 'demand for money'."[106] Instead of "money supply", it should be more accurately called "money creation", and "money demand" should be replaced by "money use". Money demand and supply mean nothing but reflect the unfolded economic exchange: the seller asks for money, and the buyer offers it. However, this means that the spotlight turns to commodity markets, whereas modern monetary literature has credit markets in mind but pretends to speak of money markets.

By clarifying the nature of money in the modern economy, the concept of economic exchange has passed its first test. This visual aid also allows us to take a closer look at the research program of the two main economic currents. Let us inspect the approach of the classics and the concept of the neoclassicists.

[106] Issing, O., Einführung in die Geldtheorie, 7th ed., München 1990, p. 70. [F. H.]

Chapter 6
Goods, Commodities and the *Homo Oeconomicus*: On the Research Programme of Economic Theory

At the top of the classical agenda was the theory of value, whose task was to get to the heart of the new economic activity sparked by the Industrial Revolution. On this basis, the founders of economics outlined the prospects of a capitalist market economy and identified the need for economic policy.

The first wave of the subsequent neoclassical attack against the approach of the progenitors was aimed at undermining the high significance of production in the classical doctrine: the neoclassicists were zealous to show that production could be interpreted as "indirect exchange". The advantageousness of production could be put on an equal footing with the increase in utility from a transaction of goods.

> . . an economic exchange," Menger argues, "contributes ... to the better satisfaction of human needs and to the increase of the wealth of the participants just as effectively as a physical increase of economic goods. All persons who mediate exchange are therefore – provided always that the exchange operations are economic – just as productive as the farmer or manufacturer. For the end of economy is not the physical augmentation of goods but always the fullest possible satisfaction of human needs.[1]

A leading figure of the "Lausanne School" expressed himself in the same vein. Vilfredo Pareto also argues in favour of viewing production as a particular form of exchange:

In a general way, when an individual gives up a certain quantity of a good in order to procure another one, we will say that he *transforms* the first good into the second. He can proceed by exchange, giving up to others the first good and receiving from them the second; he can accomplish it by production, actually transforming the first good into the second himself. In addition he can, for this operation, turn to a person who transforms goods, a producer.[2]

---

[1] Menger, C., Principles ..., op. cit., p. 190. Similarly, Jevons, W. St., op. cit., p. 241: "Both by the use of capital and by exchange we are enabled vastly to increase the sum of utility which we enjoy ...".

[2] Pareto, V., Manual of Political Economy [1927], London / Basingstoke 1971, p. 124. Hennings reproduces this passage from the Italian "Manuale" of 1906 somewhat differently. Cf. Hennings,

F. Helmedag, *Production of Commodities by Means of Labour*, Springer Studies in Alternative Economics, https://doi.org/10.1007/978-3-032-01457-3_6

From a neoclassical perspective, exchange is the theme; production appears merely as one of its possible variations. However, while the change of ownership increases welfare through a new allocation of *goods*, production increases the number of distributable *commodities*. Yet, production, which is interpreted as a special manifestation of exchange, only becomes lucrative unless ...

> ... it is more advantageous than simple exchange; that means that it will only be advantageous to convert one set of exchangeable goods into another set, by production, if the set acquired has a higher market value than the set given up.[3]

The second blow of the neoclassical attack was aimed at the "exchange of equivalents", of which the forerunners spoke in the course of their efforts to decipher the laws of exchange value. Marx was able to shift the search for the origin of profit to the sphere of production because in circulation, under conditions of free competition, performance and reward coincide and, therefore, cannot be the source of a surplus:

> If commodities, or commodities and money, of equal exchange-value, and consequently equivalents, are exchanged, it is plain that no one abstracts more value from, than he throws into, circulation. There is no creation of surplus-value.[4]

For obvious reasons, the marginal utility school—which was, among other things, a counter-revolution against certain conclusions of classical theory, particularly those that Marx advanced—had a strong interest in branding the concept of equivalent exchange as flawed. In this sense, Menger accuses economists ...

> ... to commit the error of regarding the magnitude of price as the essential feature of an exchange, and as a result of this mistake, to commit the further error of regarding the quantities of goods in an exchange as *equivalents*. The result was incalculable damage to our science since writers in the field of price theory lost themselves in attempts to solve the problem of discovering the causes of an alleged *equality* between two quantities of goods.[5]

But the polemic seems somewhat artificial. A law of commodity value claiming that physical equivalents are exchanged would indeed be utter nonsense. Who would swap a Bible for the same Bible? Of course, the classics also knew this: "... as regards the use values exchanged, both buyer and seller may possibly gain something ..."[6] In the next part, it becomes clear that the classics were concerned with exchange values. Equivalents are "made" by trade; the parity of giving and taking provides an *exchange value* equivalent, not *a use value* equivalent—what else?

It is also true of contemporary economic theory that the two economic activities based on economic exchange, business and production, *commerce and industry*, are weighted differently by the individual schools. While the followers of the neo-Ricardian or surplus approach, which is based on the classical tradition,[7] rally around

---

K. H., The Exchange Paradigm and the Theory of Production and Distribution, in: Baranzini, M., Scazzieri, R. (eds.), Foundations of Economics, Oxford 1986, pp. 221–243, p. 225.

3 Hicks, J. R., Value and Capital [1939], 2nd ed., Oxford 1946, p. 78.

4 Marx, K., Capital, vol. I, op. cit., p. 158.

5 Menger, C., Principles ..., op. cit., p. 192.

6 Marx, K., Capital, vol. I, op. cit., p. 156.

7 Cf. Garegnani, P., surplus approach to value and distribution, in: The New Palgrave, vol. IV, London / New York / Tokyo 1987, pp. 560–574.

the "Production of Commodities by Means of Commodities", the neoclassical circles primarily discuss the existence, uniqueness and stability of a general equilibrium of supply and demand. The contrast becomes particularly sharp when the variables considered exogenous by the two branches of theory are confronted with one another.

The classical approach assumes given quantities of the entire output and the goods forming the real wage bundle. Under the prevailing technical and social production conditions, the total number of workers is also fixed.[8] From these data, the social surplus product can be determined and distributed to the classes of landowners and capitalists in the form of rent and profit. Separation of value and output theory thus characterises the classical programme.[9]

Instead, neoclassicists want to derive both prices and quantities *simultaneously*. In their view, this is achieved by the opposing forces of supply and demand. As the events in goods markets, wages, profits and rents obey the universal principle of supply and demand, *scarcity* becomes the skeleton key to economic analysis. The edifice rests on three pillars: preferences, initial endowments, and production possibilities. The aim is to find a market-clearing price vector compatible with these facts.

Without going into detail about the problem-solving potential of both theoretical strands, the initial impression that the classical perspective focuses on production while the neoclassical perception is targeted at the exchange must be rejected. This assessment would be superficial. Both curricula discuss both forms of economic activity inherent in the concept of economic exchange: commerce *and* industry. However, the line of sight is diametrically opposed. If you like, the neoclassicists look at production from the vantage point of exchange; the proponents of the classical approach consider exchange from the production angle.[10]

We encounter both forms of economic activity in the behaviour of the *homo oeconomicus*. Following his mission, he attempts to *maximise* his subjective benefit in the course of income and expenditure decisions. This behaviour distinguishes economics and its image of humankind strongly from the other social sciences, which also assume rationally acting individuals but not subjects who want to *optimise* their well-being.

Admittedly, some attempts in economics purport to describe the actors' actual behaviour, e.g., through an aspiration orientation.[11] Apart from whether these

---

[8] Cf. Garegnani, P., Value and Distribution in the Classical Economists and Marx, in: Oxford Economic Papers, vol. 36 (1984), pp. 291–325, p. 293.

[9] According to Schefold, this detachment can be maintained under varying demand conditions. Cf. Schefold, B., Über Änderungen in der Zusammensetzung des Endprodukts, in: Postkeynesianismus, Ökonomische Theorie in der Tradition von Keynes, Kalecki und Sraffa, Marburg 1987, pp. 119–164. See the review of the book by Helmedag, F., in: Zeitschrift für Wirtschafts- und Sozialwissenschaften, vol. 109 (1989), pp. 148–154, pp. 151 f. This aspect is dealt with monographically by Kubin, J., Neoricardianische Gleichgewichtsmodelle und Änderungen in der Zusammensetzung der Nachfrage, Marburg 1989.

[10] Cf. Hennings, K. H., op. cit., p. 221.

[11] Cf. Kromphardt, J., Wirtschaftswissenschaft II: Methoden und Theoriebildung in der Volkswirtschaftslehre, in: Handwörterbuch der Wirtschaftswissenschaft, vol. IX, Stuttgart / Tübingen /

approaches depict a gradual process aiming at any ideal—we need only recall the comments on the economic principle—, it seems doubtful that economic theory can expect some progress in knowledge from assuming protagonists with unspecified ambitions. On the contrary, the explicit striving for an optimum allows the specification of objective functions to pave the way for an exact analysis. Furthermore, the supposed pursuit of advantage is relevant from theoretical and practical perspectives.

With the rise of utilitarianism and the expansion of the capitalist market economy, there was a growing theoretical need to explore the social implications, especially of an unbridled possessive urge. This desire became all the more pressing as the effort to maximise individual utility through economic exchange had to push back other forms of social integration …

> … because the exchange result can be improved if inhibiting feudal or religious ties and social obligations are dropped, so that the allocation of social roles is ultimately carried out by the exchange system … alone and, accordingly, social integration is brought about by economic integration.[12]

Classical economists (including Marx) faced the key issue of whether and to what degree the new economic system was entitled to life, viable and worth living.

As the discussion of the development of economic exchange and the evolution of money has shown, the epistemological interest is not merely academic; indeed, individuals are generally eager to augment their possessions. With increasing precedence, this has become a central determinant of behaviour[13]:

> Capitalism channels human aspirations in the direction of profit maximisation. Hence the homo oeconomicus is not as unrealistic as is often claimed.[14]

Although the *homo oeconomicus* is seen as constitutive for economic theory in the sense advocated here, this does not mean that processes can be observed that are *exclusively* economically initiated and therefore represent pure economic action; in reality, patterns of behaviour are regularly based on a bundle of motives. Hence, the findings of an economic theory that models the activities of *homines oeconomici* cannot be transferred to the existing world on a 1:1 scale. Instead, the extent to which purely economic calculation is modified or (over)compensated by other incitements

---

Göttingen 1982, pp. 904–936, p. 920. See also Frey, B. S., Stroebe, W., Ist das Modell des Homo Oeconomicus „unpsychologisch“?, in: Zeitschrift für die gesamte Staatswissenschaft, vol. 136 (1980), pp. 82–97 and the subsequent debate between Rothschild, K. W., Wie nützlich ist der Homo Oeconomicus? Bemerkungen zu einem Aufsatz von Bruno S. Frey und Wolfgang Stroebe, in: Zeitschrift für die gesamte Staatswissenschaft, vol. 137 (1981), pp. 289–292 and Frey, B. S., Stroebe, W., Der Homo Oeconomicus ist entwicklungsfähig, in: Zeitschrift für die gesamte Staatswissenschaft, vol. 137 (1981), pp. 293–294.

[12] Schlicht, E., Einleitung, in: Schlicht, E. (ed.), Einführung in die Verteilungstheorie, Reinbek bei Hamburg 1976, pp. 12–64, p. 16. [F. H.]

[13] Cf. Heilbronner, R. L., Die Entstehung von Märkten und Produktionsfaktoren, in: Schlicht, E. (ed.), Einführung in die Verteilungstheorie, Reinbek bei Hamburg 1976 pp. 85–99, p. 95 f.

[14] Zinn, K. G., Politische …, op. cit., p. 71. [F. H.] See as well Vogt's distinction between "conservative neoclassicism" and "neoclassical method". Cf. Vogt, W., Die Angst des kritischen Ökonomen vor der Neoklassik, in: Hickel, R. (ed.), Radikale Neoklassik, Opladen 1986, pp. 103–113.

in day-to-day existence must always be examined. The idealised activities of the *homo oeconomicus* are the driving force of the social subsystem "economy", which is intertwined with other spheres in the way of life.

From the explanations of the causes of the Industrial Revolution, it emerged that only an interplay of commercial thinking and technical mastery of nature was *sufficient* to unleash it. Since then, the *homo oeconomicus* is no longer a fictitious figure; instead, this *homunculus* proves to be the Archimedean point for (re)constructing the dialectic between productive forces and production relations in the modern era.

In this light, economic theory must be sheltered from exaggerated demands on its explanatory ability. Suppose it takes a priori only one element of human activity into account; however influential it may be, it cannot wholly disentangle one single human activity. In that case, the argument does not refer to an *empirically* delimited social subsystem of the economy but to an *analytical* entity.

The concept of economic exchange makes it possible to specify a criterion with which economic and non-economic issues can be separated. The figure of the *homo oeconomicus* also enables one to set precisely formulated goals for the parties involved in such an exchange. A seller—a term that only makes sense in the monetary economy—hands over use value and receives exchange value in return. As a *homo oeconomicus*, he wants to maximise this margin. Conversely, the buyer intends to optimise the gap between the reduction in need caused by the object received and the amount paid for it. The general rational principle loses its lack of content and gains an economic profile.

The course of action requires measuring use value in a way that allows a comparison with exchange value. Demand curves provide the necessary reference because they quantify welfare improvement by articulating the subjective monetary worth of the use value of a consumer good's last unit. It, therefore, makes sense to interpret demand curves as (marginal) additional benefit curves.[15]

In market economies, buyers pursue improving their quality of life based on use values, which minimises their wants due to an optimal consumption plan. Conversely, *capitalists* in the acquisitive economy seek to maximise profits. This group includes, on the one hand, *entrepreneurs* who endeavour to increase prosperity through their activities expressed in exchange values. For this, it is essential to maximise the margin between income and expenditure. On the other hand, *investors* strive for the highest return on financial assets, i.e., to achieve the best possible percentual yield of a pecuniary engagement. As explained at the end of this book, each of the two character types steers its own course. Until then, we shall neglect the exact destination each is heading for.

[15] Rising supply functions can be interpreted similarly: starting from a *given* stock, a vendor only sells additional quantities in return for increasing compensation. On the other hand, profit-maximising producers have no reason to construct a supply function for known demand and cost curves, as they realise Cournot's *point* where marginal costs and marginal revenue coincide.

By now, the elements to stylise the economic subject "entrepreneur" are at hand. Since profits equal the difference between revenues and costs, his activities simultaneously extend to two opposing fields. Externally, he appears as a seller in economic exchanges interested in growing sales.

In the internal relationship, the entrepreneur ensures that the expenses to produce a certain quantity of use values are kept as low as possible. In doing so, he draws on the authority to issue instructions to the staff legitimised by the employment contract: the aim is to optimally combine the workforce with the other input goods the entrepreneur procures. This aspect will play a prominent role in the following.

From the supply-side perspective, the greed for profit gives rise to the unrestricted nature of capitalist dynamics. Hence, the profit volume and its distribution among competing firms become the *key variables* in economic enquiries. Accordingly, some early neoclassicists such as Jevons, Walras, Böhm-Bawerk, Wicksell and J. B. Clark intended to answer the same fundamental question about the long-term equilibrium position as the classics, i.e., to reveal the source, scope and significance of profit.

> The real theoretical difficulty," Wicksell remarked, "is. . to explain how, under stationary conditions, the possession of capital can remain a permanent source of income. The application to *non-stationary* conditions offers no difficulty in principle.[16]

Significantly, with its universal supply–demand machinery, the neoclassical camp was eventually forced to abandon its original research program. In response to Wicksell's attempt to eradicate the shortcomings of traditional Austrian capital theory and to consistently integrate "time" as a physical index of real capital into the doctrinal system, doubts arose about the suitability of the interest rate as an indicator of scarcity: the interest rate can deviate from the marginal productivity of capital, and it may move in the same direction as the capital value.[17]

The resumption of Walras' approach of considering the vector of real capital goods as an exogenous variable instead of the capital *value* also led to a dead end: it was not possible to show that both the reproduction of all produced means of production and a uniform rate of return are compatible with the supply–demand mechanism. However, the unresolved problem was suppressed over the years and finally fell into oblivion. In modern neo-Walrasian intertemporal general equilibrium theory, the shortcomings of capital theory are no longer recognisable; the entire time horizon is split into a series of short-term market periods with given initial endowments at every beginning.[18]

---

[16] Wicksell, K., Lectures on Political Economy [1913], vol. I, London 1935, p. 154, https://cdn.mises.org/Lectures%20on%20Political%20Economy%20-%20Volume%20I%20General%20Theory_2.pdf.

[17] An exposition of the (single-sector) Wicksell model can be found in Helmedag, F., Die Technikwahl bei linearer Einzelproduktion oder Die dritte Krise der Profitrate, Frankfurt a. M. / Bern / New York 1986, p. 67 ff. On the temporal theory of capital, see Helmedag, F., Böhm-Bawerks Kapitaltheorie im Licht des Waldproblems: Eine Neubewertung, in: Trautwein, H.-M. (ed.), Studien zur Entwicklung der ökonomischen Theorie XXXV, Berlin 2020, pp. 41–55.

[18] Walras did not tackle incorporating capital formation into his system until the fourth edition of his main work. Cf. Walras, L., Elements of Pure Economics [1926], ed. by Jaffé, W., 2nd ed., Homewood

The concept of equilibrium has narrowed down to the postulate that the opposing forces of supply and demand must balance each other. The classical characterisation of the centre of gravity—reproduction of the produced means of production and the associated constant structure of relative prices—is an alien element in such a world.

This *modus operandi* worked until the results of the Cambridge-Cambridge controversy recollected that factor price and demand are not necessarily inversely related as usually supposed. Thus, the typical neoclassical nexus of a simultaneous determination of value and output was broken.[19] The subsequent neoclassical counteroffensive followed a tried and tested battle plan: similar to Keynes's attack; the eventual response was an attempted appropriation. While the "neoclassical synthesis" was born then, the thesis that the neo-Ricardian *surplus approach* was nothing more than a special case of the general equilibrium theory now saw the light of day.[20]

In reality, this claim to universality suffered from the abandonment of the analysis of the long-term equilibrium position that was intended at the beginning; tacitly, the target state had changed its content.[21] For this reason alone, the claimed superiority of the neo-Walrasian theory could be disputed, apart from the fact that the temporary version of the allegedly *general* equilibrium theory is generally incapable of deriving a uniform rate of profit, not to mention the ridiculous assumption of complete future markets on which the intertemporal variant rests.[22]

1965, p. 278 ff. Hayek interpreted this concept of capital as a remnant of the classical theory that needed to be shaken off: "... the definition of capital as produced means of production should definitely be abandoned ... Bygones are bygones in the theory of capital no less than elsewhere in economics." Hayek, F. A. v., The Pure Theory of Capital (1941), 2nd ed., London 1950, p. 89. An overview of both the difficulties that obstructed general equilibrium theory since Walras and the resulting adjustments in the research programme and method is provided by Huth, Th., Kapital und Gleichgewicht, Zur Kontroverse zwischen neoklassischer und neoricardianischer Theorie des allgemeinen Gleichgewichts, Marburg 1989.

[19] Cf. Kurz, H. D., capital theory: debates, in: The New Palgrave, vol. I, London / New York / Tokyo 1987, pp. 357–363 and Helmedag, F., Lohn- und Profitkurven, in: Wirtschaftswissenschaftliches Studium (WiSt), vol. 20 (1991), pp. 408–412.

[20] Often mentioned in this context is Hahn, F., The neo-Ricardians, in: Cambridge Journal of Economics, vol. 6 (1982), pp. 353–374. See, however, anteriorly Hahn, F., Revival of Political Economy: The Wrong Issues and the Wrong Argument, in: Economic Record, vol. 51 (1975), pp. 360–364 and Bliss, C. J., Capital Theory and the Distribution of Income, Amsterdam / Oxford / New York 1975.

[21] Garegnani worked this out quite early. Cf. Garegnani, P., On a Change in the Notion of Equilibrium in Recent Work on Value and Distribution, in: Brown, M., Sato, K., Zarembka, P. (eds.), Essays in Modern Capital Theory, Amsterdam / New York / Oxford 1976, pp. 25–45.

[22] Cf. Schefold, B., Cambridge Price Theory: Special Model or General Theory of Value?, in: The American Economic Review, vol. 75 (1985), pp. 140–145. Some authors claim that a uniform rate of return can also be determined in the general equilibrium theory, given suitable premises. They consider the interest rate that transforms the discounted prices of the intertemporal general equilibrium theory into present prices. This equilibrium interest rate corresponds to the numéraire's own rate of interest. It is, therefore, an *arbitrary* variable. Furthermore, the discount rate differs materially from the profit rate in the classical sense. Cf. Huth, Th., op. cit., p. 207 ff. It should also be noted that Sraffa's definition of the own rate of interest diverges from the neoclassical definition. Cf. Eatwell, J., own rates of interest, in: The New Palgrave, vol. III, London / New York / Tokyo 1987, p. 786 f. The topic will later be taken up again.

Actually, under the ideal–typical conditions of "perfect competition", profit by no means disappears into thin air, even with an "infinite number" of suppliers.[23] Moreover, the classical study of equilibrium models a course of conceivable events, whereas the Walrasian general equilibrium theory pursues a fiction:

i. A Walrasian equilibrium is an *ex ante* equilibrium in the sense that the equilibrium position is determined prior to any real economic activity. It is the function of the auctioneer to determine the equilibrium prices in a '*tậtonnement*' process.
ii. Conversely, a classical equilibrium is an *ex post* equilibrium, determined in the actual course of the economy.[24]

The inability to recount the play given on the stage of economic life, let alone to identify the directing instances, is ultimately rooted in the neoclassical data set. The assumption of existing initial endowments, which are transformed and allocated compliant with the technical production possibilities and driven by preference orders, leads to a dead end: from scarce resources to infinite needs.[25]

The classical project, on the other hand, although perhaps less "general" at first glance, is dedicated to the tasks to be solved *in advance*, as it deals with the operational mode and the perspective of an economic system characterised by the social division of labour and the existence *of economic* classes. Consequently, the necessity of reproduction and the circularity of economic activity are introduced into the deliberations.

In line with the list of priorities advocated here, basic economic research primarily uncovers the determinants of the structure and volume of economic exchange. However, before the level of relevant activities and possibilities for influencing them can be considered, the requirements of the division of labour in the capitalist competitive process must be formulated: the theory of value constitutes the linchpin of economics.

At the time, the classical school was not unmotivated criticised, and ultimately superseded. Just as the shortcomings of neoclassical theory, which gradually emerged in sharper contours, triggered unease among some scholars or even initiated a rethinking, the marginal revolution back then was due to the deficits inherent in the classical system, besides the ideological driving forces. In the second part of this study, the causes of the mentioned weaknesses are unearthed as a prerequisite for recovery.

---

[23] See Helmedag, F., Individuelle und kollektive Gewinnmaximierung auf homogenen Märkten, in: Oberender, P. (ed.), Private und öffentliche Kartellrechtsdurchsetzung, Berlin 2012, pp. 9–38.

[24] Duménil, G., Lévy, D., The dynamics of competition: a restoration of the classical analysis, in: Cambridge Journal of Economics, Vol. 11 (1987), pp. 133–164, p. 138.

[25] The additional difficulties in proving the unambiguousness and stability of a general equilibrium have already been indicated. Cf. Helmedag, F., Ohne Werte …, op. cit., p. 58 ff.

Part II
The Classical Theory of Value: Criticism and Counter-Criticism

Chapter 7
No Pain, No Gain: Dissemination and Suppression of a Message

Modern textbooks are dominated by neoclassical reasoning in supply and demand categories, while little attention is paid to the conception of the predecessors. Although one sometimes encounters the stereotype that the theory of value, particularly the labour theory of value, is a supporting pillar in the doctrinal system of the ancestors, there is usually no further explanation as to *why* the classics devoted themselves so intensively to this issue. Their arguments are exceptionally seldom presented true to sources, much less is the quickly stated failure of the approach substantiated. At best, after a few pleasantries, the focus regularly shifts to markets where price formation occurs through the interplay of consumers' falling marginal benefits and suppliers' rising marginal costs. This way of proceeding creates the impression that value and price theory address the same topic. Contemporary microeconomics presents itself as the accurate solution to the same problem that the discipline's founders vainly tried to tackle with their theory of value. However, the classical surplus point of view and the neoclassical supply–demand perception are far apart regarding the respective epistemological interests as well as the concrete socio-political functions.

Both doctrines rose to prominence because they promised to satisfy a pressing need. The economic classics concerned the prospects of an active bourgeoisie emancipating itself from the traditional feudal shackles. Despite all individual differences, the classics endeavoured to get to the bottom of this process. They intended to justify the actual development and pointed to possible dangers that could constrain or even stifle growth. Classical theory—especially the labour theory of value—was not an academic dry run. Instead, it was forged as the intellectual armament of the burgeoning meritocracy:

> The labour theory of value appears on the scene as a social theory of the struggle of the working civil society against the manorial system. With the labour theory of value, the active part of society, the 'third class' (which of course also includes the cultivators of the land), asserts its claim to the future as bearer of the new productive potential.[1]

[1] Hofmann, W., Wert- und Preislehre, 2nd ed., Berlin 1971, p. 23. [F. H.]

F. Helmedag, *Production of Commodities by Means of Labour*, Springer Studies in Alternative Economics, https://doi.org/10.1007/978-3-032-01457-3_7

The marginal utility revolution, on the other hand, which took up and popularised a relatively old idea in the last third of the nineteenth century, only gained a broad following when the progressive momentum of the classical school had waned. A renewed boost no longer seemed necessary, especially the labour theory of value now threatened to undermine the status the bourgeoisie had acquired in the meantime.[2] Now that the social order based on feudalism had essentially been overthrown, the assistance expected from economic theory entailed debunking the shortcomings of the classical dogma and demonstrating the superiority of a theory based on the *individual* as the decisive instance of events.

The move away from a class analysis towards examining personal behaviour was made easier because, as we shall see, the predecessors had manoeuvred *themselves* into a quagmire of inextricable complications of value theory from which they could not find a way out. In contrast, the concept of marginal utility seemed far more suitable for providing the appropriate theoretical counterpart to a liberalist society than the approach of traditional political economy, focused on the prospects of capitalism: "In a nutshell, classicism can be characterised as an apologia for the emerging future, neoclassicism as an apologia for the past."[3]

Subjectively perceived, neoclassicists rightly bear their name. In their opinion, they erected a building on the ground staked out by the ancestors. The descendants believe they are continuing the inherited project by proving that an ideal competitive economy is driven by consumer sovereignty without any exploitation. The search for the source and volume of profit, particularly the question of whether the rate of profit would inevitably fall in the course of capitalist dynamics, lost its urgency, as capitalism has de facto come to stay and no longer needed any start-up aid.

In addition, the neoclassicists gradually identified the conditions that ensure just cost-covering production. Alas, economic life did not adhere to textbooks: the facts diverging from the dogmas made amendments unavoidable.

The models of monopolistic competition and the efforts in the theory of income and employment are two examples that economics sought to satisfy the practical need for explanations. However, this reasoning followed neoclassical lines of argument. Even Keynesianism, at least in the reading of the textbooks, is permeated by neoclassicism—not least because Keynes adopted and passed on a considerable

---

[2] As the chequered history of the books by Cournot, A., Recherches sur les principes mathématiques de la théorie des richesses, Paris 1838, and Gossen, H., Entwicklung der Gesetze des menschlichen Verkehrs und der daraus fließenden Regeln für menschliches Handeln, Braunschweig 1854, powerfully demonstrates, time was not yet ripe to receive the attention the monographs deserved; both were initially a complete failure. Cournot believed that the prevailing scepticism towards the mathematical method was to blame for this, and he, therefore, published his treatise in 1863 in exclusively verbal form, which tripled the size of the book but did not promote sales. At first, Gossen's treatise was also practically unsaleable, so the embittered Gossen bought the copies himself. He died in 1858 without having received any recognition for his achievement. Thirty years later, the shrewd Berlin publisher R. L. Prager threw the old copies on the market with a new flyleaf ("New Edition") and his additional preface: this time, they sold brilliantly. Cf. Pasinetti, L., Structural Change and Economic Growth, A theoretical essay on the dynamics of the wealth of nations, Cambridge et al. 1981, p. 14 n.

[3] Zinn, K. G., Politische..., op. cit., p. 57. [F. H.]

Marshallian legacy. The 45°-Keynesianism that dominated after the Second World War, with its macroeconomic IS-LM hydraulics,[4] strikingly expresses the fixation on supply and demand categories and is, therefore, closer to the neoclassical approach than to the classical perspective, not in terms of content but in terms of method. However, Keynes classified the entire economic theory before his "General Theory" as classical.[5]

The now-beginning journey along the classical value-theoretical route stops exclusively at the main stations Smith, Ricardo and Marx.[6] The voyage is undertaken to explore where and why the authors changed direction. Only after this pilot survey will it be possible to bring classical theory, which has gone off course, back on track.

---

[4] On the classification of Keynesian schools see Coddington, A., Keynesian Economics: The Search for First Principles, in: Journal of Economic Literature, vol. 14 (1976), pp. 1258–1273.

[5] Cf. Keynes, J. M., The General ..., op. cit., p. 3. Meanwhile, the intersection of a falling *Aggregate Demand Function* (AD) with a rising *Aggregate Supply Function* (AS) directly determines the national product and the price level. Cf. Helmedag, F., Die Beschäftigungstheorie von Keynes: Dichtung und Wahrheit, in: Busch, U. (ed.), Jenseits der Orthodoxie, Ansätze für einen Paradigmenwechsel in der Wirtschaftstheorie, Berliner Debatte Initial, vol. 23 (2012), pp. 63–76, p. 68 f. Yet, Keynes's *magnum opus* contains typical classical elements that have been almost completely lost in the reception of his doctrine. This refers to the role of labour and the "wage unit": "It is preferable to regard labour ... as the sole factor of production, operating in a given environment of technique, natural resources, capital equipment and effective demand. This partly explains why we have been able to take the unit of labour as the sole physical unit which we require in our economic system, apart from units of money and of time." Keynes, J. M., The General ..., op. cit., p. 213 f. At the end of this book, the toehold of the labour theory of value in the "General Theory" is addressed again.

[6] On the more distant stages, see Immler, H., Natur in der ökonomischen Theorie, Teil 1: Vorklassik – Klassik – Marx, Opladen 1985.

Chapter 8
Adam Smith: The Component Theory of Value

Adam Smith's "Wealth of Nations" is probably affected by the same problem as other well-known scholarly works: the number of times it is mentioned does not show how often it is read. This divergence comes as no surprise: the book is "contrary", remarks Winch,[1] and Schumpeter even adjudicates on Smith: "He never moved about the heads of even the dullest readers ...; while Smith taxed the reader's patience with his masses of historical and statistical material, he did not tax his reasoning power."[2] In fact, Smith's writing hardly offers anything that on its own would do justice to the claim of originality. Instead, he was the coordinator who combined individual currents into the "system of natural liberty". Adam Smith's monograph had an epoch-making effect because the *policies* propagated by the author were in line with the spirit of the age and less because he heralded something totally new.

While Hobbes saw the wolf character of humankind as being abolished by an artificial order, Smith argued for a market system that was far more appropriate to the *zeitgeist*, enabling people, indeed even encouraging them, to grab their economic fortune by the scruff of the neck without regard for others or a higher authority.[3] The "Wealth of Nations" revolves around this idea, which is reflected in its detailed expositions. The *oeuvre*'s rich specifics made it often a quarry from which future generations of economists extracted raw materials to refine it depending on their preferences.

As the title of the inquiry proclaims, its author is concerned with the forces that determine the prosperity of nations; among these, the productivity-enhancing division of labour plays the most prominent role. However, the division of labour can only unfold and exert its beneficial effects once the necessary social structure has emerged:

---

[1] Cf. Winch, D., op. cit., p. 342. [F. H.]

[2] Schumpeter, J. A., History ..., op. cit., p. 185.

[3] Cf. Faber, M., Manstetten, R., op. cit., p. 108.

F. Helmedag, *Production of Commodities by Means of Labour*, Springer Studies in Alternative Economics, https://doi.org/10.1007/978-3-032-01457-3_8

> WHEN the division of labour has been once thoroughly established, it is but a very small part of a man's wants which the produce of his own labour can supply. He supplies the far greater part of them by exchanging that surplus part of the produce of his own labour, which is over and above his own consumption, for such parts of the produce of other men's labour as he has occasion for. Every man thus lives by exchanging ...[4]

Such a way of coexistence only meets with general approval if people have previously realised that in the market economy, things are by no means chaotic. Instead, the increasing spread of this economic organisation promises to improve productivity by extending the division of labour.[5] As had to be made public, value formation obeys laws that produce desirable results. Thus, governmental intervention in the market should be reduced.

Before Smith examines the determinants of exchange value in more detail, he points out the two (economic) meanings of the word "value":

> ... VALUE ... sometimes expresses the utility of some particular object, and sometimes the power of purchasing other goods ... The one may be called 'value in use;' the other, 'value in exchange.[6]

Immediately after mentioning this distinction originating from Aristotle,[7] Smith introduces the so-called classical value paradox:

> Nothing is more useful than water: but it will purchase scarce anything ... A diamond, on the contrary, has scarce any value in use; but a very great quantity of other goods may frequently be had in exchange for it.[8]

However, Smith did not attach great importance to this phenomenon; unlike Ricardo later, he did not explain this *seeming* paradox. Of course, diamonds have a use value—*diamonds are a girl's best friend*, which should be common knowledge since Marilyn Monroe spread this insight—and a person dying of thirst will outweigh water with diamonds—if he can do so. Instead, Smith announces his value-theoretical research program without this intermediate step. He promises to present in succession the correct measure of exchange value or the real price of goods and their parts. He also proclaims that he will explore the circumstances in which the current price of a good, the "market price", deviates from or coincides with its "natural price".[9]

Market prices fluctuate depending on the *relationship* between supply and *effective* demand:

---

[4] Smith, A., op. cit., p. 37.

[5] The passage "by exchanging that surplus part of the produce of his own labour" in the previous quote shows that Smith had no complete division of labour in mind, where production is *exclusively* destined for an a priori anonymous demand. This is not contrary to the famous pin example at the beginning of Smith's book, which illustrates the productivity gain through a more sophisticated *internal* division of labour. Cf. ibid., p. 14 f.

[6] Ibid., p. 44 f.

[7] Cf. Aristotle, op. cit., p. 92 f.

[8] Smith, A., op. cit., p. 44 f.

[9] Cf. ibid., p. 46.

> The market price of every particular commodity is regulated by the proportion between the quantity which is actually brought to market, and the demand of those who are willing to pay the natural price of the commodity … Such people may be called the effectual demanders, and their demand the effectual demand; since it may be sufficient to effectuate the bringing of the commodity to market.[10]

In modern macroeconomics, "effective" and "notional" demand indeed play a role, but the "effective" demand of the classics differs from that in the context of rationing concepts.[11] To do justice to the difference, it seems sensible to say "sufficient" demand rather than "effective" demand. This clarification appears apposite because sufficient demand allows suppliers to fetch the natural price, no more and no less.[12]

Smith then concludes that corresponding control mechanisms always push the market price toward the natural price.[13] Sufficient demand corresponds to the natural price—a *point* in a price-quantity diagram instead of a functional relationship between the two variables.[14] The deviations of market prices from natural prices would be caused on the supply side, either due to wrong decisions or a lack of competition.

From this vantage point, accounts of the classical doctrine often appear vague. The equal-ranking forces of supply and demand do not cause random fluctuations of market prices around the natural price; instead, the doctrine of Smith and his successors is hierarchically structured: the natural price, at the start of the chain of reasoning, is associated with a unique sufficient quantity of demand, which then can be taken as given. If the vendors misjudge sales opportunities or if they can keep supply short due to a lack of competition,[15] discrepancies arise between market price and natural price. Nevertheless, the natural price *must* prevail sooner or later, as relevant assumptions have been made about supply reactions. Varying market prices are only intermediate stages to the natural price and the linked demand.[16]

---

[10] Ibid., p. 73.

[11] Cf. the relevant contributions in the anthology Hagemann, H., Kurz, H. D., Schäfer, W. (eds.), Die Neue Makroökonomik, Marktungleichgewicht, Rationierung und Beschäftigung, Frankfurt a. M. / New York 1981.

[12] It would also make sense to circumscribe 'effective' and 'notional' demand as 'actual' or 'desired'. The (lower) actual demand results from (undesired) rationing.

[13] See Smith, A., op. cit., p. 75.

[14] Cf. Schefold, B., Nachfrage und Zufuhr in der klassischen Ökonomie, in: Neumark, F. (ed.), Studien zur Entwicklung der ökonomischen Theorie I, Berlin 1981, pp. 53–91. An overview of gravity models is provided by Farmer, K., Kubin, I., Marktpreise und natürliche Preise: Adam Smiths Konzeption und ihre gegenwärtige Bedeutung aus neoricardianischer und neowalrasianischer Sicht, in: Kurz, H. D. (ed.), Adam Smith (1723–1790), Marburg 1990, pp. 203–236.

[15] "The monopolists, by keeping the market constantly under-stocked, by never fully supplying the effectual demand, sell their commodities much above the natural price …" Smith, A., op. cit., p. 78.

[16] Marshall later attributed the incongruence of market price and natural price to different adjustment periods and thus suggested that the concept of supply and demand *curves* could be found in the classics. Cf. Marshall, A., Principles …, op. cit., p. 314 f. On this complex, see Bharadwaj, K., Classical Political Economy and Rise to Dominance of Supply and Demand Theories, 2nd ed., London 1986.

In truth, it is questionable whether the adjustment process always takes place, as Smith describes. In his view, the market price falls below the natural price when supply exceeds sufficient demand; in the opposite case, the reverse applies. According to Smith, such differences indicate that individual parts of the price diverge from their natural level. This discrepancy leads to corresponding capital movements.[17]

Yet, the change in total profit should not be assessed solely on the development of unit profit; the quantity component may overcompensate the price effect. If, e.g., the market price falls below the natural price, the profit share of the price possibly decreases, but higher revenues may still increase the total profit. Then, the reactions of entrepreneurs assumed by Smith—here: transfer of capital to another trade—cannot claim general validity.

By focusing not on total profit but on profit per unit, Smith paved the way for thinking conceptually in fractions rather than differences, i.e., in relative rather than absolute terms. The subsequent economic theory focused on a *quotient*—the *rate* of profit interpreted as profit per unit of capital employed—and lost sight of profit as a monetary amount—the *difference* between revenue and costs in a specific period. As we shall see, this change in perspective directed the economic theory train on a track that did not terminate at the destination station.

The hierarchical structure of classical theory stands and falls with the "natural price" or, synonymously, the "value" of a commodity. It is, therefore, not surprising that the analysis of the determinants of this magnitude was placed at the top of the agenda by Smith and his successors: if one knows the laws of natural price, one (apparently) knows the basic operation principle of the competitive economy, too.

Smith does not present a homogeneous theory of value; his explanation is historically split up. It is worth analysing Smith's presentation in more detail and backing it up with quotations, as the central questions, problems and (preliminary) judgements of the classical theory of value can be found here—at least in rudimentary form.

First, Smith presents his famous deer-beaver model, which refers to a time before capital formation and settlement:

> In that early and rude state of society which precedes both the accumulation of stock and the appropriation of land, the proportion between the quantities of labour necessary for acquiring different objects seems to be the only circumstance which can afford any rule for exchanging them for one another. If among a nation of hunters, for example, it usually costs twice the labour to kill a beaver which it does to kill a deer, one beaver should naturally exchange for or be worth two deer.[18]

Smith makes no distinction between deer hunting and beaver catching in the example, so the working hours can be directly compared. But he recognises that concrete activities can differ in the required extent of effort, dexterity and qualification; in Smith's opinion, however, wages reflect such peculiarities: "In the advanced state of society, allowances … for superior hardship and superior skill, are commonly made in the wages of labour; and something of the same kind must probably have

[17] Cf. Smith, A., op. cit., p. 74 f.

[18] Ibid., p. 65.

taken place in its earliest and rudest period."[19] Consequently, in the case of heterogeneous labour, the exchange ratio between both booties would also have to correspond to the remuneration for the particular job performance instead of only their mere duration.

On closer inspection, however, this reasoning proves to be somewhat obscure: why, in a society of free individuals in which there is neither capital nor land ownership, does Smith speak of "wages of labour", even though everyone can realise his productive potential at his *own* discretion?—But Smith does not dig that deep; instead, he continues:

> In this state of things, the whole produce of labour belongs to the labourer; and the quantity of labour commonly employed in acquiring or producing any commodity, is the only circumstance which can regulate the quantity of labour which it ought commonly to purchase, command, or exchange for.[20]

Once again, the *quantities* of labour come to the fore, but now not only in the context of producing goods but also as the effort required to *acquire* a good. Let us try to shed some light on the situation.

To stay with the example, suppose the time to kill a beaver is twice as long as the time to kill a deer. Furthermore, after returning from hunting, some of the prey is traded. There is a 1:1 exchange ratio, i.e., one beaver is worth one stag.

If this phenomenon occurs consistently, one could argue—in the spirit of Smith—that deer hunting is twice as demanding as beaver trapping; perhaps deer chasing requires more training, or predators may increase the risk of an occupational accident. If the above exchange ratio is observable, and Smith's brief remarks do not rule out such a possibility, then, contrary to popular opinion, he did not advocate a pure (quantity of homogeneous) labour theory of relative prices even for the "early and rude state of society". The unease which encounters the propagation of a value theory based solely on uniform labour quantities—though Smith restricted the doctrine to bygone times—would be unfounded.[21]

Smith devotes himself only briefly to the early and rude state of society but quickly turns to modern conditions:

> As soon as stock has accumulated in the hands of particular persons, some of them will naturally employ it in setting to work industrious people, whom they will supply with materials and subsistence, in order to make a profit by the sale of their work, or by what their labour adds to the value of the materials ... The value which the workmen add to the materials, therefore, resolves itself in this case into two parts, of which the one pays their wages, the other the profits of their employer upon the whole stock of materials and wages which he advanced.[22]

[19] Ibid.

[20] Ibid.

[21] See Recktenwald, H. C., Würdigung des Werkes, in: Smith, A., Der Wohlstand der Nationen, Eine Untersuchung seiner Natur und seiner Ursachen, translated by Recktenwald, H. C., München 1978, pp. XV-LXXIX, p. LIV f.

[22] Smith, A., op. cit., p. 65 f.

In the course of capital formation—a process that Smith does not discuss in detail—a new income category comes into sight: profit. According to Smith, profit is derived from the value that *the worker* adds to the raw material. However, as the Scotsman illustrates in a sample calculation, profit is not generated in proportion to working time but is related to the total capital invested. This sum includes wages, which in the classical view are paid upfront,[23] and the value of the raw materials.

This approach blazed the way for a far-reaching inconsistency: the increase in value of the raw material is caused solely by labour, yet the general rate of profit is calculated on total costs, which are interpreted as "capital". This method is an expression of the belief that every unit of money advanced is equally productive and, therefore, deserves the same share of profit in the competitive equilibrium: the capital gains "… are regulated altogether by the value of the stock employed, and are greater or smaller in proportion to the extent of this stock."[24] Below, it will be confirmed that this mechanism, constructed analogously to an investor's behaviour, jams and would block the gearing of the capitalist market economy—if it were really put together in this way.

As Smith's disciples either did not note this inconsistency or considered it not worthy of deeper analysis, economic theory was already on the wrong track. At a glance, it may seem plausible—especially from a microeconomic point of view based on opportunity costs—to assume that every pre-financed monetary unit in equilibrium must yield the same return. But the impression is deceptive. In fact, Smith had already taken the first step in the right direction with his component theory of value, which was to find no mercy in the judgment of Ricardo and Marx.

It is imperative, however, to proceed methodically and address each matter sequentially. Let us first look at the events in chronological order. Alongside wages and profits, a third type of income appears:

> As soon as the land of any country has all become private property, the landlords, like all other men, love to reap where they never sowed, and demand a rent even for its natural produce.[25]

And a little later, Smith sums up:

> Wages, profit, and rent, are the three original sources of all revenue as well as of all exchangeable value. All other revenue is ultimately derived from some one or other of these.[26]

According to Smith, this reveals the secret of the natural price:

---

[23] Cf. ibid., p. 73.

[24] Ibid., p. 66.

[25] Ibid., p. 67.

[26] Ibid., p. 69. Walras also attempted to dissect the price of goods ultimately into its income components. However, he does not refer to Adam Smith, as one might expect. "It was Bastia's idea," he asserts, "that, in final analysis, services are exchanged against services, but he only meant personal services, while we have in mind the services of land, persons and capital goods." Walras, L., op. cit., p. 225.

> When the price of any commodity is neither more nor less than what is sufficient to pay the rent of the land, the wages of the labour, and the profits of the stock employed in raising, preparing, and bringing it to market, according to their natural rates, the commodity is then sold for what may be called its natural price.[27]

Apart from the hardly satisfactory explanation of the "natural" price by the "natural" rates of its components, another, less popular aspect is astonishing: the advanced value of the raw materials and equipment no longer appears in the natural price because the intermediate consumption can itself be divided into the three income categories:

> But the whole price of any commodity must still finally resolve itself into some one or other, or all of those three parts; as whatever part of it remains after paying the rent of the land, and the price of the whole labour employed in raising, manufacturing, and bringing it to market, must necessarily be profit to somebody.[28]

Smith was often reprimanded for this "component theory of value": Ricardo criticised the too rapid abandonment of the labour theory of value and the incorrect treatment of rent. Marx chided, Smith confounded gross and net product and "... tries to spirit the constant part of the capital-value away from the commodity-value".[29] Smith, therefore, would assume the existence of "primary" commodities once produced without means of production.[30] When the assessment basis is available, these reproaches are evaluated.

The reflex of Smith's "divided" value theory are two different measures of value: on the one hand, he speaks of "labour embodied", i.e., the total labour content of a commodity regulates its value. On the other hand, Smith argues with "labour commanded". This quantity indicates how many labour units can be bought by a commodity. In a different light, the magnitude reflects how long a labourer must work to buy this commodity.[31] Adam Smith switched to "labour commanded" because he saw difficulties in recognising the pure duration of working time as a universally valid unit of value. However, "... different degrees of hardship endured, and of ingenuity exercised ..."[32] are equated in exchange.

---

[27] Smith, A., op. cit., p. 72.

[28] Ibid., p. 69.

[29] Marx, K., Capital, vol. II, The Process of Circulation of Capital (1885), Engels, F. (ed.) Moscow 1956, p. 377, https://archive.org/details/capitalvol2/page/376/mode/2up.

[30] Cf. Kurz, H. D., Adam Smiths Komponententheorie der relativen Preise und ihre Kritik, in: Zeitschrift für die gesamte Staatswissenschaft, vol. 132 (1976), pp. 691–709.

[31] Fourastie and Schneider call this quantity—without reference to Smith—the "real price": "By dividing the current price (or nominal price in marks, reichsmarks or DM) of a product by the hourly wage, we obtain the *real price* of this product, expressed in working hours." Fourastie, J., Schneider, J., Warum die Preise sinken, Produktivität und Kaufkraft seit dem Mittelalter, Frankfurt a. M. 1989, p. 40. In their study, the authors conclude that the real prices of almost all goods have fallen, in some cases drastically. The main factor influencing this is the increase in labour productivity. Although the law of supply and demand plays a role, "... it is ultimately only responsible for temporary fluctuations and is of secondary importance." Ibid., p. 145. [F. H.]

[32] See Smith, A., op. cit., p. 48.

> You can view the 'labour commanded' standard," Starbatty explains, "as an attempt to objectify labour quantities: we measure the value of a commodity according to how many labour quantities we can exchange for it or make them subservient, regardless of how many hours it took us to complete it ourselves.[33]

While embodied labour can be determined physically, namely in units of time, labour commanded is influenced by the wage rate. However, according to the classical view, it settles at the subsistence level in the long run: workers receive a sufficient wage to allow merely a historically given standard of living. The wage provides for the purchase of exactly the amount of food, clothing, etc., essential to make ends meet for employees and their families. Therefore, the nominal wage rate is based on prices: the cost of living. Smith's measure of labour commanded depends on magnitudes that ought to be quantified in this standard. Only in the early and rude state, before capital formation and land acquisition, do labour commanded and embodied coincide. Smith's analysis thus contains, perhaps unintentionally, a moment of social indictment:

> It may also be said that if the purchase of a certain quantum of labour by the capitalists permits the production of a commodity with which a larger quantum of labour can be obtained, this means that the exchange between the capitalist and the worker is carried out under the sign of a fundamental inequality.[34]

Smith does not address the difference between labour embodied and labour commanded any further: apart from his "natural" rates of income categories, he offers nothing on the subject. Regardless of whether Smith ultimately broke away from the labour theory of value or not,[35] the real significance of Smith's inquiry lies in the propagated *thesis* rather than in the substantiation of its correctness: the market economy does not finish in chaos; on the contrary, actions geared towards the self-interest of individuals promote the well-being of all. An "invisible hand"—which Smith admittedly only mentions once in "The Wealth of Nations"[36]—governs economic events; behind the seemingly arbitrary ups and downs of market prices, there are laws that help to enforce "natural" conditions. The seemingly inextricable economic machinery operates according to rules, whose discovery was (henceforth) the (remaining) main task of economic theory.

---

[33] Starbatty, J., Die englischen Klassiker der Nationalökonomie, Lehre und Wirkung, Darmstadt 1985, p. 60. [F. H.]

[34] Napoleoni, C., Ricardo und Marx, ed. by Pennavaja, C., Frankfurt a. M. 1974, p. 62 f. [F. H.]

[35] Cf. Starbatty, J., op. cit., p. 59.

[36] See Smith, A., op. cit., p. 456.

Chapter 9
David Ricardo: Prospects of Capital Accumulation

Classicism experienced a revival in the last third of the twentieth century; the renaissance was reflected, among other things, in Ricardo becoming the namesake of a contemporary branch of economists. Today, these aforementioned "neo-Ricardians" compete—what an irony in the history of the science—with the "neoclassicists". Indeed, there is some indication for interpreting the ramifications of economic theory as a diversification of topics in Ricardo's *oeuvre*.[1]

Ricardo himself was economically infected at the age of 27 during a stay at a spa in Bath when he came across Adam Smith's "Wealth of Nations".[2] Against this backdrop, it does not seem entirely wrong to perceive Ricardo as a scholar of Adam Smith, who renovated the latter's intellectual edifice and raised it by a few storeys, but without going beyond the terrain marked out by his inspirer. Adam Smith could, therefore, be considered the "Adam and Smith" of economics.

However, the theory of value expounded in the "Principles" is more than just a critical examination and further development of Smith's ideas. Although this moment certainly resonates and is externally recognisable in the "Principles" by multiple references to Smith, there is a deeper motive behind Ricardo's preoccupation with the theory of value. To reveal this—what the older "retellings" which merely stick to a few passages of the "Principles", insufficiently accomplish[3]—it will prove fruitful to look not only at his main work but also at the formation period of his theory above all at

[1] Cf. Schefold, B. (with the colaboration of Weihrauch, P.), Ricardo – Marshall – Sraffa, Ökonomische Theorie als Geschichte der Ricardo-Interpretation, in: das wirtschaftsstudium (wisu), vol. 16 (1987), pp. 383–387 and pp. 462–467.

[2] On Ricardo's life and work, see the informative entry by De Vivo, G., Ricardo, David, in: The New Palgrave, vol. IV, London / New York / Tokyo 1987, pp. 183–198.

[3] Ricardo's abstract, deductive approach, and the sparse explanations, which make it sometimes difficult to grasp his intentions, have often been attributed to Ricardo's Jewish origins; Marshall, e.g., criticises his 'un-English' method: "… he was more guilty than almost anyone else of the bad habit of endeavouring to express great economic doctrines in short sentences." Marshall, A., op. cit., p. 672, cf. also p. 629 n.

F. Helmedag, *Production of Commodities by Means of Labour*, Springer Studies in Alternative Economics, https://doi.org/10.1007/978-3-032-01457-3_9

the "Essay on Profits" from 1815.[4] As can be seen from his correspondence, the focus of Ricardo's research had shifted in the preceding years from currency problems to real economic issues; in particular, he was now interested in the relationship between capital accumulation and the rate of profit. In a letter to Malthus dated August 17, 1813, he uses the words "my theory" for the first time.[5]

To Sraffa's credit, he has clarified the importance of the wheat model in the ripening process of Ricardo's theory.[6] However, we must turn to the wheat economy *twice*. The first stage outlines the usual version; the second deals with the difficulties that moved Ricardo to present a theory of value in the "Principles": it was intended to broaden the validity range of his essentially existing distribution theory.

The wheat model is subsequently revisited to demonstrate that even within this elementary framework, the predominant perspective does not align with the logic of a capitalist competitive economy. In the single-sector corn economy, profit maximisation and profit rate maximisation are inherently incompatible. The relationship between wage rate and profit is, in fact, far more complex than the numerous interpreters promulgate to their readers.

Finally, we return to the "Principles" to examine the "theorem of comparative cost advantages". In this context, we can outline the explanatory power of the labour theory of value in a world of differentially productive sectors and establish the link to employment theory.

---

[4] Ricardo, D., An Essay on the Influence of a low Price of Corn on the Profits of Stock [1815], in: The Works and Correspondence of David Ricardo, ed. by Sraffa, P., vol. IV, Cambridge 1951, pp. 9–41.

[5] Cf. Ricardo, D., Letter to Malthus, August 17, 1813, in: The Works …, op. cit., vol. VI, Cambridge 1973, p. 95. Tucker has attempted to shed light on the motives that prompted Ricardo to turn to questions of capital accumulation. Cf. Tucker, G. S. L., The Origin of Ricardo's Theory of Profits, in: Economica, vol. 21 (1954), pp. 320–331.

[6] Cf. Sraffa, P., Introduction, in: The Works …, op. cit., vol. I, Cambridge 1970, pp. xiii–lxii, especially p. xxxi. During Ricardo's lifetime, 'wheat' and 'corn' were used synonymously in England, a practice we follow below. Samuel Hollander has denied the assertion of representatives of the surplus approach that the 'wheat theory of profit' plays a vital role in Ricardo. Instead, it only exists in a rudimentary form. Cf. the contributions to this discussion in: Caravale, G. A. (ed.), The Legacy of Ricardo, Oxford 1985. Without wishing to go into these questions in detail here, the following quotations, including from Ricardo's correspondence, prove that the core structure of his theory can be aptly captured by the corn model, even if it does not emerge from his writings with the clarity, we are accustomed to from modern, mathematically lined accounts. In Ricardo's contemporary Torrens, the wheat theory is more concise than in Ricardo, but Torrens explicitly accepts his conceptual authorship. Cf. De Vivo, G., Robert Torrens and Ricardo's 'corn-ratio' theory of profits, in: The Cambridge Journal of Economics, vol. 9 (1985), pp. 89–92.

9.1 Growth and Distribution in the Wheat Economy

Like other classics, Ricardo distinguishes three economic classes characterised by their roles in the economic process. The landlords own the arable land they lease to tenant farmers, who are the entrepreneurs in the agricultural economy. As consideration, landlords receive the (ground) rent: "By rent I always mean the remuneration given to the landlord for the use of the original and inherent power of the land."[7]

The agricultural entrepreneurs advance capital, which, in the corn model, consists solely of the wage fund comprising a certain amount of wheat to support the employees until the next harvest. The production period, therefore, lasts one year. Finally, the wage earners provide their labour and receive remuneration.

We denote the total quantity of wheat produced by X; it depends solely on the labour input (N)—possibly with a constant amount of seed per unit[8]:

$$X = f(N) \tag{9.1}$$

The following properties of the production function (9.1) can be derived from Ricardo's verbal explanations and his examples:

$$\frac{dX}{dN} \equiv f_N > 0 \tag{9.1a}$$

$$\frac{d^2X}{dN^2} \equiv f_{NN} < 0 \tag{9.1b}$$

$$f(0) \geq 0 \tag{9.1c}$$

$$\lim_{N \to 0} f_N(N) = a = const. 0 < a < \infty \tag{9.1d}$$

Equations (9.1a) and (9.1b) signify that the marginal revenue of labour is positive but decreasing, (9.1c) excludes the possibility of a negative output, which has no economic significance.[9] According to (9.1d), the marginal yield converges to a finite positive value as labour input decreases to zero. This assumption is otherwise not explicitly mentioned but makes sense and is included in all graphical representations of the wheat world.[10]

---

[7] Ricardo, D., An Essay ..., op. cit., p. 18 n.

[8] Cf., e.g., Pasinetti, L., A Mathematical Formulation of the Ricardian System, in: The Review of Economic Studies, vol. 27 (1960), pp. 78–98.

[9] In 1815, essays were published by Malthus, West, and Torrens, in which rent is interpreted as a phenomenon of declining marginal returns in agriculture. Incidentally, Ricardo's theory of profit is very similar to West's. Cf. Sraffa, P., Note on 'Essay on Profits', in: The Works ..., op. cit., vol. IV, Cambridge 1951, pp. 1–8, p. 5 f.

[10] Cf. the often adopted illustration in Kaldor, N., Alternative Theories of Distribution, in: Review of Economic Studies, vol. 23 (1955/56), pp. 83–100, p. 85.

Furthermore, from an economic point of view, it is reasonable to suppose that the return of the last unit of labour employed must at least be sufficient to cover its subsistence wage (w_S). Condition (9.1e) reflects this "viability condition" of the technology:

$$f_N \geq w_S \tag{9.1e}$$

The wage bill (W) is the product of the wage rate (w) and the labour input N; as already mentioned, it corresponds to the circulating capital (K):

$$K = wN = W \tag{9.2}$$

The total profit accruing to the tenant farmers (P) is calculated by multiplying the wage fund by the profit rate (r):

$$P = Kr \tag{9.3}$$

The rent (R) amounts to:

$$R = X - wN - P \tag{9.4}$$

Landowners, consequently, receive the total product minus labour and capital income.

So far, we have seven unknowns (X, K, w, N, P, r, R) and only four equations; the system, therefore, has three degrees of freedom. These are to be fixed by economically plausible assumptions to close the system. In the first step, it can be supposed that a real wage rate exists at a particular time, i.e., a certain quantity of corn, interpreted as the "natural" price of labour. This pay includes, but is not restricted to, the physical minimum subsistence level, as Ricardo explains in more detail in his main work:

> It is not to be understood that the natural price of labour, estimated even in food and necessaries, is absolutely fixed and constant. It varies at different times in the same country, and very materially differs in different countries. It essentially depends on the habits and customs of the people.[11]

Ricardo shares Malthus' view that this remuneration is linked to a stationary population:

> The natural price of labour is that price which is necessary to enable the labourers, one with another, to subsist and to perpetuate their race, without either increase or diminution.[12]

By fixing the wage rate at the subsistence level w_S, we gain the equation:

$$w = w_S \tag{9.5}$$

---

[11] Ricardo, D., On the Principles of Political Economy and Taxation [1817], in: The Works ..., op. cit., vol. I, Cambridge 1970, p. 96 f.

[12] Ibid., p. 93.

Moreover, the competition between farmers ensures that, in equilibrium, the individual capitals obtain an identical rate of profit. Consequently, the wage of the final unit of labour performed and the profit accruing to it exhaust the marginal product:

$$w(1 + r) = f_N \tag{9.6}$$

Rearranging expression (9.6) yields the profit rate equation:

$$r = \frac{f_N}{w} - 1 \tag{9.7}$$

At an infinitesimally small labour input, the profit rate r is maximal and *falls* continuously with increasing land cultivation due to (9.1b):

$$\frac{dr}{dN} \equiv r_N = \frac{f_{NN}}{w} < 0 \tag{9.8}$$

The return on capital (9.7) disappears when f_N equals w. Employment results from Eqs. (9.2) and (9.5):

$$N = \frac{K}{w_S} \tag{9.9}$$

In the Ricardian system, the demand for labour N is thus a *variable* that changes with the wage fund K and possibly the natural wage w_S. For biological reasons alone, the population size naturally reacts relatively slowly.

Now rent is also determined. Taking (9.1), (9.2), (9.3) and (9.7) into account, one calculates for (9.4):

$$R = f(N) - wN - \left(\frac{f_N}{w} - 1\right)wN = f(N) - Nf_N \tag{9.10}$$

Equation (9.10) can be labelled as the "rent formula" of the Ricardian system. In contrast to the rate of profit, rent increases with rising employment:

$$\frac{dR}{dN} \equiv R_N = f_N - (f_N + Nf_{NN}) = -Nf_{NN} > 0 \tag{9.11}$$

Thus, landowners benefit from growing employment in husbandry.

The system (9.1) to (9.4) is still not closed, as only two of the three degrees of freedom are fixed. Typically, in classical analyses, the wage fund is treated as given:

$$K = K_0 = const. \tag{9.12}$$

This capital corresponds to employment (N_0) determined via Eq. (9.9). All values of the system are now ascertained. Figure 9.1 illustrates the situation. W_0 symbolises

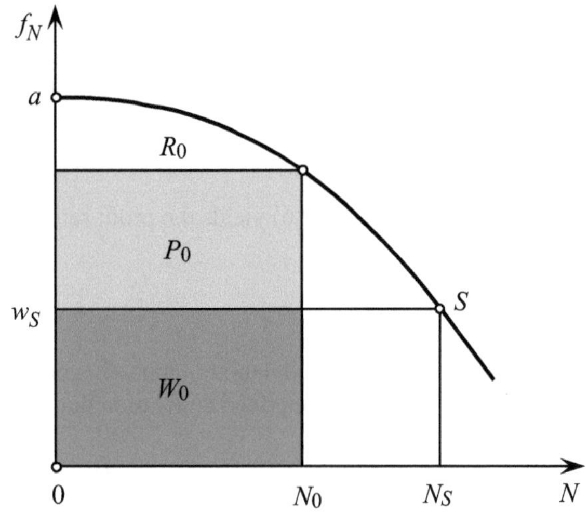

Fig. 9.1 Distribution in the wheat economy

the wage bill for wage rate w_S and employmentN_0, analogously R_0 and P_0 denote total rents and profits. If the surplus R_0 plus P_0 is wholly consumed, the economic activity remains at the same level year after year.

In fact, Ricardo characterises the landlords as an "unproductive class"[13] who use up the entire rent, while the tenant farmers consume only a little of their profit but invest the lion's share. However, the inclination of the agricultural entrepreneurs to increase the wage fund depends on the expected additional profit; "greater profits would lead to further accumulation", we read in the "Essay",[14] and in the "Principles", it says on that score:

> The farmer and manufacturer can no more live without profit, than the labourer without wages. Their motive for accumulation will diminish with every diminution of profit, and will cease altogether when their profits are so low as not to afford them an adequate compensation for their trouble, and the risk which they must necessarily encounter in employing their capital productively.[15]

Modern interpreters have supplemented Ricardo's system with an "investment function" to describe the path to long-term equilibrium. For instance, a lower limit of the profit rate is assumed, "... just enough to choke off further net saving but not so low as to dissaving and eating up of the previously existing stock of capital goods."[16] As long as the difference between the current and minimum profit rates is positive, capital, i.e., the wage fund, is augmented; if the gap disappears, the process ceases.[17]

---

[13] Cf. ibid., p. 270.

[14] Ricardo, D., An Essay ..., op. cit., p. 35.

[15] Ricardo, D., On the Principles ..., op. cit., p. 122.

[16] Samuelson, P. A., The Canonical Classical Model of Political Economy, in: Journal of Economic Literature, vol. 16 (1978), pp. 1415–1434, p. 1419.

[17] See also Brems, H., An Attempt at a Rigorous Restatement of Ricardo's Long-Run Equilibrium, in: The Canadian Journal of Economics and Political Science, vol. 26 (1960), pp. 74–86, p. 77 and

If we consider the extreme case in which the minimum profit rate is zero, the increase in (circulating) capital stops when $w_S = f_N$. This situation is shown in Fig. 9.1 at point *S*; profit has disappeared from the scene. Since the natural wage rate cannot be depressed, employment has reached its maximum (N_S). Wages and rents absorb the entire national product; the stationary state has come true.

But such mechanisations change the emphasis in Ricardo's "essay". In the disquisition, he was less concerned with spreading a gloomy prognosis of the prospects of the new era. Instead, he intended to take sides in a concrete political discussion with a *theoretically sound* contribution. As the—rarely mentioned—full title of his "essay" underlines,[18] Ricardo argued against introducing import duties on corn. According to the *theory of distribution* enunciated in the "essay", namely the economic laws that govern profit, these tariffs only benefit the established, passive class of landlords: "The consideration of those principles … which regulate the profit of stock, have convinced me of the policy of leaving the importation of corn unrestricted by law."[19] Although the direct parliamentary influence of the "essay" must be considered as insignificant—the Corn Laws were passed in 1815—it is nonetheless the *locus classicus* of an essential change of course in economic theory.

While the Physiocrats regarded nature per se as the source of surplus[20] and Adam Smith generally considered labour as the origin of the wealth of nations, David Ricardo was the first to prove in a succinct, systematic analysis that by no means do all branches of the economy contribute to the surplus. Instead, food production sets the profit rate for the other departments:

> … through the whole progress of society, profits are regulated by the difficulty or facility of procuring food. This is a principle of great importance, and has been almost overlooked in the writings of Political Economists. They appear to think that profits of stock can be raised by commercial causes, independently of the supply of food.[21]

Casarosa, C., A New Formulation of the Ricardian System, in: Oxford Economic Papers, vol. 30 (1978), pp. 38–63, p. 45 f.

[18] The full title reads: "An Essay on the Influence of a low Price of Corn on the Profits of Stock; Shewing the Inexpediency of Restrictions on Importation: With Remarks on Mr. Malthus' two Last Publications: 'An Inquiry into the Nature and Progress of Rent;' and 'The Grounds of an Opinion on the Policy of restricting the Importation of Foreign Corn." Cf. the flyleaves of the first two editions 1815, which are reproduced as facsimiles in Ricardo, D., The Works …, op. cit., vol. IV, p. 1 f.

[19] Ricardo, D., An Essay …, op. cit., p. 9.

[20] The Tableau Économique by François Quesnay offers deep insights into the circular flow of income, cf. Helmedag, F., Weber, U., Die Zig-Zag-Darstellung des Tableau Économique, in: das wirtschaftsstudium (wisu), vol. 31 (2002), pp. 115–121, pp. 135 f. and Helmedag, F., Weber, U., Die Kreislaufdarstellung des Tableau Économique, in: das wirtschaftsstudium (wisu), vol. 31 (2002), pp. 1128–1133, p. 1155.

[21] Ricardo, D., An Essay …, op. cit., p. 13 n. However, this idea can also be found in Smith: "But when by the improvement and cultivation of land the labour of one family can provide food for two, the labour of half the society becomes sufficient to provide food for the whole. The other half, therefore, or at least the greater part of them, can be employed in providing other things, or in satisfying the other wants and fancies of mankind." Smith, A., op. cit., p. 180. In a footnote, Smith also refers to Pufendorf, Cantillon and Hume, who also separate food production from the rest of production.

With his corn economy, Ricardo succeeded in cutting the Gordian knot of determining profit without recourse to a theory of value: since input and output in the wage-goods industry, i.e., in the wheat sector, are homogeneous quantities, the rate of profit results as a purely physical ratio independent of the price of wheat (cf. (9.7), p. 95). In competitive equilibrium, the other sectors have adopted the exploitation factor fixed by the agricultural industry through price adjustments:

> … in short it is the profits of the farmer which regulate the profits of all other trades, – and as the profits of the farmer must necessarily decrease with every augmentation of Capital employed on the land, provided no improvements be at the same time made in husbandry, all other profits must diminish and therefore the rate of interest must fall.[22]

This insight broke the vicious circle inherited from his predecessors: on the one hand, determining values requires the knowledge of total profit, whose calculation, on the other hand, is based on known values. "Ricardo's immortal contribution was his brilliant solution of this seemingly insoluble problem."[23]

If poorer land is tilled over time, rent also accrues to landlords who were previously left empty-handed. The development turns out to be a grandiose machinery for redistributing former profits into rents:

> Rent then is in all cases a portion of the profits previously obtained on the land. It is never a new creation of revenue, but always part of a revenue already created.[24]

The decline in profits in favour of rent can only be countered if the costs of food production decrease. According to Ricardo, this reduction is based *exclusively* on three causes. First, a fall in the real wage causes a rise in the surplus, benefitting the tenant. Second, progress in agricultural technique works in the same direction; third, importing cheaper wheat diminishes its price and thus the remuneration of labour.[25]

However, the tenor of the essay is not "wages down, profits up". The natural wage rate and the improvement in farming methods are essentially exogenous variables that hardly qualify for economic action. The only practicable possibility to compensate for the feared profit decline in the course of accumulation amounts to nothing more than lowering the prices of wage goods:

> … independently of the effect produced by liberal or scanty wages, general profits must fall, unless there be improvements in agriculture, or corn can be imported at a cheaper price.[26]

---

[22] Ricardo, D., Letter to Trower, March 8, 1814, in: The Works …, op. cit., vol. VI, pp. 103–105, p. 104.

[23] Dmitriev, V. K., Economic Essays on Value, Competition and Utility [1904], ed. by Nuti, M. D., Cambridge 1974, p. 58. For an assessment of Dmitriev's contribution, see Skourtos, M., „Der Neoricardianismus ", V. K. Dmitriev und die Kontinuität in der klassischen Tradition, Pfaffenweiler 1985. This book contains relevant quotations from Torrens, J. St. Mill, and Senior, showing that the assumption of a 'basic sector' was not an entirely exotic approach in Ricardo's time. Cf. ibid., p. 70 ff. The dissertation "Die ökonomischen Studien von V. K. Dmitriev" by Frank Schütte [2003], which is available on the Internet, offers a translation from the Old Russian together with an informative commentary, http://nbn-resolving.de/urn:nbn:de:swb:ch1-200600220.

[24] Ricardo, D., An Essay …, op. cit., p. 18.

[25] Cf. ibid., p. 22.

[26] Ibid., p. 23.

In this light, the thrust of the "essay" is less on the tension between wage rate and profit (rate), as some interpreters try to make the audience believe; instead, it addresses the conflict between landlords and tenants: "... the interest of the landlord is always opposed to the interest of every other class in the community."[27]

However, the stringency of the analysis in the "essay" stands and falls with the assumption that one branch of the economy, the wage-goods industry, keeps all other sectors on tight rein. It was, therefore, in the air that by pointing to this highly restrictive premise, the force of Ricardo's argument and the knowledge gained from his investigation into the source of profit were doubted. Indeed, the criticism of the corn model prompted Ricardo to generalise his theory in the following years. Before we study the logic of the wheat economy further, it seems helpful to shed light on the motives behind the change in his explanatory model and to outline and assess its further development.

9.2 The *Principles*: Labour Replaces Wheat

The publication of the "essay" in the last week of February 1815 gave additional impetus to the fundamental, albeit friendly, dispute between Malthus and Ricardo about the relevance of the corn economy. In March and April alone, the correspondence between the two discussion partners consists of 17 letters.[28]

In his letter of March 10, Malthus repeated his protest against Ricardo's wheat theory. Although the scepticism had already been addressed in the correspondence of the previous two years, it was only during the dialogue following the publication of the "essay" that the critique was specified in such detail as to persuade Ricardo to convert his conception.

At the outset, Malthus informs Ricardo that his "essay" has been classified by a certain James Mackintosh as pretty difficult and "... not sufficiently practical, to assist him in forming a parliamentary opinion or argument ..."[29] In addition, Malthus makes no pretence of his own assessment:

> Considering the short time you were employed about it, the essay has great merit; but it certainly might have been improved by more time and attention.[30]

[27] Ibid., p. 21.

[28] Cf. Ricardo, D., The Works ..., op. cit., vol. VI, Cambridge 1973.

[29] Malthus, Th. R., Letter to Ricardo, March 10, 1815, in: The Works ..., op. cit., vol. VI, p. 181–183, p. 182. However, about six months later, Ricardo learned from Trower what Mackintosh's judgment power was all about: the publication of the "Edinburgh Review" had to be delayed because Mackintosh was initially scheduled to write a detailed article on the Alliance's defeat against Napoleon. Then, the news about Waterloo arrived, and the newspaper had to be reprinted. Cf. Trower, H., Letter to Ricardo, September 21, 1815, in: The Works ..., op. cit., vol. VI, pp. 278–281, p. 280.

[30] Malthus, Th. R., Letter to Ricardo, March 10, 1815, in: The Works ..., op. cit., vol. VI, p. 182.

In Malthus's opinion, a growing exchange value of wheat can certainly *enhance* agricultural gain; moreover, the profitability in this sector would not at all regulate returns in the whole economy:

> ... general profits may be determined by the general supply of stock compared with the means of employing it, and not merely by the stock employed on the land. Nor can I yet satisfy myself either from theory or experience that profits depend solely on the price of corn.[31]

Ricardo answered this objection, presented in the form of a "supply–demand theory of profit", with the retort that the market price of wheat could only escalate *temporarily* due to high demand: "My opinion is that corn can only permanently rise in its exchangeable value when the real expenses of its production increase."[32]

If the opponents had continued to exchange their arguments along these predetermined lines, the discrepancy in their approaches would have been irreconcilable. However, in a letter written before Ricardo's above reply, Malthus extended the corn economy towards reality and presented the consequences to his adversary:

> Pray think once more on the effect of a rise in the relative price of corn, upon the whole surplus derived from land already in cultivation. It appears to me I confess, as clear as possible that it must be increased. The expences estimated in Corn will be less, owing to the power of purchasing with a less quantity of corn, the same quantity of fixed capital, and of the circulating capital of tea sugar cloaths &c: for the labourers; and consequently more clear surplus will remain in the shape of rent and profits together ...[33]

With this consideration, Malthus took up a point that had only been insinuated earlier. If the capital advanced in agriculture did not (realistically) consist solely of wheat,[34] agricultural profits could also go up with a higher price of corn because the value of non-wheat inputs would decline relative to the value of wheat. Accordingly, both the profit—the difference between revenues and costs—and the profit rate rise as the numerator increases and the denominator decreases.[35]

Although Ricardo initially tried to counter with reasoning based on his wheat model, he immediately recognised the strength of the argument: "Your statement is however very ingenious, and carries a great deal of plausibility with it ..."[36] In

[31] Ibid., p. 182 f.

[32] Ricardo, D., Letter to Malthus, March 14, 1815, in: The Works ..., op. cit., vol. VI, pp. 188–190, p. 189.

[33] Malthus, Th. R., Letter to Ricardo, March 12, 1815, in: The Works ..., op. cit., vol. VI, p. 185 f., p. 185.

[34] "In no case of production, the produce is exactly of the same nature as the capital advanced. Consequently, we can never properly refer to a material rate of produce ..." Malthus, Th. R., Letter to Ricardo, August 5, 1814, in: The Works ..., op. cit., vol. VI, pp. 115–118, p. 117.

[35] Cf. the numerical example in: Malthus, Th. R., Letter to Horner, March 14, 1815, in: The Works ..., op. cit., vol. VI. There Malthus comments on Ricardo's exemplary calculation in the "essay": "The fault of Mr. Ricardo's table which is curious, is that the advances of the farmer instead of being calculated in corn, should be calculated either in the actual materials of which the capital consists, or in money which is the best representative of a variety of commodities. The view I have taken of the subject would greatly alter his conclusions." Ibid., p. 187 f.

[36] Ricardo, D., Letter to Malthus, March 17, 1815, in: The Works ..., op. cit., vol. VI, pp. 192–194, p. 192.

autumn, he informed Trower, sounding almost despondent,[37] that the disagreement between Malthus and himself had not been resolved. Nevertheless, he expresses the hope that he will be able to present a revised version of his theory in the foreseeable future:

> … my opinions differ from the great authority of Adam Smith Malthus, & c[a] that I should wish to concentrate all the talent I possess, not only for the purpose of establishing what I think correct principles but of drawing important deductions from them. For my own satisfaction I shall certainly make the attempt, and perhaps with repeated revisions during a year or two I shall at last produce something that may be understood.[38]

In fact, James Mill had energetically tried to urge him two months earlier to revise the "essay",[39] and Ricardo promised, despite all his scepticism, to tackle the undertaking:

> The experiment shall however be tried, – I will devote as much time as I can to think and write on my favorite subject, – I will give myself a chance for success and at any rate the employment itself will, if nothing else comes of it, have afforded me instruction and amusement.[40]

Even later, Mill sticks to his guns: "For as you are already the best *thinker* on political economy, I am resolved you shall also be the best writer."[41] Easier said than done: the generalisation of the results of the "Essay" encountered seemingly insurmountable difficulties: "I know I shall be soon stopped by the word price," Ricardo replied, "and then I must apply to you for advice and assistance."[42] However, the price veil *had to* be lifted so that the clear and far-reaching conclusions of the wheat model could be transferred to the real world.

In Ricardo's system, the theory of value is therefore not an end in itself as for Adam Smith or in the general equilibrium theory to show that unregulated market economies would nevertheless bring about "reasonable" conditions. For Ricardo, the task of the theory of value was not limited to uncovering the laws of economic exchange. Instead, it should serve him to reveal the mechanisms determining income distribution between the economic classes.[43]

---

[37] "… never shall I be so fortunate however correct my opinions may become as to produce a work which shall procure me fame and distinction." Ricardo, D., Letter to Trower, October 29, 1815, in: The Works …, op. cit., vol. VI, pp. 314–317, p. 315.

[38] Ibid., p. 316.

[39] "… my friendship for you, for mankind, and for science, all prompt me to give you no rest, till you are plunged over head and ears in political economy." Mill, J., Letter to Ricardo, August 23, 1815, in: The Works …, op. cit., vol. VI, pp. 250–254, p. 252.

[40] Ricardo, D., Letter to Mill, August 30, 1815, in: The Works …, op. cit., vol. VI, pp. 261–265, p. 263.

[41] Mill, J., Letter to Ricardo, December 22, 1815, in: The Works …, op. cit., vol. VI, pp. 337–341, p. 340. On the significance of James Mill's influence on the making of the "Principles", see Sraffa, P., Introduction, op. cit., p. xix ff.

[42] Ricardo, D., Letter to Mill, December 30, 1815, in: The Works …, op. cit., vol. VI, pp. 347–349, p. 348. In this letter Ricardo speaks of the unchangeable value of precious metals as the anchor on which all his statements would depend. Cf. ibid.

[43] Cf. Ricardo, D., On the Principles …, op. cit., preface.

In this light, the theory of value in Ricardo's conception appears "only" as an intermediate step, which reduces the distance to the goal but without having already arrived: "If I could overcome the obstacles in the way of giving a clear insight into the origin and law of relative or exchangeable value I should have gained *half* the battle."[44] The structure of the "Principles" confirms this impression: in the first chapter, "On Value", Ricardo endeavours to lay a sufficient theoretical basis for the generalisation of the specific findings of the "essay"; not until then does he enter into details about rent, wages and profit in subsequent chapters.

In the meantime, the results of Ricardo's studies in value theory jeopardised the entire project: "You will see the curious effect," he announced to Mill, "which the rise of wages produces on the prices of those commodities which are chiefly obtained by the aid of machinery and fixed capital."[45] And in the same letter, he writes: "I have been beyond measure puzzled to find out the law of price."[46] Even the first publication of the "Principles" in 1817 does not signal the author's satisfaction with the status of the solution to the problem: apart from the addition of the chapter "On Machinery" in the third edition in 1821, Ricardo made far the most changes in this edition and the preceding second edition in 1819 to the first chapter "On Value".[47]

Now that Ricardo's motives for developing his theory of value have been reconstructed, it is interesting to see what concrete answers he found to the questions that moved him. At the beginning of the "Principles", he first eliminates the value paradox: if water is scarce, it has both a high utility and a high price. Use value, on the other hand, is a *prerequisite* for any exchange value:

> If a commodity were in no way useful … it would be destitute of exchangeable value, however scarce it might be, or whatever quantity of labour might be necessary to procure it.[48]

The value of goods that cannot be multiplied using labour is based solely on their scarcity; however, this relatively small number of goods is not at the centre of the analysis. Instead, Ricardo's attention is focused on the *production of commodities.*

> In speaking then of commodities, of their exchangeable value, and of the laws which regulate their relative prices," Ricardo delineates his research programme, "we mean always such commodities only as can be increased in quantity by the exertion of human industry, and on the production of which competition operates without restraint.[49]

[44] Ricardo, D., Letter to Malthus, February 7, 1816, in: The Works …, op. cit., vol. VII, Cambridge 1973, pp. 18–20, p. 20, own emphasis.

[45] Ricardo, D., Letter to Mill, October 14, 1816, in: The Works …, op. cit., vol. VII, pp. 82–84, p. 82.

[46] Ibid., p. 83.

[47] Cf. Sraffa, P., Introduction, op. cit., p. xxx ff.

[48] Ricardo, D., On the Principles …, op. cit., p. 11. Against this background, it is surprising that the classics are often reproached for their alleged failure regarding the value paradox.

[49] Ricardo, D., On the Principles …, op. cit., p. 12.

Consequently, Ricardo always speaks of "commodities", not "goods", as is the custom of modern neoclassicists.[50] Furthermore, supply is subject to unlimited competition—a central assumption for analysing the effects of capital accumulation. In the next step, Ricardo criticises Smith for fluctuating too often between labour embodied and labour commanded and for using one measure and then the other as if they were two arbitrarily substitutable quantities:

> If this indeed were true, if the reward of the labourer were always in proportion to what he produced, the quantity of labour bestowed on a commodity, and the quantity of labour which that commodity would purchase, would be equal, and either might accurately measure the variations of other things: but they are not equal; the first is under many circumstances an invariable standard, indicating correctly the variations of other things; the latter is subject to as many fluctuations as the commodities compared with it.[51]

With this criticism, Ricardo expresses his intention to maintain the measurement of exchange values by labour quantities longer than Smith: "... it is the comparative quantity of commodities which labour will produce, that determines their present or past relative value, and not the comparative quantities of commodities, which are given to the labourer in exchange for his labour."[52] Ricardo also assumes a given wage structure, reflected in the relative remuneration constancy. However, this fact does not influence the exchange value:

> As the inquiry to which I wish to draw the reader's attention, relates to the effect of the variations in the relative value of commodities, and not in their absolute value, it will be of little importance to examine into the comparative degree of estimation in which the different kinds of human labour are held.[53]

The level of remuneration does not affect the exchange ratios if a movement in the wage level affects all goods to the same extent. This independence can easily be demonstrated using Smith's beaver-deer model. Ricardo explicitly points out that indirect labour must also be considered to ascertain the exchange ratio.[54] Once this has been done, however, the nominal wage rate can no longer alter the exchange ratio because it cancels out, so to speak, in the numerator and denominator.

This finding is not to say that the level of payment exerts no effect on profits; quite the contrary: "... profits would be high or low, exactly in proportion as wages were low or high; but it could not in the least affect the relative value ... as wages would be high or low at the same time in both occupations."[55]

---

[50] In the German paperback edition by Neumark, which relies heavily on the translation by Waentig, there is also continual reference to goods instead of commodities. Cf. Ricardo, D., Grundsätze der politischen Ökonomie und der Besteuerung, ed. by Neumark, F., Frankfurt a. M. 1972.

[51] Ricardo, D., On the Principles ..., op. cit., p. 14.

[52] Ibid., p. 17.

[53] Ibid., p. 21 f.

[54] "Without some weapon, neither the beaver nor the deer could be destroyed, and therefore the value of these animals would be regulated, not solely by the time and labour necessary to their destruction, but also by the time and labour necessary for providing the hunter's capital, the weapon, by the aid of which their destruction was effected." Ibid., p. 23.

[55] Ibid., p. 27.

However, the harmonious appearance is distorted if the means of production are no longer of the same durability as Ricardo had initially assumed. In section IV of the first chapter, Ricardo relaxes this premise and distinguishes between fixed and circulating capital.[56] Now, the *wage rate* can affect the exchange value of two commodities:

> This difference in the degree of durability of fixed capital, and this variety in the proportions in which the two sorts of capital may be combined, introduce another cause, besides the greater or less quantity of labour necessary to produce commodities, for the variations in their relative value – this cause is the rise or fall in the value of labour.[57]

Today, the bearing of variations in wage rates or profit rates on prices is regularly categorised under the heading "Wicksell effects". Yet, Ricardo discovered the impact, causing him probably more headaches than pride.[58] The emerging difficulties can be illustrated with a simple model, regarded as the formal substrate of Ricardo's exemplary calculations.[59]

Natural prices in equilibrium are equal to their "costs", which are composed of wages and a uniform exploitation of capital.[60] In the case under consideration, it consists only of wages, which must be advanced for a particular time. The prices of any two commodities, therefore, result from the two equations:

$$p_1 = l_1 w(1 + r)^{t_1} \tag{9.13}$$

$$p_2 = l_2 w(1 + r)^{t_2} \tag{9.14}$$

The symbols denote:

p_i $\triangleq$ price of commodity i $(i = 1, 2)$
l_i $\triangleq$ quantity of labour to produce good i
w $\triangleq$ (uniform) wage rate
r $\triangleq$ (uniform) profit rate
t_i $\triangleq$ production time of commodity i

The above equations lead to:

$$\frac{p_1}{p_2} = \frac{l_1 w(1 + r)^{t_1}}{l_2 w(1 + r)^{t_2}} = \frac{l_1}{l_2}(1 + r)^{t_1 - t_2} \tag{9.15}$$

---

56 "According as capital is rapidly perishable, and requires to be frequently reproduced, or is of slow consumption, it is classed under the heads of circulating, or of fixed capital." Ibid., p. 31.

57 Remarkably, this section was not included in the first two editions of the "Principles".

58 After all, v. Hayek tried to base his business cycle theory on the 'Ricardo effect'. Cf. Hayek, F. A. v., Three Elucidations of the Ricardo Effect [1969], again in: Hayek, F. A. v., New Studies in Philosophy, Politics, Economics and the History of Ideas, Chicago 1978, pp. 165–178.

59 Cf. Ricardo's numerical examples in the "Principles", p. 33 ff. The formalisation is provided, e.g., by Blaug, M., Economic Theory in Retrospect, 5th ed., Cambridge 1997, p. 90 ff.

60 "Mr. Malthus appears to think that it is a part of my doctrine, that the cost and value of a thing should be the same; – it is, if he means by cost, 'cost of production' including profits." Ricardo, D., On the Principles ..., op. cit., p. 47 n.

Only in two specific constellations does the ratio of labour quantities alone determine the exchange relation. If the profit rate is zero, a special case in terms of *distribution* theory is present: either no agricultural entrepreneurs exist, or the stationary state has eventuated. The exceptional situation for *production* theory prevails when the two production processes coincide as to the turnover time of capital, i.e., $t_1 = t_2$ applies.[61] Usually, the relative prices differ from the corresponding labour inputs:

> The difference in value arises … from the profits being accumulated as capital, and is only a just compensation for the time that the profits were withheld.[62]

However, Ricardo's explanation (tacitly) points to a critical aspect of his reasoning. Namely, the question arises as to whether things are checked against each other whose confrontation is not meaningful in this way: the profit accruing earlier should also be capitalised to compare the processes correctly; it is pointless to lump capitalists together, some of whom strive for the (quickest possible) consumption of profit, while others accumulate profit. We shall come back to this consideration.

Although the wage rate cancels out in Eq. (9.15), this does not mean that a *change* in the wage rate usually has no consequences for the price ratio. In contrast to Smith's component doctrine, in Ricardo's theory, profit is restricted to the surplus product. As should be shown with the wheat economy, a movement in remuneration entails an opposite dynamic of profit, a connection that recurs in the "Principles": "There can be no rise in the value of labour without a fall of profits."[63] Except in the production theoretical special case, a rate of profit which follows the development of profits causes a "price revolution". Ricardo endeavours to indicate the direction of the ensuing deviation:

> … in proportion to the durability of capital employed in any kind of production, the relative prices of those commodities on which such durable capital is employed, will vary inversely as wages; they will fall as wages rise, and rise as wages fall; and, on the contrary, those which are produced chiefly by labour with less fixed capital, or with fixed capital of a less durable character than the medium in which price is estimated, will rise as wages rise, and fall as wages fall.[64]

Against this backdrop, it becomes clear why Ricardo wanted to find an absolute measuring rod that allows one to determine beyond doubt which prices rise and which fall due to wage variation. The search would have been successful if the yardstick found did not react to factors that influence the exchange value of the commodities. Ricardo indulged in the hope that the leading cause of price fluctuations, the change in the quantity of labour, would come to light if the value of goods were expressed in a unit independent of distribution. In the "Principles", Ricardo resorted to gold

---

[61] Dmitriev has also discussed these exceptions to the rule. See Dmitriev, V. K., op. cit., p. 53 and p. 69.

[62] Ricardo, D., On the Principles …, op. cit., p. 37. Torrens developed the idea that relative prices depend on the time it takes for goods to be brought to market, even if only variable capital is used. Cf. Sraffa, P., Note on Fragments on Torrens, in: The Works …, vol. IV, op. cit., pp. 305–308.

[63] Ricardo, D., On the Principles …, op. cit., p. 35.

[64] Ibid., p. 43.

despite all dissatisfaction with this "solution".[65] Nevertheless, the quest for a better measure of value occupied him for the rest of his life.[66]

Despite all that, Ricardo does not advocate an *absolute* labour theory of value in the sense that the relative prices of commodities conform to the respective quantities of labour. In numerous places in his correspondence, *two* reasons determine the exchange ratio of commodities. The amount of labour is always included; sometimes Ricardo adds the capital turnover,[67] and other times, he mentions distribution.[68] Yet he repeatedly asserts that fluctuations in the quantity of labour *mainly* cause *variations* in exchange ratios; the other determinants would merely have a modifying effect.[69]

In the aforementioned letter to Malthus, he speaks of the "... nearest approximation to truth, as a rule for measuring relative value, of any I have ever heard."[70] In the "Principles", he even quantifies the effect that would be possible through an increase in the nominal wage rate:

> The greatest effects which could be produced on the relative prices of these goods from a rise of wages, could not exceed 6 or 7 per cent; for profits could not, probably, under any circumstances, admit of a greater general and permanent depression than to that amount.[71]

Stigler used this statement to attribute a 93% labour theory of value to Ricardo.[72] Remarkably, contemporary empirical surveys confirmed the almost complete congruence of the relative prices of reproducible goods with labour values: "... we end up with a 90% labour theory of value."[73]

> In estimating, then," Ricardo sums up, "the causes of the variations in the value of commodities, although it would be wrong wholly to omit the consideration of the effect produced by a rise or fall of labour, it would be equally incorrect to attach much importance to it; and

65 Cf. ibid., p. 46.

66 Cf. Ricardo, D., Absolute Value and Exchangeable Value, in: The Works ..., op. cit., vol. IV, Cambridge 1951, pp. 361–412.

67 Cf. Ricardo, D., Letter to McCulloch, May 2, 1820, in: The Works ..., op. cit., vol. VIII, Cambridge 1973, pp. 178–183.

68 Cf. Ricardo, D., Letter to Malthus, October 9, 1820, in: The Works ..., op. cit., vol. VIII, Cambridge 1973, pp. 276–280, p. 279.

69 See also Ricardo, D., Letter to Mill, December 28, 1818, in: The Works ..., op. cit., vol. VII, Cambridge 1973, pp. 376–383, p. 377. In the "essay," Ricardo referred to the impact of escalating production costs on relative prices: "The exchangeable value of all commodities rises as the difficulties of their production increase." Ricardo, D., An Essay ..., op. cit., p. 19.

70 Ricardo, D., Letter to Malthus, October 9, 1820, op. cit., p. 279.

71 Ricardo, D., On the Principles ..., op. cit., p. 36.

72 Cf. Stigler, G. J., Ricardo and the 93% Labor Theory of Value, in: The American Economic Review, Vol. 48 (1958), pp. 357–367.

73 Petrovic, P., The deviation of production prices from labour values: some methodology and empirical evidence, in: Cambridge Journal of Economics, vol. 11 (1987), pp. 197–210, p. 209. Cf. also Grözinger, G., Konkurrenzpreise und Arbeitswerte, Ein Input–Output-Modell für die Bundesrepublik Deutschland 1960–1984, Marburg 1989. The results are confirmed by an investigation that was awarded a special prize from the German Federal Statistical Office: Fröhlich, N., Die Aktualität der Arbeitswertlehre, Theoretische und empirische Aspekte, Marburg 2009.

> consequently, in the subsequent part of this work, though I shall occasionally refer to this cause of variation, I shall consider all the great variations which take place in the relative value of commodities to be produced by the greater or less quantity of labour which may be required from time to time to produce them.[74]

So prepared, Ricardo could finally turn his attention to distribution. He starts with rent. Ricardo had already emphasised in the preface to the "Principles" that without knowledge of the "true" doctrine of rent, it "... is impossible to understand the effect of the progress of wealth on profits and wages ...".[75] Adam Smith and other authorities had therefore "... overlooked many important truths ..."[76] In terms of content, the presentation essentially coincides with his argument known from the "essay": "Corn is not high because a rent is paid, but a rent is paid because corn is high ..."[77] Once again, Ricardo criticises the widespread belief that rent reflects the contribution of nature:

> The labour of nature is paid," he comments on a quote by Smith, "not because she does much, but because she does little. In proportion as she becomes niggardly in her gifts, she exacts a greater price for her work. Where she is munificently beneficent, she always works gratis.[78]

If the view that rent is an advantage for society were correct, the newly built machines should be less efficient than the older ones, "... and a rent would be paid to all those who possessed the most productive machinery."[79] The rent is a symptom of wealth, not its source.[80] Rent is not a price-determining factor; it compensates for the varying labour productivities on soils with different fertilities. In contrast to the "essay", which emphasises the conflicting interests between the landlords and the other economic classes, Ricardo's *magnum opus* focuses on the conflict between wages and profits.

In the "Principles", Ricardo adheres to Malthus's population theory, although he expresses the wish that the workers find pleasure in "comforts and enjoyments": "There cannot be a better security against a superabundant population."[81] Ricardo does not deviate significantly from the "essay" regarding the long-term development of profit. In the course of accumulation, profits inevitably come under pressure due to the increasing effort to produce food: "The natural tendency of profits then is to fall;

---

[74] Ricardo, D., On the Principles ..., op. cit., p. 36 f.

[75] Ibid., p. 5.

[76] Ibid., p. 6.

[77] Ibid., p. 74.

[78] Yet there is also a passage in Smith where he describes rent as the result of price: "Rent ... enters into the composition of the price of commodities in a different way from wages and profit. High or low wages and profit, are the causes of high or low price; high or low rent is the effect of it." Smith, A., op. cit., p. 162. Surprisingly, Ricardo does not mention this quote even in chapter XXIV of the "Principles", which is especially dedicated to Adam Smith's theory of rent. Cf. Ricardo, D., On the Principles ..., op. cit., p. 327 ff.

[79] Ibid., p. 75 f.

[80] Cf. ibid. p. 77.

[81] Ibid., p. 100.

for, in the progress of society and wealth, the additional quantity of food required is obtained by the sacrifice of more and more labour."[82]

However, Ricardo now presents his deliberations to the public in a somewhat more refined form. According to his numerical examples, the price of corn must rise in line with the fall in labour productivity on the newly cultivated farmland. Since the adjusted natural wage rate sooner or later prevails, the exchange value of labour also increases, causing a decline in the monetary surplus of the entrepreneurial tenants.[83] And more often than in the "essay", Ricardo enunciated his credo: "... whatever increases wages, necessarily reduces profits."[84]

Malthus criticised the "essay", arguing that a higher agricultural rate of profit was conceivable due to a rise in the price of wheat, which is why the consequences described by Ricardo did not apply. Ricardo proceeds in the "Principles" to the counter-attack with his now more sophisticated argumentation.

Ricardo commences by stating that the price of wheat cannot *arbitrarily* rise since it depends on the necessary labour per unit at the cultivation margin. Moreover, an increase in the price of wheat at a given natural real wage causes a corresponding increase in the nominal wage. Because the prices of the other input goods are also determined by their labour costs according to the (approximate) labour theory, their acquisition becomes more expensive. Therefore, the capital value in agriculture rises. To boot, during accumulation, part of the previous profit is transformed into rent. Ergo, a rising wheat price *reduces* the rate of profit.

However, Ricardo's justification relies on examples; no abstract argumentation exists. This shortcoming is felt even more oppressively as soon as the workers' real wages include more than just wheat. Under these circumstances, the concept of localising the social surplus product *exclusively* in the cultivation of corn loses its persuasive power. A generalisation seems indispensable.

The theory of value was initially intended to provide a solid basis for a universal application of this explanatory model—this attempt was not convincingly successful. Only because of appropriately chosen premises, as the 93% labour theory of value and the assumption of a given value of gold, Ricardo managed to shield his concept at least partly from criticism. In doing so, his actual concern was almost lost. Despite the reference in the preface of the "Principles" regarding the importance of distribution, the book was primarily received as a contribution to value theory. The author bears part of the blame: the first, longest and repeatedly amended chapter is about *value*, and in the much shorter chapters on wages, profit and rent, the reference to the theory of value only looms shadowy.

This ambiguity made it all the easier to establish the interpretation that Ricardo's central deliberations were on value. Marx, e.g., judges: "Thus the entire Ricardian contribution is contained in the first two chapters of his work."[85] Because of

[82] Ibid., p. 120.

[83] Cf. ibid., p. 113 f.

[84] See also the chapters "Effects of Accumulation on Profits and Interest" and "Bounties on Exportation and Prohibitions of Importation", ibid., p. 289 ff.

[85] Marx, K., Theories ..., Part II, op. cit., p. 169.

the apparent dominance of value (and rent) theory, the surplus standpoint almost inevitably took a back seat. The neo-Ricardian view that in the "Principles", corn was replaced by labour for aggregating heterogeneous commodities to determine the surplus rate of the economy requires a trained eye. Even then, the usefulness of the thesis that the "Principles" are an enlarged version of the "essay" remains unclear: insofar as commodities admittedly *do not* exchange in proportion to their labour values, the profit rate derived from such an assumption is an as-if construction, a game of make-belief in economic theory—nothing more.

After all these years of wrestling with the problems of value theory, Ricardo sometimes returned to the view that the theory of production prices was not necessary to answer the central questions of distribution.

> I sometimes think," he reveals to McCulloch, "that if I were to write the chapter on value again which is in my book, I should acknowledge that the relative value of commodities was regulated by two causes instead of by one, namely, by the relative quantity of labour necessary to produce the commodities in question, and by the rate of profit for the time that the capital remained dormant, and until the commodities were brought to market. Perhaps I should find the difficulties nearly as great in this view of the subject as in that which I have adopted. After all[,] the great questions of Rent, Wages, and Profits must be explained by the proportions in which the whole produce is divided between landlords, capitalists, and labourers, and which are not essentially connected with the doctrine of value.[86]

The last statement is more of a wish than an insight: the rules that prescribe the shares of the economic classes in the national income can only be found if the operating principle of economic exchange in a competitive economy has *first* been uncovered. Because of the unresolvable difficulties of value theory, Ricardo finally hoped to be able to present the distribution of the surplus to the classes without a theory of value. In truth, this position is tantamount to a retreat to the seemingly more straightforward terrain of the wheat model. However, its intrinsic properties are more complex than one might initially think. Therefore, examining the exposition of the surplus concept within the corn-growing framework is necessary.

9.3 Once Again on the Logic of the Wheat Economy

From the above interpretation of the wheat model, which follows the traditional pathways, it emerges that in the "essay", Ricardo has no single-sector economy in mind, as texts far away from the source claim. Nevertheless, one branch of the corn

[86] Ricardo, D., Letter to McCulloch, June 13, 1820, in: The Works ..., op. cit., vol. VIII, pp. 191–197, p. 194. Ricardo expressed himself similarly in a letter to Malthus: "Political Economy you think is an enquiry into the nature and causes of wealth – I think it should rather be called an enquiry into the laws which determine the division of the produce of industry among the classes who concur in its formation. No law can be laid down respecting quantity, but a tolerably correct one can be laid down respecting proportions. Every day I am more satisfied that the former enquiry is vain and delusive, and the latter only the true objects of the science." Ricardo, D., Letter to Malthus, October 9, 1820, op. cit., p. 278 f.

economy lends it its particularity: in wheat cultivation, input and output are physically homogeneous. This property allows one to calculate a natural exploitation factor. In equilibrium, a suitable price structure ensures that the other sectoral profit rates coincide with the one determined in agriculture.

The hierarchical structure of the entire production process, coming to light in the wheat economy, thus provides the central insight that, in contrast to the conventional view, the various industries are not located on the same level. The conception is, therefore, sometimes rightly praised as a masterpiece of early economic analysis. In strange contrast is the fact that no second, closer look is bestowed on this outstanding achievement: instead of unfolding the model's inner logic, the intellectual edifice's unrealistic premises are more or less quickly criticised before it is pushed aside.

We proceed to the other extreme and subsequently consider a pure corn economy, i.e., we abstract from other branches of commodity production based on the division of labour. In an economy characterised in this way, the value problem can be ignored since measuring distribution in terms of a homogeneous, physical unit is possible. Nevertheless, this simple scenario raises questions that have recurred, albeit in different guises, throughout the history of value theory.

9.3.1 The Maximum of Total Profits

The behaviour of the agricultural entrepreneurs is decisive for the accumulation process: "The aim of the tenant farmers," it says unanimously in the usual expositions," is to maximise their profit in relation to the capital advanced."[87] To put it bluntly, Ricardo does not make it that clear; in fact, he favours the word "profit" over the word "profit rate", although he certainly often means the profit rate, even though he is talking about profit.[88] However, this rule of conduct imposed on the actors does not make sense. If entrepreneurs actually intended to maximise the profit rate, they would *never* accumulate because the rate of profit approaches its maximum when employment draws nearer to zero. With rising employment, it *must* fall, as Eq. (9.8) (cf. p. 95) testifies—what else should the rate of profit do? Maximising it is an unsuitable concept for depicting what drives the activities of profit-optimising entrepreneurs: the quotient is misleading, whereas the difference points the right way.

Ricardo indeed assumes that the tenant farmers maximise profits, which is the only way to explain the arbitrage process he often mentions: "If the profits of capital employed in Yorkshire, should exceed those of capital employed in London, capital

---

[87] Schefold, B., Ricardo ..., op. cit., p. 385. [F. H.] The quote is representative of many others with the same content.

[88] The first numerical example in the "essay" states: "... the neat profit to the owner of capital would be fifty per cent ..." Ricardo, D., An Essay ..., op. cit., p. 10. Such careless formulations occur in several places in Ricardo's work. For criticism of his language (and others), see Galbraith, J. K., Economics, Peace, and Laughter, ed. by Williams, A. D., Boston 1971, p. 26 ff.

would speedily move from London to Yorkshire …"[89] But Ricardo repeats several times that the mass of profit (and thus the rate of profit) dwindles in the course of capital accumulation; again:

> Thus by bringing successively land of a worse quality, or less favourably situated into cultivation, rent would rise on the land previously cultivated, and precisely in the same degree would profits fall; and if the smallness of profits do not check accumulation, there are hardly any limits to the rise of rent, and the fall of profit.[90]

As a result, the system contains a contradiction: on the one hand, Ricardo qualifies the tenant farmers as people who strive for maximum profit and, on the other, as "investment machines" that expand employment until the return on capital has fallen to a minimum. Yet, accumulating profit maximisers would inevitably shoot themselves in the foot if their income shrank in the course of expansion.

Numerous modern authors who have sensed a competence in reproducing Ricardo's theory juxtapose these incompatible behaviours without comment. This finding aligns with the impression that the instruction of economic thought is frequently implemented through a process akin to "Chinese whispers" [Stille Post], whereby information is transmitted orally or in written form with a degree of distortion or modification. Ricardo's original message was different: profit and the rate of profit do not always need to move in the same direction.

Suppose those economists who disseminate such formalisations really would possess the pretended analytical expertise. In that case, it should not have slipped their attention that the course of events they describe in the wheat economy is a *mirage*: profit and the rate of profit cannot always be positively correlated during accumulation.

The profit amounts to the product of the wage fund with the profit rate (cf. (9.3), p. 94). Both multiplicands must be positive for the tenant farmers to earn an income. Yet, this condition is violated twice: on the one hand, without work effort, there is no revenue, and on the other hand, at the maximum employment N_S, the rate of exploitation disappears. Hence, the profit function has two different roots depending on the labour input. According to Rolle's theorem, a continuous function has (at least) one (local) extreme value in between.[91] These conditions are met here.

In Ricardo's model, profit is the residual after the wage bill and the rent have been deducted from the social product:

$$P = f(N) - \left[f(N) - Nf_N\right] - w_S N = Nf_N - w_S N = N(f_N - w_S) \qquad (9.16)$$

The necessary condition for a profit maximum requires that the first derivative of (9.16) vanishes:

---

[89] Ricardo, D., On the principles …, op. cit., p. 134. This arbitrage process is also addressed in the "essay". Cf., e.g., Ricardo, D., An Essay …, op. cit., p. 12.

[90] Ricardo, D., An Essay …, op. cit., p. 14.

[91] Cf. Bronstein, I. N., Semendjajew, K. A., Taschenbuch der Mathematik, 20th ed., Leipzig 1981, p. 321.

$$\frac{dP}{dN} \equiv P_N = f_N + Nf_{NN} - w_S \overset{!}{=} 0 \tag{9.17}$$

The profit-maximising employment(N_P) depending on a given (subsistence) wage ($w_S < f_N$) is:

$$N_P = \frac{w_S - f_N}{f_{NN}} > 0 \tag{9.18}$$

At the maximum, the second derivative of (9.16)(P_{NN}) must be negative:

$$P_{NN} = 2f_{NN}(N_P) + N_P f_{NNN}(N_P) \overset{!}{<} 0 \tag{9.19}$$

Rearranging yields:

$$f_{NNN}(N_P) \overset{!}{<} -\frac{2f_{NN}(N_P)}{N_P} \tag{9.19a}$$

Equation (9.19a) is already fulfilled if the third derivative of the production function with respect to employment(f_{NNN}) is less than or equal to zero at employmentN_P.

Figure 9.2 shows the relationships for the production function $X = 441N - \frac{N^3}{3}$. The subsistence wagew_S was assumed to amount to 141 wheat units. As can be seen, total profit increases during employment expansion up to N_P; afterwards, it decreases. The relevant graphs in the literature are consistently incorrect.[92]

However, Ricardo knew that total profit could initially grow despite the declining rate of profit. In his numerical example, it rises from 100 wheat units in period one to a maximum of 275 in period five. Then, total profit shrinks again to 205.5 wheat units in period eight. The rate of profit diminishes continuously from 50% in the first period to 11% in the eighth.[93]

Ricardo comments on the illustrated phenomenon with the words:

> It will be seen that during the progress of a country the whole produce raised on its land will increase, and for a certain time that part of the produce which belongs to the profits of stock, as well as that part which belongs to rent will increase; but that at a later period, every accumulation of capital will be attended with an absolute, as well as a proportionate diminution of profits, – though rents will uniformly increase.[94]

---

[92] Cf. only Pasinetti, L. Lectures on the Theory of Production, New York 1977, p. 11. In Pasinetti's case, this is even more astonishing as he had previously stated: "… there must be at least one point of maximum total profits …" Pasinetti, L., A Mathematical …, op. cit., p. 89. This insight did not find its way into the corresponding diagram of his "Lectures". Even authors who rely directly on Pasinetti do not mention the profit maximum. Cf. Salvadori, N., Signorino, R., From stationery state to endogenous growth: international trade in the mathematical formulation of the Ricardian system, in: Cambridge Journal of Economics, vol. 40 (2016), pp. 895–912, p. 904.

[93] Cf. Ricardo, D., An Essay …, op. cit., p. 15 f., especially the table on p. 17.

[94] Ibid., p. 15 f.

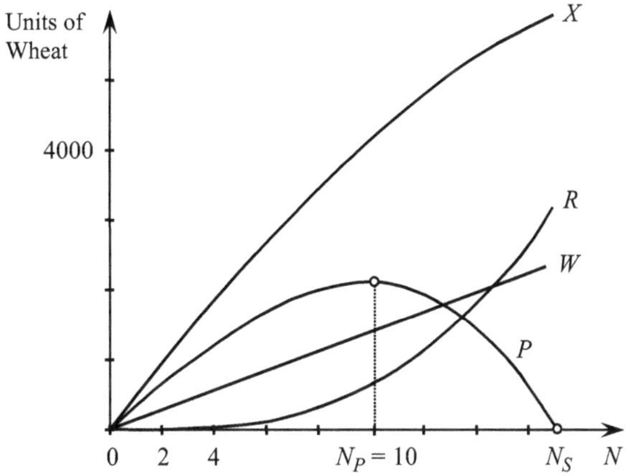

Fig. 9.2 The development of distribution in the wheat economy

This (correct) description of the development of profits is in striking contrast to the permanent reduction of profits when land cultivation expands, as Ricardo claimed two pages earlier and immediately later. The irritation intensifies even more if one considers that Ricardo attached outstanding importance to profit development: "This is a view of the effects of accumulation which is exceedingly curious, and has, I believe, never before been noticed."[95] In the "Principles", Ricardo also presented a numerical example in which profit increases at the beginning of capital accumulation, although the rate of profit decreases. Only after reaching a maximum does profit fall.[96]

Seen in this light, the thirst for knowledge is immense as to why the fact of the initially opposing relationship between profit and the rate of profit has been pushed aside. An answer seems more likely for Ricardo than for his epigones. First, it must be remembered that the "essay" was written with a practical concern: no tariffs on corn! Regardless of the concrete position of the economy on the "profit mountain", capital income always grows when the wage good becomes cheaper for a given employment.

Moreover, evidence supports Ricardo's belief that the maximum profit lies in the future. "But *after* profits have very much fallen," he warns in the "essay", "accumulation *will be checked*, and capital *will be exported* to be employed in those countries where food is cheap and profits high ..."[97] In the "Principles", he also states that the steady state is still far off. However, the longer we wait, the more difficult it will be to take what he considers to be the proper measures to eliminate the undesirable development.[98]

---

[95] Ibid., p. 16.

[96] "We should also expect that, however the rate of the profits of stock might diminish in consequence of the accumulation of capital on the land, and the rise of wages, yet that the aggregate amount of profits would increase ... This progression however is only true for a certain time ..." Ricardo, D., On the Principles ..., op. cit., p. 123.

[97] Ricardo, D., An Essay ..., op. cit., p. 16 n., own emphasis.

[98] Cf. Ricardo, D., On the Principles ..., op. cit., p. 109.

With this in mind, it becomes understandable that Ricardo handled his system "pragmatically": depending on requirements, he switches from profit maximisation to employment maximisation as the farmers' objective. But modern economists ought to evince straightness in this respect.

Since economic theory, in the sense understood here, means deciphering the laws of economic exchange between commercially oriented *homines oeconomici*, profit maximisation of entrepreneurs provides the only analytically promising guideline for action. From this perspective, the existence of an utmost business gain in the course of capital accumulation is of such significance that the phenomenon cannot be disregarded.

Initially, it is necessary to elucidate the impact of the maximum total profit on the behaviour of individual tenant farmers. Addressing this knowledge gap is essential before examining the effects on the properties of the wheat economy when profits rise while the profit rate falls. To begin with, a few remarks on the relationship between microeconomic and macroeconomic profit maximisation are appropriate.

9.3.2 Individual and Collective Rationality

EmploymentN_P would be optimal if the grain growers were striving to maximise their joint profit. However, the individual capitalist is not interested in the total profit but rather in his personal top income. One could, therefore, take the view that the total profit maximum has no further significance for the accumulation process since the profit recipients do not collectively maximise profits. Instead, each tenant continues accumulating if the profit rate exceeds the assumed minimum rate of profit. Accordingly, individual farmers only pay attention to the margin between these rates of return. In contrast, the change in profit does not send out a signal that is relevant to their decision-making.

Contrary to the prevailing Ricardo interpretation, however, such an argument does not allow for sweeping the existence of an overall profit maximum under the carpet. The justification for the sole consideration of the profit rate as an incentive to invest would only be acceptable if the profit of the individual farmer really increases with *each* individual expansion of employment. Yet, this is not true. There is a critical limit to accumulation on both a large and a small scale. It is reached as soon as two opposing effects balance each other out: the additional profit expected from higher employment is precisely compensated by the decline that the falling rate of profit, applied to the 'old capital'—the previous wage fund—entails.

For the sake of simplicity, let us assume that the number of farmers is constant throughout the growth process and that they follow the same accumulation pattern. In this situation, every tenant has hired the same number of workers and would pocket the same profit. Then, accumulation comes to a standstill at employment N_P because a further accumulation of profit would involve a more significant loss of income for each tenant than the increase in profit associated with a rising labour input. Under these circumstances, collective profit maximisation takes place behind the backs of individuals without any formal agreement.

In such a constellation, one must not arbitrarily speculate about the minimum profit rate. It corresponds to the return on invested capital, i.e., the wage fund, at employmentN_P:

$$r_P = \frac{f_N(N_P)}{w_S} - 1 \tag{9.20}$$

Circulating capital is only augmented for $r > r_P$; accumulation stops at $r = r_P$. Beyond this limit, the profit-maximising entrepreneurs' profit *must* either be consumed directly or accrue to a luxury goods industry. Of course, this possibility can only be discussed in multi-sector models. The labour input associated with r_P is always smaller than that resulting from a profit rate of $0 \leq r < r_P$, since the rate of exploitation decreases with an expansion of employment, as Eq. (9.8) (cf. p. 95) shows.

One might think that the above reasoning is correct if the number and structure of individual capitals are given. Once N_P is reached, no capitalist class member will have an alternative to improve their situation. But what happens if "new" agrarian entrepreneurs appear on the scene? The economy generates profit, and they also want to participate in the economic surplus and hire labour profitably. For that end, they must plough poorer soils. Although a decrease in overall profit accompanies this, the *newcomers* still succeed in enriching themselves. From the perspective of total capital, an accumulation beyond N_P seems irrational, but it appears plausible from the standpoint of each junior tenant.

However, there is little room for such constructions in the classical system. First, uncertainty must be mentioned regarding where the debutants can obtain capital. If, by definition, workers completely consume their wages, landlords their rent, and the "old" tenants their entire profit because an increasing wage fund beyond N_P would reduce it, there is no source to supply additional capital. Moreover, if, by Malthus' law, the population has adapted to N_P, there is not even more labour available to expand wheat production at the prevailing subsistence wage.

To boot, entrepreneurs would have arrows in their quivers to protect themselves from unwelcome competition. For example, the established farmers could rent land *without* cultivating it. Eventually, the best plot available for third parties would yield a marginal return equal to the remuneration for the required labour input. Then, some soil remains uncultivated due to a lack of profit prospects.

Establishing a cooperative "tenants league" would be an equally effective (and more stable) solution. The internal tasks of this coalition would include the cultivation of inferior land so that the modest difference between the marginal return on labour and its remuneration does not drive up rent payments. In both cases, the novices cannot find any ground to be cultivated profitably.

The actions mentioned above naturally entail a certain reduction in profit. On the one hand, fallow plots are rented; on the other, the tenants' league must advance capital for a period. However, these are not bad investments: forestalling access to the market is profitable for the farmers' association. In contrast, continued accumulation in corn production offers no advantage beyond the individual profit maximum. In addition, it should not be forgotten that fresh capital, instead of flowing into farming, whereupon the agrarian rate of profit inevitably falls, is more likely directed into other sectors that operate under linear returns to scale. There, demand alone limits expansion.

Finally, another brake should be mentioned, which blocks the excessive accrual of capital into agriculture. If, in a (theoretically) ideal case, it is possible to obtain a return in the financial sphere of the economy equal to that in wheat cultivation, no incentive exists to invest money there with the effect of lowering the farmers' profit rate.

The old tenants have, therefore, a range of instruments at their command to effectively defend their maximum profit, which is vital to all of them. Besides, other investment forms are conceivable for the "new" capital. The risk of a profit-destroying augmentation of capital in the wheat sector can be considered low.

Just as nature's stinginess with fertile soils provides a rent, the farmer's profit is only permanent if corn cultivation remains limited. The first shortage is natural; the second one is man-made. But the limit beyond which the inclination to increase output dries up is not arbitrarily imposed. The income interests of established capital stand in the way of a profit-reducing sectoral overaccumulation.

These considerations go far beyond Ricardo's analysis: the problem did not obtain sufficient weight for him, as he oscillated between the behavioural assumptions for profit maximisation and employment maximisation under the constraint of a profit rate that had not yet fallen too far. Ricardo neglected to consider the fact that he himself had mentioned, namely, that the two objectives can contradict each other.

With this suppression, Ricardo unwittingly sets the stage for the neoclassical *deus ex machina*, unbridled competition. In the absence of an equation to close the system, it regularly celebrates triumphs: because the prevailing economic theory is unable to explain profit as an independent income category due to the omission of incorporating social surplus, profit must *somehow* be eradicated from neoclassical studies, at least in the long term. Relevant prerequisites ensure that profit eventually vanishes from the scene. The uninvited actor must not put up a fuss.

Seen through this lens, to expose the Ricardo system for profit erosion to the sun of perfect competition would mean being taken in by the mainstream: the classics deem profit as a *permanent* characteristic of capitalist market economies. Neoclassicists close their eyes to this fundamental fact; as far as "profit rates" appear at all, they are assumed to be either merely interest rates—more correctly, discounting factors that (are supposed to) bridge the gap between the present and the future—or they just serve as "normal" reward for the entrepreneur's performance or "capital" productivity. The connection to the economic surplus was inevitably lost.

9.3.3 *Wage Rate and Profit*

After this digression, let us return to our wheat model. We are now interested in how a profit maximum that depends on the labour input affects the relationship between the wage rate and profit. Does Ricardo's credo of the inverse relationship between wages and profit apply in the simple experimental set-up of the "wheat economy"? Does the rate of exploitation fall as pay rises? While we previously examined profit development as a function of employment at a *given* (subsistence) wage rate, we are now studying the change in profit caused by a *variation* in earnings when capital, i.e., the wage fund, is fixed. First, we recall the profit rate Eq. (9.7a):

$$r = \frac{f_N}{w} - 1 \tag{9.7a}$$

Furthermore, the demand for labour is ascertained by the available stock of advanced wage goods(K_0):

$$N = \frac{K_0}{w} \tag{9.21}$$

Solving Eq. (9.21) for w and the ensuing insertion into the expression (9.7a) leads to the modified profit rate formula:

$$r = \frac{N f_N}{K_0} - 1 \tag{9.22}$$

The influence of a change in the wage rate on the exploitation rate can be determined by differentiation with recourse to the chain rule:

$$\frac{dr}{dw} = \frac{dr}{dN}\frac{dN}{dw} = \frac{(f_N + N f_{NN})K_0}{K_0^2}\left(-\frac{K_0}{w^2}\right) = -\frac{f_N + N f_{NN}}{w^2} \tag{9.23}$$

The effect of a wage rate variation on the profit rate is not as clear-cut as is often claimed: since by virtue of (9.1b) (cf. p. 93) $f_{NN} < 0$ applies, nothing can be said a priori about the sign of the right-hand side of (9.23). However, a case analysis allows a closer view. The fraction's numerator is equivalent to the derivative of the combined income of capitalists and workers (Q) with respect to employment. As Fig. 9.1 (p. 96) illustrates, Q is:

$$Q = W + P = N f_N \tag{9.24}$$

The first derivative yields:

$$\frac{dQ}{dN} = f_N + N f_{NN} \tag{9.25}$$

In case of a concave marginal return function of labour, i.e., $f_{NN} < 0$, employment N^*, which maximises Q, ensues from the vanishing right-hand side of the Eq. (9.25):

$$N^* = -\frac{f_N}{f_{NN}} > 0 \tag{9.26}$$

For the numerical example underlying Fig. 9.2 (cf. p. 113), one calculates $N^* = 12,124$, an employment greater than that associated with the maximum profit. A comparison of (9.18) (cf. p. 112) and (9.26) shows that this is true for each wage rate $0 < w \leq f_N$. For $N < N^*$ follows $\frac{dr}{dw} < 0$, for $N > N^*$ ensues $\frac{dr}{dw} > 0$. The relationship between the wage rate and the rate of profit turns out to be the exact opposite of what "common sense" and with it the numerous interpreters of the Ricardo system expect: the rate of profit *rises* with the wage rate if accumulation is sufficiently advanced.

Given this situation, the question emerges as to whether N^* is principally relevant when the tenants strive for profit-maximising employmentN_P at every wage rate in accordance with (9.18). It could be argued that only the "normal", i.e., the negative relationship between wage rate and profit rate was relevant since N_P would be smaller than N^*. Yet, this train of thought would derail. Despite a seeming simplicity, the wheat economy embraces further properties that have not yet been duly appreciated.

Analysing the impact of a change in the wage rate on the profit rate implies that workers can behave strategically. This way of conduct presupposes the dropping of a fixed subsistence wage. Let us go through this alternative. We assume that the workforce is unionised—what was the case with the English agricultural workers quite early[99]—and that their goal is to maximise the wage bill.[100] This strategy can only succeed in the long term if higher pay does not increase labour supply, jeopardising the achieved income level through competition for better-paid jobs. After all, the same applies to wages as to rents and profits: many hounds soon catch the hare.

The action parameter of the workers is the remuneration per unit of time; Eq. (9.18) (cf. p. 112) determines the corresponding labour demand of profit-maximising tenant farmers. The wage bill (and thus capital in the present model) is highest when

$$\frac{d(wN)}{dw} = N + w\frac{dN}{dw} \overset{!}{=} 0 \tag{9.27}$$

is valid, from which

---

[99] Cf. Webb, S., Webb, B., The History of Trade Unionism, London 1920, https://www.gutenberg.org/ebooks/66887.

[100] On trade union policy, see Helmedag, F., Möglichkeiten und Grenzen eines Beschäftigungspakts, in: Jahrbücher für Nationalökonomie und Statistik, vol. 205 (2005), pp. 151–162; cf. also Helmedag, F., Von der Sozialen Marktwirtschaft zum globalen Kapitalismus, Fehlentwicklungen und tarifpolitische Konsequenzen, in: Marquardt, R.-M., Pulte, P. (eds.), Mythos Soziale Marktwirtschaft, Arbeit, Soziales und Kapital, Festschrift für Heinz-J. Bontrup, Köln 2019, pp. 123–140.

$$w = -N\frac{dw}{dN} \tag{9.28}$$

results. Rearranging Eq. (9.18) and writing w instead of w_S gives:

$$w = Nf_{NN} + f_N \tag{9.18a}$$

The derivative of (9.18a) yields:

$$\frac{dw}{dN} = f_{NN} + Nf_{NNN} + f_{NN} = 2f_{NN} + Nf_{NNN} < 0 \tag{9.29}$$

The right-hand side of (9.29) conforms to the sufficient condition for a profit maximum (cf. (9.19), p. 112), i.e., $\frac{dw}{dN} < 0$. Inserting (9.29) into (9.28) results in a wage rate (w_W) that maximises the total payment for the workers:

$$w_W = -N(2f_{NN} + Nf_{NNN}) > 0 \tag{9.30}$$

Equation (9.18) assigns the corresponding employment to this wage rate, which is (initially) optimal from the point of view of the trade union clientele. For our numerical example, we get: $w_W = 294$ wheat units. Compared to the preliminary situation with $w_S = 141$ and $N_P = 10$, the demand for labour has now fallen to $N_W = 7$. The corresponding profit comes to:

$$P_W = N_W(f_N(N_W) - w_W) \tag{9.31}$$

Although the whole workforce would be interested in demanding payment w_W, this is not necessarily attractive for every individual: maximising the wage bill is associated with labour displacement. Although the quality of life of those still in employment improves, the resulting redundancy can significantly counter wage rate increases and make it more difficult to achieve optimum earnings. Against this backdrop, an individual reduction in working hours promotes the success of the trade union wage policy.[101]

However, the wheat economy also offers opportunities for the other side. As part of a clever policy, employers can also enhance their position. Their scope of action encompasses more than the profit-maximising adjustment of employment per (9.18) to each wage rate enforced by the workers. Astute model entrepreneurs (who appear otherwise rarely enough in economic theory) will take advantage of the fact that according to Eq. (9.26) (cf. p. 118), there is a level of activity N^* at which the *joint* income of labour and capital reaches its maximum. If the entrepreneurs

[101] Even if nominal wages rise in line with labour productivity ('golden wage rule') an individual reduction in working hours is necessary to counteract resulting job losses when growth is insufficient. Cf. Helmedag, F., Nur mehr Stundenlohn oder auch weniger Arbeitsstunden? Gewerkschaftsforderungen im Widerstreit, in: Hagemann, H., Kromphardt, J. (eds.), Keynes, Schumpeter und die Zukunft der entwickelten kapitalistischen Volkswirtschaften, Schriften der Keynes-Gesellschaft, vol. 9, Marburg 2016, pp. 273–287.

produce the corresponding output, they can offer their staff (at least) the top wage bill. Nevertheless, employers achieve a comparatively higher profit.

In this situation, the definite distribution cannot be specified a priori. Nevertheless, the margin is precisely defined. Both sides must receive not less than in case of a maximum wage bill. Thus, the minimum remuneration is:

$$w_{\min}(N^*) = \frac{w_W N_W}{N^*} \tag{9.32}$$

To obtain at least profit P_W, the tenants pay as per formula (9.31) at most:

$$w_{\max}(N^*) = \frac{N^* f_N(N^*) - P_W}{N^*} \tag{9.33}$$

In the numerical example, the wage limits are $w_{\min}(N^*) = 169.75$ and $w_{\max}(N^*) = 234.41$. Similar to the bilateral monopoly, the final distribution now depends on the threat potential and the negotiating skills of the 'bargaining partners'. The logic of the model alone does not provide any precise information about the level of remuneration and, thus, the profit rate; both variables are—within certain boundaries—indeterminate.

With these explanations, we have gone beyond the framework set out by Ricardo. The account illustrates the analytical heights that can be climbed even in a scenario as seemingly simple as the wheat economy, provided that the actors' possibilities are pursued to the utmost, given their respective objectives. Independently, which of the variants mentioned is considered particularly plausible, one thing is undoubtedly clear: the dynamics of the profit rate as an unmistakable indicator for profit development has been battered. The exploitation factor is already failing as a guideline for accumulation in the single-sector corn economy. The above exploration of the province, conducted more precisely than usual, has confirmed the earlier supposition that economic theory has determined the course without reliable navigational aid.

The reason for the unsatisfactory treatment of the wheat economy is ultimately methodological: instead of getting to the bottom of the initially always pretended profit maximisation and using this behaviour as a compass to penetrate the economic logic of the model, the focus is suddenly and tacitly shifted to a different objective.[102] To be sure, as is often the case, one can postulate that the population must be supplied; therefore, the total quantity to be produced is known. And, of course, the corresponding (natural) profit rate can then be calculated for the necessary employment. However, the analysis is no longer based on the individual profit maximisation typical of capitalist market economies but—unnoticed—on the medieval idea of food (see p. 21).

[102] In the specialised literature, volatile goal settings for entrepreneurs and investors are surprisingly often the rule rather than the exception. See Helmedag, F., Profitrate, Zinssatz, Gewinn: Irrungen und Wirrungen, in: Caspari, V. (ed.), Einkommens- und Vermögensverteilung in historischer Sicht, Studien zur Entwicklung der ökonomischen Theorie XXXVII, Berlin 2020, pp. 65–84.

It remains to be clarified whether the outcomes achieved are due to the unique nature of agriculture, where cultivation is subject to falling marginal returns. Do the previous results no longer occur if we consider industrial production operating with constant returns to scale? How is the rate of profit determined under such conditions, and what significance does it have in the accumulation process? Karl Marx's analysis of capitalism promises answers to these questions. Yet it would be rash to examine his system without looking back at Ricardo's "Principles". This book contains a theorem based on the labour theory of value, which is considered a fundamental insight and outstanding achievement of economic science.

9.3.4 Comparative Cost Advantages and Employment

In the seventh chapter, "On Foreign Trade" of his "Principles", Ricardo explains his view on the pattern of international trade by a sensation-causing illustration, probably the most reproduced numerical example in the history of economic thought.[103] Ricardo mentions cloth and wine, which can, in principle, be produced in England as well as in Portugal:

> England may be so circumstanced, that to produce the cloth may require the labour of 100 men for one year; and if she attempted to make the wine, it might require the labour of 120 men for the same time. England would therefore find it her interest to import wine, and to purchase it by the exportation of cloth.
>
> To produce the wine in Portugal, might require only the labour of 80 men for one year, and to produce the cloth in the same country, might require the labour of 90 men for the same time. It would therefore be advantageous for her to export wine in exchange for cloth …
>
> Thus England would give the produce of the labour of 100 men, for the produce of the labour of 80.[104]

The message of this quote is that, even though the production of both commodities in Portugal is less labour-intensive, strict specialisation is worthwhile for all participating nations. Each country should ultimately manufacture and export the product it can produce with the slightest efficiency disadvantage or the most significant efficiency advantage.[105]

[103] See King, J. E., David Ricardo, Houndmills / New York 2013, p. 82.

[104] Ricardo, D., On the Principles …, op. cit., p. 135. The Methuen Treaty, named after the British envoy in Lisbon, was concluded between England and Portugal in 1703, although Ricardo does not mention it. On the relationship between the maritime powers, see Helmedag, F., Komparative Kostenvorteile …, op. cit., p. 177 ff.

[105] The following presentation draws on passages from Helmedag, F., Komparative Kostenvorteile …, op. cit. and Helmedag, F., Zum Theorem komparativer Kostenvorteile: Praktische Probleme der reinen Lehre, in: Wirtschaft und Gesellschaft, 48. Jg. (2022), pp. 267–279. Transportation costs, taxes, and tariffs are neglected.

The advice was increasingly finding a sympathetic ear in theory and practice. Meanwhile, the recommendation is regarded as verified economic knowledge.[106] So, the World Trade Organization praises the doctrine on its homepage as "... arguably the single most powerful insight into economics."[107]

Concerning Ricardo's principle of the international division of labour, Paul A. Samuelson even justified the claim of economic science to provide original findings. As a young economist, he was teased by the mathematician Stanislaw Ulam with the challenge of naming a statement in the social sciences that was both true and non-trivial. Thirty years passed before, finally, the correct answer entered Samuelson's mind:

> The Ricardian theory of comparative advantage; the demonstration that trade is mutually profitable even if one country is absolutely more – or less – productive in terms of every commodity. That it is logically true need not to be argued before a mathematician; that it is not trivial is attested by thousands of important and intelligent men who have never been able to grasp the doctrine for themselves or to believe it after it was explained to them.[108]

Hence, economic theory offers (at least) with the theorem of comparative cost advantages—formulated in labour values—a profound truth precisely because it seems absurd to some people despite an extant mental power.

However, many accounts are content with the general statement that specialisation is lucrative for the weaker and the stronger partners. Nevertheless, more sophisticated authors qualify the statement by referring to the opportunity costs, which limit the permissible exchange ratio because it must not be detrimental for either side. Let us take a closer look at the matter.

Ricardo's example contains the "four magic numbers", which have since then been regularly used to demonstrate the principle.[109] In autarky, England produces one unit of cloth per year with 100 workers (N_{CE}) and one unit of wine during the same time with 120 workers (N_{WE}); Portugal produces *per annum* a unit of cloth with 90 workers (N_{CP}) and one unit of the juice from the grape with 80 workers (N_{WP}).[110]

---

[106] The precept also obtains validity in the choice of profession: "Two men can both make shoes and hats, and one is superior to the other in both employments; but in making hats, he can only exceed his competitor by one-fifth or 20 per cent, and in making shoes he can excel him by one-third or 33 per cent; – will it not be for the interest of both, that the superior man should employ himself exclusively in making shoes, and the inferior man in making hats?" Ricardo, D. Principles ..., op. cit., p. 136.

[107] World Trade Organization, The case for open trade, https://www.wto.org/english/thewto_e/whatis_e/tif_e/fact3_e.htm.

[108] Cf. Samuelson, P. A., The Way of an Economist [1969], reprinted in: Merton, R. C. (ed.), The Collected Scientific Papers of Paul A. Samuelson, vol. III, Cambridge (USA) / London 1991, pp. 675–685, p. 683.

[109] Cf. ibid., p. 678 and Maneschi, A., Ricardo's Four Magic Numbers, in: Kurz, H. D., Salvadori, N. (eds.), The Elgar Companion to David Ricardo, Cheltenham / Northampton 2015, pp. 482–489.

[110] Due to the limited length of the alphabet, some letters have different meanings in different contexts. In this section, 'W' stands for wine units; the character symbolises other magnitudes elsewhere.

To avoid putting any trading partner at a disadvantage compared to autarky, the cloth price expressed in wine (p_{CW}) must be within a specific range: at least one party is supposed to increase its benefit, and no participant should suffer reduced welfare. This condition means that there is either a weak (one wins) or a strong (both benefit) Pareto improvement, which characterises the economic exchange (cf. p. 42 ff.). The minimum wine revenue per unit of cloth demanded by the English ($p_{CW\min}$) marks the lower limit of the range in question, while the maximum willingness to pay of the Portuguese sets the upper limit ($p_{CW\max}$):

$$p_{CW\min} = \frac{N_{CE}}{N_{WE}} = \frac{100}{120} = 0.8\overline{3} \leq p_{CW} \leq p_{CW\max} = \frac{N_{CP}}{N_{WP}} = \frac{90}{80} = 1.125 \quad (9.34)$$

As can be learned from the last sentence of Ricardo's quotation with the four magic numbers (cf. p. 146), he supposes in the example that one unit of fabric is sold for one unit of beverage, i.e., $p_{CW} = 1$. The assumed *terms of trade* lie within the interval defined by Eq. (9.34).

However, this does not yet answer how a permissible exchange ratio may be established. In Ricardo's eyes, his otherwise preferred labour theory of value fails in international trade due to a lack of the worker's mobility; hence, the product of 100 Englishmen can be exchanged for the product of 80 Portuguese: "The same rule which regulates the relative value of commodities in one country, does not regulate the relative value of the commodities exchanged between two or more countries."[111]

Moreover, the transacted quantities at the ruling price must be clarified. If the same volume of work is performed in England and Portugal before and after specialisation, the additional production of cloth (ΔC) compared to the output of one unit per country in the *status quo ante* amounts to:

$$\Delta C = \frac{N_{CE} + N_{WE}}{N_{CE}} - 2 = \frac{220}{100} - 2 = 0.2 \quad (9.35)$$

The increase in wine output (ΔW) is calculated in the same way:

$$\Delta W = \frac{N_{CP} + N_{WP}}{N_{WP}} - 2 = \frac{170}{80} - 2 = 0.125 \quad (9.36)$$

How much of the increment in output will be exported? For an answer, the non-negative export quotas of the accretion in cloth (γ) and the additional juice from the grape (ω) after specialisation must be known. The upper limit of the export shares is one if the national minimum consumption of both goods is not to fall below the production quantities in autarky.

The current account equilibrium requires that the trade volume of cross-border transactions expressed in wine units coincide:

[111] Ricardo, D., Principles ..., op. cit., p. 133.

$$1 \cdot p_{CW} + \gamma \Delta C p_{CW} \overset{!}{=} 1 + \omega \Delta W \text{ with } 0 \leq \gamma, \omega \leq 1 \tag{9.37}$$

On the left-hand side of the condition (9.37) is the value of the English cloth delivery, while on the right-hand side is the quantity of wine with which Portugal settles the import bill. The rearrangement of the equalised trade balance (9.37) provides the real exchange ratio:

$$p_{CW} = \frac{1 + \omega \Delta W}{1 + \gamma \Delta C} \tag{9.38}$$

The price limits correspond to the opportunity costs already derived:

$$p_{CW\min} = \frac{1}{1 + \Delta C} = \frac{1}{1 + 0.2} = 0.8\overline{3} \text{ for } \omega = 0 \text{ and } \gamma = 1 \tag{9.39}$$

$$p_{CW\max} = 1 + \Delta W = 1 + 0.125 = 1.125 \text{ for } \omega = 1 \text{ and } \gamma = 0 \tag{9.40}$$

As an avowed supporter of Say's theorem, Ricardo saw no problem with sales since every supply creates its own demand: "... demand is only limited by production. No man produces, but with a view to consume or sell, and he never sells, but with the intention to purchase some other commodity ...".[112] Viewed in this light, it seems reasonable to interpret the total number of workers in England (N_{EA}) and Portugal (N_{PA}) in autarky as full employment:

$$N_{EA} = N_{CE} + N_{WE} = 100 + 120 = 220 \tag{9.41}$$

$$N_{PA} = N_{CP} + N_{WP} = 90 + 80 = 170 \tag{9.42}$$

If linear returns to scale prevail, feasible production increases in cloth and wine will be achieved with these national labour volumes. Obviously, at $p_{CW\min}$ Portugal appropriates the entire specialisation gain ΔW plus ΔC, while for $p_{CW\max}$ the accrual in output benefits England completely.

However, the second summands in the numerator ($\omega\Delta W$) and denominator ($\gamma\Delta C$) of the fraction on the right-hand side of the expression (9.38) do not necessarily have to disappear so that a wine price of cloth to the tune of one holds, as mentioned by Ricardo. Instead, every permissible exchange ratio, i.e., $p_{CW} = 1$, can also be accompanied by different positive values for ω and γ. The rearrangement of Eq. (9.38) yields the export share of the additional cloth:

$$\gamma = \frac{1 + \omega \Delta W - p_{CW} \cdot 1}{p_{CW} \Delta C} \tag{9.43}$$

[112] Ibid., p. 290.

Numerically, Ricardo's example yields:

$$\gamma = \frac{0,125\omega}{0,2} = 0.0625\omega > 0 \text{ for } 0 < \omega \leq 1 \tag{9.44}$$

However, the 1:1 exchange ratio, regardless of the parameter constellation on which it rests, discriminates against the more productive Portugal. Its share of the surplus product after specialisation (z) is generally:

$$z = \frac{(1-\omega)\Delta W + p_{CW}\gamma\Delta C}{\Delta W + p_{CW}\Delta C} \tag{9.45}$$

The insertion of Eq. (9.43) in formula (9.45) leads to:

$$z = \frac{1 + \Delta W - p_{TW} \cdot 1}{\Delta W + p_{TW}\Delta T} \tag{9.46}$$

With the exchange ratio $p_{CW\max}$ Portugal receives nothing from the surplus ($z = 0$), but for $p_{CW\min}$ it accrues to the Iberian Peninsula in full ($z = 1$). Ricardo's figures lead to:

$$z = \frac{1 + 0.125 - 1}{0.125 + 0.2} = 0.3846 \tag{9.47}$$

Although the Portuguese have absolute cost advantages for both products, they are fobbed off with 38.46% of the surplus at the real price $p_{CW} = 1$, whereas the less efficient English rake in $(1 - z) = 61.54\%$. For the sake of fairness, however, it can be argued that the specialisation gain should be distributed in proportion to labour productivity. This maxim can then be used to calculate the Portuguese claim ($z*$):

$$\frac{z*}{1 - z*} \overset{!}{=} \frac{N_{EA}}{N_{PA}} \Rightarrow z* = \frac{N_{EA}}{N_{PA} + N_{EA}} = \frac{220}{220 + 170} = 0.5641 \tag{9.48}$$

If the distribution of the total surplus is performance-based, the Portuguese will receive 56.41% of it, while the British will now have to be content with 43.59%.

From expression (9.46), one gets an alternative to Eq. (9.38) (cf. p. 124) for the *terms of trade*p_{CW}. The different formulation contains only the distribution parameter z in addition to the technically determined additional production quantities:

$$p_{CW} = \frac{1 + (1 - z)\Delta W}{1 + z\Delta C} \tag{9.49}$$

According to Eq. (9.49), the cloth price in wine units *does not* depend on the quantities traded despite differing factor efficiency in the countries—a significant result from the viewpoint of the labour theory of value.

The insertion of z^*, determined by condition (9.48), in Eq. (9.49) concretises the real exchange ratio p_{CW}^*, which ensures the productivity-oriented distribution of the surplus:

$$p_{CW}* = \frac{1 + (1 - 0.5641) \cdot 0.125}{1 + 0.5641 \cdot 0.2} = 0.9476 \tag{9.50}$$

A look at the right-hand sides of the equations for the *terms of trade* (9.38) and (9.49) shows that the fair exchange ratio $p_{CW}* = 0.9476$ results for $\omega = 1 - z^* = 0.4359$ and $\gamma = z^* = 0.5641$. Alas, it is questionable how the concept can come true without controlling interventions because there are "… no recognisable forces inherent in the system ensuring … that such a state occurs in reality."[113] Instead, another behaviour of autonomous actors is to be expected.

For each export ratio of the partner's surplus, Portugal's (England's) share z (1 – z) of the total surplus reaches the achievable peak value when ω (γ) vanishes. If both nations want to absorb as much surplus as possible, they will not cede any of their output growth. By hypothesis, saleability at home is guaranteed (leastwise on paper).

From this perspective, Ricardo's assumed price of one unit of wine turns out to be an equilibrium in dominant strategies with $\omega = 0$ and $\gamma = 0$. Although this result leads to an unjustifiably advantageous distribution of the surplus product for England compared to Portugal, both countries benefit more or less from cross-border trade.

However, when faced with unemployment due to inadequate sales opportunities—which in reality is the rule rather than the exception—things are different: international trade then also knows losers.

In a discussion contribution that was hardly noticed for many years, Sraffa pointed out the employment effects resulting *ceteris paribus* from the Ricardo example with the four magic numbers (cf. p. 146):

> England gives the cloth produced by 100 Englishmen in exchange for the wine produced by 80 Portuguese; and since this quantity could only have been produced by 120 Englishmen, she gains the labour of 20 Englishmen. Portugal gives the wine produced by 80 Portuguese for the cloth produced by 100 Englishmen; the production of this cloth would have required the labour of 90 Portuguese, and therefore Portugal gains the labour of 10 Portuguese.[114]

The productivity gains through trade with unchanged consumption compared to autarky are reflected in "freed" workers: 20 fewer Englishmen and 10 fewer Portuguese are needed to maintain the previous output. Nevertheless, it is not certain that lower labour requirements per product unit will automatically result in increased output. What employment effects result from Ricardo's theorem of comparative cost advantages, given autonomous demand, i.e., demand that is not dependent on the current income level?

---

[113] Helmedag, F., Komparative Kostenvorteile …, op. cit., p. 176. [F. H.]

[114] Sraffa, P., An Alleged Correction of Ricardo, in: The Quarterly Journal of Economics, vol. 44 (1930), pp. 539–544, p. 541.

In the following analysis, unchanged profits represent the fixed expenditure block for the period under consideration. Against this background, adding an ancillary interpretation to Ricardo's four magic numbers proves helpful. Let us assume that in autarky, the real wage bill in England (L_{EA}) and Portugal (L_{PA}) consists of a cloth unit, while the profit in both countries materialises in a unit of wine. The fabric is thus the primary or basic good in both countries, while the juice from the grape functions as a secondary or luxury good. It will become clear that such a distinction is hugely conducive to gaining profound insights. This separation will, therefore, be taken up several times later.

In contrast to the previous study, in which the increase in productivity brought about by specialisation served entirely to produce more, potential additional wine production is now disregarded, i.e., $\Delta W = 0$. The given profits thus have the character of autonomous demand components. Furthermore, the prevailing annual wage of a worker in both countries should remain the same. The real wage per unit of labour in Portugal (w_P) is therefore:

$$w_P = \frac{L_{PA}}{N_{PA}} = \frac{1}{170} = 0.005882 \tag{9.51}$$

The Portuguese employment to produce the total stationary profit of two wine units (N_{PS}) amounts to:

$$N_{PS} = 2N_{WP} = 160 \tag{9.52}$$

Personnel expenses in Portugal (L_{PS}) are:

$$L_{PS} = w_P N_{PS} = 0.005882 \cdot 160 = 0.9411 \tag{9.53}$$

Since England supplies a total of L_{PS} cloth units to Portugal as wage costs, the balance of trade equilibrium (9.37) (cf. p. 124) now results in the exchange ratio (p_{CWS}):

$$p_{CWS} = \frac{1}{L_{PS}} = \frac{1}{0.9411} = 1.0625 \tag{9.54}$$

The price of the fabric is within the permitted range. To calculate employment in England, one first needs to know the real wage(w_E) on the island:

$$w_E = \frac{L_{EA}}{N_{EA}} = \frac{1}{220} = 0.004545 \tag{9.55}$$

The number of workers active in England during a year (N_{ES}) results from the following condition:

$$N_{ES} w_E + L_{PS} = \frac{N_{ES}}{N_{TE}} \tag{9.56}$$

The first summand on the left-hand side of the formula (9.56) comprises the (yet unknown) English wage bill, and the second variable represents the (already determined) total remuneration in Portugal. The fraction on the right-hand side provides information on how many units of cloth the (sought-after) input quantity of English labour N_{ES} produces per year. The solution of Eq. (9.56) is:

$$N_{ES} = \frac{L_{PS}}{\frac{1}{N_{TE}} - w_E} \tag{9.57}$$

The formula encapsulates a central relationship: dividing labour costs in the secondary sector by the per capita surplus of the workers in the primary industry gives the number of employees involved there—an outcome to which we shall return later. The numerical evaluation of the expression (9.57) leads to:

$$N_{ES} = \frac{0,9411}{\frac{1}{100} - 0,004545} = 172.52 \tag{9.58}$$

With a given profit in both countries, employment obviously decreases over the year. As stated in the Sraffa quote above (cf. p. 152), the workforce in Portugal is diminished by ten men, but in England, the number of jobs falls not only by the twenty persons mentioned to 200. The decline is more than twice as substantial because a shrinking labour input reduces the necessary basic output at a fixed real wage rate, which in turn requires fewer workers, etc., until only 172.52 wage earners are needed. The corresponding wage bill in England (L_{ES}) is:

$$L_{ES} = w_E N_{ES} = 0.004545 \cdot 172.52 = 0.7841 \tag{9.59}$$

Employment in Portugal and England (N_S) sum up to:

$$N_S = N_{ES} + N_{PS} = 172.52 + 160 = 332.52 \tag{9.60}$$

The remuneration of staff in both countries (L_S) comes to:

$$L_S = L_{ES} + L_{PS} = 0.7841 + 0.9411 = 1.7252 \tag{9.61}$$

Of course, the combined payment in both countries corresponds to the ratio of the adjusted employment in England to the labour input there to produce a unit of cloth:

$$L_S = \frac{N_{ES}}{N_{TE}} = \frac{172.52}{100} = 1.7252 \tag{9.62}$$

The comparison with the total domestic workforces before specialisation (9.41) and (9.42) (cf. p. 124) reveals that with invariant profits and unchanged national per capita wages for those still employed, total labour input declines compared with the *status quo ante*:

$$N_S = 332.52 < N_{EA} + N_{PA} = 390 \tag{9.63}$$

In contrast to autarky, this is accompanied by a decimated aggregated wage bill:

$$L_S = 1.7252 < L_{EA} + L_{PA} = 2 \tag{9.64}$$

In the constellation under consideration with fixed profits, the international division of labour does not make anyone better off, while the situation of laid-off personnel worsens. Apparently, foreign trade, in compliance with comparative cost advantages, does not always improve living conditions for everyone involved. In such cases, economic policy is needed to counter detrimental effects. The subsequent examination of Karl Marx's economic system will also prompt a call for governmental action.

Chapter 10
Karl Marx: Essence and Appearance of the Capitalist Mode of Production

Karl Marx generally gets a rather bad press. Not only has his *oeuvre* constantly provoked "refutations" right up to the present day—albeit with cyclical fluctuations—but the recent developments in the countries that formerly constituted the Eastern Bloc appear to validate the critics. The tangible economic grievances contributed to the rust perforation of the Iron Curtain: existence *disgruntles* consciousness. This development is all too readily considered as empirical proof of the flawed nature of Marx's theory.

Marx's primary concern—which was directed towards denouncing capitalist conditions rather than conceptualising an ideal society—is often overlooked. In a manner unparalleled by his predecessors, he underscored the imperative of capitalism as a historical epoch whose task was to propel the advancement of the productive forces until the *pre*history of human society was fully realised.

> No social order is ever destroyed," Marx wrote in the famous preface to the volume "A Contribution to the Critique of Political Economy", "before all the productive forces for which it is sufficient have been developed, and new superior relations of production never replace older ones before the material conditions for their existence have matured within the framework of the old society.[1]

Although Marx proclaimed the inevitability of a revolution, recipes "... for the cookshops of the future"[2] are only rudimentary in his writings, if at all. Engels rejected such expectations immediately after the publication of the first volume of Capital:

> This book will disappoint many a reader ... many may have imagined, when at last they saw it announced, that they would now learn what the communist Millennium would actually be like. Anyone who had keenly awaited this pleasure made a great mistake ... Marx is and remains the same revolutionary he has always been, and in a scientific work he would

[1] Marx, K., A Contribution ..., op. cit., p. 21.

[2] Marx, K., Afterword to the Second German Edition, in: Capital, vol. I, op. cit., pp. 22–29, p. 26.

F. Helmedag, *Production of Commodities by Means of Labour*, Springer Studies in Alternative Economics, https://doi.org/10.1007/978-3-032-01457-3_10

> assuredly be the last to hide his views in this respect. But as for what is going to happen after the social revolution—on that he gives us only *very* dark hints.[3]

In this light, references to the practical failure of Marx's *analysis* are beside the point. No one who seriously wants to study economic theory can avoid carefully examining his critique of capitalism. However, popular expositions usually convey the fundamentals and main contents of Karl Marx's *oeuvre* superficially and incompletely.

> ... Marxian economics has developed in an erratic and uneven manner," Shaikh judges, "with only sporadic connection to Marx's own work: an equation here, a scheme of reproduction there, and a dialectical class struggle everywhere – with the holes in between filled in with whatever material was already at hand. *And this material, by and large, has been appropriated from orthodox economics.*[4]

If academically established economics says something good about Marx, it is certainly not the labour theory of value he propagated more radically than his predecessors. Even several Marxists consider it a foregone conclusion that the labour theory of value fails to explain relative prices in capitalism. However, as a theory of social circumstances and as a method for uncovering economic power relations, it is recognised by a minority:

> The labour theory of value has played two roles in Marxian economics. First it has been claimed to be, at some level of abstraction, a theory of prices. Second, the concept of embodied labour time has been used to define exploitation. In its first role, the labour theory of value is useless.[5]

Despite this widespread scepticism, the focus here is on the exchange-theoretical application of the labour theory of value,[6] not the "exploitation layer" as a socio-

---

[3] Engels, F., Review of Volume One of *Capital* for the *Düsseldorfer Zeitung*, in: Marx & Engels, Collected Works, vol. 20, pp. 216–218, p. 216, Electric Book, https://aaap.be/Pdf/Nachschlagewerke/MECW20.pdf.

[4] Shaikh, A., Neo-Ricardian Economics, A Wealth of Algebra, A Poverty of Theory, in: Review of Radical Political Economics, vol. 14 (1982), pp. 67–83, p. 67.

[5] Roemer, J. E., Value, Exploitation and Class, Chur et al. 1986, p. 2.

[6] Wolfstetter describes the view that exchange and labour value relations coincide in competitive equilibrium as a "vulgar price-theoretical" interpretation of the labour theory of value. Furthermore, he cites the normative variant, i.e., the labour theory of value would justify a right based on natural law to the 'full product of labour'. Cf. Wolfstetter, E., Wert, Mehrwert und Produktionspreis, in: Jahrbuch für Sozialwissenschaft, vol. 24 (1973), pp. 117–144, pp. 117 f. However, numerous passages in Marx – also in the third volume of Capital – point to a price-theoretical explanatory claim of the labour theory of value. Cf. Eberle, F., Methodisches zur Wert-Preis-Transformation, in: Gesellschaft, Beiträge zur Marxschen Theorie 13, Frankfurt a. M. 1979, pp. 140–173, in particular pp. 155 ff.

logical supplement to the economic price and quantity system.[7] Of course, this is neither a complete reproduction nor a critical appraisal of Karl Marx's entire system.

Marx's theory of value is reconstructed at the outset, where elements of philosophy and historical materialism in his *oeuvre* (must) take a back seat. In the second step, we deal with the reception of Marx's approach. Because of the enormous amount of literature on this topic, it is necessary to confine ourselves: it proves to be a fortunate circumstance that the discussion relevant to production price theory can be presented based on the contributions by Ladislaus v. Bortkiewicz.

As will also become apparent, the radical and consistent researcher Marx ultimately also fell victim to capitalism's *seemingly* obvious functional principles. As a result, he left his system with a breach into which his opponents could vehemently storm.

10.1 Surplus Value and Profit

A glance at the tables of contents of the three-volume "Theories of Surplus Value" suffices to give an idea of how intensively Marx studied the relevant literature. It would be a separate task to enquire whether Marx's fluctuating opinion on one writer or another is justified. The result would probably be that similarities between his view and that of the author in question would often be trivialised and differences exaggerated—a few examples concerning Smith and Ricardo follow immediately.

However, it is not uncommon for scientists to use the method of "pointed emphasis" in describing, if not warping, the statements of other researchers; even the rather prosaic Smith, whose work gives the impression of slowed enthusiasm rather than revolutionary zeal, used this method:

> In the technique – conscious or unconscious – of distorting preceded theories," Streissler bluntly states, "to ridicule them or to assimilate them with his own, *Smith* was also a master that even *Keynes* could not match.[8]

Well, this is (at least) equally true of Marx. On the one hand, Ricardo is accused of never (sic) caring about the origin of surplus value[9] and for constantly (sic) confusing

[7] In addition to Wolfstetter, Morishima, Baumol and Baisch, who have emphasised this aspect of the theory of value, should be mentioned. Cf. Morishima, M., Marx's Economics: A Dual Theory of Value and Growth, Cambridge 1973, Baumol, W. J., The Transformation of Values: What Marx "Really" Meant (An Interpretation), in: Journal of Economic Literature, vol. 12 (1974), pp. 51–62, Baisch, H., Wert, Preis und Allokation, Eine Verallgemeinerung des Marxschen Reproduktionsmodells, Meisenheim am Glan 1976. Petry, F., Der soziale Gehalt der Marxschen Werttheorie, Jena 1916, already championed this view. Petry's contribution is partly reprinted in: Nutzinger, H. G., Wolfstetter, E. (eds.), Die Marxsche Theorie und ihre Kritik, vol. I, Frankfurt a. M. / New York 1974, pp. 197–228.

[8] Streißler, E., Adam Smith – Der Adam oder nur Wachstum? Paradoxien einer wissenschaftlichen Revolution, in: Neumark, F. (ed.), Studien zur Entwicklung der ökonomischen Theorie I, Berlin 1980, pp. 9–52, p. 12. [F. H.]

[9] Cf. Marx, K., Capital, vol. I, op. cit., p. 483.

the value of the commodity with the cost of production (insofar as this is equal to the cost price),[10] but at least Ricardo *suspects* the discrepancy.[11] On the other hand, Marx praises his historical achievement to the skies:

> But at last Ricardo steps in and calls to science: Halt! The basis, the starting-point for the physiology of the bourgeois system – for the understanding of its internal organic coherence and life process – is the determination of *value by labour-time*. Ricardo starts with this and forces science to get out of the rut ...[12]

The above outline of Ricardo's theory of value and its origins casts doubts on whether Marx's characterisation of Ricardo's approach and intention is accurate: Ricardo's preoccupation with the theory of value was rather imposed on him from outside. Later, it seems, he felt that the labour theory of value was almost like a ball and chain he would have liked to get rid of. The motive for Marx's lavish praise is apparent; he was elevating his own concept with Ricardo. In *Marx*'s opinion, the knowledge of the dependence of value on labour time provides the necessary magnifying glass to decipher the nature of the capitalist mode of production:

> The final pattern of economic relations as seen on the surface, in their real existence and consequently in the conceptions by which the bearers and agents of these relations seek to understand them, is very much different from, and indeed quite the reverse of, their inner but concealed essential pattern and the conception corresponding to it.[13]

In compliance with this fundamental principle, which guides the acquisition of knowledge, it is imperative to ascertain the relationship between surplus value and profit: "Surplus-value and rate of surplus-value are, relatively, the invisible and unknown essence that wants investigating, while rate of profit and therefore the appearance of surplus-value in the form of profit are revealed on the surface of the phenomenon."[14] Tracing this change in the form of surplus value establishes political economy as an academic discipline: "But all science would be superfluous if the outward appearance and the essence of things directly coincided."[15]

The focal point of Marx's enquiry is the commodity, which epitomises the fundamental constituent of wealth within capitalist societies.[16] He proceeds to delineate the dichotomy between use value and exchange value, positing that use values constitute the material substructure of wealth, irrespective of prevailing social conditions. Nevertheless, what can be ascertained regarding the exchange value?

According to Marx, if two commodities are considered equivalent in trade, a common factor of the same magnitude must exist in the two entities: "Each of them, so

[10] Cf. Marx, K., Theories ..., Part III, op. cit., p. 79.

[11] Cf. ibid., p. 71, own emphasis.

[12] Marx, K., Theories ..., Part II, op. cit., p. 166.

[13] Marx, K., Capital, vol. III, The Process of Capitalist Production as a Whole [1894], ed. by Engels, F., Moscow 1959, p. 205, https://archive.org/details/capital-vol.-3/page/205/mode/2up.

[14] Ibid., p. 43.

[15] Ibid., p. 797.

[16] Cf. Marx, K., Capital, vol. I, op. cit., p. 43.

far as it is exchange-value, must therefore be reducible to this third."[17] The common ground, therefore, cannot be considered a physical property of the objects; in the allocation process, incommensurable use values are exchanged. Thus, Marx asserts that the general characterisation of commodities as products of individual labour remains. The act of equating these commodities in exchange eliminates the disparities inherent in the specific activities involved:

> Let us now consider the residue of each of these products; it consists of the same unsubstantial reality in each, a mere congelation of homogeneous human labour, of labour-power expended without regard to the mode of its expenditure. All that these things now tell us is, that human labour-power has been expended in their production, that human labour is embodied in them. When looked at as crystals of this social substance, common to them all, they are – Values.[18]

From today's perspective, Marx's approach to deriving the concept of value in this way appears (at the very least) clumsy. A whole army of critics has pounced on the operations Marx used to distil labour as the substance of value at the beginning of his *magnum opus*. Of course, you must know wherefrom you are abstracting whereto; the result is evident from the outset. The way there seems contrived, and one could have taken other forks. Böhm-Bawerk saw Marx's filtering process as "the most vulnerable point in the Marxian theory", a "great error of method",[19] and many adopted this verdict, albeit usually with less command of language.

This detour led the debate onto a side track because several misunderstandings are based on the *working hypothesis*, which Marx does not sufficiently emphasise in the first volume of Capital, only to throw it finally overboard in the third. Instead, he formulates the "law of value" quite early and without further comment: "The value of one commodity is to the value of any other, as the labour-time necessary for the production of the one is to that necessary for the production of the other."[20] This statement, often found in the first volume, is only qualified in passing:

> How can we account for the origin of capital on the supposition that prices are regulated by the average price, i. e., ultimately by the value of the commodities? I say 'ultimately,' because average prices do not directly coincide with the values of commodities, as Adam Smith, Ricardo, and others believe.[21]

Apart from the fact that the content of the assertion is incorrect—as we have seen, the divergence of prices from labour values caused Ricardo quite a headache—explanations pointing in this direction should have been made earlier and in greater detail. Besides, almost thirty years had passed until Engels published the third volume of "Capital". It would have been even more helpful to tell the public right at the beginning of the first volume that, in the author's usage, the value of a commodity coincides with its *labour value*, whereas the relationship between labour value and production price will be addressed subsequently.

---

[17] Ibid., p. 45.

[18] Ibid., p. 46.

[19] Cf. Böhm-Bawerk, E. v., Karl Marx and the Close of his System [1896], ed. by Sweezy, P. M., New York 1949, https://mises.org/library/book/karl-marx-and-close-his-system.

[20] Marx, K., Capital, vol. I, op. cit., p. 47.

[21] Ibid., p. 163 n.

This warning would not have detracted from Marx's research efforts. Of course, it is legitimate to tackle the great mystery of the capitalist mode of production—where does profit come from, despite the apparent congruence between marketable performance and money consideration?—in a first attempt under the simplifying assumption that commodities are exchanged according to their (labour) values. If it had not even been possible to explain the source of profit under these circumstances, the project would have had no chance of success right from the start.

In fact, Marx adhered to the programme just outlined. In the first volume, he examines the origin of profit, supposing the exchange relations of commodities correspond to the average amount of labour expended in their production.[22] First, he excludes the possibility that profit arises from circulation. By exchanging non-equivalents, one gains what the other loses: "The capitalist class, as a whole, in any country, cannot over-reach themselves."[23] The solution to the riddle is to be found in the sphere of production. It is a matter of discovering a commodity producing more value in its "productive consumption" than is necessary for its production, ...

> ... a commodity, whose use-value possesses the peculiar property of being a source of value, whose actual consumption, therefore, is itself an embodiment of labour, and, consequently, a creation of value. The possessor of money does find on the market such a special commodity in capacity for labour or labour-power.[24]

Since labour power is a commodity among commodities, it is also true that its value is measured by the labour socially necessary for its (re)production. The basket of goods that workers receive to maintain their labour power expresses a "historical and cultural moment" and includes the food of the "substitutes", i.e., the workers' children.[25] As a *conditio sine qua non* for the transformation of money into capital ...

> ... the owner of money must meet in the market with the free labourer, free in the double sense, that as a free man he can dispose of his labour-power as his own commodity, and that on the other hand he has no other commodity for sale, is short of everything necessary for the realisation of his labour-power ...[26]

The dissociation of the proletarian from the conditions to realise his labour power causes the antagonism between wage labour and capital:

> The process, therefore, that clears the way for the capitalist system, can be none other than the process which takes away from the labourer the possession of his means of production; a process that transforms, on the one hand, the social means of subsistence and of production into capital, on the other, the immediate producers into wage-labourers. The so-called

[22] "The exchange, or sale, of commodities at their value is the rational state of affairs," Marx explains (not earlier than) in the third volume, "i.e., the natural law of their equilibrium. It is this law that explains the deviations, and not vice versa, the deviations that explain the law." Marx, K., Capital, vol. III, op. cit., p. 184.

[23] Marx, K., Capital, vol. I, op. cit., p. 160.

[24] Ibid., p. 164.

[25] Cf. ibid., p. 168.

[26] Ibid., p. 166. Cf. also ibid., p. 668 f.

> primitive accumulation, therefore, is nothing else than the historical process of divorcing the producer from the means of production. It appears as primitive, because it forms the pre-historic stage of capital and of the mode of production corresponding with it.[27]

This division means that the labourer must work over and above the "necessary labour time" to reproduce the value of his labour power. In the additional working hours, "surplus labour time" is performed:

> It is every bit as important, for a correct understanding of surplus value, to conceive it as a mere congelation of surplus labour-time, as nothing but materialised surplus-labour, as it is, for a proper comprehension of value, to conceive it as a mere congelation of so many hours of labour, as nothing but materialised labour. The essential difference between the various economic forms of society, between, for instance, a society based on slave-labour, and one based on wage labour, lies only in the mode in which this surplus-labour is in each case extracted from the actual producer, the labourer.[28]

Excess work is not an invention of capital.[29] It exists in all societies as soon as labour has reached a certain level of productivity:

> If the labourer wants all his time to produce the necessary means of subsistence for himself and his race, he has no time left in which to work gratis for others. Without a certain degree of productiveness in his labour, he has no such superfluous time at his disposal; without such superfluous time, no surplus-labour. and therefore no capitalists, no slave-owners, no feudal lords ... It is only after men have raised themselves above the rank of animals, when therefore their labour has been to some extent socialised, that a state of things arises in which the surplus-labour of the one becomes a condition of existence for the other.[30]

In the earlier cultures oriented towards use value, more or less "external" needs limit excess hours. By contrast, in societies dominated by the acquisitive drive, the "greed for surplus labour" becomes irrepressible.[31] Besides, another aspect deserves attention.

In past eras, extra work was visible to the naked eye—just think of the feudal services—but this phenomenon is not readily apparent under capitalism. Here, it must be unveiled that unpaid overtime is systematically performed despite the seeming exchange of equivalents between employee and employer. According to Marx, the concept of *labour power* was the decisive breakthrough, allowing the look behind the scenes: surplus labour generates surplus value, and the source of profit appears to have been localised.

"The Ricardian school suffered shipwreck about the year 1830 on the rock of surplus-value", Engels laconically records in the preface to the second volume of Capital[32]; Marx, on the other hand, by differentiating between labour and labour power had solved "with one stroke" one of the difficulties responsible for the decline

[27] Ibid., p. 668.

[28] Ibid., p. 209.

[29] Cf. ibid., p. 226.

[30] Ibid., p. 479.

[31] Cf. ibid., p. 226 ff.

[32] Engels, F., Preface to Marx, K., Capital, vol. II, op. cit., pp. 1–20, p. 18.

namely "... the impossibility of harmonising the mutual exchange of capital and labour with the Ricardian law that value is determined by labour."[33] At this point, we will not go into further detail as to whether this concept was as new as Marxists like to claim—in terms of content, Smith's distinction between *labour embodied* and *labour commanded* (cf. p. 105 f.), e.g., amounts to the same thing[34]—what is essential here is to assess what has been accomplished so far.

> "Every condition of the problem is satisfied," Marx triumphs in the first volume, "while the laws that regulate the exchange of commodities, have been in no way violated."[35] However, this success message only refers to the questions that were asked at the time. In the introduction to the second volume of Capital, Engels again explained what still had to be done. "In actual fact," he remarks, "equal capitals, regardless of how much or how little living labour is employed by them, produce equal average profits in equal times. Here there is therefore a contradiction of the law of value ..."[36] Against the background of this inconsistency, later often referred to as the 'price puzzle', Engels called on Marx's critics to present a solution which reveals "... in which way an equal average rate of profit can and must come about, not only without a violation of the law of value, but on the very basis of it ..."[37]

The springboard for the solution to the problem proposed by Marx (or Engels?) in the third volume of Capital is Marx's breakdown of the value of a commodity into three components:

$$W = c + v + s \tag{10.1}$$

W symbolises the total labour value of a commodity under consideration, c is "constant capital", i.e., the value of the consumed means of production and raw materials, and v represents "variable capital".[38] In contrast to constant capital, the part of capital v that is transformed into labour power changes its value in the production process. The performed work not only reproduces as "necessary labour" the value of labour power v, but also creates surplus value s.[39] Of course, all quantities in formula (10.1) must be expressed in the same units—here: labour time per unit of the good—otherwise, using the plus sign on the right-hand side would be inadmissible.

---

[33] Ibid., p. 17.

[34] Though Marx judges "Adam Smith is superior to Ricardo", he criticises that Smith "... does not distinguish surplus-value as such as a category on its own, distinct from the specific forms it assumes in profit and rent. This is the source of much error and inadequacy in his inquiry, and of even more in the work of Ricardo." Marx, K., Theories of Surplus Value, Part I, Moscow 1963, p. 81 and 82, https://archive.org/details/marxtsvpart1.

[35] Marx, K., Capital, vol. I, op. cit., p. 189.

[36] Engels, F., Preface ..., op. cit., p. 18.

[37] Ibid.

[38] In Capital, vol. III, op. cit., p. 25, the letter C symbolises the labour value of a commodity. But on p. 49 and on p. 204 in the first volume of Capital, C stands for the sum of constant and variable capital: $C = c + v$. To avoid misunderstandings, we use W for the labour value of a commodity, as in the German edition of the first volume. Cf. Marx, K., Das Kapital, vol. I, Der Produktionsprozess des Kapitals [1867], in: Marx Engels Werke, vol. 23, Berlin 1977, p. 34.

[39] Cf. Marx, K., Capital, vol. I, op. cit., p. 201.

However, violations of this elementary requirement for dimensional consistency are often encountered, which we shall criticise when the opportunity arises.

As stated by Marx, "unpaid labour" can increase for two reasons:

> The surplus-value produced by prolongation of the working-day, I call *absolute surplus-value*. On the other hand, the surplus-value arising from the curtailment of the necessary labour-time, and from the corresponding alteration in the respective lengths of the two components of the working-day, I call *relative surplus-value*.[40]

If the surplus value is related to the variable capital, the result is the rate of surplus value $\frac{s}{v}$, which Marx abbreviates as s'.[41] This pure percentage serves him as a measure of exploitation.

Since, in Marx's conception, the entire surplus value of an economy constitutes its profit, it seems clear "... that the average profit can be nothing but the total mass of surplus-values allotted to the various quantities of capital proportionally to their magnitudes in the different spheres of production."[42] Marx defines the rate of profit (*p*') as follows[43]:

$$p' = \frac{s}{c + v} \tag{10.2}$$

Marx believes this profit rate is adopted to form production prices. However, the symbolism is not entirely clear. If profit accrues in proportion to the *total* capital advanced, formula (10.2) can only be correct if *c* includes all components of constant capital. Indeed, Marx is conscious of the discrepancy between fixed and circulating constant capital:

> Portion c of the value, representing the constant capital *consumed* in production, does not coincide with the value of the constant capital *employed* in production. True, the materials of production are entirely consumed and their values completely transferred to the product. But only a portion of the employed *fixed* capital is wholly consumed and its value thus transferred to the product. Another part of the fixed capital, such as machines, buildings, etc., continues to exist and function the same as before, though depreciated to the extent of the annual wear and tear.[44]

The "cost price" category developed by Marx also contains, in addition to the variable capital *v*, only that part of the constant capital passed on to the product.[45] In his examples of converting surplus value into profit, he also explicitly distinguishes between the constant capital advanced as a whole and the constant capital consumed.[46] But the rate of profit is always calculated on constant capital *in all*. Thus, *c* in (10.2) does not always merely symbolise the circulating portion of constant capital.

---

[40] Ibid., p. 299.

[41] Cf. Marx, K., Capital, vol. III, op. cit., p. 49.

[42] Marx, K., Capital, vol. III, op. cit., p. 174.

[43] Cf. Marx, K., Capital, vol. I, op. cit., p. 490 and Marx, K., Capital, vol. III, p. 49.

[44] Marx, K., Capital, vol. II, op. cit., p. 400.

[45] Cf. Marx, K., Capital, vol. III, op. cit., p. 33.

[46] Cf. ibid., p. 155 f.

Then, however, serious dimensional problems arise: if s and v are related to a *period*, e.g., a working day, no stock variable for the fixed constant capital dated to a specific *point in time* can be added to the necessary labour v in the denominator of the profit rate Eq. (10.2).

To be sure, the treatment of fixed capital is more complex than Marx believed—we shall delve into this problem later. In the first instance, the difficulty mentioned is cleared away by assuming there is no fixed but only circulating constant capital, which, needless to say, turns over entirely in the period under consideration.

In deriving production prices, Marx assumes an equal rate of surplus value in all branches of the economy[47]; the individual sectors should generate the same surplus value relative to the respective variable capital:

> Such a general rate of surplus value – viewed as a tendency, like all other economic laws – has been assumed by us for the sake of theoretical simplification. But in reality it is an actual premise of the capitalist mode of production, although it is more or less obstructed by practical frictions ... But in theory it is assumed that the laws of capitalist production operate in their pure form. In reality there exists only approximation; but, this approximation is the greater, the more developed the capitalist mode of production and the less it is adulterated and amalgamated with survivals of former economic conditions.[48]

The distribution of profit takes place in proportion to the total capital input $c + v$. The surplus value that morphs into profit, on the other hand, accrues depending on the respective labour expended v. Thus, a producer who employs a relatively large share of direct labour would enjoy a high individual profit rate, while an entrepreneur who uses a relatively large portion of constant capital ought to settle for a lower profit rate.

> If a capital, consisting in per cent of 90 c + 10 v," Marx illustrates the dilemma, "produced as much surplus-value, or profit, at the same degree of exploitation as a capital consisting of 10 c + 90 v, it would be as plain as day that the surplus-value, and thus value in general, must have an entirely different source than labour, and that political economy would then be deprived of every rational basis.[49]

Knowing the source of profit, in Marx's eyes, it did not seem particularly difficult to bridge the gap between value and price calculation: he determined the overall economic average profit rate by dividing the sum of surplus values (S) by the aggregates of constant (C) and variable capital (V). According to Marx, in a competitive equilibrium, the individual profit rate must be equal to the average profit rate:

$$p' = \frac{S}{C + V} \tag{10.3}$$

---

[47] Cf. ibid. p. 154 ff.

[48] Ibid., p. 175.

[49] Ibid., p. 149. Of course, the values in the commodity value formula (10.1) (cf. p. 165) can differ in individual cases. Therefore, strictly speaking, the symbols should bear an index related to the respective good under consideration.

The profit rate p' determined in this way must also be a pure number due to the required dimensional homogeneity of the variables on the right-hand side of the formula (10.3).

In Marx's system, particularly in connection with "The Law of the Tendency of the Rate of Profit to Fall", discussed in the third part of the third volume of Capital, the "organic composition of capital" assumes a prominent position. This quantity, in turn, is based on the "technical composition of capital", by which Marx understands "... the mass of the means of production employed, on the one hand, and the mass of labour necessary for their employment on the other."[50] After disclosing the labour embodied in the numerator and denominator, the result is the ratio of "dead" to "living" labour.

The microeconomic organic composition of capital is denoted by $q\left(\equiv \frac{c}{v}\right)$.[51] The macroeconomic organic composition of capital is abbreviated as $Q\left(\equiv \frac{C}{V}\right)$. If we divide the numerator and denominator of the right-hand side of Eq. (10.3) by V, we obtain the dimensionless rate of profit, since the result again contains only pure numbers:

$$p' = \frac{s'}{Q+1} \tag{10.4}$$

Now, we can trace the relationship between value and price. If we symbolise the price of a unit of a good by Π, the first result is:

$$\Pi = (c+v)(1+p') \tag{10.5}$$

The rearrangement of this price equation gives:

$$\begin{aligned}\Pi &= c+v+(c+v)\left(\frac{s'}{Q+1}\right) = c+v+\frac{s'c+s}{Q+1} = c+v+\frac{s(q+1)}{Q+1} = \\ &= W + s\left(\frac{q+1}{Q+1} - 1\right) = W + \frac{s}{Q+1}(q-Q)\end{aligned}$$

And thus:

$$\Pi = W + p'v(q-Q) \tag{10.6}$$

The price is higher than the labour value if the individual organic composition of capital exceeds the macroeconomic composition; if smaller, the price falls short of the value. In exceptional situations where the individual organic composition of

[50] Cf. Marx, K., Capital, vol. I, op. cit., p. 574. Obviously, "the mass of the means of production" is not a homogeneous aggregate but a (fictitious) list of all fixed capital components, such as buildings and machines.

[51] Again, indexing the respective constant and variable capitals would be appropriate.

capital coincides with the average one, no gap occurs between the labour value and the production price.

Marx does not use an expression corresponding to the formula (10.6).[52] Nevertheless, the founder of scientific socialism provides a numerical example in which differences between values and prices emerge.[53] There can be no question of a correct solution to the price puzzle, as Engels claimed. In the usual case, a uniform average rate of profit ostensibly only establishes itself when the law of value is *violated*.

However, Marx's transformation method guarantees the validity of two "invariance postulates" of his theory: on one side, the added profits of the branches of production are equal to the added surplus values; on the other side, the prices of production as a whole correspond to the total amount of values.[54] The secret of profit seems to have been revealed: it does not arise from a price surcharge—the sum of values is identical to that of prices—but is, in fact, surplus value—surplus value in a misleading disguise[55]:

> The actual difference of magnitude between profit and surplus-value – not merely between the rate of profit and the rate of surplus-value – in the various spheres of production now completely conceals the true nature and origin of profit not only from the capitalist, who has a special interest in deceiving himself on this score, but also from the labourer.[56]

Shortly afterwards, it says:

> 'The individual capitalist ... whose outlook is limited, rightly believes that his profit is not derived solely from the labour employed by him, or in his line of production. This is quite true, as far as his average profit is concerned. To what extent this profit is due to the aggregate exploitation of labour on the part of the total social capital, i.e., by all his capitalist colleagues – this interrelation is a complete mystery to the individual capitalist; all the more so, since no bourgeois theorists, the political economists, have so far revealed it.[57]

It cannot be doubted that Marx's analysis, if it were tenable, would represent an unparalleled advance in the basic research of economic theory. But it collapses in the form of how Marx couched it. And he at least suspected the inadequacy of his transformation method; his "cost price" $c + v$ never became a *price*; it remains in the sphere of value:

> But for the buyer the price of production of a specific commodity is its cost-price, and may thus pass as cost-price into the prices of other commodities. Since the price of production may differ from the value of a commodity, it follows that the cost-price of a commodity

---

[52] Bortkiewicz derives a similar relationship, but he operates with a q whose denominator is $c + v$. Cf. Bortkiewicz, L. v., Wertrechnung und Preisrechnung im Marxschen System, in: Archiv für Sozialwissenschaft und Sozialpolitik, vol. 24 (1907), pp. 10–51, pp. 13 f. (This is the second of three articles published in 1906/7. An English translation of the second and third articles is available under the title "Value and Price in the Marxian System", http://gesd.free.fr/bortk7b.pdf.

[53] Cf. Marx, K., Capital, vol. III, op. cit., p. 156 f. The literature provides numerous other examples. A particularly simple one presents Napoleoni, C., op. cit., p. 184 ff.

[54] Cf. Marx, K., Capital, vol. III, op. cit., p. 155 ff. and p. 173.

[55] Cf. ibid., p. 36.

[56] Ibid., p. 168.

[57] Ibid., p. 170.

> containing this price of production of another commodity may also stand above or below that portion of its total value derived from the value of the means of production consumed by it. It is necessary to remember this modified significance of the cost-price, and to bear in mind that there is always the possibility of an error if the cost-price of a commodity in any particular sphere is identified with the value of the means of production consumed by it. Our present analysis does not necessitate a closer examination of this point.[58]

Even later, Marx refrained from elaborating on this aspect, although he had noticed where the cause of the problem came from:

> The whole difficulty arises from the fact that *commodities* are not exchanged simply as commodities, but as *products of capitals*, which claim participation in the total amount of surplus-value, proportional to their magnitude, or equal if they are of equal magnitude.[59]

Marx's transformation of values into prices is ultimately not a conversion at all: his prices are merely corrected *labour values*, and the promised expedition to the surface gets stuck halfway. However, the formal turbulence can be removed. Indeed, Marx himself indicates how a correct transformation ought to happen. To achieve the goal, the fact should be considered that …

> … under capitalist production the elements of productive capital are, as a rule, bought on the market, and that for this reason their prices include profit which has already been realised, hence, include the price of production of the respective branch of industry together with the profit contained in it, so that the profit of one branch of industry goes into the cost-price of another.[60]

Such a procedure paves the way for a reappraisal of the problem within the "production of commodities by means of commodities" framework. The question is what then remains of Marx's theory of value—it will be far more than commonly admitted.

10.2 From Value to Price and Back Again

The relevant publications of Ladislaus v. Bortkiewicz provided the decisive breakthrough towards a positive critique of Marx's system. He sees "the useful and truly significant aspect of Marx's (but also Ricardo's) system" in the perception "… that labour or 'surplus labour' is the sole originator of capital profit."[61]

---

[58] Ibid., p. 164 f., see also p. 207.

[59] Ibid., p. 175.

[60] Ibid., p. 160.

[61] Bortkiewicz, L. v., Wertrechnung und Preisrechnung im Marxschen System, in: Archiv für Sozialwissenschaft und Sozialpolitik, vol. 23 (1906), pp. 1–50, p. 50. [F. H.] This first article in a series of three mainly deals with the contemporary reception of Marx. Bortkiewicz presents his analytical investigations primarily in the second and third article (see p. 170, n. 52) and in a paper entitled: Zur Berichtigung der grundlegenden theoretischen Konstruktion von Marx im dritten Band des „Kapital ", in: Jahrbücher für Nationalökonomie und Statistik, vol. 34 (1907), pp. 319–335. 86 years later, a critical examination of the article appeared in the same journal. Cf. Helmedag, F., Zur Berechtigung der grundlegenden theoretischen Konstruktion von Marx im ersten Band des "Kapital", in:

Bortkiewicz also reproaches Marx's opponents for taking the easy way out by merely repeating Marx's own doctrine, according to which price and value only match in rare cases.[62] Instead, whether a correct derivation of production prices from values would be possible must be examined. Bortkiewicz has taken on this task. The following section is devoted to his propagated transformation of labour values into production prices. However, his proposal does not enjoy a monopoly position: as is subsequently shown, there is a more powerful alternative in every respect among the competitors.

10.2.1 *The Contribution by Ladislaus v. Bortkiewicz*

In his analysis, Bortkiewicz assumes a stationary three-sector economy in which the entire constant capital turns over in one period.[63] In department I, the means of production are produced, department II manufactures the workers' consumer goods, and department III makes the capitalists' luxury goods. The rate of surplus value s' is uniform in all sectors.[64] With "simple reproduction"—input and output coincide in the aggregate—the economy is structured as follows:

$$c_1 + v_1 + s_1 = c_1 + v_1(1 + s') = c_1 + c_2 + c_3 \tag{10.7}$$

$$c_2 + v_2 + s_2 = c_2 + v_2(1 + s') = v_1 + v_2 + v_3 \tag{10.8}$$

$$c_3 + v_3 + s_3 = c_3 + v_3(1 + s') = m_1 + m_2 + m_3 \tag{10.9}$$

The "trick" to getting to the price calculation is to include the relationships of values to prices as unknowns in the system and then solve it. Bortkiewicz writes x as the ratio of the price to the value of the goods produced in industry I; y and z stand analogously for the corresponding relations in departments II and III, respectively.[65] ρ symbolises the profit rate in the following system of equations, C, V and S again figure as the

---

Jahrbücher für Nationalökonomie und Statistik, vol. 212 (1993), pp. 442–450. This contribution is based on the following deliberations.

[62] Cf. Bortkiewicz, L. v., Wertrechnung ..., Erster Artikel, op. cit., p. 5.

[63] Cf. also Bortkiewicz, L. v., Zur Berichtigung ..., op. cit., p. 319 ff. English translation: "On the Correction of Marx's Fundamental Theoretical Construction in the Third Volume of *Capital*", in: Böhm-Bawerk, E. v., Karl Marx and the Close of his System [1896], ed. by Sweezy, P. M., New York 1949, pp.199–221, https://mises.org/library/book/karl-marx-and-close-his-system. In the following, references are to this source.

[64] The symbols used here essentially correspond to those of Marx. Bortkiewicz sometimes employs other abbreviations.

[65] In his outline of Bortkiewicz's approach, Pasinetti mistakenly multiplies the labour values by the respective prices. However, the magnitudes x, y, and z reflect the *relationships* between prices and values, so labour time units cancel out. Cf. Pasinetti, L., Lectures ..., op. cit., p. 23.

aggregates of the variable and constant capitals as well as the surplus values:

$$(1+\rho)(c_1x+v_1y)=Cx \tag{10.10}$$

$$(1+\rho)(c_2x+v_2y)=Vy \tag{10.11}$$

$$(1+\rho)(c_3x+v_3y)=Sz \tag{10.12}$$

In his approach, Bortkiewicz shares the classical hypothesis advocated by Marx and others that profits accrue proportionally to the sectoral total capital in equilibrium. However, because the assessment bases differ, the price-oriented Bortkiewicz profit rate ρ is no longer the same as Marx's labour value-related profit rate p'.
The three Eqs. (10.10–10.12) contain four unknowns x, y, z andρ. Bortkiewicz eliminates the degree of freedom by assuming that the price unit is identical to the value unit. In addition, the good that serves as the price measure (e.g., gold) is produced in division III. Therefore, $z \equiv 1$ applies *by definition.* Bortkiewicz introduces abbreviations to make the formulas shorter:

$$\frac{v_1}{c_1}\equiv f_1,\quad \frac{v_1+c_1+s_1}{c_1}\equiv g_1$$

$$\frac{v_2}{c_2}\equiv f_2,\quad \frac{v_2+c_2+s_2}{c_2}\equiv g_2$$

$$\frac{v_3}{c_3}\equiv f_3,\quad \frac{v_3+c_3+s_3}{c_3}\equiv g_3$$

If we further write σ for $(1+\rho)$, the system (10.10–10.12) boils down to:

$$\sigma(x+f_1y)=g_1x \tag{10.13}$$

$$\sigma(x+f_2y)=g_2y \tag{10.14}$$

$$\sigma(x+f_3y)=g_3 \tag{10.15}$$

(10.13) gives:

$$x=\frac{f_1y\sigma}{g_1-\sigma} \tag{10.16}$$

Substituting this outcome for x in (10.14), we obtain a quadratic expression:

$$(f_1-f_2)\sigma^2+(f_2g_1+g_2)\sigma-g_1g_2=0 \tag{10.17}$$

Bortkiewicz shows that there is only one solution for a non-negative σ:

$$\sigma = \frac{-(f_2 g_1 + g_2) + \sqrt{(f_2 g_1 + g_2)^2 + 4(f_1 - f_2) g_1 g_2}}{2(f_1 - f_2)} \tag{10.18a}$$

To prove this, Bortkiewicz rearranges Eq. (10.18a). He multiplies the numerator and denominator on the right-hand side by (– 1) and simplifies the discriminant:

$$\sigma = \frac{f_2 g_1 + g_2 - \sqrt{(g_2 - f_2 g_1)^2 + 4 f_1 g_1 g_2}}{2(f_2 - f_1)} \tag{10.18b}$$

Bortkiewicz then considers two cases.[66] For $f_1 - f_2 > 0$ would $\sigma < 0$ result if there were a minus sign in front of the root in (10.18a). When $f_1 - f_2 < 0$ applies and ignoring the last summand in the discriminant, a plus sign in front of the root in (10.18b) leads to:

$$\sigma > \frac{g_2}{f_2 - f_1} \tag{10.19}$$

It follows *a fortiori*:

$$\sigma > \frac{g_2}{f_2} \tag{10.20}$$

However, (10.20) contradicts Eq. (10.14), from which the relation

$$\sigma < \frac{g_2}{f_2} \tag{10.21}$$

can be inferred. The expressions (10.18a) and (10.18b) therefore provide a positive σ.

Equations (10.14) and (10.15) now enable us to calculate y:

$$y = \frac{g_3}{g_2 + (f_3 - f_2)\sigma} \tag{10.22}$$

Finally, after inserting σ and y in (10.16), the value of x is obtained. The value-price ratios and the profit rate are found.

Bortkiewicz also proves that the rate of profit determined by (10.18a) or (10.18b) is—with one exception—*lower* than the rate of surplus value.[67] This theorem later caused a sensation—in the context of n-dimensional models—as the "fundamental

[66] Cf. Bortkiewicz, L. v., On the correction …, op. cit., p. 203.

[67] Cf. Bortkiewicz, L. v., On the Correction, … op. cit., p. 217 f. The constellation in which the rate of profit corresponds to the rate of surplus value plays an essential role in what follows.

theorem of Marx's theory". In modern literature, it is called the Morishima-Okishio-Seton theorem[68]—probably due to a lack of knowledge in the history of economic thought. The tenet states that profit can only occur if there is exploitation, i.e., the rate of profit is only positive if the rate of surplus value is positive, too. However, the quantitative relationship between the two ratios is unknown: "But 1 and 2 are positive like 1 and 10 000"[69]—this argument will be discussed shortly.

Equation (10.17) is of particular interest: it reveals that the profit rate is determined *exclusively* by the production conditions in sectors I and II.

> "...this result is hardly surprising," Bortkiewicz remarks, "from the point of view of the theory of profit which sees the origin of profit in 'surplus labour.' Ricardo had already taught that a change in the relations of production which touches only such goods as do not enter into the consumption of the working class cannot affect the height of the rate of profit."[70]

Bortkiewicz's deduction is indeed based on the requirements of simple reproduction expressed in labour values, i.e., Eqs. (10.7–10.9) (cf. p. 144). Yet the rate of profit could also be obtained from the scheme (10.10–10.12), even without recourse to a stationary economy: no variables of division III appear in the derived formula for the rate of profit either.[71] With the conversion of values into prices recommended by Bortkiewicz, a gap between Marx's and Ricardo's theory seems to be closed. A central, if not the most crucial, finding of Ricardo's research was that profit is solely determined in the wage-goods industry, thus regulating the overall economic rate of profit.

In Marx's system, however, only the rate of surplus value depends on the real wage and the state of the productive forces in the wage goods industry, i.e., on the ratio of surplus labour to necessary labour. But Marx includes the capitals of all sectors in the formation of the average rate of profit. As a result, a change in capital in the luxury goods industry influences the general rate of profit. Based on this

---

[68] Cf. Morishima, M., Seton, F., Aggregation in Leontief Matrices and the Labor Theory of Value, in: Econometrica, vol. 29 (1961), pp. 203–220, Okishio, N., A Mathematical Note on Marxian Theorems, in: Weltwirtschaftliches Archiv, vol. 91 (1963), pp. 287–299. The classification of this finding as fundamental comes from Morishima; in his opinion, it is "... the heart and soul of Marxian philosophy, since it implies that exploitation is necessary for the continued existence of a capitalist economy ..." Morishima, M., Marx's Economics, op. cit., p. 6.

[69] Cogoy, M., Wertstruktur und Preisstruktur, Die Bedeutung der linearen Produktionstheorie für die Kritik der politischen Ökonomie, Frankfurt a. M. 1977, p. 37. [F. H.) Incidentally, Bortkiewicz's result is more precise. He not only determines the sign of the rate of surplus value and the rate of profit – as has become customary today – but also makes a statement regarding their order. Morishima, M., Seton, F., op. cit., p. 209, also comment on the ranking: "... the rate of exploitation will always *exceed* the rate of profit ...".

[70] Bortkiewicz, L. v., On the correction ..., op. cit., p. 209. Elsewhere, Bortkiewicz has presented an algebraic solution to the price problem, which he, by his own admission, "essentially adopted from a paper by W. K. Dmitrieff". [F. H.] In this framework, the price of a commodity can be traced back equally to its production technique and to that of the commodity labour power. Cf. Bortkiewicz, L. v., Wertrechnung ..., Zweiter Artikel, op. cit., p. 34 f.

[71] Cf. Winternitz, J., Values and Prices: A Solution of the So-Called Transformation Problem, in: The Economic Journal, vol. 58 (1948), pp. 276–280, p. 279.

Table 10.1 Value calculation

Department of production	Constant capital	Variable capital	Surplus value	Value of products
I	225	90	60	375
II	100	120	80	300
III	50	90	60	200
I–III	375	300	200	875

Table 10.2 ρ- or Bortkiewicz-prices

Department of production	Constant capital	Variable capital	Profit	Price of product
I	288	96	96	480
II	128	128	64	320
III	64	96	40	200
I–III	480	320	200	1000

assessment, Marx often criticised Ricardo, who conflated the surplus value rate with the profit rate. Since Bortkiewicz has shown that the "correct" rate of profit arises in departments I and II, Ricardo's core idea comes to light again; Marx's criticism seems obsolete. Moreover, Marx's doctrine appears unfavourable when viewed from another perspective.

Bortkiewicz's correction suggests that Marx's assertion regarding the congruence of the total amount of values and the sum of prices is no longer generally valid. This discrepancy can best be illustrated by a numerical example, which will also serve to examine Bortkiewicz's price calculation critically. The labour values are given in Table 10.1, overleaf.[72]

The criteria for simple reproduction are met, the row totals match the column totals. The uniform rate of surplus is $s' = \frac{2}{3}$. With the help of the appropriate formulas, one gets $\sigma = \frac{5}{4}$, $\rho = \frac{1}{4}$, $y = 1.0\overline{6}$ and $x = \frac{32}{25} = 1.28$.

Table 10.2 shows the ρ- or "Bortkiewicz-prices" calculated with the above variables. Since we shall learn about other pricing methods, it makes sense to distinguish the individual alternatives by the name of the appertaining author.

The ρ-prices guarantee reproduction: the aggregated input prices equal the corresponding output values.

As a matter of interest, let us look at Table 10.3, where the p'- or "Marx-prices" are displayed. With the present data, Marx would have obtained $p' = \frac{200}{675} = \frac{8}{27} = 0.\overline{296}$ according to formula (10.3) (cf. p. 140). Marx's procedure ensures the equivalence of the total surplus value with the total profit and the identity of the added-up prices with the sum of values. But, the costs of this congruence are unbearable: the consistency

---

[72] Cf. Bortkiewicz, L. v., On the correction ..., op. cit., p. 204. Bortkiewicz refers to an example by Tugan-Baranowsky. Cf. ibid., p. 205 n.

Table 10.3 p′- or Marx-prices

Department of production	Constant capital	Variable capital	Profit	Price of product
I	225	90	$93.\overline{3}$	$408.\overline{3}$
II	100	120	$65.\overline{185}$	$285.\overline{185}$
III	50	90	$41.\overline{481}$	$181.\overline{481}$
I–III	375	300	200	875

of reproduction is violated as the column and row totals diverge from each other.[73] The constant and variable capitals must be converted into prices, too.

The method *à la* Bortkiewicz has led to a different distribution of the given total profit compared to the value calculation. The beneficiary of this procedure is division I. As Table 10.2 shows in comparison to Table 10.1, the earnings of branches II and III decrease, while the profit of department I increases from 60 to 96. This redistribution comes about because sector I absorbs relatively more of the total profit in this reckoning. The share of industry I in the value calculation was $\frac{v_1}{V} = 0.3$, in the system of ρ-prices it is $\frac{c_1x+v_1y}{Cx+Vy} = 0.48$. Accordingly, the profit of department I has risen by 60%.

After all, the standardisation $z \equiv 1$ ensured that the total surplus value matched the total profit. Yet, the prices sum up to 1000, whereas the sum of values taken from Table 10.1 only amounts to 875.

The transformation of values into production prices seems analytically correct; however, the identity of the value and price sums was lost along the way. Due to the normalisation, the aggregate profit is equal to the total surplus value, but this result cannot be adduced to counter the view that profit would simply be a surcharge on prices or costs.

Numerous other solutions achieve the same sum of values and prices through a suitable determination of the degree of freedom. Then, the aggregate surplus value generally differs from the total profit, which is also a hard nut to crack for Marx's doctrine since this result casts doubt on surplus labour as the source of profit.

Hence, the thesis that Bortkiewicz's contribution is *qualitatively* different from a mere "correction" of a formal blunder by Marx gains persuasive force; in truth, Bortkiewicz's investigation accelerated the *decline* of the classical theory of value. The operation, carried out by every trick in the book, weakened the patient instead of strengthening him. Competition in the form of the subjectivist theory of value and price undoubtedly achieved a competitive advantage because the labour theory of value had fallen into a crisis of meaning: why should one start from values to transform them into prices? Why not focus directly on production prices? Through this lens, the calculation of labour value appears to be a superfluous detour.—When dealing with modern production price theory, we shall again encounter the questions just raised.

[73] The example also shows that the solution to the transformation problem proposed by Winternitz, J., op. cit., suffers from the same shortcoming. Moreover, in this approach, the profit sum is smaller than the total surplus value.

However, the "Bortkiewicz method" is by no means the only pricing technique vying for the public's favour. Therefore, we look at the rivals, not just because of a cardinal flaw in the ρ-prices that will soon be highlighted. As will come to the surface, the economic theory train has again failed to choose the right track at this stage.

10.2.2 Two Alternative Calculation Methods

In his improvement, Bortkiewicz adopted the distribution relative to the total capital employed as intended by Marx (and others) without raising any objections to this basis of distribution. But what does "total capital employed" signify? Suppose capital comprises only the money that entrepreneurs must actually disburse before production begins. In that case, the extent to which capital must be advanced depends on the payment modalities (and the creditworthiness). Are the production *costs* always and in complete "capital"?

Marx himself stated, as is often forgotten, that wages, in reality, are typically paid *post-festum*:

> In every country in which the capitalist mode of production reigns, it is the custom not to pay for labour-power before it has been exercised for the period fixed by the contract, as for example, the end of each week. In all cases, therefore, the use-value of the labour-power is advanced to the capitalist: the labourer allows the buyer to consume it before he receives payment of the price; he everywhere gives credit to the capitalist.[74]

However, Marx adds in context that it is expedient to assume *for the time being* that wages are handed over with the sale of labour power.[75]

Let us examine the consequences of converting values into prices if, instead of the total costs, only the circulating constant capital is chosen as the assessment basis for profit distribution. Accordingly, we assume that "living labour" is remunerated *ex post* and that only the means of production must be invested at the beginning of the period. Incidentally, this is the prevailing view in modern literature; therefore, we shall subsequently call the prices calculated in this way "Sraffa-prices".

Furthermore, it has become customary to abbreviate the rate of profit calculated on this basis as r. If, moreover, we denote $(1 + r)$ by u, the scheme (10.13–10.15) (cf. p. 145) is replaced by the following equations:

$$ux + f_1 y = g_1 x \tag{10.23}$$

$$ux + f_2 y = g_2 y \tag{10.24}$$

---

[74] Marx, K., Capital, vol. I, op. cit., p. 170.

[75] Cf. ibid., p. 171.

$$ux + f_3y = g_3 \tag{10.25}$$

From (10.23) we get:

$$x = \frac{f_1y}{g_1 - u} \tag{10.26}$$

Inserting (10.26) in (10.24) gives at first:

$$uf_1 + f_2(g_1 - s) - g_2(g_1 - u) = 0$$

Rearranging the above expression yields:

$$u(g_2 + f_1 - f_2) + g_1(f_2 - g_2) = 0$$

Solving for u leads to:

$$u = \frac{g_1(f_2 - g_2)}{f_2 - g_2 - f_1} \tag{10.27}$$

Undoing the abbreviations makes it easy to verify that $u > 1$ and thus $r > 0$ applies. With recourse to (110.26 and (10.27) expression (10.25) yields:

$$y = \frac{g_3}{g_2 - f_2 + f_3} \tag{10.28}$$

The corresponding formulas are now much more straightforward than in the case of Bortkiewicz-prices. We obtain $r = 0.\overline{36}$, i.e., the profit rate is now greater than $\rho = 0.25$. In addition, x and y have increased, $x = 1.\overline{46}$ and $y = 1, \overline{1}$. $y = 1, \overline{1}$.

As Table 10.4 shows, the reproduction condition is satisfied: the r-pricing also results in a principally viable system; this proviso for participation in the competition is fulfilled. Albeit, with an increasing price sum, the profit distribution has changed compared to the ρ-prices. Once again, sector I is the beneficiary. Because its share of the value of constant capital is 60%, it receives the corresponding part of the unaltered total profit.

Table 10.4 r- or Sraffa-prices

Department of production	Constant capital	Variable capital	Profit	Price of product
I	330	100	120	550
II	$146.\overline{6}$	$133.\overline{3}$	$53.\overline{3}$	$333.\overline{3}$
III	$73.\overline{3}$	100	$26.\overline{6}$	200
I–III	550	$333.\overline{3}$	200	$1083.\overline{3}$

The possibilities of price formation, however, have not yet been exhausted. As the capitalistic practice teaches us, entrepreneurs *regularly* grant each other payment terms, especially if they have had commercial connections for quite some time. Marx already pointed out the existence of credit chains, i.e., business people make promises of payment among themselves—e.g., in the form of bills of exchange. In this complex network of relationships, the default of just a few claims triggers an avalanche with the potential for a general crisis:

> The flax-grower has drawn on the spinner, the machine manufacturer on the weaver and the spinner. The spinner cannot pay because the weaver cannot pay, neither of them pay the machine manufacturer, and the latter does not pay the iron, timber or coal supplier … Thus the general crisis comes into being … we can already see the connection between the mutual claims and obligations, the sales and purchases, through which the possibility can develop into actuality.[76]

The empirical argument is allied with a theoretical one. The model is tailored to an *equilibrium situation* of perfect competition, i.e., economic activity repeats itself at the same level daily. Let us look at any "day" in this series on which—as on every day—the processing of a constant number of goods in the sectors is started, continued, and finished. Nothing contradicts the view that today's payments come from yesterday's proceeds.

In addition, there is something left over every day: profit in the form of capitalist consumption. However, the distribution of a given total profit to the sectors is subject to the respective calculation basis. Thus, a method must be discovered that appears "fair" to the capitalists and which they therefore accept and practice. The objective is to identify the mechanism that underlies the rationality of the social division of labour within the context of capitalist commodity production.

Before this problem becomes the focus of our further enquiry, we shall complete the spectrum of alternative pricing techniques with a version that has not yet been examined: allocating profit in proportion to variable capital. The hunch as to the result becomes a certainty when we formulate and recalculate the relevant equations. The profit rate of this system is denoted asε, e stands for $(1 + \varepsilon)$. Then we get:

$$x + ef_1y = g_1x \tag{10.29}$$

$$x + ef_2y = g_2y \tag{10.30}$$

$$x + ef_3y = g_3 \tag{10.31}$$

From (10.29) follows:

$$x = \frac{ef_1y}{g_1 - 1} \tag{10.32}$$

---

[76] Marx, K., Theories …, Part II, op. cit., p. 511 f.

(10.32) in (10.30) leads to:

$$e = \frac{g_2(g_1 - 1)}{f_1 + f_2(g_1 - 1)} \tag{10.33}$$

It would be a serious omission to abort the analysis at this stage. Instead, the abbreviations (see p. 145) are worth undoing. First, we ascertain:

$$e = \frac{V(v_1 + s_1)}{v_1 c_2 + v_2(v_1 + s_1)} \tag{10.34}$$

Expansion and subtraction of 1 yield:

$$e - 1 = \varepsilon = \frac{v_1 s_2 + v_1 s_1 + v_3 s_1}{v_1 c_2 + v_2 v_1 + v_2 s_1} \tag{10.35}$$

Dividing the numerator and denominator of the right-hand side of (10.35) by v_1 yields the following expression, where the uniform rate of surplus was considered:

$$\varepsilon = \frac{s_1 + s_2 + s_3}{c_2 + v_2 + s_2} = \frac{S}{V} = s' \tag{10.36}$$

Our supposition was not deceiving: if variable capital serves as the basis for allotting profits, the profit rate corresponds to the rate of surplus value. And what about the price-value ratios? After inserting (10.36) and (10.32) into (10.31), we first gain:

$$(1 + s')\frac{f_1 y}{g_1 - 1} + (1 + s')f_3 y = g_3 \tag{10.37}$$

Some rearrangements result in:

$$y = \frac{g_3 c_3}{c_3 + v_3 + s_3} = \frac{M}{M} = 1 \tag{10.38}$$

After recourse to (10.36) and the insertion of (10.38) in (10.32), we immediately see that x equals 1, and the prices match the values. Therefore, Table 10.1 (cf. p. 148) displays the labour values and the s'-prices. Since the value scheme presented ensures simple reproduction, the consistency condition is met.

Accordingly, *three* principles can be considered to ensure that capitalists behave like communists,[77] i.e., practise a *competitive* mode of profit distribution. Table 10.5 lists the sectoral profits that are recorded in each of these calculation variants. The total profit to be apportioned is the same for all alternatives.

The maximum profits of each department are printed in italics and bold; as can be seen, *no* sector prefers the calculation Marx had in mind and that Bortkiewicz

[77] Cf. Marx, K., Theories ..., part III, op. cit., p. 83.

Table 10.5 Sectoral profits of alternative price systems

Department of production	ρ-Prices	r-Prices	s'-Prices
I	96	***120***	60
II	64	$53.\overline{3}$	***80***
III	40	$26.\overline{6}$	***60***
I–III	200	200	200

corrected. Sector I would like constant capital alone as the benchmark to distribute total profit, while the other two favoured the value calculation. Therefore, the labour theory of value would have most capitalists' backing. This result may surprise some people, especially those who—for obscure reasons—believe that only labour income is compatible with the labour value theory. Accordingly, Recktenwald opines:

> The only thing that remains incomprehensible is how, by demanding the practical application of the labour theory of value, highly developed industrial nations ought to be rolled back to the level of primitive hunter-gatherers by seeing the value of a commodity only in the contribution of labour and leaving the other two factors of production unremunerated.[78]

Yet, in the preceding model, the amount of the surplus product to be distributed is not affected by its allocation; profit also exists with the value calculation. How much of it flows into the individual pockets depends on the respective calculation method.

However, deciding how competitive prices are formed does not occur in a democratic "one sector, one vote" style. As with the creation of money, it is a *social* process.[79] A numéraire fulfils its function because *all* those belonging to a monetary community use it in their accounting. In the same way, money acquires its quality as general remuneration, as a universal good, by being accepted by *every* seller in all economic exchanges as consideration from the customer. The same must pertain to the calculation rule we seek: it only generates a competitive equilibrium if *all* entrepreneurs are content with its results. Which pricing rule can expect general acceptance in the present context?

If one takes the intensity of the discussion of this question as an indicator of its importance, one would indeed think that it does not arise at all. Since the matter is seemingly apparent, arguably, no one has come up with the idea of examining which effects could occur due to a distribution of the surplus proportional to the total capital. Hence, doubts about whether this procedure is principally suitable for depicting a competitive equilibrium did not even take root. What price-setting procedure keeps no producer from participating in the social division of labour?—The solution must

[78] Recktenwald, H. C., op. cit., p. LV. [F. H.] Something similar can be read in the works of well-known older authors: "The central proposition of the socialist theory of value was that the value of a commodity is equal to the amount of labour it costs to produce it under normal conditions. This completely arbitrary proposition, which is in sharp contradiction to reality, naturally excludes from the outset not only interest itself, but also any reasonable theory of interest." Cassel, G., Theoretische Sozialökonomie (1918), 5th ed., Leipzig 1932, p. 170. [F. H.]

[79] Cf. Helmedag, F., Ohne Fleiß kein Preis: Nochmals zur Erklärungskraft der Arbeitswertlehre, in: Jahrbücher für Nationalökonomie und Statistik, vol. 214 (1995), pp. 470–482, p. 481.

be found based on "methodological individualism", pursuing personal economic advantage.

Table 10.5 (see p. 154) shows that *no* capitalist would vote for the traditional method, i.e., the Bortkiewicz-prices. Furthermore, as already mentioned, it has another serious shortcoming: it sometimes *fails* to accomplish a competitive equilibrium at all!

Bortkiewicz proved that "his" rate of profit is lower than the rate of surplus value, except in one special case. The extreme constellation occurs if department II produces without constant capital. In this situation, the rate of profit is directly determined by the equation of sector II in the system of ρ-prices. For $c_2 = 0$, one ascertains directly from (10.11) (cf. p. 145) and (10.8):

$$\sigma = 1 + \rho = \frac{V}{v_2} = \frac{v_2 + s_2}{v_2} = 1 + s' \tag{10.39}$$

In this situation, Bortkiewicz's profit rate coincides with the surplus value rate determined by industry II. But now, a problem arises: under certain circumstances, the other branches cannot adopt this rate of profit. "The truth of the matter, however, is that the share of constant capital in the total investment of Departments I and III cannot exceed a certain limit if the rate of profit in these two departments is also to equal ρ[*]."[80] Let us outline the deliberation.[81]

The stepping stone is Eq. (10.10) (see p. 145), which can be written for$\rho = s'$ and $c_2 = 0$ as follows:

$$(1 + s')(c_1 x + v_1 y) = (c_1 + c_3)x \tag{10.40}$$

From (10.7) (cf. p. 144), we get in the present case:

$$c_3 = \left(1 + s'\right) v_1 \tag{10.41}$$

The insertion of (10.41) in (10.40) yields:

$$(1 + s')(c_1 x + v_1 y) = c_1 x + (1 + s')v_1 x \tag{10.42}$$

This equation can be transformed into the inequality:

$$c_1 x s' < (1 + s')v_1 x \tag{10.43}$$

Simplification leads to:

$$c_1 < \frac{1 + s'}{s'} v_1 \tag{10.44}$$

[80] Bortkiewicz, L., On the correction ..., op. cit., p. 214. [*] Bortkiewicz writes r instead of ρ.

[81] Cf. ibid., p. 214 ff.

Accordingly, the following relation applies:

$$C = c_1 + c_3 < v_1(1 + s')\left(\frac{1}{s'} + 1\right) \tag{10.45}$$

From (10.8), we know that

$$V = v_2(1 + s') \tag{10.46}$$

is valid. *A fortiori* one gets:

$$v_1 < v_2 s' \tag{10.47}$$

Because of (10.45) and (10.46) we obtain:

$$\frac{C}{V} = Q < \frac{v_1(1 + s')\left(\frac{1}{s'} + 1\right)}{v_2(1 + s')} \tag{10.48}$$

Consideration of (10.47) finally entails:

$$Q < \frac{v_2 s'\left(\frac{1}{s'} + 1\right)}{v_2} = 1 + s' \tag{10.49}$$

Since c_1 and thus Q are not subject to any restrictions, it is easy to construct numerical examples in which the inequality (10.49) is violated. Then, setting up a ρ-price system à la Bortkiewicz that incorporates a uniform profit rate is impossible.

Similarly, Sraffa-style r-pricing is for $c_2 = 0$ incapable of generating a competitive price system: now y approaches zero since the denominator of the fraction in expression (10.28) (cf. p. 151) becomes infinitely large. According to the right-hand side of Eq. (10.24) (cf. p. 150), there would thus be no profit in division II, although a positive physical profit rate could be observed there. The value calculation profiles itself as the *only* consistent competitive price system.

The obvious objection is that the recently analysed production of division II without capital hardly reflects reality. Agreed; regardless of this, the reference to empiricism does not take the wind out of the sails of the argument: "... what does not hold in the special case," Bortkiewicz rightly observes, "cannot claim general validity."[82] Instead, the functionality of the s'-price calculation in circumstances in which the other two methods fail points to its general superiority. There is also another argument.

The requirements of simple reproduction imply that c_2 and c_3 are not "historical" values inherited from the past but represent living labour of the *current* period. Two

[82] Bortkiewicz, L. v., On the correction …, op. cit., p. 200. Bortkiewicz aims with this dictum at simplifying the analysis on the assumption that all capital, including constant capital, turns over in one period.

equilibrium conditions can be derived from the scheme (10.7–10.9) (cf. p. 144):

$$c_2 = v_1 + v_3 - s_2 \tag{10.50}$$

$$c_3 = s_1 + s_2 - v_3 \tag{10.51}$$

Nonetheless, in addition to the fallacious opinion that the value calculation does not permit profit, the equally erroneous assertion can be found that labour values must be reckoned by regression into the depths of time immemorial. Joan Robinson, e.g., expressed this view:

> The constant capital was produced in the past by labour-time working with then pre-existing constant capital and so on, *ad infinitum* backwards. It therefore cannot be reduced simply to a number of labour hours that can be added to the net value of the current year.[83]

Yet, it would be false to regard the activities of earlier times as determining today's value: "The value of every commodity", Marx clarifies, "– thus also of the commodities making up the capital – is determined not by the necessary labour-time contained in it, but by the *social* labour-time required for its reproduction."[84] Only present work is crucial.

The criteria that decide whether the entrepreneurs accept a pricing rule are now available. They know the topical value of the means of production and, in principle, nothing, and no one prevents departments II and III from manufacturing the necessary inputs *themselves* in a parallel process. For this purpose, the available labour force must be allocated within the company in suitable proportions to produce the material inputs internally.

Because of the feasible alternative to manufacturing intermediate products in-house, the general profit rate must match the rate of surplus value in equilibrium. If the rate of profit were lower, at least one sector would leave the division of labour.[85] Industries can only expect to find buyers for their commodities if the exchange ratios correspond to the values; this is the only method of "correctly" distributing surplus products as profit, meeting with the unanimous approval of entrepreneurial colleagues.

Under the present circumstances, only the law of value enunciates the rational formation of exchange values. The transformation of labour values into production prices turns out to be a pseudo-problem. However, it is essential to pay attention to the hierarchical structure of the economy: it is about Ricardo's insight that the wage-goods sector—in his case, food production, i.e., wheat cultivation—determines the rate of surplus value alias the profit rate in the system. Trade between the basic sector

[83] Robinson, J., Ideology and Analysis, in: Schwartz, J. (ed.), The Subtle Anatomy of Capitalism, Santa Monica 1977, pp. 364–370, p. 365.

[84] Marx, K., Capital, vol. III, op. cit., p. 150.

[85] Strictly speaking, this statement only applies under constant economies of scale. In fact, the exploitation of economies of scale – which allow *other* forms of production – is one of the main motives of the social division of labour. More on this topic at the end of this book.

and the "luxury division" then complies with the labour theory of value to establish a uniform rate of profit throughout the economy.

The analysis of the exchange between the two "subsystems"[86] proves to be a methodological "trick" that affords considerable gains in knowledge. We have already acquired an initial impression of the usefulness of the separation into a primary and secondary sector in studying the employment effects of the international division of labour according to the theorem of comparative cost advantages (cf. p. 145 ff.). Further evidence concerning the fruitfulness of this approach follows immediately.

10.3 Maximal Rate of Profit? Optimal Real Wage!

The starting point of the ensuing investigation is Marx's profit rate formula 10.3 (cf. p. 140), which, after dividing the numerator and denominator by the aggregate variable capital V, leads to the expression 10.4 (cf. p. 141). Thus, the double equation applies:

$$p' = \frac{M}{C+V} = \frac{s'}{Q+1} \tag{10.52}$$

Marx believed that for a given rate of exploitation s'—a precondition which, as will be shown shortly, seems stricter than it actually is—the rate of return on capital "tends" to fall because the organic composition of capital Q increases. Certain "retarding" moments could slow down the development or reverse it in the short term, but the capitalist mode of production would inevitably come to an end.[87]

Yet, it is not only a question of when the exploitation by capital would be eliminated but also of what peak value the rate of profit could ever reach. Heinz D. Kurz has repeatedly referred to the alleged existence of an upper limit for the rate of profit in Marx's system.[88] He starts from the assumption that the "… total amount of direct labour performed during a year (the total economic net value added) is equal to L."[89] We stick to the previous notation and continue to write N instead of L for employment

---

[86] Cf. Sraffa, P., Production …, op. cit., p. 89. Marx's theory of the circlar flow already contains the idea of 'integrated industries' or 'subsystems'. The equilibrium condition of a two sector economy developed by him postulates the equality of living labour in department I and constant capital in department II: "It follows that, on the basis of simple reproduction, the sum of the values of v + s of the commodity-capital of I … must be equal to the constant capital II_c, which is likewise taken as a proportional part of the total commodity product of department II; or $\text{II}_{(v+s)} = \text{II}_c$." Marx, K., Capital, vol. II, op. cit., p. 406.

[87] Cf. Marx, K., Capital, vol. III, op. cit., p. 211 ff.

[88] The presentation can be found almost identically in several articles and repeatedly in Kurz, H. D., Ökonomisches Denken in drei Jahrhunderten, vol. I: Bedeutende Ökonomen, Marburg 2021, p. 201 and p. 238. In the second volume with the subtitle "Ausgewählte Felder und Themen", published in the same year and at the same place, one encounters on p. 206 the reasoning once more.

[89] Kurz, H. D., Ökonomisches …, vol. I, op. cit., p. 201. [F. H.]

and S for total surplus value. In mathematical terms, Kurz's initial premise reads:

$$N = S + V \tag{10.53}$$

Equation (10.53) expresses a stringent assumption because, ostensibly, no constant capital is produced in the current period; gross and net value added are identical. Kurz thus concludes:

> But the reciprocal value of the organic composition is now equal to the *maximum rate of profit*, R, of the system, which would be realised if the real wage and with it the variable capital, V, were equal to zero if the workers could live on air and love, so to speak …[90]

The statement arouses astonishment: for $V = 0$, the reciprocal of the organic composition of capital $\frac{1}{Q} = \frac{V}{C}$ also vanishes instead of reaching a finite positive maximum. But Kurz probably has something else in mind. In the case of costless labour, value creation consists solely of profit or surplus value, and the maximum profit rate would, therefore, emerge as:

$$0 < R = \frac{S}{C} = \frac{N}{C} < \infty \text{ fü r } V = 0 < S = N, C < \infty \tag{10.54}$$

Yet the train of thought only does not derail when the constant capital consists exclusively of "dead" labour, i.e., is a fixed positive quantity. But then unresolved dimensional problems arise (cf. p. 167 f.): a flow quantity referring to a period is related to a dated stock; the character of the profit rate as a pure number (cf. p. 168) falls by the wayside.

However, the situation changes fundamentally if the total labour N is also employed to produce constant capital, whether in the form of intermediate products or means of production:

$$N = C + S + V \tag{10.55}$$

Rearranging gives:

$$C = N - V - S \tag{10.56}$$

According to Eq. (10.56), the general rate of profit p', as posited by Marx, is expressed as follows:

$$p' = \frac{S}{C + V} = \frac{S}{N - S} \tag{10.57}$$

Now, for a vanishing wage bill, the maximum profit rate R knows no limit:

$$R = \frac{N}{0} = \infty \text{ for } N = S \tag{10.58}$$

---

[90] Ibid., p. 238. [F. H.]

The hypothesis that there is an upper limit to the rate of profit will be addressed again shortly (cf. III.14, p. 212 f.). The examination of the classical theory of value in this section of the book culminates in the demonstration that not all profit-maximising employers endeavour to elevate the rate of profit to a higher level or even to maximise it. Instead, a "focal point" exists towards the exploitation of wage labour is heading within the context of perfect competition.

This movement presupposes the existence of a more or less large "industrial reserve army", i.e., there is basically unemployment, which characterises capitalism for most of its lifetime. For this reason, output can usually be expanded in volume without reaching capacity limits. The following model is intended to reproduce essential elements of Marx's analysis of capitalism compactly and consistently.[91]

In quantitative terms, it is striking that Marx repeatedly assumes a rate of surplus value of 100% in all three volumes of his main work.[92] The founder of scientific socialism probably chose this "round" value to create the simplest possible numerical examples. However, it will be shown below that the *one-hundred percent* exploitation of labour power should not merely be chosen for convenience since it represents "capitalistic communism" in its purest form. The key variable of capitalism is a system-immanent result of conflicts of interest in the *entrepreneurial* camp.

In the first step, we sort the almost multitudinous variety of products in a modern economy—which includes services—into two baskets of commodities. One contains all wage goods and intermediate products finally acquired from labour income. The other basket comprises the rest of the products, which are also manufactured by vertical integration.[93] The individual objects within the two categories of goods do not necessarily differ materially but only in terms of *who* acts as the buyer: if employees appear as purchasers, they always acquire wage articles, while all other products will alternatively be declared as luxury, surplus or surplus goods.[94] Against this background, e.g., a pencil or an envelope may principally fall into both demand categories.

Indeed, a supplier often does not know the financial background of a customer he is serving. Hence, it is usually unclear from which income source the money comes that makes the cash tills ring. Nevertheless, it is worth conceptually grouping the variety of commodities into wage and luxury goods, even though this distinguishing

[91] The account draws on sections and arguments from Helmedag, F., Kapitalistischer Kommunismus, in: Ökonomie und Gesellschaft, Jahrbuch 24: Entfremdung – Ausbeutung – Revolte, Karl Marx neu verhandelt, Marburg 2012, pp. 111–126, Helmedag, F., Principles of capitalistic commodity production, in: European Journal of Economics and Economic Policies: Intervention, vol. 9 (2012), pp. 23–34 and Helmedag, F., Über Kapital im „Kapital": Einige elementare Überlegungen, in: Wirtschaft und Gesellschaft, vol. 40 (2014), pp. 405–415.

[92] Cf. Marx, K., Capital, vol. I, op. cit., p. 543, vol. II, op. cit., p. 299, vol. III, op. cit., p. 28 and p. 211.

[93] Such separation into subsystems is feasible using input–output analysis methods, as shown in the next part of this investigation.

[94] The dichotomisation made here from the perspective of demand distinguishes the approach from Garegnani's "Integrated Wage-Goods Sector", in which the production of wage goods is separated from the production of other goods. Cf. Garegnani, P., Value and Distribution ..., op. cit., p. 313 ff.

feature is not based on specific use values. Thanks to this *virtual* decomposition of the economy, its inner workings can be revealed, and it is also possible to concretise the structural proportions with easily accessible statistical data.

We now declare a fictitious standard article of the sector under consideration as its output in a certain period. For example, the secondary department weekly produces X 'units' of surplus goods. Dividing the employment per week in the stylised multi-product industry N_X by the quantity X leads to the vertically integrated labour value of the imaginary surplus good v_X:

$$v_X = \frac{N_X}{X} \tag{10.59}$$

The same happens in the basic industry. Dividing the employmentN_B by the homogenised virtual output per period B provides the labour value v_B:

$$v_B = \frac{N_B}{B} \tag{10.60}$$

Workers pay the pricep_B per unit of the normalised foodstuff. Multiplying the uniform real remuneration (w) *pro rata temporis* in quantities of the wage good by its price provides the nominal wage rate (typically per hour) wp^{B}. The existence of profit requires that the price of a good is higher than the unit costs by a markup factor$\varepsilon > 0$. Then, the price equation of the basic good is:

$$p_B = v_B w p_B (1 + \varepsilon) \tag{10.61}$$

After cancellation of price p_B—which may be chosen to serve as a numéraire—and after rearranging, the exploitation factorε is determined from Eq. (10.61) as a pure positive number. This magnitude must, therefore, not be confounded with an interest rate, as this always refers to a period, usually one year. The profit rate alias rate of surplus value is positive if the output of a working hour in the wage-goods sector, the productivity $\frac{1}{v_B}$, exceeds the real wage w:

$$\varepsilon = \frac{1 - v_B w}{v_B w} > 0 \text{ for } \frac{1}{v_B} > w \tag{10.62}$$

The *markup* $(1 + \varepsilon)$ determines an amount that encompasses, in addition to wages, the *gross* profit from which depreciation and interest payments must be deducted to obtain the *net* profit. The number $(1 + \varepsilon)$ can be interpreted as an indicator of the *production price level*.[95] Of course, the magnitude only refers to processes of arbitrarily reproducible goods. If one likes, this index corresponds to so-called core inflation, which excludes the prices of natural resources and agricultural goods.

The reciprocal of the production price level corresponds to the average *real* unit labour costs as a percentage of total wages to gross domestic product. The fraction

[95] Cf. Helmedag, F., Ultra posse ..., op. cit., p. 53 f.

also reveals the cause of exploitation: employees cannot buy back the product they produce. This finding confirms Adam Smith's theory: more labour can be acquired with a commodity (labour commanded) than it contains (labour embodied) because the price level is above 100% (cf. p. 105 f.)

Likewise, the price of the luxury good p_X results from a markup calculation. However, there is a hierarchical relationship between the sectors: Eq. (10.63) comprises the nominal wage rate $w_{nom} = wp_B$,, which is determined in the basic industry:

$$p_X = v_X w p_B (1 + \varepsilon) \tag{10.63}$$

It is in the wind to calculate the price ratio of our two categories of goods in equilibrium, i.e., with a uniform rate of exploitationε. From (10.61) and (10.63) we get:

$$\frac{p_X}{p_B} = \frac{v_X w p_B (1 + \varepsilon)}{v_B w p_B (1 + \varepsilon)} = \frac{v_X}{v_B} \tag{10.64}$$

This upshot is significant: the relative prices of the stylised commodity categories do not change with real or nominal wage variations! Contrary assertions with a universal validity claim prove to be a fallacy. Instead, under free competition, the quantities of labour embodied in the two classes of goods alone determine the exchange ratio.

An economic consideration enables one to ascertain employmentN_B in the integrated basic sector. In capitalism, human labour is ultimately demanded to produce secondary goods for non-wage earners; the surplus of primary goods production supports the workforce in the luxury industry. Of course, both variables hinge on the real remuneration.

The division of the wage good requirements in the luxury sector $N_X w$ by the surplus product per hour in the basic department yields the necessary labour input there:

$$N_B = \frac{N_X w}{\frac{1}{v_B} - w} = \frac{N_X v_B w}{1 - v_B w} = \frac{N_X}{\varepsilon} \tag{10.65}$$

Evidently, the rate of surplus value or rate of profit ε influences the activity level in the primary industry. The total employment adds up to:

$$N = N_X + N_B = N_X \left(1 + \frac{1}{\varepsilon}\right) = \frac{N_X}{1 - v_B w} \tag{10.66}$$

The volume of labour increases with employment in luxury production N_X or a rise in the real wage w. Nevertheless, in Marx's terminology, the "value of labour power" $v_B w$ will remain below 100% if the rate of surplus value respective to the rate of profit is positive (cf. 10.62, p. 161).

Next, we make use of the insight that, in the present model, the wage costs of the luxury sector constitute the basic sector's nominal profit:

$$N_X w p_B = X_B p_X \tag{10.67}$$

Considering the employment in the secondary sector N_X taken from (10.59) (cf. p. 161) and the price ratio (10.64), Eq. (10.67) yields the real profit in the basic sector (X_B):

$$X_B = X v_B w \tag{10.68}$$

The wage goods industry thus reaps a "virtual physical" profit, which corresponds to the product of the total quantity of the imaginary secondary product X with the value of the labour power $v_B w < 1$. The profits in the luxury sector, therefore, amount to:

$$X_X = X(1 - v_B w) \tag{10.69}$$

As a key variable behind the scenes, the rate of surplus value structures the economy:

$$\varepsilon = \frac{N_X}{N_B} = \frac{X_X}{X_B} = \frac{X_X p_X}{X_B p_X} = \frac{1 - v_B w}{v_B w} \tag{10.70}$$

In fact, the uniform exploitation rateε is not an indicator of the total profit level. Instead, it determines the allocation of labour and the distribution of profits across the stylised sectors. As illustrated in Fig. 10.1, sectoral profits develop in *opposite directions* depending on the value of labour power or real unit labour costs$v_B w$. Who would have thought that in the entrepreneurial camp, opposing objectives regarding wage levels prevail behind the scenes?

Fig. 10.1 Profits in the wage and luxury sector

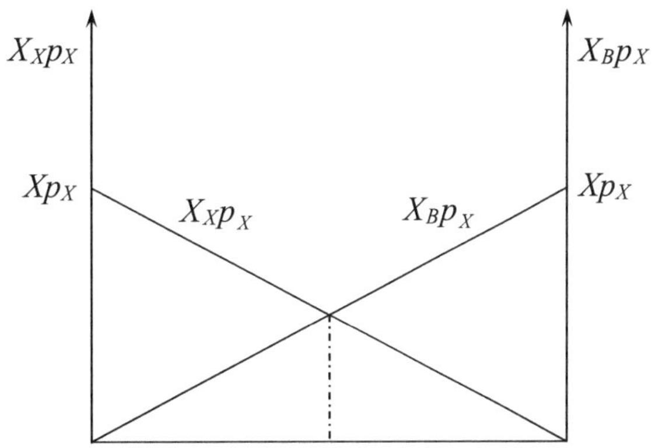

Unit labour costs ($v_B w$)	0	0.5	1
Profit rate (ε)	∞	1	0

Suppose the profit opportunities of the suppliers who sell to the two customer groups differ. In that case, some will switch the sector sooner or later until there are no more arbitrage opportunities. During such processes on sufficiently open markets, existing profit differentials are reduced: "What competition between the differently composed masses of capital residing in the different spheres of production strives for is *capitalist communism*, namely that the *mass of capital belonging to each sphere of production* … receives an aliquot share of the total surplus value."[96]

The intersection of the profit functions at$\varepsilon = 100\%$ carries significant weight, as this specific level of the surplus value rate is optimal because the conflicting profit interests of the two industries are balanced at this point. A transition between sectors then does not appear lucrative. However, the basic industry holds the reins: the real wages paid there voluntarily for its own benefits lead to real unit labour costs$v_B w$ of 50% or a profit rate of 100%.

What conclusions can be drawn from the above considerations? One characteristic of the Smith–Ricardo–Marx line is that the successor criticised the predecessor for having deviated too early from the labour theory of value. Because of the preceding analysis, this accusation can also—what a surprise!—be raised against Marx. In this light, his criticism of Smith and Ricardo pales into insignificance: the net product splits, in fact—apart from rent—into the categories of wages and profit and the profit rate is determined by the ratio of surplus labour to necessary labour.

Like Ricardo, Marx thought "successivistically",[97] and his treatment of the transformation of values into prices bears witness to this.[98] For the early classics, the idea that the accumulation of a capital stock *preceded* all production arose from their immediate experience. In the almost entirely agricultural mode of production at the time, food for humans and animals had to be stored and pre-financed for an extended period until the next harvest. This capital stock, including seed, became the quasi-natural basis for allocating the surplus. This financial need also applies to small tradesmen: "What the worker lacked in Smith's time was not a workshop and tools – he had these in or behind the house – but money to buy supplies and feed his family

---

[96] Marx, K., Letter to Engels, 30. April 1868, in: Marx and Engels, Collected Works, vol. 43, Letters 1868–1870, Electric Book, pp. 20–25, p. 23, https://www.koorosh-modaresi.com/MarxEngels/V43.pdf.

[97] Marshall characterised Ricardo's method with this attribute: "He does not state clearly, and in some cases he perhaps did not fully and clearly perceive how, in the problem of normal value, the various elements govern one another *mutually*, and not *successively* in a long chain of causation." Marshall, A., Principles …, op. cit., p. 672.

[98] Cf. in more detail Bortkiewicz, L. v., Wertrechnung …, Zweiter Artikel, op. cit., p. 37 ff. According to Bortkiewicz (ibid., p. 38), Walras has earned the merit of "liberating modern theory from successivistic prejudice". [F. H.]

while these goods were being produced."[99] Against this backdrop, the classic bridge from calculating labour values to supposedly "normal" prices, including interest on the advanced costs of materials, is understandable; nevertheless, the practised allotment of profit is conceptually flawed.

Modern theorists, however, are less excusable for the unreflective application of the "agrarian" way of thinking in an industrial world of *simultaneous* production. However, costs are still constantly identified with disbursals, which in turn are classified as invested capital without any intermediate step. In the next part, there are several opportunities to substantiate this criticism.

---

[99] Starbatty, J., op. cit., p. 61. See also Bortis, H., Structure and Change Within the Circular Theory of Production, in: Baranzini, M., Scazzieri, R. (eds.), The Economic Theory of Structure and Change, Cambridge et al. 1990, pp. 64–92.

Part III
Production of Commodities and the Law of Value

Chapter 11
Piero Sraffa's Production Price Theory

Published in 1960, the slim book "Production of Commodities by Means of Commodities" is undoubtedly one of the most important pieces of modern economic literature, the "… true watershed in critical discussion dividing the older and newer climates of opinion …"[1] Sraffa's work is regarded as the culmination of the objectivist theory of value, and not only by his followers. As Sraffa stated in the preface, his theory was intended as a *platform* for a later dispute about the neoclassical theory of prices and distribution: "If the foundation holds, the critique may be attempted later, either by the writer or by someone younger and better equipped for the task."[2]

Although an essay by Joan Robinson, written several years earlier, marked the beginning of the modern debate on capital theory[3], the Cambridge-Cambridge controversy moved into gear after a larger audience became aware of the critical potential in Sraffa's *oeuvre*. Indeed, the greater formal coherence and substance of Sraffa's conception made it more attractive in the long term than Joan Robinson's rather metaphorical contribution. In retrospect, the claim expressed in the subtitle of Sraffa's work proves to be justified: "Prelude to a Critique of Economic Theory". The outwardly brief prelude was to be followed by an echo that has not faded away until now.

During the discussion, Sraffa's system underwent an adaptation—the more compact matrix notation has now practically completely replaced Sraffa's notation of the single equations—and the approach's coverage and content were also expanded. With the help of certain theorems of matrix calculus, it was possible, on the one hand, to present this or that statement by Sraffa more accessible and, on the other hand, to gain insights into more complex cases, such as joint production, that go beyond Sraffa's issues.

---

[1] Dobb, M., Value and Distribution Theories since Adam Smith, Cambridge 1973, p. 248.

[2] Sraffa, P., Production …, op. cit., p. vi.

[3] Cf. Robinson, J., The Production Function and the Theory of Capital, in: The Review of Economic Studies, vol. 21 (1953/54), pp. 81–106. Cf. also Helmedag, F., Die Technikwahl …, op. cit., pp. 30 ff.

F. Helmedag, *Production of Commodities by Means of Labour*, Springer Studies in Alternative Economics, https://doi.org/10.1007/978-3-032-01457-3_11

As is often the case, however, the *irreparable* damage is to be found in the underpinnings. Once again, it will turn out that the subsequent literature adopted the basis of Sraffa's analysis axiomatically, as it were, while the test of its stability that Sraffa himself admonished was not carried out. If one likes, his disciples took the second step without the first: *If the foundation holds*, the critique may be attempted later …

Nonetheless, Sraffa's theory of value has had to put up with reproaches from sceptics. Sometimes, he received criticism for being out of date with his way of arguing. The models associated with Leontief and v. Neumann should be regarded as *state-of-the-art*, at least in formal terms. In this wake follows (with strange linguistic logic) the thesis: "None of the new things that Sraffa proclaims in his book … were unknown in 1960 when the book was published."[4] From another source, one learns that the efficiency of the neo-Ricardian theory is downright "pathetic"[5]. It lacks a monetary theory, does not take the financial markets into account, and ignores the role of uncertainties and expectations—in one word: "The Neo-Ricardian model belongs in every textbook on the history of economic thought in the appendix to the chapter on Ricardo as a modern reconstruction of his theory of value."[6]

Such a complaint is not plausible: although it is true that all the blank areas mentioned (and others) should be covered by truly universal economics, there is undoubtedly still a long way to go before this happens. In this light, the whole economic theory can be dismissed as miserable if the level of ambition is appropriate—an opinion that may have some merit but does not help.[7] If one criticises a field of research for what has not yet been achieved, it is merely a complaint that an enhanced performance is needed. Without a doubt, neo-Ricardianism only covers a few problem areas in economics, while members of the neoclassical clan appear in practically all places. However, efforts to expand the neo-Ricardian doctrinal edifice have existed for some time.[8]

---

[4] Stamatis, G., Zur Entmythologisierung Sraffas, in: Staatsgrenzen, Argument-Sonderband AS 89, Berlin 1982, pp. 168–182, p. 168. Cf. also Stamatis, G., Sraffa und sein Verhältnis zu Ricardo und Marx, Göttingen 1984.

[5] Cf. Schneider, J., Die Fortsetzung eines Irrwegs, Replik, in: Matzner, E., Kregel, J., Roncaglia, A. (eds.), Arbeit für alle ist möglich, Berlin 1987, pp. 35–38, p. 38.

[6] Ibid. [F.H.].

[7] In the introduction to their seminal work, John v. Neumann and Oskar Morgenstern compare the state of economic theory with that of physics in the Middle Ages—the time of the alchemists, as is well known. Cf. Neumann, J. v., Morgenstern, O., Theory of Games and Economic Behavior [1943], 2nd. ed., London/Oxford 1953, p. 3, https://archive.org/details/in.ernet.dli.2015.215284.

[8] Kurz and Kalmbach, e.g., promote a *new-classical* perspective, i.e., *Sraffa plus Keynes*, as a competitive substitute for neoclassicism, which (admittedly) more or less monopolises all submarkets of economic theory as ever. Cf. Kurz, H. D., Kalmbach, P., Elemente einer neuklassischen Analyse von Verteilung, Wert, Akkumulation und Beschäftigung: eine Skizze, in: Mückl, W. J., Ott, A. E. (eds.), Wirtschaftstheorie und Wirtschaftspolitik, Gedenkschrift für Erich Preiser, Passau 1981, pp. 283–311. See also the discussion in Hödl, E., Müller, G. (eds.), Die Neoklassik und ihre Kritik, Frankfurt a. M. 1986, pp. 133 ff. On the applicability of "commodity production by means of commodities" in foreign trade theory, see Nobel, K., Außenhandelseffekte in linearen Wachstumsmodellen, Berlin 1982. An environmental economics approach in the tradition of Ricardo and Sraffa is offered by Kratena, K., Produktion, Umweltpolitik und Einkommensverteilung, in: Jahrbücher für Nationalökonomie und Statistik, vol. 207 (1990), pp. 417–431.

Even if this were not the case, it cannot be claimed that Sraffa's book addresses a marginal problem despite all the requests for additions. On the contrary, as was explained in detail in the first part of this book, the laws of economic exchange in societies based on the division of labour and commercial interests form the core of the science around which the other topics revolve. The classical theory of value was chosen to provide a look behind the superficial explanation of price phenomena through supply and demand and to show the hidden mechanism of the emerging new economic society. The research was intended to unveil the characteristics of an equilibrium towards the real economic activity is *tendentially* heading. Hence, the reference system is provided against which observed deviations can be measured. The classical object of knowledge focuses on the permanent and dominant factors, not the temporary and accidental ones.[9]

If a conception claims to have completed this "classical" project, then its relegation to the appendix of an exposition on the history of doctrine defies the true significance: Sraffa's analysis represents fundamental economic research *par excellence.* The criticism that individual statements are not necessarily "new" or are served up in a somewhat antiquated form does not harm Sraffa's highbrow ambition. The follow-up or even the completion of a program naturally presupposes that contributions to the field have already occurred. Incidentally, the intensive study of sources increases the reluctance to proclaim that one or another idea is unprecedented. Such references do not exempt one from grappling with the content of the work.

This scrutiny is provided below. It is less a matter of an explanatory commentary on the Sraffa system—there is no shortage of that nowadays. Instead, its premises and *economic* implications are at the centre of the enquiry. Based on the results of this study so far, it makes sense to pay particular attention to the relationship between Sraffa's theory of production prices and the labour theory of value. As we have seen, the latter is not as damaged as it is generally enunciated. Conversely, the supposedly more attractive concept of production prices, which reflect a uniform rate of profit on "capital", has experienced a debacle time and again. Even in the single-sector wheat economy, the rate of profit proved to be a poor indicator for obtaining reliable information about the accumulation behaviour of profit-maximising tenants. Bortkiewicz's transformation of values into production prices via calculating the *return on material costs*, alias the profit rate, was also not precisely the ideal solution. Instead, the value calculation emerged as the only consistent and problem-adequate method. Sraffa's theory is confronted with these insights below.

The method employed for this can be characterised as *Reductio ad absurdum*: it is gradually revealed and substantiated through concrete numerical examples that, in specific constellations which cannot be ruled out a priori, Sraffa's price theory produces results incompatible with the requirements of a competitive capitalist economy. Hence, his model cannot correctly reflect its operational mode. Sraffa's propositions are mainly attacked where they seem well-embedded: in the framework of single production.

[9] Cf. Kurz, H. D., Kalmbach, P., op. cit., p. 286 f.

Some "oddities" of joint production give even neo-Ricardians such a headache that they—one sometimes has the impression—would like to suppress them with a head-in-the-sand attitude. Nevertheless, some of their disciples have used joint production to demonstrate the (alleged) paradoxes of the labour theory of value. Joint production theory served them as a reference base, without mentioning its anomalies, which were swept under the carpet. Fortunately, it is much easier to deal with joint production once one knows how to get to grips with single production. Therefore, let us first review the fundamentals and main propositions of that part of the neo-Ricardian theory which addresses processes producing one distinct commodity.

11.1 From the Subsistence Economy to Capitalism

Sraffa begins his book with the most spartan production economy, where an exchange value problem can arise: each of two sectors manufactures an output of its typical good that just suffices to replace the input in both industries. In this economy, the exchange relation—there is only one—is identical to the *quantity ratio* of the mutually supplied use values. This simple rule does not apply to higher-dimensional economies. We are familiar with Sraffa's example: as emerged from the analysis of the wheat-iron-pig economy (cf. p. 67 ff.), the reference to a unit of account is an indispensable prerequisite for determining a consistent exchange structure in an economy with more than two commodities.

It was demonstrated there that the direct juxtaposition of physical trade quantities in the three-sector economy evoked a contradictory system of exchange values. A numéraire is indispensable to reduce the heterogeneous inputs and outputs to a common denominator for expressing the budget restrictions. Nevertheless, without a general medium of exchange, despite knowledge of the correct relative values, a triangular exchange was necessary for reproduction: first, the wheat and pig sectors had to settle their business so that the wheat sector could fully pay its iron bill.

The formation of exchange value in subsistence economies can be generalised. We shall abandon Sraffa's exposition and introduce matrix notation on this occasion. Let n be the positive natural number of goods produced and, in the case of single production, the number of sectors synonymous with industries, departments, branches, divisions or factories. If we divide each of the n production equations by its output, we obtain the quantity $a_{ij} \geq 0$ of good i to produce one unit of good j. Since at least one coefficient is positive, the elements a_{ij} form a semi-positive, n-dimensional "direct requirement" matrix $\mathbf{A}$. Its *columns* are the input vectors of the sectors to produce one unit of a specific commodity.[10] Under the conditions of a pure subsistence economy, the system of price equations is as follows:

---

[10] Pasinetti, L., Lectures ..., op. cit. offers on pp. 226–277 a well-made compendium of the relevant mathematics, containing the pertinent theorems of matrix calculus and their proofs, in particular the theorems of Perron and Frobenius on non-negative matrices. The mathematically less interested reader can skip the relevant passages without losing crucial information. The later argumentation is based on simple models that do not require in-depth knowledge of matrix calculus.

$$\mathbf{p}A = \mathbf{p}I = \mathbf{p} \tag{11.1}$$

p denotes the n-dimensional row vector of prices and **I** the unit matrix, i.e., the output matrix of a single production run at unit level. The system (11.1) is nothing other than a special eigenvalue problem of the form $pA = \lambda p$ with $\lambda = 1$:: a (positive) row vector **p** is sought, whose multiplication with the columns of **A** leads to **p** again. In the subsistence economy, $\lambda = 1$ corresponds to the maximum eigenvalue λ_{max} of **A**, which is generally between the minimum and the maximum of the row sums of the coefficient matrix.

In the given situation, the elements of each row add up to one; hence, the minimal and maximal row sums coincide. If **A** is indecomposable, a positive eigenvector **p** is assigned to the largest eigenvalue of **A**. Economically, this means that all products are basic goods in Sraffa's sense, as they enter mutually into their production.[11] From the matrix Eq. (11.1) follows:

$$\mathbf{p}(A - I) = 0 \tag{11.2}$$

The non-trivial solution of (11.2) requires that the determinant of $(A - I)$ vanishes:

$$|A - I| = 0 \tag{11.3}$$

This condition applies in the present stationary production: because the sum of the inputs must equal the sum of the outputs, each of the n equations can be ascertained when the others are known. Thus, only (n—1) independent equations are available to calculate n exchange ratios. The missing nth equation is obtained after defining a numéraire.

Sraffa has not dwelt on the subsistence economy for long. What happens if the economy under consideration produces more than the inputs into the production processes? What criterion serves as a benchmark for distributing the surplus product that is now available? For Sraffa, the matter is straightforward: "... the surplus (or profit) must be distributed in proportion to the means of production (or capital) advanced in each industry..."[12] Oops, the sensitised reader will think: just a page earlier, we had a pure subsistence economy, which was merely capable of producing the food of those who work plus the consumed means of production, and now we already have profit and capital, as soon as there is a surplus product![13]

---

[11] Cf. Sraffa, P., Production ..., op. cit., p. 8. The distinction between basic and non-basic goods plays an important role in the literature. This classification will be taken up later.

[12] Ibid., p. 6.

[13] Moreover, even in the two-commodity case, the matter is more complex than Sraffa states: the (missing) profit rate equation has two positive solutions, one of which is ruled out because it is associated with a negative price for a good. Cf. in detail Helmedag, F., Die arbeitsteilungskompatible Kalkulation von Produktionspreisen, in: das wirtschaftsstudium (wisu), 26. vol. (1997), pp. 573–582, pp. 575 f.

The identification of surplus and profit on the one hand and the equalisation of the value of physical inputs with capital on the other is due to a barely noticeable but—as will be shown—even more serious congenital disability of the Sraffian system. The very second sentence of his book states succinctly: "Commodities are produced by separate industries and are exchanged for one another at a market held after the harvest."[14] According to Sraffa's casual comments, the market day is held once a year.

Neo-Ricardian theory has never questioned this "peasant" approach, let alone attempted to emancipate from it. This omission is loyalty in the wrong place. Among the classics, successivistic thinking arose, as noted, from the immediate experience of an agrarian society. In the modern industrial economy, which was undoubtedly already evident in 1960, the fewest products are only offered for sale at fairs: our supermarket is open every working day.

Of course, the "year" does not have to last twelve months—Marshall's "week" served the same (formal) purpose. However, two things should be pointed out in this context. First, countless passages in the literature prove that neo-Ricardians (and others) actually believe that all material costs over the assumed period are to be pre-financed. In this context, it is even claimed that "… the period of production is generally longer than the period over which the wage contract is made …".[15]

In truth, the assumption of a uniform production period rests on a *convention*—at the time, the "year" was widely accepted, as can be seen in the definition by James Mill quoted earlier (see p. 67 n.). The actual completion period of individual goods is, by the nature of things, highly individual: in an economy in which not only paper clips are bent, and daily newspapers are printed, but also skyscrapers are erected, and ships are launched, *any* uniform production interval is an arbitrary construct. As a result, one is entitled to abandon the classical view when choosing a standard production period: why not a day, an hour and—in the borderline case—a "logical" second? The unfinished goods are interpreted as intermediate products anyway.—More on this below.

Another aspect deserves attention. The theory of production *naturally* has to do with *flows*—this is undisputed and emerges from the considerations just made.[16] Hence, we proceed on thin ice if we elevate the post-harvest *market* to the institution for price setting. This peril arises because stocks are offered at a trade centre; such stocks are strongly influenced by non-economic, above all climatic, conditions in an agricultural economy. For some reason, the classics kept market and production prices apart. The explanation of such prices, which originate from an exchange out of stocks, cannot dispense with the categories supply and demand—i.e., scarcity relations—in contrast, determining the value of commodities that, given idle capacities, can be produced as desired is another story.

---

[14] Sraffa, P., Production …, op. cit., p. 3.

[15] Steedman, I., Marx After Sraffa, London 1977, p. 103.

[16] "All inputs are flows" asserts Kesting, H., Produktionspreise, Wachstum und Verteilung, Marburg 1990, p. 34. See also Pasinetti, L., Lectures …, op. cit., p. 26.

Deciphering the law of value is the be-all and end-all of the classics' research program. They wanted to reveal the rules that establish the values of goods whose production is limited exclusively by the reservoir of human labour, with nature's greater or lesser assistance. If some of the original factors of production are involuntarily unused, the concept of scarcity loses its guiding cognitive function. More powerful explanations need to be developed to provide an impressive answer to the questions posed.

Sraffa's "market after the harvest" brings the analysis unintentionally close to neoclassical theory, whose central theme is the optimal allocation of resources to alternative uses. In this framework, production merely figures as an indirect exchange; distribution atrophies into an appendage of the universal supply–demand machinery: "... a sound distribution theory is hardly more than a corollary or footnote to an exposition of the mechanics by which resources are apportioned among different uses."[17]

According to Sraffa's hypothesis, if a surplus is registered, the prices consist of the value of the intermediate products plus a markup according to a uniform profit rate r:

$$\mathbf{pA}(1+r) = \mathbf{p} \tag{11.4}$$

With the definition

$$\frac{1}{1+r} \equiv \lambda \tag{11.5}$$

results from (11.4) an eigenvalue task again:

$$\mathbf{p}(\mathbf{A} - \lambda\mathbf{I}) = 0 \tag{11.6}$$

The interesting solution for λ_{max} is less than one because it is associated with non-negative prices: a surplus product appears if the production of leastwise one good exceeds its consumption in the production process; at a minimum, the sum of one row is less than one. The maximum eigenvalue of the coefficient matrix, the Frobenius root, can be used to make a statement about the economy's productivity. Under the given conditions, this is not only based on the state of the art, because qua assumption, the direct requirement matrix **A** also includes the workers' food "... entering the system on the same footing as the fuel for the engines or the feed for the cattle."[18]

The wage goods bundle can turn out more or less copious; hence, the surplus rate is smaller or larger. As the real wage increases, the maximum eigenvalue of the coefficient matrix rises since the Frobenius root grows with the matrix elements. The profit rate results from the rearrangement of (11.5):

---

[17] Knight, F. H., The Ricardian Theory of Production and Distribution, in: The Canadian Journal of Economics and Political Science, vol. 1 (1935), pp. 171–196, p. 171.

[18] Sraffa, P., Production ..., op. cit., p. 9.

$$r = \frac{1}{\lambda \max} - 1 \tag{11.7}$$

The markup factor decreases with an increasing Frobenius root and disappears when $\lambda_{\max}$ equals one. We are then back in a stationary economy. In this case, the *workers* consume everything that emerges as a net surplus in the economy. Such a situation, of course, requires relevant social conditions. However, when forming the price according to the system of Eqs. (11.4), Sraffa probably considered the world of the classics, in which the "natural" wage rate merely allowed subsistence.

Does speaking of a "profit rate" in this model make sense? Sraffa begins his analysis with a pre-capitalist society without a surplus product; in this case, the values arise directly from production conditions. Systematically, the next step should have been to take a pre-capitalist commodity production *with* a surplus product under the microscope, albeit *with* a discernible division of labour. Sraffa takes a different approach: without revealing the allocation of social labour to the sectors, all things that enter the product directly or indirectly via the food of an (unknown) number of workers are declared "capital". Although Ricardo had also "capitalised" the hunter's weapons (cf. p. 123), he 'only' intended to specify Adam Smith's labour theory of value in the early and rude state. In addition to direct labour, indirect labour is also relevant for value.

Similarly, Sraffa's "capital" initially exists, yet the appertaining capitalists remain hidden. They stay behind the scenes until Sraffa makes the respective sectoral part of the total labour visible in his production equations.[19] It would have been more convincing if Sraffa had exposed the direct use of labour *from the outset* before clarifying the prerequisites for initiating and establishing the division of labour.

In place of this, Sraffa—in the style of his predecessors –takes the existence of the individual sectors for granted. Furthermore, a uniform *markup* on the respective inputs—vulgo: the capital advanced—allegedly characterises the equilibrium of free competition. The relationship between this profit rate and the remuneration of labour is now the subject of our attention. This way, we create a formal basis to answer questions raised earlier.

11.2 Wage Rate and Profit Rate

When drawing up his general price equations, Sraffa abandons the classical assumption that wages are advanced at the beginning of the production period. But he explicitly abides by the "agricultural conception" of his treatise: "We retain, however, the supposition of an annual cycle of production with an annual market."[20] For Sraffa, the postulated ability of working people to live off the air for a year did not seem too much to ask. Yet a year is just not a year …

[19] Cf. ibid., p. 9 ff.

[20] Ibid., p. 10.

Sraffa's treatment of the individual work qualities is very much in Ricardo's style. The differences are levelled out by counting more complicated work as a corresponding multiple of "simple" work. It remains unclear what concrete solution to the reduction problem he has in mind: "... we assume any differences in quality to have been previously reduced to equivalent differences in quantity so that each unit of labour receives the same wage."[21] If w denotes this wage rate and $\mathbf{a}_0$ signifies the *positive* row vector of direct labour input—direct labour a_{0j} is performed in *each* sector—we gain the central formula of the neo-Ricardian theory:

$$\mathbf{p} = \mathbf{pA}(1 + \mathrm{r}) + \mathbf{a}_0 w \tag{11.8}$$

While the system of Eqs. (11.4) can be interpreted as the counterpart of the Bortkiewicz- or ρ-prices, as they were labelled earlier (cf. p. 173 ff.), the matrix Eq. (11.8) is the complement of the *r-prices* there. For this reason, the prices calculated according to the *hypothesis* (11.8) were called "Sraffa-prices" (cf. p. 180 ff.). This account was followed by the proof that neither the ρ- nor the r-prices provide a valid calculation rule to distribute the surplus product according to the principles of a capitalist competitive economy. We shall now examine what can be said *in principle* about Sraffa prices in this respect. Before, it is worth paying attention to the extreme values of (11.8).

Let us assume that the rate of profit is zero, i.e., the capitalists are (still) conspicuous by their absence. Then (11.8) is simplified to:

$$\mathbf{p} = \mathbf{pA} + \mathbf{a}_0 w \tag{11.9}$$

In the first step, one obtains:

$$\mathbf{p}(\mathbf{I} - \mathbf{A}) = \mathbf{a}_0 w \tag{11.10}$$

The solution of the above system is:

$$\mathbf{p} = \mathbf{a}_0 w\,[\mathbf{I} - \mathbf{A}]^{-1} \tag{11.11}$$

$[\mathbf{I} - \mathbf{A}]^{-1}$ is the "total requirement" matrix, often referred to as the Leontief-inverse, denoted by $\mathbf{L}$. Its non-negative elements express how many units of good i are needed *in total* to produce one unit of good j. Multiplying the columns of the Leontief-inverse from the left by the row vector of direct labour inputs yields the positive vector of labour values $\mathbf{v}$:

$$\mathbf{v} = \mathbf{a}_0[\mathbf{I} - \mathbf{A}]^{-1} = \mathbf{a}_0\mathbf{L} \tag{11.12}$$

[21] Ibid.

In the given situation, prices are parallel to labour values:

$$\mathbf{p} = w\,\mathbf{v} \tag{11.13}$$

Since there are n equations, whereas the n prices and the wage rate are sought, the system is only determined after selecting a unit of account. Standardising the price of commodity j to one, yields a wage rate $w = \frac{1}{v_j}$, where v_j symbolises the labour value of commodity j. The exchange ratio of two commodities corresponds to the quotient of the respective quantities of labour embodied in the particular commodities. The prices are identical to the labour values if we choose w as numéraire in (11.13): labour embodied and labour commanded coincide under these circumstances.

The Eqs. (11.13) reflect the formation of prices in, if one likes, the "early and rude state" (cf. p. 101). In pre-capitalist societies, in which everyone is free to realise their labour power at will, there would, in the theoretical ideal, be no exchange in which more labour is given than received. Without considering the increase in productivity resulting from the division of labour, in equilibrium, it must be immaterial whether a good is vertically integrated, produced in-house or externally procured.

In reality, specialisation increases the total output, making it worthwhile for *everyone* to exchange their work for others (cf. p. 146 n. on occupational choice). The more the effectiveness of the individual activity increases in relation to the average, the more units of 'simple' work it represents. The labour quantity theory becomes a *labour cost theory*. The price formation (11.13) ensures that all producers receive a performance-related share of the social product.

Let us look at the other extreme: the wage rate is zero—after all, Sraffa's workers can live on air for a year. The system (11.8) is now transformed into:

$$\mathbf{p} = \mathbf{pA}(1 + R) \tag{11.14}$$

R is the maximum profit rate associated with the zero-wage rate. The analogy with Eq. (11.4) (cf. p. 209) is striking. Once again, we face an eigenvalue problem. However, the coefficient matrix $\mathbf{A}$ no longer contains the workers' food. According to (11.7), this matrix's maximum eigenvalue determines the profit rate's permissible range as a purely "technical" quantity. But does R have any relevance in a world where all means of production can be produced in any quantity at will using costless labour?

Sraffa provides some (brief) literature references in Appendix D of his book. There, one learns that the idea of a maximum rate of profit would come from Marx. According to Sraffa, Marx expressed this doctrine directly when he incidentally hinted at the possibility "... of a fall in the rate of profits 'even if the workers could live on air' ..."[22]. It can hardly be a lack of practice when Sraffa, who otherwise almost wholly dispenses with literal quotations in his book but whose Ricardo edition

[22] Ibid., p. 94. Perhaps Kurz had this passage in mind when he intended to prove that in Marx, a maximum rate of profit would exist, cf. p. 191 f.

meticulously registers even the most minor nuances of the individual editions, does *not* quote correctly here. In the relevant paragraph, Marx discusses that the total surplus value might be exposed to two opposing influences as the productive power increases. Since it results from the product of the rate of exploitation and the value of labour power, a substantial decline in variable capital possibly compensates for an increase in the rate of surplus value. As the section title indicates, Marx addresses the conflict between expanding and exploiting production. To avoid misunderstandings, let us look at the passage in the edition used by Sraffa:

> "To the extent that the development of the productive power reduces the paid portion of employed labour, it raises the surplus-value, by raising its rate; but to the extent that it reduces the total mass of labour employed by a certain capital, it reduces the factor of numbers with which the rate of surplus-value is multiplied in order to calculate its mass. Two labourers, each working 12 hours daily, cannot produce the same mass of surplus-value as 24 labourers each working only 2 hours, even if *they* could live on air and did not have to work for themselves at all."[23]

In the last sentence, "they" refers to the "labourers" *mentioned in the preceding example.* The bonding in this context remains hidden if one—tacitly—replaces "they" with "the workers" and thus creates the impression that Marx is talking about a maximum profit rate in a situation that would occur if all workers lived off the air. Instead, Marx merely states that with a uniform rate of surplus value, regardless of its concrete level, not as much surplus value can be created in 24 working hours as in 48. So, this card of Sraffa fails to trump.

Sraffa believes he has another ace up his sleeve. He bases his argument on Marx's critique of Smith's component theory of price. The complete dissolution of price into the income types implies "final commodities" produced without means of production. According to Sraffa, this contradicts a fixed upper limit for the profit rate.[24] This (mis)assessment is evident if one has a special way of presenting Sraffa's prices in mind.

To illustrate this, let us look at the solution of (11.8) (cf. p. 211). A first rearrangement leads to:

$$\mathbf{p}[\mathbf{I} - (1 + r)\mathbf{A}] = \mathbf{a}_0 w \tag{11.15}$$

This results in:

$$\mathbf{p} = \mathbf{a}_0 w[\mathbf{I} - (1 + r)\mathbf{A}]^{-1} = \mathbf{a}_0 w\ \mathbf{S} \tag{11.16}$$

---

[23] 23Marx, K., Capital, vol. III, Chicago, 1909, p. 290, own emphasis. In the original German text this passage is also clear: "... even if they could live on air ..." [F. H.] Marx, K., Das Kapital, vol. III, Der Gesamtprozeß der kapitalistischen Produktion [1894], ed. by Engels, F., in: Marx Engels Werke, vol. 25, Berlin, 1976, p. 257. The editors of the German translation of Sraffa's book, which was 1968 initially published in the former German Democratic Republic, rendered Marx correctly and added the parenthetical phrase "die Arbeiter, d. Hrsg." [the labourers, ed.] after "sie" [they]. Cf. Sraffa, P., Warenproduktion mittels Waren, Frankfurt a. M., 1976, p. 126.

[24] Cf. Sraffa, P., Production ..., op. cit., p. 94.

The "Sraffa-inverse"$\mathbf{S} \equiv [\mathbf{I} - (1 + r)\mathbf{A}]^{-1}$ only has positive elements for a feasible r, i.e., $0 \leq r < R$ must apply. Under these circumstances, (11.16) can be expanded according to the infinite series:

$$\mathbf{p} = \mathbf{a}_0 w\left[\mathbf{I} + (1 + r)\mathbf{A} + (1 + r)^2\mathbf{A}^2 + (1 + r)^3\mathbf{A}^3 + \ldots\right] \tag{11.17}$$

Sraffa calls this form of price decomposition very vividly, but, as will be explained shortly, somewhat misleadingly, "reduction to dated labour quantities"[25]. If there were no interdependence between the distribution parameters w and r—a view for which Adam Smith is held responsible—the influence of their development on prices would be clear: they would follow the "natural" rates of w and r.[26] However, as Ricardo taught, there is an inverse relationship between wage and profit rates.

The system (11.16) comprises n equations with $n + 2$ unknowns: the n prices, the wage rate, and the profit rate. Again, one degree of freedom can be eliminated by choosing a unit of account. It now makes sense to select a price; let us assume that $p_j \equiv 1$. It is necessary to extract the price equation for commodity j from Eqs. (11.16) to determine the relationship between the wage and profit rates. To that end, we multiply (11.16) from the right by $\mathbf{e}_j$, an n-dimensional column vector whose jth element is one and in which otherwise only zeros occur:

$$\mathbf{pe}_j = \mathbf{a}_0 w^{(j)}\mathbf{Se}_j \equiv 1 \tag{11.18}$$

$w^{(j)}$ stands for the wage rate measured in commodity j. From (11.18), one obtains after rearrangement:

$$w^{(j)} = \frac{1}{\mathbf{a}_0\mathbf{Se}_j} \tag{11.19}$$

Since the elements of $\mathbf{S}$ grow with r according to (11.17), $\frac{dw}{dr} < 0$. The wage rate falls when the profit rate rises and vice versa. Yet, no general statement can be made about the second derivative. Although the "wage curve" falls in a w-r-diagram, convex and concave sections can alternate in higher-dimensional models.[27]

Due to the opposing relationship between the wage rate and the profit rate, it is impossible to predict a priori what course the price of a commodity will take as soon as a distribution parameter changes. After expanding the right-hand side of (11.17), it becomes clear that each summand of the series is exposed to the divergent movements of the wage rate and the profit rate. It is impossible to predict which effect will gain the upper hand.

---

[25] Cf. ibid., p. 34 ff.

[26] Modern authors also view the profit rate as unrelated to the real wage rate, e.g., Preiser, E., Wachstum und Einkommensverteilung, 3rd ed., Heidelberg 1970, p. 19.

[27] Cf. in detail Helmedag, F., Die Technikwahl …, op. cit., p. 189 ff. As will be shown with an example, the choice of the accounting unit is reflected in the shape of the negatively sloped w-r-curve.

As Sraffa demonstrates through an example, complicated patterns of price fluctuations are conceivable for a continuous variation of the profit rate, a phenomenon with which he criticises the attempt of Austrian capital theory to consider a period of production autonomous from distribution as a quantitative measure of capital.[28] Furthermore, according to Sraffa, the concept of a macroeconomic production function with "capital" as an independent variable is also doomed to failure: "The reversals in the direction of the movement of relative prices, in the face of unchanged methods of production, cannot be reconciled with *any* notion of capital as a measurable quantity independent of distribution and prices."[29]

From the Eqs. (11.17), it was (wrongly) concluded that they were suitable for depriving Smith's component theory of its foundation.

> "In fact," Roncaglia opines, "whenever there is at least one commodity directly or indirectly necessary for the production of all other commodities in the economy (a 'basic product' in Sraffa's terminology), the cost of production of each commodity will include a residual of such commodities, and no matter how many times the process of reduction is repeated this residual cannot be eliminated, even as the process of reduction tends to infinity ... it is impossible to arrive at a commodity whose cost of production consists solely of wages, profits, and rents, because, by definition, there exists no commodity which does not require at least one basic commodity for its production."[30]

As indicated earlier, such an interpretation does not stand to reason. The reduction process is by no means lost in an infinite historical regress. Although (11.17) consists of an endless series, it only contains data and parameters of the current period. Dmitriev has already formulated this unambiguously[31], and other post-Sraffian neo-Ricardians have not contested it. Steedman, e.g., states, "... the backward resolution of means of production into dated labour quantities is a purely conceptual resolution, and *not* a 'historical story' ..."[32] And Garegnani assists: "... the reduction to dated labour constitutes a more logical device, as is shown by the fact that, when the production of a commodity is 'circular', it cannot be conceived as starting with unassisted labour."[33]

---

[28] Sraffa's assertion is too sweeping because in Böhm-Bawerk's capital theory, a physically determined production period can be identified. Cf. Helmedag, F., Böhm-Bawerks Kapitaltheorie ..., op. cit.

[29] Sraffa, P., Production ..., op. cit., p. 38.

[30] Roncaglia, A., Sraffa and the Theory of Prices, Chichester et al. 1978, p. 9.

[31] "... we can always find the total sum of the labour directly and indirectly expended on the production of any product *under present-day production conditions*, ... the fact that all capital under *present-day* conditions is itself produced with the assistance of other capital in no way hinders a precise solution of the problem." Dmitriev, V. K., op. cit., p. 44.

[32] Steedman, I., Marx ..., op. cit., p. 73.

[33] Garegnani, P., Value ..., op. cit., p. 315 n. Incidentally, with this explanatory scheme, an attempt was made to scotch the neo-Austrian capital theory: "It is sometimes argued that if history could be traced back far enough, the production of every capital good must be explained by labour inputs alone. This argument ... is entirely fallacious ... *it may never again be efficient to produce hammers by the process which uses labour alone.* All that is required is the existence of a (sufficiently productive) alternative process for producing hammers using labour *and* a machine ... When such realistic simultaneity is admitted, the neo-Austrian description of the feasible technology becomes

For this reason, the term "reduction to dated quantities of work", which initially seems descriptive, was classified as misleading. It encourages a successivistic approach to the problem, which is misguided in a model of simultaneous production. Those who think along these lines tend to treat something as "advanced" and, therefore, as a stock variable, which in reality is produced *during* a period in a circular production process and *must* consequently be a flow variable.

Significantly, neo-Ricardians ignore that the decomposition of a commodity price, as expressed in (11.17) (cf. p. 214), refers to the current period. At any rate, Sraffians disregarded the *convergence* of the infinite series. The motive for the omission can easily be traced. If one accepts the existence of a limit of convergence, then, in plain terms, separating the price into a wage and a profit component à la Smith must be feasible. As a result, (at least) Sraffa's postulate of a maximum profit rate would hang in limbo:

> "If the 'total decomposition' were possible, the rate of profits corresponding to a zero wage rate would be infinite, for the rate of profits would be obtained from the division of a finite quantity (total profit, which would be equal to the value of output) by a zero quantity (capital advanced which would be composed entirely of wages and thus zero)."[34]

An infinite rate of profit may not seem very realistic, but the same applies to a zero-wage rate. After all, who said in such an extreme situation—free labour input!—is the value of output positive and finite? Wouldn't it be more conceivable that if wages vanish, prices and costs would also disappear, resulting in a profit rate of "$\frac{0}{0}$", a mathematically indeterminate expression? Is capitalism without *wage* labour still capitalism?

Such a reasoning could also refer to an essential result of input–output analysis. It is undisputed that, within this framework, all goods—including those that return into production, i.e., the intermediate products—can be reduced solely to the *only* input that is not (capitalistically) produced: labour. "It is characteristic of Leontief's model that it reduces the primary factors to one only—homogeneous labour, the inputs of each industry are the outputs of other industries."[35] As will be shown later, this result also applies to the Sraffa analysis; it is not for nothing that we speak of the Sraffa-Leontief model.

It gets even better. Some neo-Ricardians *explicitly* admit that "total dissolution" is possible. One of the most prominent among them is Luigi Pasinetti. In his argument, he subtracts **pA** on both sides of the neo-Ricardian price formula in the first step (11.8) (cf. p. 211):

$$\mathbf{p} - \mathbf{pA} = \mathbf{pA}r + \mathbf{a}_0 w \tag{11.20}$$

inadequate." Burmeister, E., Synthesizing the Neo-Austrian and Alternative Approaches to Capital Theory: A Survey, in: Journal of Economic Literature, vol. 12 (1974), pp. 413–456, p. 416.

[34] Roncaglia, A., op. cit., p. 9.

[35] Hicks, J. R., Linear Theory [1960], reprinted in: Surveys of Economic Theory, vol. III (Resource Allocation), London et al. 1966, pp. 75–113, p. 104. In a review, Solow used the remarkable phrase: "The intermediate goods are *spurlos versenkt* [*sunk without trace*] inside the process." Cf. Solow, R. M., Review of "Capital and Time" by J. Hicks, in: The Economic Journal, vol. 84 (1974), pp. 189–192, p. 189.

Right multiplication with $\mathbf{L} \equiv [\mathbf{I} - \mathbf{A}]^{-1}$ yields:

$$\mathbf{p} = \mathbf{pAL}r + \mathbf{a}_0\mathbf{L}w = \mathbf{pH}r + \mathbf{v}w \tag{11.21}$$

On the right-hand side of (11.21), the "Pasinetti-matrix"$\mathbf{H} \equiv \mathbf{AL}$ contains all goods directly and indirectly involved in the production of the means of production.[36] Obviously, $\mathbf{v}w$ encompasses the wage components of prices, while the interpretation of the vector $\mathbf{pH}r$ as profit shares is evident and seems to confirm the "advance thesis", i.e., "capital" is construed as a pre-financed material input. "This is a remarkable expression," Pasinetti promotes (11.21), "as it explicitly shows that each price is ultimately made up of only two components: wages and profits."[37] So the good Adam Smith may have shot in the dark with his much-maligned component theory, yet he hit the bull's eye!—Such a conclusion, however, would be rash.

As a second look at the expression (11.21) reveals, the prices $\mathbf{p}$ appear on *all* sides of the equations: Pasinetti's explanation, therefore, by no means substantiates that they are *ultimately* composed solely of wages and profit; the solution of the matrix Eq. (11.8) is not (11.21), but (11.16) (cf. p. 214), and this system is inapt to approve the component theory.

Heinz D. Kurz took another way to examine Smith's approach. He operates with the subsystem concept—we shall discuss the details later. In this model, which considers rent, Kurz intends to demonstrate that the price of a good can be divided wholly into wages, profit, and rent. The dissection reflects "… in a purely formal way *Smith*'s 'adding-up'-theory".[38] This finding contrasts sharply with Kurz's initial statement, after which scepticism towards the component theory is appropriate.[39] Immediately before the result that production prices finally split up into wages, profit and rent, he again states the shipwreck of the component theory.[40]

Hence, Smith's proposal is wrong on the one hand, although formally right on the other. This ambiguity in judgment rests on confusion about the "statics and dynamics" of the component theory of value. It is different to say the price of a commodity ultimately consists of wages and profit (if we disregard rent) than to claim that there is no relationship between incomes. The first (static) statement is correct, but the second (dynamic) is not.

What is the use of a doctrine that posits the existence of an advanced capital value to be "remunerated" with a uniform rate of profit if labour is the only original factor

---

36 Cf. Pasinetti, L., The Notion of Vertical Integration in Economic Analysis [1973], reprinted in: Pasinetti, L. (ed.), Essays on the Theory of Joint Production, London/Basingstoke 1980, pp. 16–43, p. 20 f.

37 Ibid., p. 22.

38 Cf. Kurz, H. D., Adam Smiths Komponententheorie …, op. cit., p. 707. [F. H.] Kurz's representation also suffers from the shortcoming that the price sought appears on the left and right in the 'solution'. Cf. ibid., Eq. (17a).

39 Cf. ibid., p. 691.

40 "Due to his inadequate understanding of the distributional context, *Smith*'s additive component theory of relative prices was also bound to fail." Ibid., p. 706. [F. H.].

and wages and profit altogether constitute the price? Against this backdrop, would it not be more plausible to make labour the basis for calculating profit? To be sure, we shall continue to focus on this question. For this purpose, an apparent detour turns out to be a shortcut. To wit, the Sraffian work was not only opposed to neoclassicism. Instead, it served as an armoury for a (renewed) attack on Marx's theory of value. Once again—as with Bortkiewicz's correction of the value calculation—scrutinising the critique will prove fruitful.

11.3 Exploitation and Profit: The Fundamental Theorem

Sraffa's analysis was, by his own account, intended to provide the platform for an attack against neoclassicism, but he, *nolens volens,* became the incriminating witness in the Marx case. Sraffa (supposedly) unveiled how a correct transformation of labour values into production prices occurs. Actually, converting values into Sraffa-prices can be carried out without great difficulty. To achieve this, we multiply the value system (11.12) $\mathbf{v} = \mathbf{a}_0\mathbf{L}$ from the right by $w\mathbf{L}^{-1}\mathbf{S}$ to immediately obtain (11.16) (cf. p. 214)[41]:

$$\mathbf{v}w\mathbf{L}^{-1}\,\mathbf{S} = w\mathbf{a}_0\mathbf{L}\mathbf{L}^{-1}\,\mathbf{S} = w\mathbf{a}_0[\mathbf{I} - (1+r)\mathbf{A}]^{-1} = \mathbf{p} \qquad (11.22)$$

This procedure shows clearly how the transformation proceeds: first, the Leontief-inverse is "eliminated" by multiplying it by its inverse. All that remains of the values is the vector of direct labour inputs (multiplied by a unit matrix), which is required to calculate the Sraffa prices. The missing elements needed for the desired outcome—the Sraffa-inverse **S** and the wage rate—are, as expected, brought along, too. From this point of view, Samuelson hit the bull's eye with his oft-cited polemic:

> "... the 'transformation algorithm' is precisely of the following form: 'Contemplate two alternative, and discordant systems. Write down one. Now transform by taking an eraser and rubbing it out. Then fill in the other one. *Voilà*! You have completed your transformation algorithm.' By this technique one can 'transform' from phlogiston to entropy; from Ptolemy to Copernicus; from Newton to Einstein; from Genesis to Darwin—and, from entropy to phlogiston again ..."[42]

Therefore, the solution to the transformation problem definitively establishes that the calculation of values is tantamount to pointless occupational therapy since prices can

---

[41] Cf. Wolfstetter, E., Wert, Profitrate und Beschäftigung, Frankfurt a. M. 1977, p. 78.

[42] Samuelson, P. A., Understanding the Marxian Notion of Exploitation: A Summary of the So-Called Transformation Problem Between Marxian Values and Competitive Prices, in: Journal of Economic Literature, vol. 9 (1971), pp. 399–431, p. 400. Further approaches to transforming labour values into production prices, not discussed here, are reviewed by Fröhlich, N., op. cit., pp. 137 ff.

be determined without knowing the values. In this light, Marx's theory of value—at least as a quantitative theory of equilibrium prices—appears superfluous,[43] the transformation problem reveals itself as an "intrinsically unimportant problem",[44] and in general, the analysis of value should be replaced by an examination of the production relations "in the field".[45]

Of course, there were dissenting voices: "Marx would call Sraffa's economic theory vulgar economics."[46] Others, probably with the reduction to dated quantities of labour in mind, tried to take a balancing position:

> "By solving the problem of the transformation of Marxian values into long-run competitive prices, Sraffa provides a viable labour theory of value ... It is a labour theory in the limited sense that relative prices can be shown to be determined by amounts of direct and indirect labour."[47]

However, this interpretation is dubious. In contrast to the value calculation, Sraffa prices assign weights to the individual labour quantities that depend on the distribution. It was even concluded from this that "... no systematic relationship can exist between value variables and production prices."[48] But Sraffa's place in the spectrum of economic theory should prevent him from being played off too harshly against Marx; it is not only at the surface that both felt committed to the "classical" mission, despite their autonomy otherwise:

> "In this respect," Kurz judged at the time, "the position of some representatives of the new critique is astonishingly ahistorical, for obviously their attack on Marx is not restrained by the awareness of their common affiliation to *one and the same theoretical-historical tradition*."[49]

For those neo-Ricardians who take the view that Marx and Sraffa stand in a complementary relationship to one another, it is relatively easy not to regard the transformation problem as a severe difficulty: in their opinion, after all, they have an ironclad theory of production prices, which has also proven itself in the critique of neoclassicism. Furthermore, exploitation and profit are linked by *the fundamental theorem*. As a result, an essential element of Marx's critique of capitalism would remain intact.

As mentioned, v. Bortkiewicz has already seized the connection between the surplus value rate and the profit rate. It pays to present this relationship within the framework outlined here. Expediently, one starts from the quantity system of the

---

[43] Cf. Fees-Dörr, E., Die Redundanz der Mehrwerttheorie, Ein Beitrag zur Kontroverse zwischen Marxisten und Neoricardianern, Marburg 1989 and Stanger, M., Krisententendenzen der Kapitalakkumulation, Berlin 1988, p. 177.

[44] Steedman, I., Marx ..., op. cit., p. 29.

[45] "Hence, we conclude that value analysis should be displaced by a direct investigation of the production process." Nutzinger, H. G., Concepts of Value in Linear Economic Models, in: Operations Research Verfahren, vol. 26 (1977), pp. 717–724, p. 717.

[46] Stamatis, G., Zur Entmythologisierung ..., op. cit., p. 180. Cf. also, Shaikh, A., op. cit.

[47] Harcourt, G. C., The Rate of Profits in Equilibrium Growth Models: A Review Article, in: Journal of Political Economy, Vol. 81 (1973), pp. 1261–1277, p. 1262.

[48] Wolfstetter, E., Wert, Profitrate ..., op. cit., p. 137. [F. H.].

[49] Kurz, H. D., Zum Problem der Rente in der Wert- und Produktionspreistheorie, in: Gesellschaft, Beiträge zur Marxschen Theorie 13, Frankfurt a. M. 1979, pp. 174–200, p. 175. [F. H.].

economy. Surplus value and profit are only observable if the technique is productive, i.e., the following condition applies:

$$\mathbf{Ae} \leq \mathbf{e} \tag{11.23}$$

e symbolises the summation vector in which only ones occur.[50] Condition (11.23) is fulfilled for all coefficient matrices **A** whose largest eigenvalue $\lambda_{\max} < 1$. Subtracting the goods consumed in the production process from the (column) vector **q** of total production yields the net product **y**:

$$\mathbf{q} - \mathbf{Aq} = \mathbf{y} \tag{11.24}$$

The system (11.24) consists of $2n$ unknowns, **q** and **y**. Solving for the gross quantities **q** to manufacture an exogenous output vector **y** gives:

$$\mathbf{q} = \mathbf{Ly} \tag{11.25}$$

The n degrees of freedom are reduced by one if we—like Sraffa—fix the social volume of work in a given period as unity[51]:

$$\mathbf{a}_0\mathbf{q} \equiv 1 \tag{11.26}$$

Left multiplication of (11.25) with $\mathbf{a}_0$ gives:

$$\mathbf{a}_0\mathbf{q} = \mathbf{a}_0\mathbf{Ly} = \mathbf{vy} = 1 \tag{11.27}$$

The total work performed is thus reflected in the sum of the labour values of the net product. In the period under consideration, the labourers receive a bundle of goods as real wage, which is listed in a semi-positive column vector **d**. Then the rate of surplus value comes to:

$$s' = \frac{\mathbf{vy} - \mathbf{vd}}{\mathbf{vd}} \tag{11.28}$$

The fundamental theorem states that a positive profit rate indicates exploitation. To prove this, we turn to the price system. If the nominal wage rate w is set to one, we

[50] In Eqs. (11.23), the less-than sign must apply at least once. Strict productivity exists when the output of *every* good exceeds its total input requirement.

[51] Cf. Sraffa, P., Production …, op. cit., p. 10. The normalisation leads to a pure number since the dimensions cancel out. With constant returns to scale, the definition can be interpreted as a per capita view, as is customary, e.g., in neoclassical growth theory. The expression also illustrates that 'effective demand', which comprises intermediate and consumer products, determines total employment.

obtain a standardisation for prices, since the pay suffices *ex hypothesi* to acquire the wage goods bundle **d**:

$$w \equiv 1 = \mathbf{p}^*\mathbf{d} \tag{11.29}$$

The labour commanded prices $\mathbf{p}^*$ are measured in a timespan indicating how long a labourer must work for a particular commodity at the wage rate $w \equiv 1$. If the rate of profit is positive, the prices expressed in this way exceed the values. The difference becomes immediately apparent by juxtaposing the expanded forms of the two variables:

$$\mathbf{v} = \mathbf{a}_0\mathbf{L} = \mathbf{a}_0\left[\mathbf{I} + \mathbf{A} + \mathbf{A}^2 + \mathbf{A}^3 + \ldots\right] \tag{11.30}$$

$$\mathbf{p}^* = \mathbf{a}_0\mathbf{S} = \mathbf{a}_0\left[\mathbf{I} + (1+r)\mathbf{A} + (1+r)^2\mathbf{A}^2 + (1+r)^3\mathbf{A}^3 + \ldots\right] \tag{11.31}$$

From the comparison between (11.30) and (11.31) results for $0 < r < R$:

$$\mathbf{p}^* > \mathbf{v} \tag{11.32}$$

Combining Eqs. (11.27) and (11.29) leads to:

$$\mathbf{vy} = 1 = \mathbf{p}^*\mathbf{d} \tag{11.33}$$

Rearranging (11.28) under consideration of (11.33) and (11.32) yields:

$$s'\mathbf{vd} = \mathbf{vy} - \mathbf{vd} = \mathbf{p}^*\mathbf{d} - \mathbf{vd} = (\mathbf{p}^* - \mathbf{v})\mathbf{d} > 0 \tag{11.34}$$

If the value of labour power **vd** is positive, this also applies to s' according to (11.34): a positive rate of profit goes hand in hand with a positive rate of surplus value.[52]

Fatally, however, the fundamental theorem amounts to a *statement of equivalence*: the positivity of r and s' is mutually dependent. *This* theorem, therefore, does not confirm that profit is the manifestation of surplus value. From a formal point of view, one could just as well have started with the positivity of the rate of surplus value to identify surplus value subsequently as an appearance of profit.[53] But that is not all.

Suppose the real wage defrayed by the individual sectors—which can be written as a dyadic product $\mathbf{da}_0$—is integrated into the matrix **A** of direct requirements. In

---

[52] Numerous variants of the derivation of the fundamental theorem can be found in the literature. Cf., e.g., Morishima, M., Marx' Economics, op. cit., p. 53 ff. and Roemer, J. E., Analytical Foundations of Marxian Economic Theory, Cambridge 1981, p. 16 f.

[53] Cf. Samuelson, P. A., Understanding …, op. cit., p. 416 f. See also Steedman, I., Marx …, op. cit., p. 58: "The very fact that the proposition in question 'runs both ways' … means at once that it does not constitute a theory of why r is positive.".

that case, the coefficient matrix **M** is augmented by workers' consumption:

$$\mathbf{M} = \mathbf{A} + \mathbf{d}\mathbf{a}_0 \tag{11.35}$$

Assuming that **M** is productive, the ability exists to generate surplus products in addition to the workers' wage goods. However, labour is hidden in the production equations; it no longer emerges as a source of added value.[54] In such a "slave economy", if one likes, people are "manufactured" like machines in a capitalist production process and treated like commodities. Under such conditions, as several authors have pointed out, the productivity of **M** can be linked to the "exploitation" of any commodity. Apparently, it is not necessary to attribute the surplus product to labour exploitation.

Roemer, e.g., calculates a value system based on steel. According to his analysis, the productivity of **M** is sufficient for "… the steel value of steel is less than one, and hence that steel is exploited."[55] This property applies to all goods in a productive system: "Hence profitability of capitalism is not explained by the exploitation of labour unless some other reason can be provided to choose labour as the value numeraire instead of steel."[56]

This standpoint is not new; Dmitriev had already developed the same idea. Yet there is no suggestion in his work that labour should perhaps be given a unique role for other reasons:

> "... whenever a known quantity of some product α has been used up in the production of α and we can obtain a *larger* quantity *of the same* product within some definite period of time as a result of the production process, the profit rate in the given branch of industry will be a fully-determined quantity *greater than zero, irrespective of the price of the product* α. If the production costs of the other goods ... are reduced *in the final analysis* to the same productα, the same profit rate should also be established in these branches under conditions of free mobility from one branch of production to another..."[57]

Dmitriev then mentions a purely robotic economy in which profit is conceivable without human labour[58], and he concludes: "… the origin of industrial profit does not stand in any 'special' relationship to the human labour used in production."[59]

But this conclusion throws the baby out with the bathwater. Of course, there is no exploitation of labour without labour input.[60] In such a situation, using the word profit is problematic—despite surplus product. Incidentally, fiction does not invalidate reality: human labour is still performed in the production process, as everyone can see. No change is to be expected in this respect in the foreseeable future.

---

[54] Cf. Schneider, J., Der Beitrag der Arbeitswertlehre zur Theorie der kapitalistischen Warenproduktion, Frankfurt a. M./New York 1980, p. 13.

[55] Roemer, J. E., Value …, op. cit., p. 26.

[56] Ibid.

[57] Dmitriev, V. K., op. cit., p. 62 f.

[58] Cf. ibid.

[59] Ibid., p. 64.

[60] Cf. on this complex Pichler, E., Vollautomatische Güterproduktion, Marburg 1990.

Moreover, labour is the *only* original factor in the present framework: steel—like all commodities—is *produced* by labour (and by means of production); this remains the case whether one "hides" the real wage in the enriched coefficient matrix **M** or not. In Ricardo's wheat economy, it is also possible to express the labour employed in terms of a corresponding quantity of corn paid as wages. Then, one could come up with the idea that grain would be "exploited". In truth, however, there is no exploitation of the crop. Instead, a "material rate of produce" only occurs as a matter of fact after people have been (more or less) industrious.

This consideration applies to all pre-products. As noted, the linear single production models have been attested that their output can be reduced entirely to labour: "Remember, however," says the "bible" of linear optimisation, "that everything is congealed labour in a Leontief system."[61] How can this statement be reconciled with the thesis that profit comes from "exploited" intermediate products, which are also elevated to the benchmark of its distribution? To get down to basics, we need to dig deeper.

11.4 Demand and the Choice of Technique: The Non-Substitution Theorem

In the context of single production, the fundamental theorem proves the reciprocal positivity of the rate of surplus value and the rate of profit. Of course, it cannot be concluded from *this* statement that profit is the manifestation of surplus value, although this view does not contradict the theorem. If it could be proven that labour values play a key role in capitalist market economies, the causality between values and prices would remain relevant. However, according to the prevailing opinion, prospects look bleak for the value theory in this regard.

The surplus product is the material form of surplus value and profit, and its extent depends on the technique used. Practically, several alternatives to produce a commodity exist. The chosen method is a means to an end: profit maximisation. According to orthodox doctrine, this objective is guided by prices, not values. Labour values are regarded as *ex post* magnitudes, which can only be calculated once the employed techniques are known; the profit rate ostensibly governs the rate of surplus value:

> "The determination of the profit rate is thus *logically prior* to any determination of value magnitudes—it is hardly surprising, then, that the latter have nothing to contribute to the former ... All value quantities are purely derivative of the physical conditions of production and the real wage, and, indeed, in the presence of a choice of technique—which does always exist—those value quantities can only be determined *after* the rate of profit has already been determined in the profit maximising choice of technique."[62]

[61] Dorfman, R., Samuelson, P. A., Solow, R. M., Linear Programming and Economic Analysis, New York/Toronto/London 1958, p. 249.

[62] Steedman, I., Marx ..., op. cit., p. 65.

The selection of the coefficient matrix **A** occurring in the value and quantity system is—according to the unanimously advocated view—made exclusively in the price system; only the profit rate or the wage rate decides on the preferred technique. Marx's doctrine of the hierarchy of values and prices thus seems to have been turned upside down.

Under certain conditions, the non-substitution theorem shows that demand does not influence the profit-maximising technique. The theorem rests on three pillars: linear returns to scale, single production and one primary factor—labour. The model to be studied here rests on the same premises; this is not the only reason the non-substitution theorem deserves closer attention. The effect of a change in demand on the established profit-maximising production processes can only be analysed if the production methods have been chosen earlier—a central point of this enquiry.

In this context, as already indicated, remarks are repeatedly made, giving rise to a certain uncertainty as to whether labour values are actually irrelevant to the choice of production methods. Instead, at first glance, there is a contradiction between the distribution-dependent prices of a Sraffa economy and the *unchanging* price ratios embedded in the Leontief system. Let us listen to a characterisation of the Leontief input–output model, sounding like the labour theory of value in its purest form. The constancy of the incorporated exchange relations is explained as follows:

> "The reason is essentially that there is *by assumption* only one fixed factor, only one true social cost. Relative prices of commodities will depend only on their direct and indirect labor content. A change in wage rates, for example, will simply increase the prices of all commodities in the same proportion, leaving relative prices unchanged. Since there is only one thing to be economized, labor, it is perhaps plausible that one set of activities should turn out to be the most economical of labor, regardless of what final goods are desired."[63]

Against this background, a closer examination of the non-substitution theorem seems worthwhile. It will emerge that Sraffa's account of the choice of technique has disregarded significant findings of input–output analysis and instead relies on assumptions that may appear plausible but are questionable. As the history of the non-substitution theorem confirms once again, one direction was prematurely favoured at the junctures of economic theory without seriously considering whether another course might have been the right one.

As Samuelson reports[64], the original version of the theorem was formulated independently by N. Georgescu-Roegen and him in 1949 and published in an anthology containing several contributions to this topic.[65] The characteristic style was initially neoclassical; the aim was to work out the compatibility of Leontief's fixed production coefficients with the substitutability between inputs, a typical feature of neoclassical analyses: "Actually, *all* his theory in its present form is compatible with the

---

[63] Dorfman, R., Samuelson, P. A., Solow, R. M., op. cit., p. 225. See also Bliss, C. J., op. cit., p. 252 ff.

[64] Cf. Samuelson, P. A., A New Theorem on Nonsubstitution, in: Hegeland, H. (ed.), Money, Growth and Methodology and Other Essays in Economics in Honor of Johan Åkerman, Lund 1961, pp. 407–423, p. 408.

[65] Cf. Koopmans, T. C. (ed.), Activity Analysis of Production and Allocation, New York/London/Sydney 1951.

more general case of substitutability."[66] Even in the situation of two factors, the isoquant diagram familiar from standard microeconomics illustrates the existence of a continuum of alternatives to produce a specific good. Nevertheless, a constant factor input ratio could be observed regardless of the level of output: "This appears to be, in fact, a revival of the Walrasian assumption regarding the constancy of production coefficients under a more general form."[67] In this light, the seemingly absurd use of language, namely to refer to the non-substitution theorem occasionally as the "substitution theorem", right up to the present day, becomes understandable.

The creation not only has a double name, but it also exists in two forms. The simple or static version assumes a profitless economy. In any case, this was pretended in the early proofs—a further indication of the theorem's neoclassical origins since, for neoclassicists, there is no such thing as "pure" profit, at least in the long run. We discuss the non-substitution theorem in a framework that suits this enquiry's concerns: linear programming.[68] It allows us to assess the general or dynamic variety subsequently.

Let several production options be available for some or all goods, with each of these activities comprising n input coefficients.[69] When there are more methods (m) than goods (n), i.e., $n < m$, it is impractical to identify the individual processes solely by reference to their input coefficients. For this reason, we agree on a sign rule, as is usual in activity analysis[70]: inputs are noted with a negative sign in the column relating to an activity, whereas a positive value indicates the respective output. If necessary, the methods can be so proportioned that outputs consist of one unit.

The possibilities are combined in a rectangular $n \times m$ technology matrix $\mathbf{T}$, where the rows correspond to the commodities and the columns refer to the activities. If the element t_{ij} of this matrix is positive or one, the ith good represents the production result of the jth process. Of course, at least one positive element exists in every row and column: all goods can be produced, and all processes have an output.[71]

---

66 Samuelson, P. A., Abstract of a Theorem Concerning Substitutability in Open Leontief Models, in: Koopmans, T. C. (ed.), op. cit., pp. 142–146, p. 142 f. Leontief also sees his approach in the tradition of neoclassical theory. Cf. Leontief, W., The Structure of the American Economy 1919–1935, An Empirical Application of Equilibrium Analysis, 2nd ed., New York 1960, p. 33 ff.

67 Georgescu-Roegen, N., The Aggregate Linear Production Function and Its Applications to von Neumann's Economic Model, in: Koopmans, T. C. (ed.), op. cit., pp. 98–115, p. 98.

68 One encounters this derivation method first in Gale, D., The Theory of Linear Economic Models, New York/Toronto/London 1960, p. 301 ff., who owes the idea to the pioneer of linear optimisation, G. Dantzig. Cf. ibid., p. 318.

69 In the limiting case, even the continuous substitution of inputs characteristic of neoclassicism is covered: "... in the Sraffa-Leontief model, it is usual to consider discrete techniques ... but continuous substitution could also be allowed. It would simply require the existence of an infinite number of techniques each differing in an infinitesimal way from its 'neighbor'." Mainwaring, L., Value and Distribution in Capitalist Economies, Cambridge 1984, p. 177.

70 Cf. Hildenbrand, K., Hildenbrand, W., Lineare ökonomische Modelle, Berlin/Heidelberg/New York 1975, p. 22 ff.

71 If there is only one process for each product—i.e., the coefficient matrix $\mathbf{A}$ is square—$\mathbf{T}$ becomes $(\mathbf{I}—\mathbf{A})$.

Operating the m processes at a level prescribed by the vector $\mathbf{q} \geq \mathbf{0}$ results in the net output $\mathbf{y}$:

$$\mathbf{Tq} = \mathbf{y} \tag{11.36}$$

If the system (11.36) contains m variables q_j, while only $n < m$ equations exist, several results are conceivable. An objective function must be formulated to transform the problem into a solvable optimisation task. What is the plan? Correct; because labour is the only non-produced input, it is crucial to minimise the expenditure for this original factor, i.e., wages subject to (s. t.) (11.36).[72]

If we set the wage rate equal to one, then the objective function minimises the total demand for labour. We denote the m-dimensional row vector of labour inputs by $\mathbf{t}_0$. The element t_{0j} represents the direct labour performed in activity j. The linear program thus reads:

$$\mathbf{t}_0\mathbf{q} \rightarrow \text{Min} \quad \text{s. t.}\mathbf{Tq} = \mathbf{y}, \mathbf{q} \geq \mathbf{0} \tag{11.37}$$

From the theory of linear programming, it is known that every basic solution of (11.37) includes at most n positive elements of $\mathbf{q}$. Under the condition that the n goods are all to be produced in exogenously fixed, positive quantities, the optimal solution determines exactly n activities in $\mathbf{T}$, each producing one good. Unneeded columns of the technology matrix $\mathbf{T}$ are irrelevant.

The optimal basic solution does not change if the final demand $\mathbf{y}' \neq \mathbf{y}$ is to be produced instead of net output $\mathbf{y}$. If the coefficient matrix $\mathbf{A}$ and the corresponding labour input $\mathbf{a}_0$ are employed to produce output $\mathbf{y}$ with minimal labour input, this also applies to production $\mathbf{y}'$. With linear techniques, the labour values do not vary with the process levels.[73] Despite a growing or shrinking demand, the optimal technique remains the same; the individual activities are merely expanded or contracted as required.

Let us look at the dual of (11.37). Since the primal is a quantity minimisation problem, it is now a price maximisation problem:

$$\mathbf{py} \rightarrow \text{Max} \quad \text{s. t.} \quad \mathbf{pT} = \mathbf{t}_0, \quad \mathbf{p} \geq \mathbf{0} \tag{11.38}$$

[72] Cf. Gale, D., op. cit., p. 304, Lancaster, K., Mathematical Economics, New York 1968, p. 82, Bliss. C. J., op. cit., p. 254.

[73] Of course, the programme must be feasible, i.e., the minimum amount of labour required to produce a desired bundle of goods must not exceed the amount of labour available. A formal proof is provided by Lancaster, who calls the corresponding theorem the "basic theorem of linear programming". Cf. Lancaster, K., op. cit., p. 39. The same statement can be found without this name in Gale, D., op. cit., p. 304 (Lemma 9.3). Similar considerations exist in the theory of centrally planned economies. Novoshilov, e.g., presents a linear programme for minimising the amount of work. Cf. Novoshilov, W., Arbeitswerttheorie und Mathematik, in: Sowjetwissenschaften, 1965, pp. 1029–1047. Such approaches also appear in the business management literature. See Weitzman, M., On Choosing an Optimal Technology, in: Management Science, vol. 19 (1967), pp. 413–428.

This programme produces the same optimal value of the objective function as the primal, and the same processes are activated. If we write $\mathbf{a}_0$ for the vector selected from $\mathbf{t}_0$, the following applies:

$$\mathbf{a}_0\mathbf{q} = \mathbf{p}\mathbf{y} \tag{11.39}$$

In this model, the total labour $\mathbf{a}_0\mathbf{q}$ also coincides with the sum of the labour values of the net output $\mathbf{v}\mathbf{y}$. Accordingly, we get from (11.39):

$$\mathbf{p} = \mathbf{v} \tag{11.40}$$

The Leontief system, therefore, implicitly embraces a labour theory of value. If the wage rate serves as a unit of account, the labour values correspond directly to the equilibrium prices of a "profitless" economy. In such a situation, neoclassicists (for some inexplicable reason) occasionally speak of a "timeless economy", a confusion of language that probably goes back to Mirrlees.[74] In reality, neither the allegedly missing factor "time" is responsible for a price system (11.40) or (11.13) (cf. p. 212) nor a special distribution situation. As will be shown in a moment, this price formation can claim validity not only for exceptional cases of distribution or production theory.

Extending the simple non-substitution theorem to situations characterised by a positive profit rate was in the air for several years[75] before it was analytically established that the price structure is generally not linked to demand. The work of Mirrlees and Stiglitz[76] from the late 1960s is usually cited in this context. Yet, Samuelson's disciple Levhari had noted a few years earlier: "… in each rate of interest r there exists a matrix a composed of pure activities which will minimize prices in terms of wages, or rather, maximize real wages."[77] All proofs of the "dynamic" non-substitution

[74] Cf. Mirrlees, J. A., The Dynamic Nonsubstitution Theorem, in: The Review of Economic Studies, vol. 36 (1969), pp. 67–76. Of course, there is no lack of attempts to justify the vocabulary: "The optimal technique minimises the use of the primary factor labour and thus ensures efficiency. In timeless production, the labour input embodies the only real costs, and cost-covering production prices and labour values are therefore understandably identical (or proportional to each other for a different standard of account)." Kesting, H., op. cit., p. 141 f. [F. H.] In the footnote on p. 141, Kesting even claims: "Because of the assumed timeless production, the net social product consists only of the consumption of households …" [F. H.].

[75] Cf. Bliss, J., C., op. cit., p. 251 n.

[76] Cf. Mirrlees, J. A., op. cit. and Stiglitz, J. E., Non-Substitution Theorems With Durable Capital Goods, in: The Review of Economic Studies, vol. 37 (1970), pp. 543–553.

[77] Levhari, D., A Nonsubstitution Theorem and Switching of Techniques, in: The Quarterly Journal of Economics, vol. 79 (1965), pp. 98–105, p. 102. a corresponds to the coefficient matrix $\mathbf{A}$. Levhari then made a *false* deduction, implying that the recurrence of a technique does not occur if the distribution changes. This proposition got the debate about 'reswitching' going. Cf. Morishima, M., Refutation of the Nonswitching Theorem, in: The Quarterly Journal of Economics, vol. 80 (1966), pp. 520–525, Levhari, D., Samuelson, P. A., The Nonswitching Theorem is False, in: The Quarterly Journal of Economics, vol. 80 (1966), pp. 518 f. The topic will be discussed promptly in more detail.

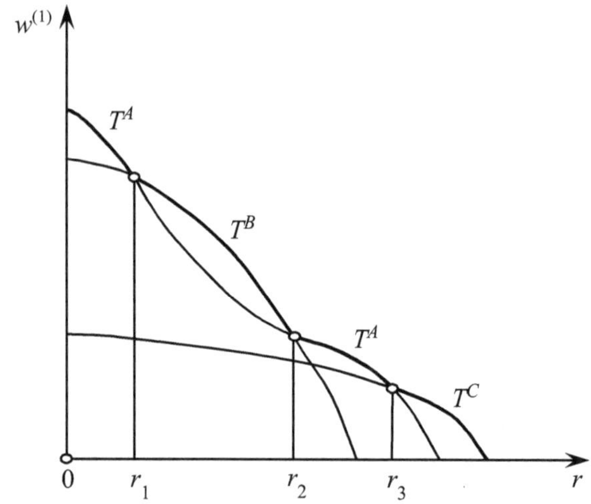

Fig. 11.1 The wage curves of three techniques

theorem proclaim this message. Another example may suffice: "The nonsubstitution theorems assert that ... only one vector of relative prices is possible for the economy ... In equilibrium, the price of each produced commodity is equal to the *minimum cost of producing it* ...".[78]

On the one hand, the last quote was chosen to prove again—better safe than sorry—that the general non-substitution theorem certifies the independence of the price structure from final demand. On the other hand, the passage reveals a competitive economy's assumed mode of operation to determine the price vector. Neoclassicists *and* neo-Ricardians believe the decision between the production methods "... will be exclusively grounded on cheapness ..."[79] Under competitive conditions, the (supposedly) most cost-effective technique will gain the upper hand. For a fixed profit rate, this generates the least possible prices. Then, *ipso facto* the real wage is maximised. But it may well be that with a *different* rate of profit, a *different* choice from **T** will entail even lower Sraffa-prices, on the contrary.

If several techniques alternate on the so-called wage frontier, varying methods would be applied depending on the distribution constellation. Figure 11.1 shows the wage curves of three techniques T^A, T^B, and T^C, which result according to (11.19) (cf. p. 215), when the price of commodity 1 is chosen as the numéraire.

The slightly thicker segments of the three wage curves located furthest to the north-east form the wage *frontier*. It provides information on the highest possible remuneration for each profit rate, or—which amounts to the same thing—it assigns the highest achievable profit rate to the respective wage rates. Between $0 \leq r < r_1$

[78] Mirrlees, J. A., op. cit., p. 67, own emphasis. See also Weizsäcker, C. C. v., Steady State Capital Theory, Berlin/Heidelberg/New York 1971, p. 53. Bliss prefers the label "general non-substitution theorem": "This is to be greatly preferred to Mirrlees' unfortunate terminology—dynamic non-substitution theorem. There is nothing dynamic about these results." Bliss, C. J., op. cit., p. 260 n.

[79] Sraffa, P., Production ..., op. cit., p. 83.

method T^A is used, for $r_1 < r < r_2$ technique B is implemented. In the interval $r_2 < r < r_3$ technique A again entails lower prices: *reswitching* occurs, the previously employed and later replaced method A now seems to be more profitable again.

Finally, for $r \geq r_3$ the previously inferior technique C forges ahead. It remains at the helm until the wage rate measured in good 1 is zero, i.e., until the maximum profit rate of this process. At the intersections of two wage curves, the switch points, the neighbouring techniques could coexist. At least, that is what the neo-Ricardian doctrine (erroneously) propagates.

As widespread as the belief is that the competitive process leads to the lowest prices, the general non-substitution theorem does not show that this really happens. For what can indeed be demonstrated within the framework of this theorem? Only the independence of a particular pricing *hypothesis* from final demand is brought to light—nothing else.[80] In no way is it brought to light that profit-maximising entrepreneurs always prefer the technology appearing on the wage frontier.

One can only be surprised that the simple theorem was extended by a (supposedly) general non-substitution theorem. Actually, there was no need to extend the "timeless" variant to a "profitable" economy: the solution of the program (11.37) (cf. p. 230) and the derivation of the non-substitution theorem based on it already covers this case. If the initial net output vector $\mathbf{y}$ merely contained the real wage bundle, a different output vector $\mathbf{y}' \geq \mathbf{y}$ does not cause a change in technique—as the gist of the non-substitution theorem states. Nothing prevents anyone from interpreting the semi-positive difference $\mathbf{y}'$—$\mathbf{y}$ as the surplus product.

The programme's dual also instructs how the vector of the physical surplus product is to be valued to calculate the scalar quantity profit: with prices corresponding to labour values. This calculation rule determines the minimal prices towards which free competition can, should and will move.

Unlike Sraffa pricing, the *law of value* considers the corresponding (optimal) quantity system. The total profit *pro rata temporis* does not simply consist of a profit per unit. In fact, overall profit results from multiplying the gain per unit by the (sold) output in the selected period.[81]

In Sraffa's approach, the classical idea that surplus limits profit fell by the wayside—against his will. Indeed, a particular surplus product can be generated with various techniques, but the most favourable for entrepreneurs is the one that

---

[80] Pasinetti also points out that the price independence from the level of production shown in the non-substitution theorem has nothing to do with substitution: "…'non-variation of prices' and the 'possibility of variation of prices' are something quite different from 'non-substitution' and 'substitution'." Pasinetti, L., On 'non-substitution' in production models, in: Cambridge Journal of Economics, vol. 1 (1977), pp. 389–394, p. 390.

[81] In business administration this insight has long been accepted as accurate: "We know that the maximum unit profit does not have to coincide with the maximum total profit for the period … the entrepreneur (disposes) with the highest economic efficiency only when he attains the maximum profit for the period, i.e., the maximum absolute profit for the reference period." Koch, H., Das Wirtschaftlichkeitsprinzip als betriebswirtschaftliche Maxime, in: Zeitschrift für handelswirtschaftliche Forschung, vol. 3 (1951), pp. 160–170, p. 166 f. [F. H.].

minimises the necessary labour input; there are no other original factors. Price formation *à la* Ricardo, Marx, Dmitriev, Bortkiewicz, Sraffa and whatever they are all called simply assumes—without examination!—that a higher rate of return or profit rate on (any) supposedly "advanced" capital value promises more profit. However, the seemingly reliable profit indicator of an incorrect calculation rule never provides the correct decision criterion for the choice of technique.

Contrary to the dogma presented at the beginning of this section, labour values fulfil a central function in capitalist market economies. The analytically obtained results are in the further course confronted with examples. The by now well-founded superiority of labour value calculation is also and especially confirmed when the modern form of the classical theory of value, the neo-Ricardian doctrine, experiences a fiasco.

Chapter 12
Paradoxes and Anomalies of Sraffa-Pricing in Single Production

The starting point for the following deliberations is an elementary but straightforward detection. Under capitalist conditions, the price of a commodity must at least cover its (variable) unit costs to be manufactured:

$$\mathbf{p} \geq \mathbf{pA} + \mathbf{a}_0 w \tag{12.1}$$

This fundamental fact is, as Dmitriev rightly remarks, "... not a result of a scientific analysis of the phenomena of economic life, but a simple statement of the self-evident fact that production cannot continue (at least for any appreciable length of time) if the price of the product does not cover the costs incurred."[1] The interesting question is how the gap is closed if the greater-than sign applies in the above equations.

Economic theorists—from the classics to the present day—have never seen a problem in this: in their eyes, it always seems to be as obvious a fact as the system (12.1) itself that profit must be allotted in proportion to the sectoral *material expenditure*—nothing else is **pA**. An *existing* sector-specific division of labour is always *assumed* without ever approaching the idea that the usual distribution procedure could lead to downright absurd results. These outcomes would prevent the "discriminated" entrepreneurs from engaging in the social division of labour. As will be seen from the garnered evidence, the Sraffa approach is either fundamentally unsuitable as a pricing rule or only conceivable if the profit maximisation objective is abandoned.

At the same time, the criticism will reveal which pricing method excludes the "irregularities" from the outset: value calculation. This principle refers to a surcharge method that leads to prices proportional to the labour values or—with appropriate standardisation—matching them. The observations on the non-substitutions theorem have shown that this pricing policy corresponds to the choice of the profit-maximising technique. Furthermore, it avoids the misguided successivistic treatment of the problem in the context of simultaneous production processes. The value calculation

[1] Dmitriev, V. K., op. cit., p. 39.

F. Helmedag, *Production of Commodities by Means of Labour*, Springer Studies in Alternative Economics, https://doi.org/10.1007/978-3-032-01457-3_12

harmonises with a flow analysis typical for production processes, while Sraffa-prices are based on a disguised stock reckoning.

The above considerations on the (in)dependence of the optimal technique on final demand were based on a macroeconomic level. However, the "invisible hand" coordinates the *microeconomic* behaviour. How must prices be determined at this level to prevent the announced irregularities? Yes, the price system we are looking for gains ground when profit in the individual calculation is a markup on the real, because not capitalistically reproduced cost factor, labour:

$$\mathbf{p} = \mathbf{pA} + \mathbf{a}_0 w\ (1 + \varepsilon) = \mathbf{pA} + \mathbf{a}_0 we \tag{12.2}$$

The symbol for the wage cost surcharge is the same as that already used in the analysis of Bortkiewicz's proposal to transform values into prices (cf. p. 173 ff.). The solution of (12.2) yields prices that are parallel to labour values:

$$\mathbf{p} = \mathbf{a}_0 \mathbf{L} we = \mathbf{v} we \tag{12.3}$$

This pricing method does not owe its existence to a shot in the dark. Instead, as explained later, it is the only rational method of setting production prices on open markets under linear returns to scale from a seller's perspective.

One may object that with a calculation *à la* (12.2), the entrepreneur no longer earns profit on (allegedly) advanced money to buy intermediate products. Besides, wages do not need to be pre-financed because they are paid *post-factum.* This protest misjudges the actual facts. First, interest on one's own or other people's money invested has the character of *fixed costs* and is therefore *irrelevant* for short-run decisions (and possibly for some time beyond). With that said, it makes sense to interpret the "profit" that is constantly referred to here as the *gross margin*, i.e., the contribution to fixed cost and profit combined. This approach also fits in with the correct management perspective.

Furthermore, in the modern economy, entrepreneurs usually carry out deliveries among themselves on account and disburse wages only periodically. However, the grant of a payment term generally requires *solvency*, i.e., the debtor is regarded as financially sound and reliable. Then, the conditions for participating in commercial life as a creditworthy business partner are met.

A commodity is regularly produced *during* a specific interval, whereas payment for the intermediate goods is typically made at a certain *point* in time after their supply. This distinction is not contradicted by the fact that down payments or instalments must be made for some projects. In such cases, this amount of money quasi acts as an entrance fee entitling one to participate in the event. Whatever the individual case may be, financial relations do not override the regularities of the production sphere.

From this perspective, the Sraffa-pricing approach is less *realistic* than the recommended contrast programme: material costs of established companies are rarely procured by upfront payment, at least not in full. Furthermore, the ex-post settlement of liabilities is increasingly being extended to final demand; mentioning the cue "credit card" may suffice.

The Eqs. (12.3) have the advantage of being mathematically simpler than the system (11.16) $\mathbf{p} = \mathbf{a}_0 w\mathbf{S}$ (cf. p. 214), which is, after all, a polynomial of the nth degree in r. Furthermore, they also work if (11.16) fails. The system (12.3) consistently delivers quality products, whereas the Eqs. (11.16), as we shall shortly see, only produce rejects.

12.1 Basic and Non-Basic Commodities

The concrete problems of forming Sraffa prices under certain circumstances were publicised soon after the appearance of "Production of Commodities by Means of Commodities". In a review article restricted to single production, Peter Newman presented for the first time a numerical example in which a price becomes negative at a uniform rate of profit.[2]

Following Ricardo's wheat economy, corn figures in Newman's two-sector model as a basic commodity that appears as an input in both processes, be it as a means of production or as a consumer good for workers. The other commodity, iron, has the character of a luxury good; as a non-basic commodity, it only enters its own production.

The existence of non-basic goods in Sraffa's sense implies that the coefficient matrix $\mathbf{A}$ can be decomposed by a suitable interchange of rows and columns, i.e., it can generally be brought to the following form[3]:

$$\mathbf{A} = \begin{pmatrix} \mathbf{A}_{11} & \mathbf{A}_{12} \\ \mathbf{0} & \mathbf{A}_{22} \end{pmatrix} \tag{12.4}$$

$\mathbf{A}_{11}$ and $\mathbf{A}_{22}$ are square submatrices, not necessarily of the same order. For a decomposable coefficient matrix $\mathbf{A}$, submatrix $\mathbf{A}_{21}$ vanishes. In the two-dimensional model, it corresponds to the coefficient a_{21}. Commodity 2, in this case, iron, is therefore not used to produce commodity 1, wheat. In his example, Newman adds the real wage to the coefficient matrix; a_{11} and a_{12} represent the respective labour input per unit in addition to corn as a means of production. Normalising the wheat price to one and writing p for the iron price results in the two price-determining equations:

$$1 = a_{11}(1 + r) \tag{12.5}$$

[2] Cf. Newman, P., Production of Commodities by Means of Commodities, in: Schweizerische Zeitschrift für Volkswirtschaft und Statistik, vol. 98 (1962), pp. 58–75, p. 66 f.

[3] Cf. the clear explanation of the permutation procedure in Takayama, A., Mathematical Economics, 2nd ed., Cambridge et al. 1985, p. 368 ff.

$$p = (a_{12} + a_{22}p)(1 + r) \tag{12.6}$$

From (12.5), we obtain the rate of profit directly as the net reproduction rate of the grain:

$$r = \frac{1 - a_{11}}{a_{11}} > 0 \quad \text{for} \quad 0 < a_{11} < 1 \tag{12.7}$$

In Ricardo's style, the profit rate is specified solely by the basic goods industry. For the other sectors, it is a datum; in equilibrium, they must accept the physically determined wheat profit rate. "The fact, however, that they *must* accept it, does not mean that they *can* accept it."[4] To reveal when the non-basic sector cannot apply the profit rate of the wheat sector, even if it wanted to, we calculate the profit rate of the iron industry from (12.6):

$$r = \frac{(1 - a_{22})p - a_{12}}{a_{12} + a_{22}p} \tag{12.8}$$

If the wheat consumption per iron unit a_{12} approaches zero, the rate of profit (12.8) tends towards its maximum value $\left(r^I_{\max}\right)$. With $a_{12} = 0$ Eq. (12.8) morphs into the rate of self-reproduction of iron:

$$r^I_{\max} = \frac{1 - a_{22}}{a_{22}} > 0 \quad \text{for} \quad 0 < a_{22} < 1 \tag{12.9}$$

In equilibrium, (12.7) and (12.8) should coincide. For $a_{11} < a_{22}$, however, even the maximum profit rate of the non-basic sector (12.9) is lower than that of the wheat industry (12.7).[5] If we equate (12.7) and (12.8), we obtain after a short rearrangement for p:

$$p = \frac{a_{12}}{a_{11} - a_{22}} \tag{12.10}$$

If $a_{11} < a_{22}$, the condition of positive prices is violated: the price of iron becomes negative.[6] Since there are no opposing economic reasons, Newman concludes: "… 'non-basics' do not exist, if we are not to confine ourselves to a rather odd and

[4] Zaghini, E., On Non-Basic Commodities, in: Schweizerische Zeitschrift für Volkswirtschaft und Statistik, vol. 103 (1967), pp. 257–266, p. 261. Zaghini classifies the different types of non-basic goods that can appear in a decomposable sub-matrix $\mathbf{A}_{22}$.

[5] In general, the maximum profit rate of the non-basic sector is lower than that of the basic industry if the maximum eigenvalue of $\mathbf{A}_{11}$ is smaller than that of $\mathbf{A}_{22}$.

[6] Kurz, H. D., Zur neoricardianischen …, op. cit., p. 67, provides a graph of the development of the price of iron as a function of the rate of profit.

restricted class of situations."[7] This assessment contradicts the high status that Sraffa grants to non-basics in his work. He, therefore, rejects the conclusion drawn by Newman.

In a letter to Newman, Sraffa first points out that he had commented on the issue[8]: "Have you not overlooked my Appendix B, to which the reader was referred to by a footnote on p. 28?"[9] Furthermore, he remarks that the problem only arises if the maximum rate of profit of non-basic production is sufficiently low. This constellation would hardly occur in reality: "I certainly failed to discover any faintly realistic example of this which I could use, and had to invent those 'beans'."[10]

Seeing how Sraffa deals with the exceptional but not entirely impossible problem is instructive. Suppose bean cultivation yields a relatively (too) low self-reproduction rate (12.9). Then, there is—according to Sraffa—nevertheless a method of saving the uniform profit rate at positive prices: "The 'beans' could however still be produced and marketed so as to show a normal profit if the producer sold them at a higher price than the one which, in his book-keeping, he attributes to them as means of production."[11]

Yet, neither the reference to the allegedly rare existence of such phenomena in reality is convincing, nor does the solution to the ensuing difficulties, if they do occur, appear acceptable: the event *can* happen, although the probability of its emergence decreases the more the workers participate in the surplus.[12] Instead, the failure of a theory in borderline and extreme cases—which should nevertheless be covered by it—is a symptom of its weakness. The exception *disproves* the rule and is the harbinger of a new one.

Bortkiewicz's correction of the value-price transformation also fails if the constant capital of department II is zero. In this constellation, which is analogous to the one given here, the profit rate corresponds to the rate of surplus value determined exclusively in division II. However, the other sectors cannot adopt this profit rate under certain conditions. It is then futile to set up the Bortkiewicz price system, which corresponds to Eqs. (12.5) and (12.6). *Only* the value calculation has been able to assert itself in this exaggerated situation.

---

[7] Newman, P., Production ..., op. cit., p. 67.

[8] The reprint of the correspondence between Sraffa and Newman is published in Bharadwaj, K., On the Maximum Numbers of Switches Between Two Production Systems, in: Schweizerische Zeitschrift für Volkswirtschaft und Statistik, vol. 106 (1970), pp. 409–429, p. 425 ff.

[9] Sraffa, P., Letter to Newmann, June 4, 1962, op. cit., pp. 425 f., p. 425.

[10] The beans are the hypothetical example Sraffa chose in Appendix B of his book to illustrate the possibility of negative prices of non-basic goods. Cf. Sraffa, P., Production ..., op. cit., p. 90 f. Newman shares the view that the question must be treated empirically: "It seems to me that more empirical considerations would have to be brought in." Newman, P., Letter to Sraffa, June 8, 1962, in: Bharadwaj, K., On the ..., op. cit., pp. 426 f., p. 427. In his second letter, Sraffa repeats his assessment that the case is empirically extremely improbable: "It has not been possible to find a reasonable case in reality in which the rate is smaller ..." Sraffa, P., Letter to Newman, June 19, 1962, in: Bharadwaj, K., On the ..., op. cit., pp. 427 f., p. 428.

[11] Sraffa, P., Production ..., op. cit., p. 91. Note the wording: In the style of Ricardo, the term 'normal profit' is used, whereas the 'normal *rate* of profit' is meant.

[12] Cf. Kurz, H. D., Zur neoricardianischen ..., op. cit., p. 69.

Sraffa's proposal to cure the disease is like bloodletting: it weakens the patient without providing relief or healing. No bean producer should be prevented from trying to kid oneself by manipulating the accounts—paper is patient, an attribute that has also made life easier for economic theory throughout its history.

Nevertheless, implementing Sraffa's recommendation encounters unexpected troubles: given two unknowns, one equation is one too few. Even with knowledge of r, (12.6) (cf. p. 239) is not sufficient to determine a "selling price"—to the left of the equal sign—and an "accounting price"—to the right of the equal sign. The production conditions alone are insufficient in this setting to derive an unambiguous price system. However, the task can be accomplished without seeking refuge in demand or the arbitrary occupation of the degree of freedom (or many degrees of freedom in the case of several types of iron and beans).

The way out of the impasse remains blocked as long as the labour expended is shifted into the coefficient matrix. The direct labour inputs a_{0j} must be made visible to form the prices according to (12.2) (cf. p. 237). Under the same assumptions on which (12.5) and (12.6) are based, we obtain:

$$1 = a_{11} + a_{01}we \tag{12.11}$$

$$p = a_{12} + a_{22}p + a_{02}we \tag{12.12}$$

From (12.11) we get:

$$e = \frac{1 - a_{11}}{a_{01}w} \tag{12.13}$$

Inserting (12.13) in (12.12) yields:

$$p = \frac{a_{12} + \frac{a_{02}(1-a_{11})}{a_{01}}}{1 - a_{22}} \tag{12.14}$$

(12.14) exhibits that p is now always positive. The exchange ratio of iron to wheat can be further simplified by taking the value system into account:

$$v_1 = v_1a_{11} + a_{01} \tag{12.15}$$

$$v_2 = v_1a_{12} + v_2a_{22} + a_{02} \tag{12.16}$$

The solutions are:

$$v_1 = \frac{a_{01}}{1 - a_{11}} \tag{12.17}$$

$$v_2 = \frac{v_1 a_{12} + a_{02}}{1 - a_{22}} \tag{12.18}$$

With (12.17) and (12.18) in (12.14), p emerges as:

$$p = \frac{a_{12} + \frac{a_{02}}{v_1}}{1 - a_{22}} = \frac{v_2}{v_1} \tag{12.19}$$

Irrespective of the exploitation factor $e = (1 + \varepsilon)$, the labour values determine the exchange ratio between iron and wheat. The number is always positive; once again, the value calculation beats the Sraffa-prices.

Furthermore, the result indicates which commodities should indeed be assigned a basic character: wage goods. This classical point of view is further consolidated as soon as profit appears explicitly in the analysis. This remains to be done. So far, it has only been proven that value accounting works well where the neo-Ricardian doctrine is at a loss. The task now is to highlight that in situations where Sraffa's pricing hypothesis is formally applicable, results that contradict the premises are obtained.

12.2 Profit Rate, Capital Value and Total Profit

At least in one respect, Sraffa's work caused a withering effect: the *unrestricted* claim regarding the validity of the "neoclassical postulate", which asserts the aligned movement of the wage rate and the capital value[13], was deprived of its foundation. However, this qualification did not eradicate the view that the positive correlation dominates reality. The neoclassical "rule of thumb" that an increase in the wage rate triggers a substitution of labour with "capital" continues to attract economists in theory and practice. For many, the *modus vivendi* consists of not (or no longer) doubting as a *theoretical* possibility the extreme swings in capital value and per capita national income to be expected according to Sraffa's theses on the choice of technique. In the same breath, the *empirical* relevance of the aforementioned model properties is denied in the face of facts.

In the end, those blessed with "common sense" are right—albeit for the wrong reason: the findings of the neo-Ricardian doctrine are not irrelevant because reality—for whatever motive—favours the relatively stable conditions that fit the neoclassicists' concept. The amplitudes of capital intensity—not only conceivable in the light of the Sraffa approach but even very likely—stay away, as reality ignores putative operating principles of capitalist market economies concocted in the study room.

[13] Sato, K., The Neoclassical Postulate and the Technology Frontier in Capital Theory, in: The Quarterly Journal of Economics, vol. 88 (1974), pp. 353–384.

A simple multi-purpose model substantiates the statement. It illustrates the neo-Ricardian theory of the choice of technique and pricing and reduces it to *absurdity*. The 'book of blueprints' of the considered economy is limited to two techniques: A (T^A) and B (T^B). Both methods produce two identical goods in two single production processes. The coefficients of technology A are specified as follows:

$$a_{01} = 0.002 \qquad a_{02} = 0.01$$
$$a_{11} = 0.35 \qquad a_{12} = 0.1$$
$$a_{21} = 0.05 \qquad a_{22} = 0.1$$

In contrast to the case just discussed, both goods are now "basics"; each enters into the production of the other. The same applies to technology B, which differs from technology A only in the coefficients of sector 1:

$$b_{01} = 0.001 \qquad b_{02} = 0.01 = a_{02}$$
$$b_{11} = 0.254542 \qquad b_{12} = 0.1 = a_{12}$$
$$b_{21} = 0.161435 \qquad b_{22} = 0.1 = a_{22}$$

The Sraffa price system has two degrees of freedom; one can be eliminated by defining a counting unit. The relationship between the wage and profit rates is of interest here. According to (11.19) (cf. p. 215), two wage curves can be derived for each technique, depending on which price serves as the standard.

Figure 12.1 overleaf shows the wage curves for techniques A and B, with product 1 initially acting as the numéraire ($p_1 \equiv 1$). For this reason, the ordinate is labelled $w^{(1)}$. The two wage curves intersect at $r_{S1} = 0.11193$ and $r_{S2} = 1.10928$.

In the context of the non-substitution theorem, it was outlined how the neo-Ricardian theory conceives the choice of technique: if, e.g., the wage rate falls starting from the maximum wage rate of technology B ($w_{\max B}$), would at first T^B be preferred because it initially assigns a higher profit rate to each wage rate (and vice versa). At the wage rate w_{S1}, both techniques are considered equally profitable, and it is said that they could exist side by side: "The point of intersection ... is where the two alternative methods of production are equally profitable ...".[14]

If the wage rate continues to fall, the economy supposedly switches: T^A delivers a higher profit rate for $w_{S2} < w < w_{S1}$. If the wage rate falls below w_{S2}, "reswitching" follows: the economy returns to the previously used, temporarily abandoned, but now apparently more lucrative technique B.

Generally, in the Sraffa system, the macroeconomic capital intensity (k) is calculated to:

$$k = \frac{\mathbf{pAq}}{\mathbf{a}_0\mathbf{q}} \tag{12.20}$$

[14] Sraffa, P., Production ..., op. cit., p. 85.

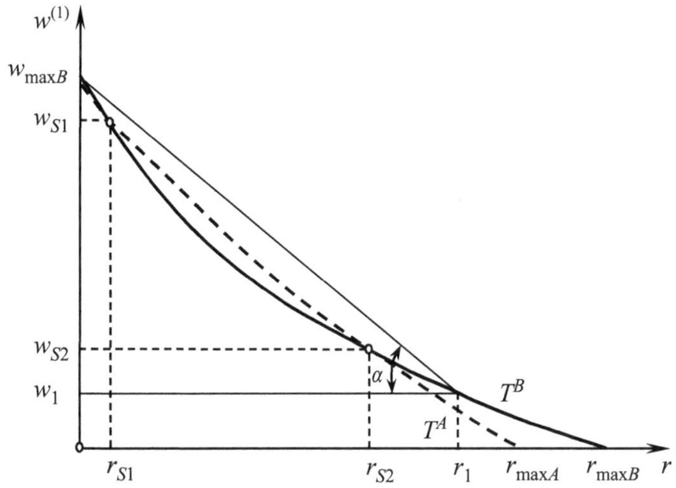

Fig. 12.1 The $w^{(1)}$-r relationships of techniques A and B

The gross production vector **q** must be known to say something about the capital intensity k. Actually, wage curves are almost always presented without stating how the n degrees of freedom of the quantity system (11.25) $\mathbf{q} = \mathbf{Ly}$ (cf. p. 222) have been fixed. After standardising the total labour to one, there are still (n—1) degrees of freedom left in the quantity system. These can be determined exogenously: changes in final demand do not affect prices. If we set all components of **y** except one (y_i) equal to zero, the equations for calculating output provide the number of units produced in the subsystem of good i.

Let us take a closer look at the integrated industry of commodity 1. The net output vector is written as $\mathbf{y}_1$, a column vector that contains only zeros apart from y_1. Then we have:

$$\mathbf{q} = \mathbf{L}\mathbf{y}_1 \tag{12.21}$$

Left multiplication by $\mathbf{a}_0$ leads in consideration of (11.26) $\mathbf{a}_0\mathbf{q} \equiv 1$ to:

$$1 = \mathbf{a}_0\mathbf{L}\mathbf{y}_1 = \mathbf{v}\mathbf{y}_1 = v_1 y_1 \tag{12.22}$$

Thus, the quantity y_1 amounts to:

$$y_1 = \frac{1}{v_1} \tag{12.23}$$

Generally, the net output of a selected commodity's subsystem is the quotient of the total labour by its labour value. This result will be processed further in a moment. Before we do so, let us look at Fig. 12.1 again.

Assume that the model economy represents the integrated production of good 1, whose price is taken as the unit of account. Then, the techniques generate a net output of good 1 that corresponds to the ordinate intercept of the respective wage curve. In this case, the capital value—corresponding to the capital intensity because the labour input is normalised to one—can be read from the wage rate-profit rate diagram straightforwardly. The distribution equation $y = kr + w$ immediately yields $k = \frac{y-w}{r}$. In this equation, y and w are physical quantities of commodity 1, the sole net output.[15] In the given situation, e.g., tan α measures the capital value of technology B at the wage rate w_1 and the profit rate r_1. If this method is applied to the wage *frontier*, i.e., the segments of the wage curves furthest to the northeast, a negative correlation between the profit rate and capital intensity is determined in the range $0 \leq r < r_{S1}$, which is known as a "*positive price*-Wicksell effect". At the switch point r_{S1}, the transition to T^A results in a "*positive real* Wicksell effect". Between r_{S1} and r_{S2} the price Wicksell effect remains positive. Up to this point, the neoclassical world is in order.

This situation is now changing: if the rate of profit rises to r_{S2}, the capital value increases abruptly in the wake of the (alleged) switch to technique B, resulting in a *negative* real Wicksell effect. The renewed use of T^B is associated with "paradoxical consumer behaviour" since the national product grows with the rate of profit—a relation that appears absurd from a neoclassical perspective.[16] However, if the rate of profit is greater than r_{S2}, capital intensity decreases again, and a positive price-Wicksell effect reoccurs.

The "backward switch" at r_{S2} in Fig. 12.1 results in "capital reversing", as the movement of the profit rate and capital value in the same direction is called, regardless of its cause. Reswitching is, therefore, a sub-case of capital reversing. Given such phenomena, neo-Ricardians assess the concept of basing income distribution on the opposing forces of supply and demand as a failure.[17]

Because of the convex shape of the two wage curves, each technique in Fig. 12.1 exhibits a positive price Wicksell effect. This property explains the neoclassical endeavour to prove that the wage curves are convex in reality and have, at most, one intersection with another w-r-relationship.[18]

---

[15] The modelling is less restrictive than one might think *prima facie*. Even with heterogeneous net output, the non-substitution theorem allows us to identify the subsystem for each particular good analytically. The observed gross output is the aggregate of the subsystems with the corresponding weight.

[16] Cf. Burmeister, E., Capital Theory and Dynamics, Cambridge 1980, p. 116 f.

[17] Cf. the pioneering work in this field by Garegnani, P., Heterogeneous Capital, the Production Function and the Theory of Distribution, in: The Review of Economic Studies, vol. 37 (1970), pp. 407–436.

[18] Krelle, in particular, has attempted this in several articles. Cf., e.g., Krelle, W., Die kapitaltheoretische Kontroverse, Test zum Reswitching-Problem, in: Zeitschrift für Wirtschafts- und Sozialwissenschaften, vol. 98 (1978), pp. 1–31.

Remarkably, however, some neo-Ricardians are also keen to *rule out* reswitching. First, one must remember that the number of conceivable switch- and reswitch-points would be enormous in practice. As can be shown, techniques that replace each other in switch points differ only in the production of a (basic) commodity; thus, the maximum number of switch points of two techniques is determined by the number of basic commodities in both systems (without double counting).[19] In reality, several methods are regularly available to produce thousands and thousands of goods. Regarding switching and reswitching possibilities, astronomical orders of magnitude are obtained[20]: "So that as the rate of profits rises", oracles Sraffa, "there will be a *rapid succession* of switches in the methods of production of one or other of the commodities."[21] Even the slightest variations in the rate of profit or the wage rate would have to be characterised by enormous changes in the mode of production—which is obviously not the case. Instead, economists rightly speak of certain "stylized facts", i.e., certain economic variables or stable relations between them that remain pretty constant over time. These empirical facts stand in strange contrast to neo-Ricardian theory, for which the permanent switch should actually be the norm.

With this in mind, it is not surprising when Sraffa's supporters—and neoclassicists alike—search for motives why reswitching spares the world: "One has to show that wage curves do, under realistic assumptions, not deviate to any considerable extent from straight lines, and if they intersect at all, they should intersect to the right of the actual rate of profit."[22]

This endeavour is rooted in the fact that reswitching deprives the theory of technical progress of any material basis. If the return on material costs, alias the profit rate, controls the choice of process, a technique entailing a *decline* in net output might be used. This upshot would result in Fig. 12.1 if technique A, whose ordinate intercept is below technique B's, were to prevail.

In the framework of the Sraffian conception, it ultimately remains open "... whether technical change represents progress or regress because there is no technical-physical basis for judgment that is independent of distribution."[23] The neo-Ricardian doctrine allows space for a conceivable spectrum of variants that easily exceed the observed processes in reality:

> "The theory, therefore, appears like a razor," Cogoy judges, "the sharpness of which bears no relation to the practical problems to be mastered with this instrument; the theoretical sharpness with which neoclassical or Marxist value theory approaches can be criticised does

[19] Cf. Sraffa, P., Production ..., op. cit., p. 82, Bharadwaj, K., On the Maximum ..., op. cit. and Helmedag, F., Die Technikwahl ..., op. cit., p. 212 ff. Therefore, in the numerical example, technique B differs from technique A only in the production coefficients of commodity 1.

[20] See Schefold, B., Capital, Growth, and Definitions of Technical Progress, in: Kyklos, vol. 32 (1979), pp. 236–250, p. 244.

[21] Sraffa, P., Production ..., op. cit., p. 85, own emphasis.

[22] Schefold, B., Capital ..., op. cit., p. 244 f. See also Schefold, B., Different Forms of Technical Progress, in: The Economic Journal, vol. 86 (1976), pp. 806–819.

[23] Cogoy, M., Produktion, Markt und technischer Fortschritt, in: Analyse und Kritik, vol. 4 (1982), pp. 39–70, p. 59. [F. H.].

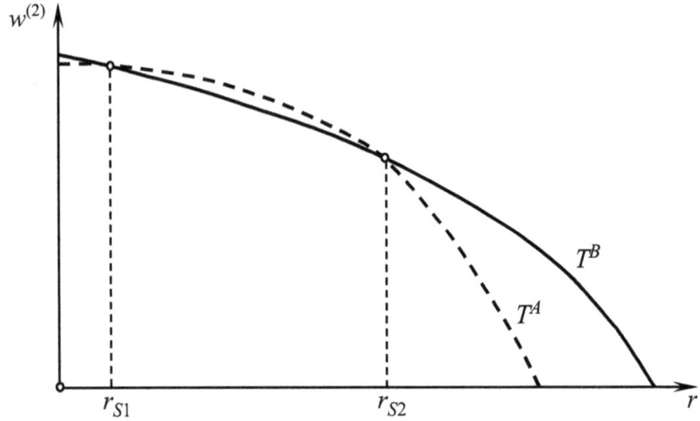

Fig. 12.2 The $w^{(2)}$-r relationships of techniques A and B

not correspond to any parallel successes in the empirical analysis of technical change, and the sharpness of the instrument seems to exceed the requirements of the targeted practical activity by far."[24]

Incidentally, the research objective of identifying the causes of wage curves that are as linear as possible is a double-edged affair. If this succeeds (contrary to expectations), the neo-Ricardians will have extinguished the fire they kindled in the neoclassical building with their own hands. In any case, the flames could have been fought earlier and more effectively. After all, a movement of the profit rate and capital intensity in the same direction can already be established using a suitable unit of account.

The definition of a numéraire is an arbitrary decision. Figure 12.2 shows the wage curves for T^A and T^B, where the price of commodity 2 has now been chosen for measurement. The ordinate label $w^{(2)}$ expresses this.

A first glance confirms that the unit of account does not influence re-switching; regardless of the standard, the methods in the switch points r_{S1} and r_{S2} each produce the same price system.[25] However, the absolute value of the wage rate, which corresponds to a certain profit rate, has varied. Furthermore, the *shape* of both wage curves has changed significantly compared to Fig. 12.1. They are now concave, although the calculations are based on the same technical coefficients.

Suppose the development of the capital values is examined as shown in Fig. 12.1. In that case, it becomes apparent that the real Wicksell effects occur as before: they are positive for r_{S1} and negative for r_{S2}. In contrast to Fig. 12.1, however, the price Wicksell effects are always negative. This phenomenon means that capital reversing

[24] Ibid., p. 60. [F. H.].

[25] Cf. Pasinetti, L., Lectures …, op. cit., p. 181.

appears even without altering the technique used upon distribution shifting.[26] Price-Wicksell effects can be produced at will by selecting a suitable unit of account.[27] The arbitrary choice of the numéraire affects the analysis results, as it influences the shape of the wage curves and, consequently, the relationship between the profit rate and the capital value.[28]

From this angle, reswitching alone, which is detached from the unit of account, causes uneasiness. Neo-Ricardians have repeatedly complained that the phenomenon has not been duly appreciated: "… distinguished economists …, when coming across the reswitching phenomenon, instinctively shied away from it, by reacting with illogical exorcizing sentences—as if against the appearance of a dangerous demon."[29] The behaviour is perhaps due to cognitive dissonance: on the one hand, the analysis appears logically watertight; on the other, common sense raises legitimate doubts, not least because there is virtually no known empirical evidence for the return of a technique. If an attempt is nevertheless made to interpret an observation accordingly, this is done with shielding reservations.[30]

However, the problem is not empirical but theoretical: the choice of technique to maximise the profit rate must not be equated with profit maximisation. Regardless of the wage rate, the method that generates the highest net output always yields the highest profit. The profit is shown in Figs. 12.1 and 12.2 as the difference between the maximum wage rate, i.e., the per capita output, and the actual remuneration: in the example, technique B is associated with a higher profit for *each* (permissible)

---

[26] The effort to exclude such undesirable consequences culminates in the dogma prohibiting the free determination of the unit of account. Cf. Helmedag, F., Kapitale Böcke in der Kapitaltheorie: Der Test zum Protest, in: Jahrbücher für Nationalökonomie und Statistik, vol. 216 (1997), pp. 744–760, p. 745 ff.

[27] Cf. Burmeister, E., On the Social Significance of the Reswitching Controversy, in: Revue d'Economie Politique, vol. 87 (1977), pp. 335–350, p. 340. Against this background, the assertion that price-Wicksell effects are more critical than reswitching seems incomprehensible. This opinion is held by Backhouse, R., A History of Modern Economic Analysis, Oxford / New York 1985, p. 450 n.

[28] In Sraffa's book, the construction of a standard commodity as a unit of account ranks high. If the wage rate-profit rate relationship is expressed in this way, the wage curve becomes a straight line. Of course, each technique generally has its own standard commodity, so distinct techniques cannot be compared. In fact, the standard product does not have the properties that Sraffa ascribes to it. Cf. paricularly Helmedag, F., Die verteilungsinvariante Messung von Produktionspreisen, in: das wirtschaftsstudium (wisu), vol. 27 (1998), pp. 266–274, p. 284 f. Sraffa himself describes the standard product quasi as an aid to interpretation: "The Standard system is a purely auxiliary construction. It should therefore be possible to present the essential elements of the mechanism under consideration without having recourse to it." Sraffa, P., Production …, op. cit., p. 31. Cf. also Flaschel, P., Sraffa's Standard Commodity: No Fulfillment of Ricardo's Dream of an "Invariable Measure of Value", in: Journal of Theoretical and Institutional Economics, vol. 142 (1986), pp. 588–602, Schefold, B., The Standard Commodity as a Tool of Economic Analysis: A Comment on Flaschel, ibid., pp. 603–622 and Flaschel, P., The Standard Commodity as a Tool of Economic Analysis: A Reply to Schefold, ibid., pp. 623–625.

[29] Pasinetti, L., The Unpalatability of the Reswitching of Techniques, in: Revue d'Economie Politique, vol. 89 (1979), pp. 637–642, p. 638.

[30] Cf. Albin, P. S., Reswitching: An Empirical Observation, a Theoretical Note, and an Environmental Conjecture, in: Kyklos, vol. 28 (1975), pp. 149–153.

wage rate. Nevertheless, T^A delivers a higher profit rate than T^B for all wage rates $w_{S2} < w < w_{S1}$. How can this be reconciled with the fact that T^B always leads to a higher profit?

Formally speaking, the answer should not be complicated: because profit results from the multiplication of capital value and profit rate, a higher profit rate goes hand in hand with a lower profit, provided the basis of assessment is low enough. After all, the capital value is not a predetermined quantity; in the Sraffa economy, it is ascertained *simultaneously* with the prices. It is enough to take a close look at a switch point to expose the representation of the profit volume by the profit rate as a bogus claim.

Allegedly, both techniques can coexist at a switch point, as the profit rate and the price system are the same. Yet, the capital values of both techniques differ. T^B produces a higher capital value if we apply the method already used to determine the capital intensity graphically. Undoubtedly, entrepreneurs who use T^B *make more profit at the same profit rate* as those who use T^A.

Contrary to the opinion of Sraffa and his disciples, the techniques are, therefore, *not* equally profitable at a switch point. Furthermore, it can be shown that T^A has a lower total profit than T^B despite the higher profit rate between the switch points.[31] Sraffa's theory of the choice of technique must be wrong.

What needs to be clarified is whether the higher total profit is sufficient to assess the choice of technique conclusively. According to methodological individualism, the individual capitalist is not interested in how high the total surplus is. Instead, they are guided by what they personally receive. Does it then perhaps make sense to pay attention to the profit rate after all? This problem we shall now address.

12.3 The Individual Profit

Surprisingly enough, the previous deliberations regarding total profit were not expressed earlier. Although wage curves are probably among the most common diagrams in the economic literature, the very easily recognisable capital income of techniques was overlooked or passed over. The profit rate was unquestioningly accepted as the profit indicator, keeping attention away from the ordinate intercepts.

Moreover, the unwavering trust in the return on material costs hindered the examination of how sectoral profit distributions can arise through uniform profit rates. The minimisation of input costs per unit during the competitive process seems so plausible that all parties have unanimously accepted cost-effectiveness as a decisive criterion for technique selection.

Yet, the crucial question should be asked previously: costs are valued quantities, but *how* are they valued? It has never been proven that Sraffa's calculation engenders prices compatible with the principles of a competitive economy based on the division of labour. It was always supposed, without further justification, that all industries

[31] Cf. Helmedag, F., Die Technikwahl ..., op. cit., p. 226 ff.

accepted a profit distribution proportional to the material costs as a "fair" share of the surplus.[32]

The right way to confirm that the choice of technique is governed by minimising Sraffa-prices would have been to explicitly derive sectoral profit functions providing the individual capital incomes. Of course, it is correct that competitive entrepreneurs do not act as a class pursuing collective profit maximisation. The respective industrialist is not interested in the gain of others; he individually wants to pocket as much as possible.

Although it can be unequivocally determined which technique maximises total profits, a particular department may prefer a different method. As expected, our multi-purpose model is tailored to allow the study of such a situation. First, we search for the profit equations for the two industries.

Let us start with the quantity system of an economy with two sectors, each represented by a typical enterprise. Assuming good 2 is a means of production and good 1 is a consumption article constituting the net output, we apply the subsystem method[33]:

$$q_1 - (a_{11}q_1 + a_{12}q_2) = y_1 \tag{12.24}$$

$$q_2 - (a_{21}q_1 + a_{22}q_2) = 0 \tag{12.25}$$

The labour input of the integrated industries is standardised to unity[34]:

$$a_{01}q_1 + a_{02}q_2 \equiv 1 \tag{12.26}$$

(12.24), (12.25) and (12.26) yield after a short calculation:

$$q_1 = \frac{1 - a_{22}}{a_{01}(1 - a_{22}) + a_{02}a_{21}} \tag{12.27}$$

$$q_2 = \frac{a_{21}q_1}{1 - a_{22}} \tag{12.28}$$

$$y_1 = \frac{(1 - a_{11})(1 - a_{22}) - a_{12}a_{21}}{a_{01}(1 - a_{22}) + a_{02}a_{21}} \tag{12.29}$$

---

[32] Neoclassicists can easily align with this perspective, as the appropriate language seems clear: "By pure profits I understand the difference between receipts and costs where the latter include the opportunity cost of investment by r times the value of the investment." Hahn, F., The neo-Ricardians, op. cit., p. 306 n. However, the cost of materials is not an "investment", and the next best alternative merely serves as a lower limit for profit.

[33] See Helmedag, F., Technikwahl, Profitstruktur und Arbeitsproduktivität, in: Jahrbücher für Nationalökonomie und Statistik, vol. 203 (1987), pp. 408–421, p. 411 ff.

[34] This convention does not imply a full employment assumption. With a linear technique, the level of employment has no effect on the issues to be discussed here. Cf. Helmedag, F., Profit-Raten mittels Profitraten, in: Jahrbücher für Nationalökonomie und Statistik, vol. 207 (1990), pp. 67–83, p. 80 f.

(12.23) (cf. p. 246) also instructs that y_1 is the reciprocal of the labour value of commodity 1; the technique that requires less labour—the only non-produced resource—per unit yields a higher net output. The social product is distributed between the entrepreneurs in sectors 1 (P_1) and 2 (P_2) and the workers. Because of (12.26), the wage bill corresponds to the wage rate w. It is expedient to declare the price of the consumption good as the accounting unit. This way, the nominal and real values of wages and profit coincide. The total profit (TP) is therefore calculated as follows:

$$TP = P_1 + P_2 = y_1 - w \tag{12.30}$$

Subtracting the sectoral costs from the respective revenues provides information on the individual profits:

$$P_1 = q_1(1 - a_{11} - p_2 a_{21} - a_{01} w) \tag{12.31}$$

$$P_2 = q_2(p_2 - a_{12} - p_2 a_{22} - a_{02} w) \tag{12.32}$$

But trying to determine the unknowns P_1, P_2 and p_2 from the Eqs. (12.30), (12.31) and (12.32) is a futile endeavour: equating the sum of (12.31) and (12.32) with (12.30) results in $p_2 = \frac{0}{0}$, an indeterminate expression. One escapes this impasse when introducing a hypothesis regarding the profit distribution mode. According to the generally accepted conjecture, the profit-capital ratio of all branches must coincide in equilibrium:

$$\frac{P_1}{q_1(a_{11} + p_2 a_{21})} = \frac{P_2}{q_2(a_{12} + p_2 a_{22})} \tag{12.33}$$

Equation (12.33) reflects the assumption of a uniform profit rate r on the material costs identified with the capital value. For this reason, the profits formed in this manner will be called "Sraffa-profits" in reference to the calculation rule heeded. P_1 can be derived from the formulae (12.30), (12.31), and (12.33). After a few intermediate steps, the solution of a quadratic equation is obtained:

$$P_1 = -\frac{z}{2} \pm \sqrt{\left(\frac{z}{2}\right)^2 - u}$$

The abbreviations mean: (12.34)

$$z = q_1\{a_{11} - a_{22} - 2 + w[a_{01}(2 - a_{22}) + a_{02} a_{21}]\}$$

$$u = q_1(1 - a_{22})(y_1 - w)(1 - a_{01})$$

Furthermore, the root in (12.34) must be taken negatively, as $\left(-\frac{z}{2}\right)$ is greater than the total profit for all w. A few manipulations confirm the assertion. Obviously, z increases with w. Therefore, the statement is already true if $\left(-\frac{z}{2}\right)$ exceeds y_1 for $w = 0$. Therefore

$$\frac{(1-a_{22})(2+a_{22}-a_{11})}{2[a_{01}(1-a_{22})+a_{02}a_{21}]} > \frac{(1-a_{11})(1-a_{22})-a_{12}a_{21}}{a_{01}(1-a_{22})+a_{02}a_{21}} \tag{12.35}$$

has to apply. Via

$$(1-a_{22})(2+a_{22}-a_{11}) > 2(1-a_{22})(1-a_{11}) - 2a_{12}a_{21} \tag{12.36}$$

one gets:

$$(1-a_{22})(a_{11}+a_{22}) > -2a_{12}a_{21} \tag{12.37}$$

The condition (12.37) is always valid: in (12.34), only the negative sign in front of the root is relevant. Now, p_2 and P_2 can be determined from (12.30) and (12.33).

Figure 12.3 shows the profit functions of sector 1 when Sraffa-pricing prevails. The techniques were chosen so that the curves intersect. Thus, the profit-maximising sector 1 faces a single process alternative depending on the wage rate.

For wage rates above $\overline{w} = 104.13$, technique B, which leads to higher total profit, is beneficial for industry 1. At $\overline{w}$, the two methods are equivalent from the sector's point of view; the profit is $P_1 = 143.349$ in both cases.

If the wage rate is lower than $\overline{w}$, there appears to be a contradiction between the technique that maximises the sector profit and the one that maximises total profit: the profit of division 1 with T^A is higher than that of T^B. Is there a switch of techniques after all? To be sure, by focusing on profit instead of the profit rate, there is no longer any trace of *re*switching—despite identical technical coefficients; nevertheless, the impression arises that in competitive capitalism, the most economically productive technique may remain unemployed.

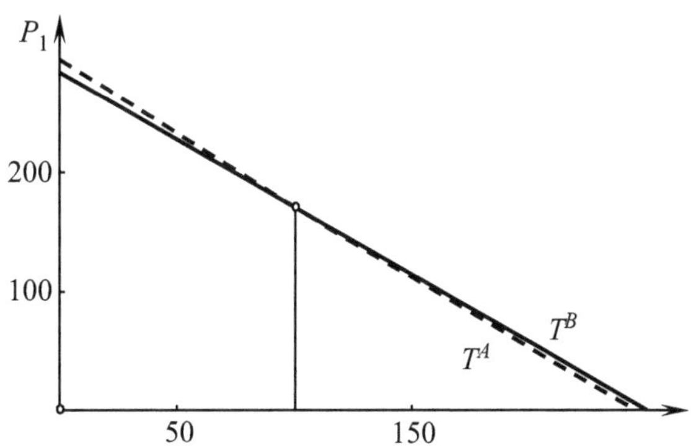

Fig. 12.3 The Sraffa-profits of sector 1

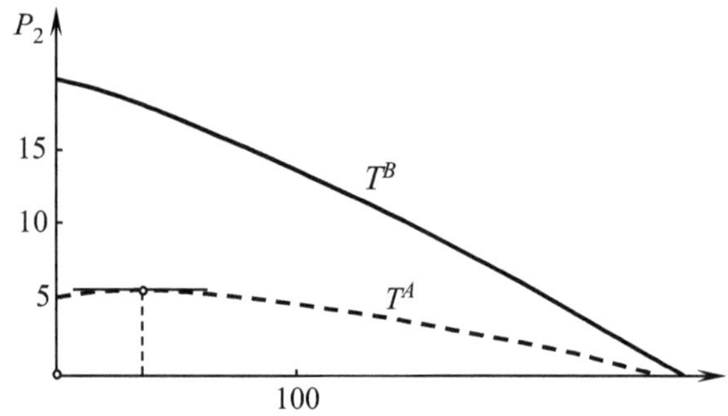

Fig. 12.4 The Sraffa-profits of sector 2

Before drawing such a far-reaching conclusion, the profit situation of sector 2 should be considered. As Fig. 12.4 illustrates, the choice of technique does not raise any questions for this sector: T^B yields a more or less significantly higher profit than T^A for each wage rate.

A detailed comparison shows that switching to technique A, provided the wage rate is correspondingly low, would entail a more significant profit decline in sector 2 than the profit increase in sector 1.[35] Since the representative entrepreneur in industry 2 also acts as a profit maximiser, he has the alternative of preventing a change of technology by disbursing compensation to the industrialist in department 1. Then, the global profit-maximising technique would prevail—to the advantage of both branches. However, there could be no talk of a uniform profit rate in the various sectors of the economy. Ideas pointing in this direction had been advanced.[36] To be sure, such plausibility considerations do not apply if an identical capital return is required as a constitutive characteristic of a perfect competition equilibrium in the classical sense. Then, it is necessary to clarify which assessment basis can achieve the desired profit breakdown.

In truth, the thesis that the overall profit-maximising technique to the benefit of *all* entrepreneurs gains the upper hand due to side payments (or price discounts) stands on a shaky pedestal. It expresses the (still) unshaken belief in the dogma that the Sraffa calculation is the *gold standard* in profit distribution under competitive conditions. Evidently, the accumulation of paradoxical results and anomalies did not lead to a critical examination of the standard premise on page one, which underlies the entire further analysis: the distribution of profits according to the material costs. Instead, an attempt was made to tame the recalcitrant troublemakers through special treatments—the epicycle theory sends kind regards.

Sraffa-pricing has another effect that cannot be rationalised even with the best will in the world. Technique A was additionally designed to demonstrate an extraordinarily astonishing curiosity. Let us assume that there is only this technique; the problem of choosing a method does not (yet) arise.

[35] Cf. tables 2 and 3 of the (slightly different) numerical example in Helmedag, F., Technikwahl ..., op. cit., p. 415 f.

[36] Cf. ibid., p. 417 f.

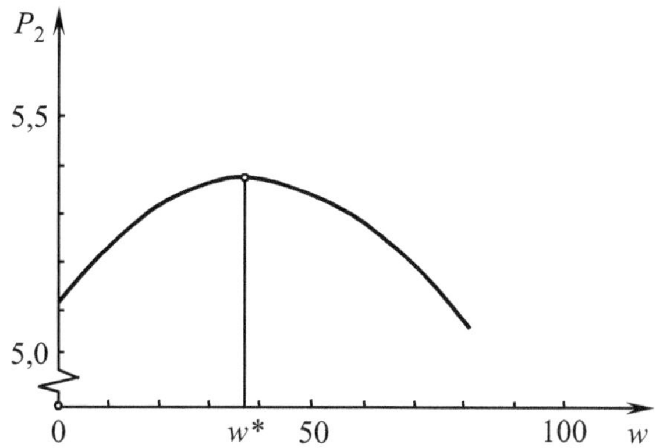

Fig. 12.5 The Sraffa-profit of sector 2 for T^A as a function of the wage rate

Table 12.1 Selected wage rates, Sraffa-profits and profit rates for T^A

w	TP	P_1	P_2	r
0.00	252.174	247.064	5.110	1.71286
10.00	242.174	236.937	5.237	1.61686
20.00	232.174	226.854	5.320	1.52457
30.00	222.174	216.810	5.364	1.43568
36.87	215.304	209.932	5.372	1.37643
40.00	212.174	206.803	5.370	1.34992
50.00	202.174	196.831	5.343	1.26707
60.00	192.174	186.890	5.284	1.18692

Figure 12.5 overleaf shows, in magnification, a phenomenon already indicated in Fig. 12.4: the existence of an *absolute* sectoral profit maximum with a *positive* wage rate.[37] Because of the particular importance, Table 12.1 lists some selected values on which Fig. 12.5 is based. Other variables of interest are also shown.

When technique A is employed, the net output of the economy under consideration comprises 252.174 units of good 1, which also serves as the accounting unit. At a zero wage rate, this net output equals total profit. If the wage rises, the neo-Ricardian worldview collapses: although, as expected, the profit of sector 1 decreases with total profit, how does the profit of sector 2 develop? It initially grows, only to diminish after reaching a maximum!

Up to $w^* = 36.87$, the profit of industry 2 rises with a falling profit rate, i.e., the opposing movement of the wage rate and total profit is reversed at the sectoral level. In this range, division 1 even records a declining income greater than the reduction in total profit. Indeed, with a wage rate lower than w^*, sector 2 could raise its gain

[37] The investigation into the possibility of a sectoral profit maximum at a positive wage rate using the Sraffa-calculation – given its numerous other 'irregularities' – was initiated by a student named Rosi Schings, who posed a question to this effect in a special seminar.

through a voluntary wage increase that would spill over to sector 1 under competitive conditions.[38]

The fiasco of the neo-Ricardian profit rate as an indicator of the profit level and its development is complete: what can one do with this profit rate if it is established that it may grow despite a declining sectoral profit? With the proof of this possible "perversity", the production price *approach* of Ricardo, Marx, Dmitriev, Bortkiewicz, Sraffa and others is entirely up in the air. The last vestige of confidence that may still have existed—regardless of the upstream weaknesses of the (individual) doctrine(s) uncovered here—has lost all ground: the distribution of the surplus product in relation to the material expenditure is not a characteristic of classical competition; this emperor is also naked.

In reality—if it were to be found as pure as on the drawing board—the now shattered Sraffa calculation would never have had a serious chance. With the given conditions—labour as the only non-produced input and constant returns to scale—*every* entrepreneur has a reference system against which he can test whether the division of labour pays off for him: "his" subsystem.

The social division of labour cannot simply be assumed to exist, as the prevailing theory tries to make us believe; instead, the concrete conditions must be uncovered, whose fulfilment brings about sectoral specialisation in the economy. Horizontal differentiation must not lead to a worse result than vertical integration. A company only orders from a supplier if the external procurement pays off at least equally as an integrated in-house production of its inputs.

Let us look at the alternatives that are always available to our model entrepreneurs. It is helpful to distinguish between two cases. First, we consider a situation in which there is only *one* technique. With linear production processes, each industrialist would be free to use part of the total labour employed in his sector so that only consumer goods appear in the net product. Of course, individual profits add up to the total profit as before. The sectoral profit functions are:

$$P_1 = a_{01}q_1(y_1 - w) \tag{12.38}$$

$$P_2 = a_{02}q_2(y_1 - w) \tag{12.39}$$

What kind of pricing must be employed so that the profit determined by (12.38) and (12.39) accrues to the specialised industries? Based on our investigations above, it is obvious what the correct answer must be: yes, the assessment basis for allocating profit can only be the respective wage bill $a_{0j}q_jw$ $(j = 1, 2)$. Then, as we know from the corresponding calculation (12.3) (cf. p. 237) the production prices are parallel to the labour values.

Let us look at the standardisation of the consumer good price:

[38] Techniques exhibiting the same properties can be constructed at will once the sectoral profit function à la (III.74) (cf. p. 254) is known. The coefficients have merely to be chosen so that the first derivative of the profit curve with respect to the wage rate vanishes at a positive wage rate.

$$p_1 = v_1 w(1 + \varepsilon) \equiv 1 \tag{12.40}$$

Considering the inverse relation between the labour value and the productivity in division 1 (cf. (12.23), p. 246), the 'new' rate of profit ensues:

$$\varepsilon = \frac{y_1 - w}{w} \tag{12.41}$$

In both sectors, the unit profit is now $a_{0j}w\varepsilon = a_{0j}\,(y_1—w)$. After multiplication by the respective quantity q_j, the profits according to (12.38) and (12.39) result. No entrepreneur would participate in the social division of labour if they had less profit to collect. It can also be seen that when this pricing rule is applied, the sectoral profit curves are *straight lines*. Thus, there is no maximum of a profit function at a positive wage rate.

Moreover, this calculation method guarantees the *constancy* of profit *ratios*, irrespective of the wage rate. With Sraffa pricing, the percentage share of the sectors in the total surplus varies with the labour remuneration.[39] Even this fact raises massive doubts about whether all entrepreneurs will embrace a procedure that expects them to accept such irregularities.

It becomes all the more exciting when *several* techniques are known. At the first attempt, one might believe that if profit is allotted in compliance with employment, the rational microeconomic calculus would be to make the relative sectoral labour input as large as possible. This extension of the assessment basis would increase the share of total profit $(y_1—w)$ that a sector might claim. Still, this hypothesis does not stand up to scrutiny.

Our multi-purpose model is also appropriate for illustrating the current situation. Figure 12.6 shows the profits of division 1 for techniques A and B as functions of the wage rate. $P^A_{1\,\max}$ and $P^B_{1\,\max}$ represent the maximum profit of Sector 1 for technique A and technique B respectively. Evidently, the profit lines intersect. However, it would be premature to conclude from this that there is a distribution-dependent change of technique in the case of the value calculation.

If the entrepreneurs use the labour value calculation, T^A brings sector 1 for a wage rate w between $0 \leq w < \hat{w}$ a higher profit than T^B, which maximises total profit. Therefore, sector 1 would prefer T^A in this range. Industry 2, conversely, earns consistently higher profits with T^B compared to T^A. Again, the difference would suffice to compensate sector 1 to dispense with T^A.

The reason for the good performance of sector 1 when using T^A is simply because this method absorbs significantly more of the total labour than T^B. The respective gross production of department j at T^A or T^B is symbolised by $q_j{}^A$ or $q_j{}^B$. With technique A, the employment of sector 1 amounts to $a_{01}q_1{}^A = 0.782608$, i.e., almost eighty per cent of the total work. On the other hand, the share is much lower when technique B is employed: $b_{01}q_1{}^B = 0.357945$. Now we know why sector 1 would

---

[39] Cf. the columns of relative profits in Tables 2 and 3 in Helmedag, F., Technikwahl …, op. cit., p. 415 f.

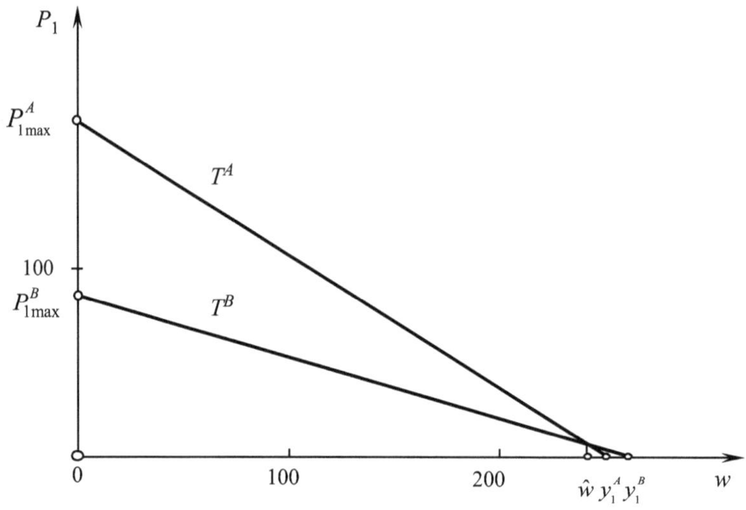

Fig. 12.6 Profit curves of sector 1 for T^A and T^B

favour technique A if the branches absorbed the profit based solely on labour input: the more than doubled employment level overcompensates for wage rates up to $\hat{w}$, the higher total profit that T^B yields.

However, the comparison in this form is misguided. Department 2 would not give in to sector 1 if the latter insists on using technique A. Without a division of labour between industries, sector 1 would also employ the profit-maximising technique B. Consequently, in this case, the (final) consumer good is manufactured by a vertically integrated production in both branches. The labour-minimising technique then rules the roost. In equilibrium, the congruence of profit *per unit of labour* in every division ensues. The societal division of labour requires the "competitiveness" of the techniques, i.e., a method must not require more than the *socially necessary* labour at the given level of technical knowledge. Of course, each entrepreneur accepts the sectoral differentiation if he is not better off with a corresponding internal allocation of his available labour.

From an individual economic perspective, in-house making of the means of production is always worthwhile if it entails lower costs than external procurement. To boot, the recourse to outsourcing would inherently diminish the employment of profitable labour. Inter-industrial value chains only emerge if the acquisition of upstream products offers advantages over integrated in-house fabrication: the market price of the input must be lower than the costs of complete interior production. Intermediate solutions in the form of purchasing from a range of finished intermediate goods are possible and realistic.

The supplier's profit is based on the most cost-effective technique he can use, e.g., due to mass production advantages. Specialisation gives him a level of labour productivity that his customers are denied. Competition between the manufacturers of means of production and intermediate goods calls for further efforts to increase labour productivity. The same applies to their customers, who gain a competitive edge by using the cost-cutting lever to reduce the labour required to manufacture their goods. This typical pressure to act sheds light on the energy source that feeds the engine of process innovations in capitalist market economies.

These considerations should counteract the idea that entrepreneurs could increase their profits at will by artificially raising personnel costs beyond the socially necessary norm. The opposite is true: they are only price-competitive if they opt for the technique that *minimises labour costs* from a macroeconomic perspective. At the enterprise level, this technique asserts itself as the most cost-effective. Likewise, with the Sraffa calculation, a sector cannot increase its profit by inflating input coefficients: free competition enforces the lowest conceivable prices. These are, however, not those which distribute the surplus in proportion to material costs but allocate the profit to the minimum labour costs. Value calculation gains the upper hand without exhibiting the paradoxes owed to Sraffa's approach, which contradicts profit maximisation and, thus, the principles of market capitalism.

Before outlining the consequences that the new old theory demands, the viability of this approach is subjected to a further severe test. Does the concept prove itself in the case of joint production? The hunch is not deceptive: value calculation is *in every respect* more powerful than Sraffa-pricing.

Chapter 13
Value and Price in General: Joint Production

Sraffa attaches great importance to the phenomenon that a manufacturing process produces more than one commodity: he devotes the second part of his book, which makes up more than half of the account, to joint production. This province of value theory is usually not paid the same attention as single production. In contrast to Ricardo, Marx does make a few scattered notes on the simultaneous production of several goods. Still, he does not take them up in his analytical-formal discussion of the formation of production prices.[1] By extending his investigation to processes that generate a mixed output, Sraffa entered a field that had been sparsely explored before.

Moreover, locating joint production processes exclusively in the secondary sector, e.g., in the chemical industry, would be unrealistic. Numerous examples cited in the literature relating to arable and livestock farming societies raise awareness that joint production is the order of the day in such economies, if it does not dominate. In a hunter-gatherer society envisioned by Adam Smith, the chasing of deer and beaver is by no means only for meat:

> "Skins and hides are used for clothing and tent construction, bones, teeth and sinews are used to manufacture hunting weapons and jewellery, etc. Each object mentioned is therefore a *compositum mixtum* of different use values or goods (and possibly some non-goods) that arise as joint products when the animal is cut up."[2]

Therefore, it seems necessary to widen the problem area. Joint production is not merely a special case of production theory. Instead, it can claim general validity: "… these cases of joint production", already Jevons remarked in his criticism of Mill's

[1] On the history of joint production theory, see Kurz, H. D., Classical and Early Neo-classical Economists on Joint Production, in: Metroeconomica, vol. 36 (1986), pp. 1–37.

[2] Kurz, H. D., Adam Smith, die Regel der freien Güter und die > vent for surplus < -Begründung des Außenhandels, in: Kurz, H. D. (ed.), Adam Smith (1723–1790), Marburg 1990, pp. 237–260, p. 239 f. [F. H.]

F. Helmedag, *Production of Commodities by Means of Labour*, Springer Studies in Alternative Economics, https://doi.org/10.1007/978-3-032-01457-3_13

treatment of the subject, "far from being 'some peculiar cases' form the general rule, to which it is difficult to point out any clear or important exceptions."[3]

Moreover, the significance of joint production for the theory of value is not influenced by the frequency of such processes in reality. The existence of a process that produces more than one good is taken by itself sufficient to change the characteristics of an economy that might otherwise consist only of single production industries.[4]

Generally, the formal mastery of joint production obviously allows one to cope with less complex tasks. Thus, fixed capital can be understood as a joint product: with the application of a new machine and other inputs, a specific output is produced and a used apparatus. In Sraffian theory, the prices of the used machines of the individual age groups and consequently their *economic* life depend on the distribution.[5] Finally, joint production allows the integration of other original inputs besides labour. These include natural resources such as pasture and arable land, which enter and leave manufacturing.[6] Against this backdrop, we shall discuss joint production in general terms and do not treat the sub-issues of fixed capital and land separately.

First, Sraffa's solution is presented and evaluated. In this context, the question arises about how the "irregularities" associated with his explanatory scheme have been assessed and processed. However, we do not merely discuss the shortcomings of Sraffa's theory of joint production. Instead, the essential defects of the concept are illustrated precisely by the concrete model brought forward to deny any sense of the labour theory of value. Despite the weaknesses of Sraffa's doctrine, it seemed to some people robust enough to demonstrate that a negative surplus value could arise in joint production, even though prices and profits were positive.

However, under the microscope, we shall confirm what we suspected due to the foregoing experience: the neo-Ricardian production price theory is incurably ill; the supposedly dead labour theory of value, on the other hand, is not merely twitching. On the contrary, a closer examination of the example mentioned above reinforces the impression that the apparent corpse has the potential to turn out to be a princess.

[3] Jevons, W. St., op. cit., p. 215.

[4] Cf., e.g., Steedman, I., Joint Production and the Wage-Rent Frontier, in: The Economic Journal, vol. 92 (1982), pp. 377–385.

[5] Cf. Sraffa, P., Production …, op. cit., p. 63 ff., Varri, P., Prices, Rate of Profit and Life of Machines in Sraffa's Fixed-Capital Model, in: Pasinetti, L. (ed.), op. cit., pp. 55–87, Baldone, S., Fixed Capital in Sraffa's Theoretical Scheme, in: Pasinetti, L. (ed.), op. cit., pp. 88–137 and Schefold, B., Fixed Capital as a Joint Product and the Analysis of Accumulation with Different Forms of Technical Progress, in: Pasinetti, L. (ed.), op. cit., pp. 138–217.

[6] Cf. Sraffa, P., Production …, op. cit., p. 74 ff. and Kurz, H. D., Rent Theory in a Multisectoral Model, in: Oxford Economic Papers, vol. 36 (1978), pp. 16–37.

13.1 Sraffa's Approach, Its Shortcomings and Their Echo

Unlike in single production, where neo-Ricardians (mistakenly) recognise no obstacles to applying Sraffa-pricing, the literature teems with curiosities that can occur under joint production conditions. Therefore, as in the case of single production, we are not forced to demystify the idyll systematically. Instead, it is now sufficient to refer to the scepticism sometimes entertained even by neo-Ricardians regarding what has been achieved. Accordingly, Pasinetti's introduction to the relevant collection of essays published by him contains the following assessment:

> "... on the wave of enthusiasm and mathematical elegance, there has been a tendency to concentrate efforts on the most general possible case of joint production. Unfortunately, this case is so general as to allow too many possibilities, and these have indeed led to many negative conclusions and to very few positive ones."[7]

The first difficulty in calculating the exchange ratios under joint production conditions is that the number of equations typically falls behind the number of prices to be determined. This deficit is ruled out in the case of single production: the separated processes can be identified with "their" representative commodities.

If, e.g., iron and wheat are produced in one process, it is impossible to speak of the iron or wheat industry. How does Sraffa deal with this problem? "In these circumstances," he placates, "there will be room for a second, parallel process which will produce the two commodities by a different method and, as we shall suppose at first, in different proportions."[8]

Sraffa's model for price determination necessarily postulates a "quadratic" system; the number of commodities must equal the number of processes. Against this background, *Sraffa simply assumes* that a sufficient number of processes would be used: "… the number of processes should be equal to the number of commodities."[9] With this economically completely unmotivated hypothesis, the path to tackling the upcoming workload in a promising way was already obstructed right out of the gate. The central premise of Sraffa's deliberations, which is decisive but free-floating, has initiated many proposals to erect the construction on firm ground. Schefold, in particular, has attempted in numerous works to justify the, as he concedes, "strange and crucial assumption"[10] by plausibility and probability considerations.[11]

---

[7] Pasinetti, L., Introductory Note: Joint Production, in: Pasinetti, L. (ed.), op. cit., pp. xii-xvii, p. xv. Cf. also Steedman's sober preliminary remarks to the volume "Sraffian Economics II", in which selected articles on joint production are reprinted. There it says, "… it is only especially restricted forms of fixed capital system that are free from the general complexities of joint production …" Steedman, I., Introduction, in: Steedman, I. (ed.), Sraffian Economics II, Aldershot 1988, pp. 1–7, p. 5.

[8] Sraffa, P., Production …, op. cit., p. 43.

[9] Ibid., p. 44.

[10] Schefold, B., Sraffa and Applied Economics: Joint Production, in: Political Economy, vol. 1 (1985), pp. 17–40, p. 23.

[11] See Schefold, B., Mr Sraffa on Joint Production and Other Essays, London 1989 and the articles cited there.

The most convincing of such rescue attempts complete the system by referring to disposal processes to eliminate damages or "bads" which emerge quasi as joint products. Of course, this reasoning will only impress those who want their beliefs reinforced. As is well-known, injuries are often quite persistent, not to mention that not all by-products can be classified as "harmful" needing to be neutralised. However, if you do the Neo-Ricardians the favour of pretending that the system is square, one immediately encounters new turbulence.

It is customary to write **B** for the square output matrix. Its columns, which contain the output of the respective process, can have more than one positive element. Each row vector of this matrix is semi-positive because each good is produced with at least one method. **B** occupies the position of the unit matrix **I,** representing the unit output matrix in single production. Production prices now result from the following system:

$$\mathbf{pA}(1+r) + \mathbf{a}_0 w = \mathbf{pB} \tag{13.1}$$

The solution is:

$$\mathbf{p} = \mathbf{a}_0 w[\mathbf{B} - (1+r)\mathbf{A}]^{-1} \tag{13.2}$$

A solution requires that $[\mathbf{B} - (1+r)\mathbf{A}]$ is regular, i.e., the determinant of this matrix must exist. However, this by no means guarantees economically acceptable results. In this respect, a contribution by Manara was groundbreaking.[12] He formulated the second part of Sraffa's book mathematically precisely, like what Newman did with the first half. Manara proves that Sraffa's standard commodity can contain, in addition to negative quantities—what Sraffa knew,[13] even *complex* elements.[14] In the face of these outcomes, there is no need for a lengthy plea to justify the serious doubts about the significance of the standard commodity and the linear wage rate-profit rate relationship obtained with it.

Even if one does not attach great importance to the standard system as a purely auxiliary construction—an approach adopted here in the context of single production—further curiosities emerge in Sraffa's theory of joint production, which are difficult to interpret. By way of example, it will be shown soon that labour quantities attributable to diverse commodities, and thus Sraffa-prices, can be negative. Furthermore, "bumps" in the wage rate-profit rate graph are conceivable. In such cases, the distribution variables move in the same direction within a certain range.[15] Thus, it seems conceivable that a wage rate corresponds to several profit rates. Consequently,

---

[12] Cf. Manara, C. F., Sraffa's Model for the Joint Production of Commodities by Means of Commodities [1968], in: Pasinetti, L. (ed.), op. cit., pp. 1–15.

[13] Cf. Sraffa, P., Produktion …, op. cit., p. 47 ff.

[14] Cf. Manara, C. F., op. cit., p. 9 f.

[15] This should not be confused with the possibility described above, according to which a *sectoral* profit positively correlates with the wage level in single production systems (cf. p. 258). In these models, wage and profit rates constantly change in opposite directions at the macroeconomic level.

the Sraffa model advertises attractive opportunities: in contrast to Ricardo's credo, rising pay may also lead to an increasing profit rate.

In the context of single production, the criterion for the choice of technique, cost minimisation, coincided with maximising the real wage at a given profit rate. The technique located furthest to the northeast on the wage front generated the lowest Sraffa-prices. This property is no longer valid for joint production. The Sraffa calculation possibly identifies a system as cost-minimal when the real wage is *not* the highest. Furthermore, the cost-minimising technique may be associated with negative prices at particular profit rates. And—to finally break the camel's back—the existence of a cost-minimising system is by no means guaranteed[16]: from the Sraffa-prices of technique *A*, technique *B* appears more cost-effective, while from the vantage point of technique *B*, technique *A* is estimated to be more lucrative!

In addition to the formal calamities of the Sraffian joint production doctrine, the identified weaknesses of his single production treatment persist. The cost-minimising Sraffa system fails to maximise profits and distributes the surplus differently from the demands of free competition. With this in mind, one should not attach too much weight to the constructed irrationalities of capitalism: since neo-Ricardian theory fails in general, entrepreneurs, in particular, are certainly not tormented by the nightmare that the choice of technique degenerates into an event resembling the race between the Hare and the Hedgehog.

Despite the looming difficulties of single and joint production, people shied away from the obvious consequences. Instead of checking the sustainability of the cornerstones of the Sraffian price theory laid down in the first few pages, it was concluded with razor-sharp precision that which must not, cannot be. The doyen has also provided relevant exercise material to this effect. If some prices become negative due to a change in wages, this is nothing sensational in Sraffa's opinion:

> "All that it implies is that, although in actual fact all prices were positive, a change in the wage might create a situation the logic of which required some of the prices to turn negative: and this being unacceptable, those among the methods of production that gave rise to such a result would be discarded to make room for others which in the new situation were consistent with positive prices."[17]

In principle, this method was never abandoned by Sraffa's disciples. Suppose the doctrine allows for upshots that, with the best will in the world, are no longer accessible to any valid justification. In this instance, the trouble is eliminated by banishing the cause of the problem. Since the explanatory pattern does not exclude negative prices, but these are unobservable in reality, there are consequently no processes that generate negative prices. Should such a situation arise, other processes with the appropriate properties are conjured up, which—what luck!—are available in the right place at the right time.

---

[16] Cf. Salvadori, N., Existence of Cost-Minimizing Systems within the Sraffa Framework, in: Zeitschrift für Nationalökonomie, vol. 42 (1982), pp. 281–298. In another article, Salvadori presented numerical examples of the phenomena mentioned. Cf. Salvadori, N., Switching in Methods of Production and Joint Production, in: The Manchester School, vol. 53 (1985), pp. 156–178.

[17] Sraffa, P., Production ..., op. cit., p. 59.

Therefore, the "dominant technique" is the one that fits into the concept. It comes as no surprise when profiles of this planned child involuntarily turn into caricatures. Schefold claims he has shown that …

> "... the dominant technique, *appropriately defined*, exists in the *relevant range*, ... that it is unique, 'square', and that the wage curve is *essentially* monotonically falling."[18]

In plain language, this statement is an admission of failure of the neo-Ricardian joint production theory: only the "appropriately defined" technique has the desired properties in the "relevant range" alone, and the wage curve only falls "essentially", i.e., if it does not rise. After all, this bitter medicine is not administered without a sedative pill. Despite the concept's undeniable flaws, it deserves to be trusted:

> "The important assertions have been proven; it is of interest only to the specialist that some details have turned out to be incorrect, especially regarding Sraffa's description of the choice of technique in the joint production case. We are now free to turn to new tasks like the analysis of the social forces defining the socially necessary technique..."[19]

Although the specialists have by no means achieved anything impressive so far, the advice given is heeded: some experts may (continue to) devote themselves to the detailed questions of the Sraffian thought model, the study of the forces that determine the socially necessary technique, on the other hand, is not always a new task for others—it has long been a subject of this investigation. To be continued.

13.2 From Steedman via Morishima to von Neumann

It is one of the ironies in the history of economic thought that Sraffa's theory, which was intended as the basis for a critique of the neoclassical tenets of value and distribution, was not only turned against the labour theory of value in the context of the transformation problem but was also used as a means of razing the (supposed) last bastion of the labour theory of value: the fundamental theorem. In the mid-1970s, Ian Steedman opened fire on what appeared to be the only reliable statement of the labour theory of value, after which exploitation and profit were positively correlated. With the aid of a numerical example, he attempted to prove the invalidity of the fundamental theorem in the case of joint production: "In brief, in the presence of joint production, the existence of positive surplus value is neither a necessary nor a sufficient condition for the existence of positive profits and prices."[20]

Since Steedman was undoubtedly aware of the considerable hardships of the Sraffian joint production approach, one can only admire his audacity in relying on such an ally in his attack. Although the outcome of the case is to his disadvantage,

---

[18] Schefold, B., The dominant technique in joint production systems, in: Cambridge Journal of Economics, vol. 12 (1988), pp. 97–123, p. 102, own emphases.

[19] Ibid., p. 111.

[20] Steedman, I., Positive Profits With Negative Surplus Value, in: The Economic Journal, Vol. 85 (1975), pp. 114–123, p. 114.

Table 13.1 Steedman's example

	Product 1	Product 2	Labour		Product 1	Product 2
Process 1	5	0	1	→	6	1
Process 2	0	10	1	→	3	12

he has nevertheless rendered outstanding services to the further development of the theory of value: Steedman's attack underlines the strength of the labour theory of value in general. The analysis of the example he presented serves as a litmus test of the comprehensive superiority of the value theory over Sraffa's pricing model, which has already been irrefutably proven for single production.[21]

Table 13.1 overleaf shows the numerical example with which Steedman wanted to deal the final blow to the labour theory of value. He considers a situation in which two processes can each produce two products. The input is to the left of the arrows, and to the right is the output.[22] One labour unit is performed in both processes. Furthermore, both methods are subject to linear returns to scale, i.e., the input coefficients do not vary with the quantity produced.

The data in Table 13.1 can be used to formulate the equations to determine the variables l_1 and l_2, which Steedman interprets as labour values:

$$5l_1 + 1 = 6l_1 + l_2 \tag{13.3}$$

$$10l_2 + 1 = 3l_1 + 12l_2 \tag{13.4}$$

Hence, the Sraffa-Steedman values are obtained as:

$$l_1 = -1 \tag{13.5}$$

$$l_2 = 2 \tag{13.6}$$

[21] In his book "Marx After Sraffa", Steedman advocates that the value calculation is superfluous in principle—i.e., not only under joint production conditions. Concerning single production, he states: "What have any value magnitudes to contribute to this analysis? Nothing. The labor values of commodities, or of any aggregates of commodities, are known only when it is known which methods of production are in use. The choice of production methods is itself determined, however, only in the process of determining the maximum achievable rate of profit … The determination of the profit rate is thus *logically prior* to any determination of value magnitudes—it is hardly surprising, then, that the latter have nothing to contribute to the former." Steedman, I., Marx …, op. cit., p. 64 f. Since, as we have seen, Sraffa's profit rate is not a helpful indicator for determining the maximum profit and its distribution in single production, we shall not take a closer look at this part of Steedman's critique in detail. Nevertheless, one or two comments on Steedman's text would be on the tip of the tongue. A critical review of the book provides Kurz, H. D., Sraffa After Marx, in: Australian Economic Papers, vol. 18 (1979), pp. 52–70.

[22] Cf. Steedman, I., Positive …, op. cit., p. 115 ff. The same example can be found in Steedman, I., Marx …, op. cit., p. 150 ff.

Apparently, commodity 1 "contains" a *negative* amount of total labour expended in its production; indeed, it is a surprising and grotesque discovery.[23] However, Sraffa would have interpreted the phenomenon in the final analysis differently, though he admitted at first: "This looks at first as if it were a freak result of abstraction-mongering that can have no correspondence in reality."[24] But anyone who thinks this (correct) impression would finally prompt him to scrutinise the premises responsible for this bizarre result has rejoiced too soon. A little later, the kind reader learns: "... nothing abnormal will be noticeable ..."[25] How come?

The absurdity does not penetrate to the "surface" because the Sraffa-prices of both commodities only become positive *above* a certain level of the profit rate. The values (**l**) calculated by Steedman are nothing else than the labour-commanding Sraffa-prices (cf. (13.2) on p. 267 with $w \equiv 1$) at a profit rate of zero. In general:

$$\mathbf{l} = \mathbf{a}_0[\mathbf{B} - \mathbf{A}]^{-1} \tag{13.7}$$

As noted above, Sraffa ruled out negative prices simply by claiming that process alternatives without this embarrassing side effect would be used promptly when the rate of profit (in his view) turns out to be undesirably low. If one regards this construction as wishful thinking, it appears not too far-fetched that both the negative values and the negative prices point in truth to a disaster of the neo-Ricardian theory. At the very least, a tolerant Sraffa supporter—who grants others the same right that he claims on his behalf—should have considered the thesis that any new processes or changes in the structure of the labour input vector would make negative values and, consequently, negative prices disappear.

Steedman does not follow this path; in his steadfast confidence, the choice of technique is based on Sraffa's prices, the calculation of which, as he never tires of asserting, does not require labour values. Instead, he wants to scotch the fundamental theorem. For that purpose, he invoked the possibility of negative labour values already mentioned by Sraffa. For the desired result, the *surplus value* must be negative to boot. No witchcraft is needed to achieve this: one must only postulate that capitalists mainly acquire commodities with a negative Sraffa-Steedman labour value.

To this end, Steedman fixes a real wage, causing the remainder of the net product accruing to the entrepreneurs to comprise more than twice as much of good 1 as good 2. He assumes first that five units of labour are performed in process 1 and one unit of labour in process 2. The net product then amounts to eight units of product 1 and seven of product 2. Next, Steedman fixes the wage basket: the six workers earn three units of commodity 1 and five units of commodity 2. The remaining five units of good 1 and the leftover two of good 2 go to the capitalists. In this aggregate, the Steedman labour value of product 1 predominates. Ergo, the surplus value becomes negative; an important interim stage seems to have been reached.

---

[23] Cf. Kurz, H. D., Zur neoricardianischen ..., op. cit., p. 185.

[24] Sraffa, P., Production ..., op. cit., p. 60.

[25] Ibid.

Remarkably, during the following intensive discussion, the dual paradox of negative surplus value was not discussed: the value of labour power, i.e., the labour time "embodied" in the real wage, amounts to seven units and is thus *greater* than the total employment of six units. This abstruse result is also hardly appropriate for enhancing trust in Steedman's argument.

Of course, the coup could only be successful if the prices and the profit rate were positive in this constellation. The data in Table 13.1 allow us to obtain two equations determining the labour-commanding prices, i.e., $w \equiv 1$:

$$(1 + r)5p_1 + 1 = 6p_1 + p_2 \tag{13.8}$$

$$(1 + r)10p_2 + 1 = 3p_1 + 12p_2 \tag{13.9}$$

The real wage bundle put together by Steedman provides another equation:

$$3p_1 + 5p_2 = 6 \tag{13.10}$$

From the system (13.8), (13.9) and (13.10) a profit rate of 20%[26] and $p_1 = \frac{1}{3}$ and $p_2 = 1$ are calculated. The objective of the exercise seems to be accomplished: positive profit with negative surplus value. "Marxists should therefore concentrate on developing the materialist account of why production conditions and real wages are what they are", Steedman lectures the proponents of the fundamental theorem, "leaving the discussion of 'value magnitudes' to those concerned only with the development of a new Gnosticism."[27]

As expected, Steedman attempts to explain why a negative labour value under conditions of joint production is nothing special. In such a world, it was generally impossible to produce *exactly* one commodity and thus ascertain its labour value. Because of this, the correct way to determine the values would be to interpret the change in *employment* resulting from an increase in net output by exactly one unit of a commodity as its value.

In Steedman's example, the increase in the output of good 1 by one unit is achieved by *reducing* the labour input by one unit. If three instead of five labour units are employed in process 1 and two instead of one in process 2, the total net output is nine units of good 1 and seven of good 2. Although the total employment *decreases* by one unit compared to the initial situation, the net output *increases* by one unit of commodity 1: "This is the meaning of the result that commodity 1 has a value of—1 ... there is nothing at all strange about a negative value. It follows that there is nothing strange about negative surplus value."[28]

---

[26] There is a second solution for r, but it is associated with a negative price of product 1: "The negative price p_1 makes this solution economically insignificant." Steedman, I., Positive ..., op. cit., p. 115 n.

[27] Steedman, I., Marx ..., op. cit., p. 162.

[28] Steedman, I., Positive ..., op. cit., p. 119.

Steedman's provocative theses met with a significant response in the economic literature. Several authors have localised the cause of Steedman's results, which run counter to common sense, in the premises. Therefore, the data Steedman presented in his numerical example are the linchpin of further analysis.

A glance at Table 13.1 (see p. 272) is enough to recognise that the processes listed there are in a strange proportion to each other: the labour performed in process 2 is far more productive than that in process 1. This direct comparison is possible because both methods produce more than their necessary input themselves; they are viable on their own and do not depend on each other, as in the case of single production. The net output of process 1 per unit of labour amounts to one unit of each of the two commodities, while process 2 produces three units of good 1 and two units of good 2.

This difference raises the question of whether the same homogeneous labour is employed in both processes and, if so, whether process 1 has any real chance of asserting itself against process 2. In fact, a negative labour value of a commodity always indicates that the corresponding subsystem can be divided into two divisions with different productivity:

> "... the labour value of a commodity will only be negative if, in the subsystem that produces the commodity in question in isolation, more labour is expended in the processes that must be contracted to produce the commodity in isolation than in those that expand."[29]

From this angle, it is evident that labour can be multiplied in the two processes of Steedman's example by a productivity index $\pi_i (i = 1,\ 2)$, that weighs the labour input. The calculated values in "simple labour" are positive, provided the relation of the weighting factors $\frac{\pi_1}{\pi_2}$ is selected from the interval $\left(\frac{1}{3},\ \frac{1}{2}\right)$, defined by the productivities of the two processes.[30]

The weakness of such concepts for modifying labour input is palpable: although the number of products and processes coincide, the values depend on the arbitrary ratio of the productivity indices. If, on the other hand, a theoretically sound deduction is targeted, one is situated at the centre of the "reduction problem", likewise not a particularly pretty spot in economic theory.[31] It should be possible to clarify the case without seeking salvation by resorting to heterogeneous labour, which only shifts the problem to another field but does not contribute to its solution in the given setting.

The objection tackling the issue on the other end was first put forth by Morishima: is the use of the less productive method 1 economically reasonable at all to determine values? Morishima was particularly destined to comment on Steedman's approach: in a published inaugural lecture, he propagated both a generalisation of the fundamental

[29] Schefold, B., Sraffas Theorie der Kuppelproduktion, in: Zeitschrift für Wirtschafts- und Sozialwissenschaften, vol. 103 (1983), pp. 315–340, p. 323. [F. H.] Cf. also Cogoy, M., Wertstruktur ..., op. cit., pp. 160 ff.

[30] Cf. Kurz, H. D., Sraffa ..., op. cit., p. 66 f. On the 'dogma of homogeneous labor', see Krause, U., Elemente einer multisektoralen Analyse der Arbeit, in: Gesellschaft, Beiträge zur Marxschen Theorie 13, Frankfurt a. M. 1979, pp. 15–53.

[31] For a critique of Kurz's contribution, see Fujimori, Y., Modern Analysis of Value Theory, Berlin/Heidelberg/New York 1982, p. 154 n.

theorem and, based on this, a "new" labour theory of value.[32] However, the doctrine does not refer to values that can be empirically observed but to "optimal" values, which are the shadow prices of a labour minimisation programme:

> "As soon as joint production and choice of techniques are admitted, we must discard the labour theory of value, at least in the form Marx formulated it ... There is an alternative way to formulate the labour theory of value, not as the theory of 'actual values' calculating the embodied-labour contents of commodities on the basis of the prevailing production coefficients as Marx did, but as the theory of 'optimum values' considering values as shadow prices determined by a linear programming problem that is dual to another linear programming problem for the efficient utilisation of labour."[33]

Morishima defines "necessary" labour as the *minimum* amount of labour time required to produce the commodities, given the current level of technical knowledge. The surplus labour results from the difference between the actual work performed and the necessary work interpreted in this way. Based on this, Morishima shows that exploitation must exist for the economy to grow and for capitalists to make profits. This view of things completely contradicts Steedman's example. Morishima, therefore, took the floor to explain the discrepancy.

Morisima's main criticism against Steedman is that the latter expresses the relevant relationships in the form of *equations* instead of presenting them in *inequalities*, as it would be appropriate for joint production systems:

> "... Steedman simply extends the value equations so as to include joint outputs and calls formal solutions to them 'values' with a wrong justifi- cation ... As far as his example is concerned, these Steedman values have nothing to do with the labour values of commodities, nor with Marxian values, because the latter should be non-negative by definition, while the former contain negative ones. Thus the Steedman equations fail to determine the labour values. Nevertheless, he continues his mathematical exercise and calculates the 'surplus value' at a negative amount on the basis of his 'values' or pseudo-values. It is clear, however, that the pseudo-surplus value obtained from the pseudo-values has nothing to do with Marx's surplus value ..."[34]

Morishima's values ensue from an activity vector $\mathbf{q}$, minimising the labour input required to produce (at least) a net output bundle $\mathbf{y}$[35]:

$$\mathbf{a}_0\mathbf{q} \rightarrow \text{Min} \quad s.\,\text{t.} \quad \mathbf{Bq} \geq \mathbf{Aq} + \mathbf{y} \tag{13.11}$$

---

[32] Cf. Morishima, M., Marx in the Light of Modern Economic Theory, in: Econometrica, vol. 42 (1974), pp. 611–632.

[33] Ibid., p. 615 f.

[34] Morishima, M., Positive Profits With Negative Surplus Value—A Comment, in: The Economic Journal, Vol. 86 (1976), pp. 599–603, p. 600.

[35] Cf. ibid., p. 601 f.; the symbolism has been adapted to that introduced here. For a full account of the model, see Morishima, M., Catephores, G., Value, Exploitation and Growth, London 1978, p. 22 ff.

According to Morishima, the value of the objective function provides the "true" labour value of the *basket* of products **y**.[36] The optimal activity vector is not necessarily unique, but the objective value always is. Under certain circumstances, the net output of a good is greater than it is requested by **y**.

As can be seen without much arithmetic, Steedman's postulated net output of eight units of product 1 and seven of product 2 can be produced by three-and-a-half labour units instead of six. These are employed exclusively in process 2; process 1 is no longer needed at all. The net output now consists of ten and a half units of good 1 and seven of good 2. Two and a half units of good 1 beyond Steedman's specification are manufactured; thus, the inequality sign of the constraint in (13.10) comes into operation. As a result, the labour required to produce the real wage can be determined in Morishima's sense; his proposed rate of exploitation is always positive.

Joint production systems are put into a straitjacket if one demands that a particular output be produced precisely, i.e., without making even one additional good. By that very fact, the higher yield of such techniques is annihilated in principle, if not reversed, by an economically unfounded restriction. The ability of a process to produce *several* goods prevents the fulfilment of the obligation to manufacture precisely one unit of it.

In the Sraffian joint production approach, the universal productive power of a process leads to a negative value because (at least) one further but inferior process must be implemented to complete the system. In Steedman's example, process 1, which is at a disadvantage compared to process 2 in all aspects, is *only* used to obliterate the excess over the exogenously determined net output.

In the final analysis, Steedman's reasoning rests on a premise "… which ultimately boils down to the hardly creditworthy Say's Law …"[37] Instead of considering profit maximisation based on microeconomic foundations to determine activities, Steedman is guided by the condition, plucked out of thin air, that the quantities produced must coincide entirely and without exception with an arbitrarily fixed final demand vector. This provision theoretically and empirically contradicts the operating mode of a capitalist market economy.

However, Morishima mixes normative and positive statements. On the one hand, he advocates recognising true values as a measure of necessary labour; on the other hand, he states that Steedman's method 1 is not applied. Yet, Morishima does not claim that his true values can be observed in reality; neither does he fundamentally criticise Sraffa's conception of the choice of technique, and nowhere does he brand Sraffa's price formation hypothesis as wrong.

Morishima's comments on the joint production topic do not contradict the finding that the realised employment regularly exceeds the lowest possible labour input. Thus, in Morishima's opinion, exploitation means that wage earners must systematically work longer under capitalist conditions than using the technique with the highest

---

[36] Morishima's "true values" differ conceptually from his earlier proposed "optimum values", which the programme $\mathbf{vy} \rightarrow Max$ s. t. $\mathbf{vB} \leq \mathbf{vA} + \mathbf{a}_0$ yields. Cf. Morishima, M., Positive …, op. cit., p. 601 f.

[37] Kurz, H. D., Zum Problem …, op. cit., p. 178. [F. H.]

labour productivity. To be sure, supporters of Sraffa's price theory can certainly live with this message.

In this sense, Steedman could take the easy way out in responding to Morishima's comment.[38] Without discussing the issue of equations versus inequalities, he pointed out that Marx considered the minimal amount of labour to be decisive for determining value in only *one* place—and that in an early work.[39] Later, this view is no longer found in Marx's writings.

Although Steedman accepts the logic of the general fundamental theorem and Morishima's concept of true values, these creations are, as Steedman emphasises, far removed from Marx. Since the methods that gain the upper hand in practice are usually not the most labour-efficient,[40] the value calculation *à la* Morishima had to put up with the accusation that it "… in no way reflects the functional mechanisms of the capitalist system …".[41]

Nevertheless, such a view can only be justified if the Sraffian theory of joint production proves correct. However, protests were voiced at that score. Wolfstetter, e.g., passed censure on Steedman's argumentation in a contribution to the discussion:

> "... the possibility of negative labour value, and the more extreme possibility of a negative surplus value coexisting with positive prices and profits, indicate a fundamental weakness in Sraffa's (1960) theory of joint production, which deprives that theory of valid economic meaning. Thus we hope both to comment on Steedman, and to contribute to a comparative evaluation of Sraffa's and von Neumann's (1937) theories of joint production."[42]

As Wolfstetter explains, the labour values differ in sign if one process—here method 1 of Steedman's example—can be classified as "absolutely inferior", i.e., it cannot measure up to the other technique.[43] Subsequently, Wolfstetter criticises Sraffa's joint production theory for being inadequate because it operates with equations instead of inequalities. The Sraffian approach lacks a decision criterion for the choice of technique: "… the formulation of the restrictions in terms of equalities prevents the application of any choice criterion to determine how the activity vector is chosen."[44] In comparison, the von Neumann approach would be more fruitful. Wolfstetter, therefore, attacks not only Sraffa's equation method for calculating the *values* but also the treatment of joint production in equations per se. Let us pursue this hint.

---

[38] Cf. Steedman, I., Positive Profits With Negative Surplus Value: A Reply (cited hereafter as "A Reply"), in: The Economic Journal, vol. 86 (1976), pp. 604–608.

[39] "It is important to emphasize the point that what determines value is not the time taken to produce a thing, but the minimum time it could possibly be produced in, and this minimum is ascertained by competition." Marx, K., The Poverty of Philosophy [1847], 3rd ed., Beijing 1977, p. 57, https://foreignlanguages.press/wp-content/uploads/2021/11/C30-The-Poverty-of-Philosophy-1st-Printing.pdf.

[40] Cf. Steedman, I., A Reply, op. cit., p. 607. See also Steedman, I., Marx …, op. cit., p. 192 ff.

[41] Cogoy, M., Traditionelle und neue Arbeitswerttheorie, in: Gesellschaft, Beiträge zur Marxschen Theorie 13, Frankfurt a. M. 1979, pp. 115–139, p. 132. [F. H.]

[42] Wolfstetter, E., Positive Profits With Negative Surplus Value: A Comment, in: The Economic Journal, Vol. 86 (1976), pp. 864–872, p. 864.

[43] Cf. ibid., p. 867.

[44] Ibid., p. 870.

The problem that von Neumann addresses in his famous article is so general that it also covers joint production. Initially, he notes that goods are primarily produced "from each other" and that there may be more production processes than goods. In contrast to Sraffa, however, v. Neumann does not postulate a quadratic system of equations. Thus, "... 'counting equations' is of no avail ... The way in which our questions are put leads of necessity to a system of inequalities ...".[45]

According to Steedman, Sraffa's and von Neumann's theories are compatible despite this fundamental discrepancy: "... a particular piece of analysis which is very much in the 'spirit' of von Neumann (1945–6) yields certain results which are perfectly compatible with those of Sraffa's analysis, the implication for Wolfstetter's remarks will be clear."[46] To be sure, evidence must be taken before judging whether Steedman's analysis is really in Neumann's spirit. For this purpose, let us inspect the source text.

Since von Neumann assumes that "... all income in excess of necessities of life will be reinvested",[47] the subsistence wage, like the other means of production, figures as an input; the labour directly employed in the processes is not perceptible:

> "Wage costs are not considered as such, for labourers are not separately considered any more than are farm animals. It is supposed that they will do their work in return for rations of shelter, fuel, food and clothing, just as a horse works when it is fed and cared for ... The essential point about v. Neumann's theory of prices is that goods are made out of goods *alone* and that the cost price of any good or collection of goods consists of the value of the goods from which they are made plus an interest charge."[48]

With recourse to the already familiar tokens—**M** symbolises the coefficient matrix augmented by the workers' food and **B** the output matrix of a joint production system—the central inequalities (7) and (8) of v. Neumann's approach[49] can be written down as follows:

$$\alpha \mathbf{Mq} \leq \mathbf{Bq} \tag{13.12}$$

$$\beta \mathbf{pM} \geq \mathbf{pB} \tag{13.13}$$

---

[45] Neumann, J. v., A Model of General Economic Equilibrium, in: The Review of Economic Studies, vol. 13 (1945), pp. 1–9, p. 1, http://piketty.pse.ens.fr/files/VonNeumann1945.pdf.

[46] Steedman, I., Positive Profits With Negative Surplus Value: A Reply to Wolfstetter (henceforth cited as "A Reply to Wolfstetter"), in: The Economic Journal, Vol. 86 (1976), pp. 873–876, p. 873.

[47] Neumann, J. v., A Model ..., op. cit., p. 2.

[48] Champernowne, D. G., A Note on J. v. Neumann's Article on "A Model of Economic Equilibrium", in: The Review of Economic Studies, vol. 13 (1945), pp. 10–18, p. 12, own emphasis, https://competitionandappropriation.econ.ucla.edu/wp-content/uploads/sites/95/2017/08/ChampernowneOnVonNeumann.pdf. In the first footnote of this commentary, Champernowne thanks Sraffa, among others, "for instruction in subjects discussed in this article". According to the preface of Sraffa's book, he was busy drafting his theory of joint production during the 1930s and early 1940s—i.e., around the same time. However, Sraffa's familiarity with Neumann's approach to "commodity production by means of commodities" is not apparent. Cf. Sraffa, P., Production ..., op. cit., p. vi.

[49] Cf. Neumann, J. v., A Model ..., op. cit., p. 3.

The matrices **M** and **B** record the diverse process alternatives in the columns, while the rows refer to the commodities. The system is not necessarily quadratic. Of course, **q** and **p** are suitably adapted. The scalar α represents an "expansion coefficient" in the quantity scheme (13.12), β serves as an 'interest factor' in the price terms (13.13), i.e., $\beta = 1 + \frac{z}{100}$, with z as the percentage interest rate per time unit. Furthermore, two provisions are of crucial significance. The "rule of free goods" requires the price of the product in question to vanish if the less-than sign in (13.13) holds. Formally, this principle seems reasonable: in this situation, the production of a good exceeds demand, and it is available in excess supply.[50] Analogous applies in the price Sect. (13.14). The "profitability rule" states that a process is not activated if the costs, including the interest markup, are not covered by revenues.

These precepts are employed to obtain the two groups of equations

$$\mathbf{p}(\mathbf{B} - \alpha\mathbf{M})\mathbf{q} = 0 \tag{13.14}$$

and

$$\mathbf{p}(\mathbf{B} - \beta\mathbf{M})\mathbf{q} = 0 \tag{13.15}$$

In addition, a positive output value can be postulated:

$$\mathbf{pBq} > 0 \tag{13.16}$$

Employing topological concepts, v. Neumann proves that the problem has (at least) one solution characterised by the interest factor and the expansion coefficient correspondence.[51]

What has become of v. Neumann's model in the discussion? Steedman (like numerous other authors) serves up a linear program that is supposed to correspond to v. Neumann's concept.[52] In our notation, Steedman's primal problem is:

$$\mathbf{pd} \rightarrow \text{Max} \quad \text{s. t.} \quad \mathbf{pB} \leq (1 + r)\mathbf{pA} + \mathbf{a}_0, \quad \mathbf{p} \geq \mathbf{0} \tag{13.17}$$

The vector **d** comprises the workers' consumer goods bundle, and vector **p** contains the labour-commanded prices. In the first instance, the change in Steedman's method compared to v. Neumann's leaps to the eye; linear programming was developed later, although v. Neumann played a decisive role in this process.[53] Undoubtedly,

[50] Another question is whether the price of an overproduced good actually has to fall to zero. We will come back to this issue later.

[51] With his generalisation of Brouwer's fixed point theorem, v. Neumann anticipated the core of Kakutani's theorem from 1941. Cf. Nikaido, H., Introduction to Sets and Mappings in Modern Economics, Amsterdam/London 1970, p. 309 ff.

[52] Cf. Steedman, I., A Reply to Wolfstetter, op. cit., p. 874.

[53] Cf. Dantzig, G. B., linear programming, in: The New Palgrave, vol. III, London/New York/Tokyo 1987, pp. 203–206.

using the more modern calculus would not be objectionable if it were employed to answer the same set of economic questions. However, this is not the case.

The system (13.13) corresponds only at first glance with the constraints of the program (13.17). In the latter, direct labour input is explicitly shown, and the profit rate is calculated only on the means of production. In contrast, v. Neumann includes the worker's subsistence goods in the coefficient matrix, which are thus also interest-bearing. When analysing Bortkiewicz's proposal on transforming values into prices, it was shown that the two calculation methods produce qualitatively different results. However, they share the common property of being wrong. There is another aspect to mention.

As was made evident in connection with the fundamental theorem, including the direct labour input in a coefficient matrix **M** augmented by the real wage is detrimental to studying the premises of a social division of labour. Only because of such an approach was it possible to derive the surplus from the "exploitation" of a commodity, e.g., steel. Furthermore, it is then impossible to check whether the distribution of the surplus product in the form of a uniform "interest rate" on the material costs is generally accepted: at least for single production, this is *not* true. Since v. Neumann's general theory should do justice to the specific situations, we know that the pricing method he favours runs counter to the requirements of a company-specific division of labour under competitive conditions. The system of v. Neumann is by no means the answer to everything either.

By "cleverly" transferring von Neumann's inequalities into the Steedman programme, it was also possible to usher them out the back door again without attracting attention. The objective function of the programme (13.17) postulates maximising the labour commanded prices of the wage basket. A normalised nominal wage $w \equiv 1$ means nothing other than minimising the real wage: "... the primal problem thus determines the *lowest* real wage rate and the associated prices consistent with the given value of r, under competitive conditions."[54] At the same time, the constraints *dictate* that prices must be calculated according to the Sraffian hypothesis: revenues must not be greater than the material costs plus interest surcharge at a *given* rate of return (alias profit rate r) and the remuneration of labour. Yet, the less-than sign does not apply because the uniform profit rate r is (supposedly) adopted in every implemented process in equilibrium.

The constraints ultimately turn out to be Sraffa's price *determination* Eqs. (13.1) (cf. p. 267) for joint production. The race is already run when—as Steedman does—the profit rate is fixed exogenously. The non-negativity condition of prices was added to ensure nothing could go wrong. We have thus returned to Sraffa's system: the objective function of the primal (13.17) is redundant, and the drama takes place behind the scenery of the constraints. Now we understand why Steedman has no doubts about recognising the efficiency of this approach, which, in his opinion, exudes the spirit of v. Neumann: "The most powerful analysis available of a capitalist, joint production economy is that due to von Neumann ...".[55]

[54] Steedman, I., A Reply to Wolfstetter, op. cit., p. 874.

[55] Steedman, I., Marx ..., op. cit., p. 186.

However, sacrificing the (in truth dispensable) objective function of Steedman's linear programme creates a dilemma for the neo-Ricardian theory. If the real wage is a datum, as in v. Neumann, maximising the value of the workers' consumption goods bundle for a fixed nominal wage would cause the real wage to fall. Assumedly, this should not happen. According to Schefold, the programme leads to a choice of technique that *minimises* the rate of profit:

> "This minimization of the rate of profits is usually interpreted as the result of a competitive process ... It appears to be paradoxically opposed to the classical principle of a maximization of the rate of profit (given the real wage)."[56]

Schefold, therefore, rebukes Steedman's recourse to the "minimum real-wage frontier"[57] and adds that this reference is superfluous:

> "Steedman has succumbed to the temptation of introducing a minimum wage curve in the Sraffa approach in order to make it comparable with von Neumann, but it turns out that this is not necessary. We can prove that the processes which are activated and the commodities which are produced but not overproduced according to the solution of the linear programme define the *same* Sraffa system in a simultaneous determination as would be chosen according to the Sraffa approach in a finite number of successive comparisons of different Sraffa systems, taking into account processes which could be used but which are ultimately discarded in the final solution."[58]

Since Schefold starts from the same primal as Steedman, we know what the power of the constraints can achieve; the objective function becomes functionless, and the pressure for failing to offer an explanation disappears:

> "The apparent contradiction between the maximisation of the real wage according to Sraffa and its minimisation according to von Neumann is thus resolved: if we compare systems which are technically feasible ... the real wage is maximised, whereas the rule 'Max $\mathbf{d}'\mathbf{p}$' of the primal plays no rôle whatsoever in this comparison."[59]

Thus, to prove the correctness of a theory, the audience is served a linear program whose constraints presuppose the application of the doctrine in question, whereby the problems of this very doctrine do not arise. The *petitio principii* sends congratulations. But the end justifies the means: the objective function must vanish. Neo-Ricardians do not shed a tear over the loss anyway because the primal is appertaining to a dual, which packs a punch indeed:

---

[56] Schefold, B., Von Neumann and Sraffa: Mathematical Equivalence and Conceptual Difference, in: The Economic Journal, Vol. 90 (1980), pp. 140–156, p. 144.

[57] "The analysis referred to is that embodied in Burmeister and Kuga's Minimum Real-Wage Frontier (1970), as modified by Fujimoto (1975) in his discussion of von Neumann equilibria." Steedman, I., A Reply to Wolfstetter, op. cit., p. 873. Meant are the contributions by Burmeister, E., Kuga, K., The Factor-Price Frontier, Duality and Joint Production, in: Review of Economic Studies, vol. 37 (1970), pp. 11–19 and Fujimoto, T., Duality and the Uniqueness of Growth Equilibrium, in: International Economic Review, vol. 16 (1975), pp. 781–791.

[58] Schefold, B., Von Neumann ..., op. cit., p. 144.

[59] Schefold defines **d** and **p** as column vectors. Therefore, the objective function of his primal is $\mathbf{d}'\mathbf{p}$, which corresponds substantially to our **pd**.

$$\mathbf{a}_0\mathbf{q} \rightarrow \text{Min} \quad \text{s. t.} \quad \mathbf{Bq} \geq (1+g)\mathbf{Aq} + \mathbf{d}, \quad \mathbf{q} \geq \mathbf{0} \tag{13.18}$$

As expected, the constraints here also ensure that with steady-state growth according to the Golden Rule, i.e., profit rate equals growth rate (g), the Sraffian world ("flukes apart", as the phrase always goes at this point) remains a realm of peace. But the objective function of the dual: minimising labour input ...—praise be to the constraints.

After neo-Ricardians believed to have demonstrated that the v. Neumann model does not elude their view of things, a plea for the superiority of their own vantage point must not be missed:

> "It is clear," Schefold proclaims, "that the two approaches are *conceptually* different in that the Sraffa method allows one to view the adoption of a preferred method as a transition, facilitated by surplus profits accruing to innovating entrepreneurs, from one system to another, with the preferred system yielding a *higher* real wage, given the rate of profit."[60]

Hence, the touchstone that will decide whether Sraffa's joint production concept deserves recognition or not is mentioned. What about the profits generated by the different processes? What influence does a varying profit rate exert on profit and its distribution? In short, does Sraffa's approach satisfy the premises of a capitalist competition economy based on the division of labour? Contrary to widespread custom, however, jumping to foregone conclusions should be avoided: before speculating on the extra profits of dynamic entrepreneurs, it is worth paying attention to the earnings in the Steedman economy.

13.3 Putting Steedman's Example to the Test

Sraffa's central theme was the criticism of those approaches, suggesting that capital could be determined without knowledge of prices. Yet, due to the open reaction of Sraffa-prices to changes in distribution, it is impossible to say a priori in which direction the value of the aggregated means of production will move. Notwithstanding, Sraffa attempted, with his analysis, to undermine the common notion of an inevitable substitution of capital for labour after a wage increase. However, the discussion of this topic took place almost exclusively in the context of single production. This confinement is hardly surprising: if one considers the development of Sraffa-prices as a function of the functional distribution of income under joint production conditions, the neo-Ricardian reluctance to offer the argument a broader basis through such models becomes understandable. As described above, Sraffa's joint production theory does not stint with exotic oddities that raise doubts as to whether it can hold steady in our latitudes. The Steedman economy was cradled with a lot of these.

Steedman determined the two prices and the rate of profit in his example by specifying the real wage (cf. (13.9), p. 274). However, if one wants to study the

[60] Ibid., p. 143.

Fig. 13.1 Profit rate and Sraffa prices in the Steedman example

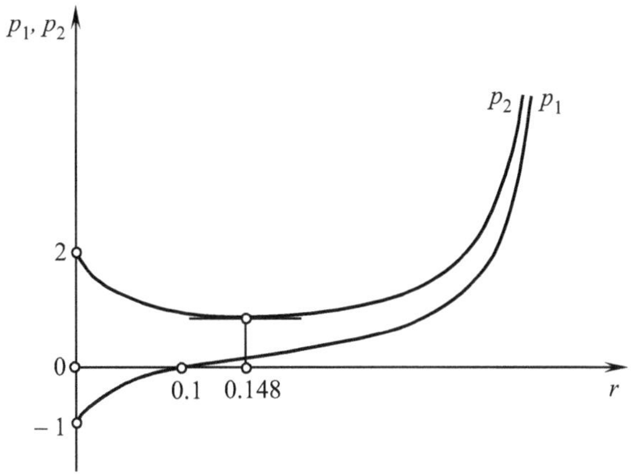

influence of a varying profit rate on prices, it is appropriate to use the standardisation $w \equiv 1$. For the labour-commanded prices, we then obtain from (13.7) and (13.8):

$$p_1 = \frac{1 - 10r}{50r^2 - 20r - 1} \tag{13.19}$$

$$p_2 = \frac{-(2 + 5r)}{50r^2 - 20r - 1} = p_1(5r - 1) + 1 \tag{13.20}$$

Figure 13.1 shows the graphs of the two prices as a function of the profit rate. Apparently, Steedman's example, with which he wanted to make nonsense of the labour theory of value, is also suitable for illustrating the previously mentioned "unpleasant" situations for Sraffa's price theory.

It is challenging to decide which shape of the two curves may claim the higher degree of curio: for $0 \leq r < 0.1$, the price of commodity 1 is negative, but at least it rises with the profit rate. The price of commodity 2 is always positive, but it initially falls, reaching a minimum at $r \approx 14.8\%$, only to increase thereafter. Suppose the wage is expressed in units of commodity 2. In that case, this phenomenon initially causes a "bump" in the $w^{(2)}$-r-relationship: the wage curve has an absolute maximum at a positive rate of profit; Steedman's example suffers from the defects that should be alien to a "dominant" technique.

Of course, Steedman knew what could happen to the Sraffa-prices in his example; he even provided a relevant illustration towards the end of his article.[61] However, Steedman does not go into the unusual features of the curves in any detail but merely lists their peculiarities. Evidently, neo-Ricardians have internalised the singularities of their theory, which go beyond any economic norm, to such an extent that comment seems redundant to them: *Credo, quia absurdum.*

---

[61] Cf. Steedman, I., Positive..., op. cit., p. 122 f. Steedman presents the relationships using the standard net product as the unit of account. Therefore, his curves look somewhat different at first glance; nevertheless, they show the same abnormalities.

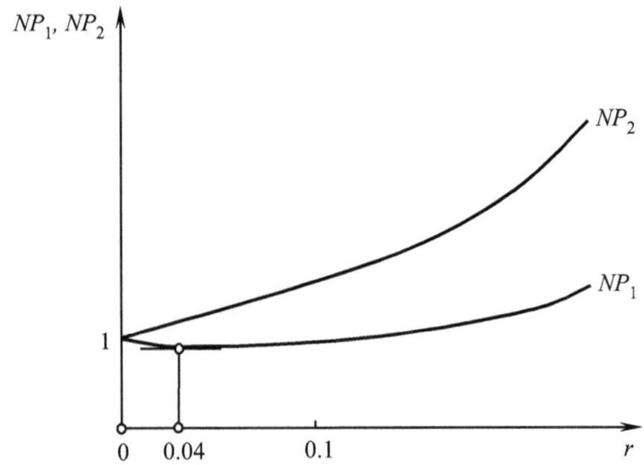

Fig. 13.2 Profit rate and Sraffa-net products ne in the Steedman example

Instead, Steedman immediately ups the ante and tries to draw attention back to the negative values in his model. If one interprets his two processes as a basic system, numerous economies that produce non-basic goods with a negative labour value are conceivable. Analogous to constructing a negative surplus value, the consumption of commodity 1 in the corresponding non-basic commodity would only have to be sufficiently high.[62]

However, Steedman applies double standards: the economically absurd results of the Sraffa theory are simply excluded by claiming that they do not occur. If the profit rate falls below 10%, another process is activated—how practical. Needless to say, the theory of value must not venture such whims. Yet, a negative Sraffa-Steedman labour value *always* means that the corresponding Sraffa-price is also negative up to a specific profit rate. If the Sraffa-prices are positive over the entire interval $0 \leq r < R$, the values are also positive. The direction of the thrust should have been reversed: with an abolition of the anomalies of prices, those of labour values disappear.

As demonstrated in the context of single production, the Sraffian profit rate is neither suitable as an indicator of total profit nor does it achieve an acceptable distribution of the surplus among the sectors. The same applies to joint production processes.

Figure 13.2 shows the value added or net product NP_1 and NP_2 of the two Steedman's processes as a function of the profit rate. The wealth creations are equivalent to the differences between the outputs and inputs valued at the respective Sraffa-prices. The labour costs—the same in both Steedman processes—must be deducted from value added to quantify the profit of the distinct methods. A comparison on this basis makes economic sense because each process is viable on its own, provided the real wage is not too high. This concept has already proven successful in single production.

As absurd as the results of Sraffa's calculation may otherwise be, this time, the fundamental economic fact of the significantly higher productivity of process 2 is

[62] Cf. ibid., p. 123.

not covered up. At *any* positive profit rate, the net product of the superior technique 2 is greater than that of the inferior process 1. Therefore, the profit of process 2 always exceeds the gain of method 1. Process 1 would even incur a loss at a sufficiently high wage rate, while process 2 remains in the black.

Another nice effect is that the value added of process 1 initially *falls* as the profit rate rises, only to increase beyond a critical limit (at $r \approx 4\%$). This shape is nothing new for us: we have already seen the counterpart in single production as the Rosi-Schings curiosity (see p. 257 n.).

Under these circumstances, is there any industrialist at all who is prepared to use method 1? Even if one gives Steedman and the other neo-Ricardians the pleasure that, for some reason, the profit rate is precisely 20%, an entrepreneur striving to maximise profits who preferred process 1 to process 2 would obviously not be a representative of the genus *homo oeconomicus*.

Neo-Ricardians are presumably sceptical about Fig. 13.2: it is based—as the response is likely to be—on the assumption that the net product valued at Sraffa prices can be sold. However, if the final demand is so fixed that the sole utilisation of process 2 manufactures more of a good than is demanded, process 1 must come on board to prevent overproduction.

At this point, it is important to recall an essential divergence between single and joint production. In the context of single production, it is palpable to characterise a sector of the economy by its product and the appertaining production method. This identification can no longer be maintained in the case of joint production. Nevertheless, the decision between several processes suggests that only *one* process is operated in each branch of the economy. Accordingly, to meet the final demand exactly, one entrepreneur has the fate of having to operate with method 1. In contrast, the other is lucky enough to be able to use the more profitable technique 2. However, this interpretation is by no means comprehensible.

The problem to be solved is not merely determining the activity levels of the processes that serve a given demand without surplus. What is really missing is the knowledge of which price calculation is compatible with a sectorally differentiated economy. The arbitrary allocation of activity levels of individual processes to the sectors does not satisfy this thirst for knowledge. Instead, it must be assumed that industries can choose between the known processes at will, a premise that is easy to make when returns to scale are constant.

If overproduction—whatever the cost—is prohibited, a suitable *combination* of the *two* processes is implemented in *every* sector in the Steedman economy. In this case, only one technique exists, which is made up of just two methods. Production takes place in all departments similarly and is fully integrated. Under other circumstances, the social division of labour is also impossible in Steedman's example.

In the context of single production, the alternative available to every entrepreneur of producing his goods *ab ovo* provided the decisive aid in deciphering the puzzle of the choice of technique: those processes that minimise labour costs manifested as profit-maximising. As a result, the exchange ratios correspond to the labour values. Pricing under conditions of free competition thus drives process innovations that reduce the "socially necessary labour time" in the longer term.

An entrepreneur is certainly only involved in sectoral specialisation if he is at least not worse off than operating his own subsystem. Even in integrated production, labour is the only non-produced resource.[63] That is why profit maximisation in free competition, regardless of joint or single production, means minimising wage costs!

If one accepts Steedman's (unfounded) condition and prohibits an output surplus, the programme to find the profit-maximising activity levels is:

$$\mathbf{a}_0\mathbf{q} \to \text{Min} \quad \text{s.t.} \quad \mathbf{Bq} = \mathbf{Aq} + \mathbf{y} \tag{13.21}$$

The equal sign in the constraints indicates that $\mathbf{y}$ specifies the *exact* net output to be manufactured. Several processes can be used in a sector for this purpose. Applied to Steedman's example, this prevents the assignment of labour values, and much less negative ones, to the individual components of the final demand, which is unchanging in its structure. Instead, the fixed bundle of goods $\mathbf{y}$ is to be interpreted as a *mixed product* whose value results from the objective function of (13.20) or its dual. Due to the discontinuation of the isolated process implementation in the sectors, one only knows how many labour units are embodied in $\mathbf{y}$; the breakdown into the components remains in the dark—one equation is insufficient to determine two unknowns.

However, the condition of competitive equilibrium must be observed: extra profits compared to other divisions are not permitted. In contrast to the Sraffian explanation scheme, compliance with this rule now poses no difficulties. In the context of Steedman's example, this prevents assigning labour values, particularly negative ones, to the individual components of the final demand, which remains unchanged in its structure.

As far as a process's mixed output is marketed separately, the price ratio of the components is known. In practice, however, the number of absolutely superior processes is likely to be relatively small. Typically, joint production methods are hardly ever carried out because of the arising by-products: "… the more conspicuous part consists of the marketable commodity that is the primary object of the process."[64]

The analysis is put in a straitjacket when it is required to produce final demand without a remainder. The substitution of the Sraffian approach by the theory propagated here makes it possible to cast off this shackle. Excess supply is a typical feature of real capitalist market economies.

If Steedman's example is interpreted so that every manufacturer has to choose only *one* process, the postulate of equality of production and sales becomes particularly questionable. *No* profit-maximising industrialist would vote for process 1, even at the risk of a partial lack of sales:

> "Since the battle of competition is fought by the cheapening of commodities", Kurz criticises Steedman's argumentation, "the capitalists that use process II will drive their competitors

[63] Once land and natural resources are regarded as factors of production, rent rates can be understood—in Ricardo's style—as compensation for the differing labour productivity on various fertile soils. More details will follow at the end.

[64] Sraffa, P., Production …, op. cit., p. 63.

that use the inferior process I out of the market. This can lead to an overproduction and hence wastage of one of the commodities that may be compared, for example, to the wastage of energy in connection with fast breeders as it is observable in terms of the heating up of rivers whose water is used for cooling purposes ... Competition weeds out any potential method of production that is inferior and that endangers the survival of the individual capitalist, who uses it."[65]

Provided one does not want to exclude overproduction from the outset, the constraints of (13.20) can be relaxed:

$$\mathbf{a}_0\mathbf{q} \rightarrow \text{Min} \quad \text{s. t.} \quad \mathbf{Bq} \geq \mathbf{Aq} + \mathbf{y}, \quad \mathbf{q} \geq 0 \tag{13.22}$$

The dual of this program yields the labour-commanded prices which are parallel to the values:

$$\mathbf{py} \rightarrow \text{Max} \quad \text{s. t.} \quad \mathbf{pB} \leq \mathbf{pA} + \mathbf{a}_0, \quad \mathbf{p} \geq 0 \tag{13.23}$$

What happens to the prices of commodities produced in excess? If the rule of free goods applies, they fall to zero. But the answer does not always have to be so radical. Perhaps, e.g., the export price limits the decline. It is also conceivable to look for and, if necessary, find alternative uses for goods that are initially unsaleable. Incidentally, the possibility should not be overly dramatised: joint production processes are often characterised by a certain variability concerning the mixing ratio of the heterogeneous output; scope for adjustment then allows for the synchronisation of production and disposition.

No matter how you look at it, under free competition, labour-minimising techniques prevail—they alone maximise profits. Moreover, in the case of constant returns to scale, the industry-specific division of labour forces sectoral profits to be distributed proportionately to the respective labour costs. No other price calculation is compatible with the assumptions made.

There is no trace of negative labour values; it is not the theory of value to be jettisoned, but Sraffa's concept of production prices and, thus, his hypotheses. Kurz's surmise has proven to be correct:

"Many people have maintained that the labour theory of value is dead. However, as is the case with Nietzsche and God, after a while the critics die, whereas the labour theory of value lives on. On the basis of overwhelming historical evidence in support of this fact I presume that Steedman will not be the exception to the rule."[66]

Given the results obtained, it should not be impossible to impress critics of Steedman's stature. In his opinion, the joint production problem represents the *experimentum crucis* for obtaining a watertight argument: "The challenge is, of course, to create an alternative and superior theory, able to take the fact of joint production

---

[65] Kurz, H. D., Sraffa ..., op. cit., p. 68.

[66] Ibid., p. 58.

in its stride."[67] However, the alternative and superior theory must not be created first—certainly not by revitalising the Sraffian model. Instead, the original approach of the ancestors, adequately handled, already accomplishes all that a production price theory ought to achieve.

[67] Steedman, I., Joint Production and Technical Progress, in: Political Economy, vol. 1 (1985) pp. 41–52, p. 52. Steedman references this sentence to neoclassical theory, whose performance is considered modest.

Chapter 14
Law of Value and Economic Theory

In the course of this enquiry, a statement that is as simple as it is momentous has become increasingly prominent: in economies based on the division of labour and integrated by economic exchange, gross sectoral profits, including interest and rents, accrue in equilibrium proportional to wage costs, which thus determine the exchange ratios of commodities. This practice is the *only* calculation method that does justice to profit maximisation under common knowledge conditions of free competition, constant returns to scale and labour as the single original factor. It is not the candidate labour theory of value that has turned out to be unqualified, but the standards adduced to evaluate it. The view that has prevailed for a long time and is repetitively invoked anew, namely that the law of value as a production price theory is shipwrecked, must be revised.[1]

On the one hand, an economic law has to be logically correct, and on the other hand, it must not be factually refuted if it is to be recognised as having a function beyond academic art for art's sake. As noted in the first part of this book, looking at empirical truth checks the degree to which the analysis reflects a relevant section of reality.

As far as the labour theory of value is concerned, we are (so far) in the unusual situation that, although (allegedly) theoretically wrong, it does not (at least) fail in reality. This phenomenon is underlined by the earlier mentioned, relatively recent publications, which prove a broad congruence of the exchange ratios of commodities that are discretionarily (re)producible in any quantity up to the capacity limit by the exertion of labour (cf. p. 127 n.). Hence, contrary to the prevailing view, the labour

[1] "Marx's labor theory of value, one can thus conclude, no longer serves a useful purpose ... Having had a function in the past, it must no longer confuse us today, and it now can be disposed of." Weizsäcker, C. C. v., On Ricardo and Marx, in: Brown, E. C., Solow, R. M. (eds.), Paul Samuelson and Modern Economic Theory, New York et al. 1983, pp. 203–210, p. 208. Similarly, Haberler demanded "as the first task the elimination of the labour theory of value" when incorporating the theory of international trade into the modern economic equilibrium theory. Cf. Haberler, G., Der internationale Handel, Berlin 1933, p. 132. [F. H.]

F. Helmedag, *Production of Commodities by Means of Labour*, Springer Studies in Alternative Economics, https://doi.org/10.1007/978-3-032-01457-3_14

theory of value asserts itself on the market. In this light, it is critical that the law of value demonstrably expresses the logic of the economic exchange of commodities in a specialised, profit-oriented, competitive economy.

The credit that one is inclined to give to the labour theory of value depends on its logical and factual confirmation and the extent to which it promises to provide "better" information than other concepts about economic facts, relationships, and alternative courses of action. This investigation will, therefore, be completed with a few brief theses on the status to be attributed to the law of value regarding the interpretation of reality and its shaping.

14.1 The Entrepreneur, the Capitalist and the Return on Investment

Remarkably, at the beginning of the 1960s, a controversy in the German-language business management literature related to the issue addressed in this study took place. In that debate, it was argued whether the corporate goal of profit maximisation goes hand in hand with maximising profitability, i.e., a rate of return. Formally speaking, it is a matter of weighing up the optimisation of a difference—profit as the margin between revenues and costs—and that of a quotient—the ratio of profit to capital.[2]

As on the macroeconomic level here and the microeconomic plane there, the maximisation of quotients has drawn the short straw: "The profitability maximum can deviate from the profit maximum," Hax rightly stated at the time, "if the decision to be made influences not only the profit but also the respective reference value, i.e., capital employed or turnover."[3] Accordingly, he classifies the objective of maximising profitability "as less important for practical company policy".[4]

The discrepancy between profitability and profit maximisation reflects a more profound difference between the two types of capitalists pointed out earlier. Still, it can only now be brought to the point: the separation between entrepreneurs and investors (cf. p. 87). Identifying these two actors is responsible for the collapse of classical production price theory.

The cliché that, in equilibrium, the return on material costs, alias the profit rate, must be the same in all sectors of the economy corresponds to the mindset of those *capitalists* who invest a *sum of money* and expect a *return* as high as possible on it. From Smith to Sraffa, it has always been assumed that this calculation also characterises the entrepreneur.

---

[2] Helmedag, F., Indikatoren erwerbswirtschaftlichen Erfolgs, in: das wirtschaftsstudium (wisu), vol. 35 (2006), pp. 1294–1299, p. 1318 and p. 1320, offers an appraisal of the various corporate targets mentioned in the literature.

[3] Hax, H., Rentabilitätsmaximierung als unternehmerische Zielsetzung, in: Zeitschrift für handelswissenschaftliche Forschung, vol. 13 (1963), pp. 337–344, p. 338. [F. H.] In this article, other relevant business management publications are mentioned. Cf. ibid., n.

[4] Cf. ibid., p. 344. [F. H.]

In this enquiry, the strange effects that would occur if the *profit maximisers* were to set prices "capitalistically" have been expounded. In order to show that the value calculation rules out these paradoxes, it was assumed that there were credit links between the businesses, which made pre-financing material costs unnecessary. This supposition was intended to counteract the investor mentality and illustrate the entrepreneurial reasoning: the equilibrium of free competition is established *solely* by the distribution of profit as a wage premium. The law of value does justice to the typical behavioural patterns of capitalists acting as entrepreneurs.

The working hypothesis of existing payment terms was not entirely out of thin air; it undoubtedly reflects a property of modern market economies. Schumpeter, e.g., believes that a credit theory of money may be preferable to a monetary theory of credit: "It may be more useful … to look upon capitalist finance as a clearing system that cancels claims and debts and carries forward the differences—so that 'money' payments come in only as a special case without any particularly fundamental importance."[5]

For this reason alone, the labour theory of value is closer to reality than Sraffa's price theory. The cost of materials and "capital" do not correspond quantitatively, nor are the inputs—at least not in full—immediately covered. Nevertheless, assets or creditworthiness must be available as a springboard for entrepreneurial activity. A homeless person will almost certainly have to abandon his plan to start a steelwork.

It is no coincidence that the major firms today are primarily corporations. The combined monetary resources finance those investments, which serve, so to say, as an entry ticket to operate in specific markets with a chance of success, i.e., as a platform for entrepreneurial activity in the Schumpeterian sense. In his eyes, entrepreneurs are …

> "... the economic subjects whose function is the implementation of new combinations and who are the active element in this ... even if, as is increasingly common at present, they are 'dependent' employees of a public limited company—but also private companies—such as directors, members of the board of directors etc. … Ownership of the business—or any 'assets' at all—is not an essential characteristic for us ... Not only farmers, craftsmen, members of the liberal professions—who are *sometimes* included—but also 'factory owners' or 'industrialists' or 'merchants'—who are *always* included—need not necessarily be 'entrepreneurs'."[6]

From the entrepreneur's perspective, the return on capital represents a cost factor that must be accepted to make a profit. Interest on borrowed capital and the imputed interest on equity (which does not necessarily impact cash flow) are *fixed costs*. If the company is to survive, these expenditures must not exceed the contribution margin in the long term. In an equilibrium economy, as shown, this occurs proportionally to

[5] Schumpeter, J. A., History …, op. cit., p. 717. Minsky's 'Wall Street paradigm' for analysing a capitalist economy goes in the same direction. Cf. Minsky, H. P., John Maynard Keynes, London / Basingstoke 1975, http://digamo.free.fr/minsky75.pdf.

[6] Schumpeter, J. A., Theorie der wirtschaftlichen Entwicklung [1912], 6th ed., Berlin 1964, p. 111 f. [F. H.] The passage in the English translation "The Theory of Economic Development ", Cambridge (Mass.) 1949, p. 74 f. deviates appreciably from the German original, https://archive.org/details/theoryofeconomic0000schu/page/n7/mode/2up.

wages, not commensurate to the money advanced. Through this lens, interest can be interpreted as a kind of tax on company profits,[7] even though the tax is not levied by the revenue department but by the owner-financiers.

The classical theory of production prices has a crucial flaw: it conflates the capitalist, who is eager to exploit *money*, with the entrepreneur, who seeks to exploit *labour*. From an analytical point of view, the two must be strictly separated, although, in practice, one person often pursues both aspirations.

The *conditio sine qua non* of operating a production process in the long term requires that the price of a product is at least equal to the entire unit cost. The profit accruing to industries in proportion to the labour expenses must be sufficient to pay interest on borrowed or equity capital.

For this reason, the level of interest rates in financial markets, indirectly controlled by monetary policy,[8] significantly influences the companies' interest payments. A higher yield on financial assets than company funding harms pecuniary engagement in production economics.

In this sense, the monetary realm restrains the real sphere: investment in tangible assets is curbed because there are more profitable dispositions of financial resources. The input and use of the common good, money, is *both a condition and restriction* for producing consumable goods, the entrepreneurial exploitation of labour.

14.2 Process Innovations, Vertical Integration and Rents

Under the given circumstances, the social division of labour presupposes that profit in equilibrium is calculated as a wage cost markup instead of a return on the material costs. This insight makes it possible to address Ronald Coase's question posed in the 1930s: "… why the allocation of resources is not done directly by the price mechanism."[9]—For what reason do companies exist? In response, Coase presents "… a cost of using the price mechanism."[10] In his view, transaction cost savings justify the firm as a permanent economic institution. This topic ranks right at the top of the agenda within the New Institutional Economics.[11]

---

[7] Cf. Schumpeter, J. A., Theorie …, op. cit., p. 317. However, the comparison is somewhat flawed, as interest on credits is payable irrespective of the amount of profit.

[8] Cf. Helmedag, F., Getrennt marschieren, vereint schlagen: Nationale Geldpolitik im Euro-Raum, in: Ohr, R. (ed.), Internationalisierung der Wirtschaftspolitik, Berlin 2009, pp. 39–51 and Helmedag, F., Europäische Geldpolitik in der Krise, in: Chaloupek, G., Kromphardt, J. (eds.), Finanzkrise und Divergenzen in der Wirtschaftsentwicklung als Herausforderungen für die Europäische Währungsunion, Schriften der Keynes-Gesellschaft, vol. 3, Marburg 2009, pp. 108–121.

[9] Coase, R., The Nature of the Firm, in: Economica, vol. 4 (1937), pp. 386–405, p. 393.

[10] Ibid., p. 390.

[11] For an overview, see Richter, R., Sichtweise und Fragestellung der Neuen Institutionenökonomik, in: Zeitschrift für Wirtschafts- und Sozialwissenschaften, vol. 110 (1990), pp. 571–591 and in-depth Erlei, M., Leschke, M., Sauerland, D., Institutionenökonomik, 3rd ed., Stuttgart 2016.

Even if the approach's explanatory power is considered high, it inevitably collapses if vertical integration is based *solely* on market utilisation costs. Oliver E. Williamson, one of the most renowned representatives of new institutional economics, also considers production cost differences when discussing the factors determining the extent of vertical integration.[12] Like many other authors, Williamson, awarded the Central Bank of Sweden Prize for Economic Science (alias Nobel Prize) in 2009, builds on plausibility considerations whose neoclassical provenance is unquestionable. The findings obtained in this enquiry provide a more robust foundation for the argumentation.

Inter-industrial supply chains would make no sense in a world where all companies could use the same linear technique. All final products would be manufactured in a fully integrated manner. Each company can use the labour-cost-minimising technique to manufacture the means of production at the required level without resorting to a supplier.

This theoretically correct outcome contradicts the actual situation: there are evidently advantages to procuring specific inputs from other companies. This study revealed the conditions that cause operational divisions in labour. In a two-stage economy divided into an intermediate and a final product industry, external sourcing is profitable if the market price of the upstream product is lower than the labour costs of fully integrated in-house production in the consumer goods sector. The supplier then uses a more labour-saving technique than the downstream user. This difference also applies *mutatis mutandis* to more deeply structured economies. Therefore, the premise of constant returns to scale across the entire range of alternative outputs must be abandoned.

Moreover, there is another reason why consistently linear returns to scale conflict with the functioning of modern economies. Strictly speaking, there should be no involuntary unemployment under such conditions: All income-seekers could work in their own mini-factory and then sell the fruits of their labour at the prevailing competitive prices: "Involuntary unemployment is logically impossible in a strict constant-returns-to-scale world of one-person firms."[13] If it were in everyone's discretion to use the labour-minimising technique on *any* scale, they could realise their labour power autonomously, independent of the provision of means of production by others. Then, no 'doubly free' (cf. p. 163) wage labourers exist, and the business basis of separating wage labour and capital would be lacking.

The motive for process innovations can be surmised—and recognised—in enhanced labour productivity. The theoretical foundation now joins the empirical evidence: superior know-how, effective incentive systems, lower administrative costs,

[12] Cf. Williamson, O. E., The Economic Institutions of Capitalism, New York / London 1985, p. 103 ff.

[13] Weitzmann, M. L., Increasing Returns and the Foundations of Unemployment Theory: Rejoinder, in: The Economic Journal, vol. 98 (1988), pp. 172–174, p. 173.

economies of scale and scope, etc., which are reflected in increased labour productivity and, thus, in individual profits. On the one hand, value reckoning ensures temporary productivity advantages. On the other hand, this calculation method requires a permanent rise in labour efficiency during the competitive process.

The rivalry between entrepreneurs, spurred on by the hunt for profits, *necessarily* increases labour productivity insofar as the new combinations affect production processes. Precisely, this driving torque to burgeon the productive forces is slowed down when the labour theory of value, *genuinely* a theory of competitive capitalist economies, is merely conceptually superimposed on a centrally planned economy. From this point of view, the economic failure of trying to outstrip capitalism in its home territory without tapping its energy sources was programmed: increases in labour productivity can be decreed only to a limited extent; the economic compulsions of competition generate the most substantial pressure.

Capitalism has always legitimised, channelled and institutionalised the more or less pronounced pursuit of acquisitiveness; this also explains *why* firms exist. The extent of vertical integration is based less on transaction costs and more on the labour productivity of the supplier compared to that of in-house production. As long as there is (still) a difference compared to the socially (otherwise) necessary work, specialised production generates extra profits that have the character of *rent*. Whether and how quickly this differential income is eroded depends on the intensity of competition and access to the more productive technique.

In reality, besides labour, there are other original, i.e., non-capitalistically produced inputs, such as land and raw materials. Once the model analysis has solved the puzzle of which technique is chosen in a scenario where just labour and the produced means of production are used in manufacturing, the rents of natural resources can be ascertained. This requires supply and demand categories: the law of scarcity applies in this area.

In the style of classical rent theory, the next best alternative available to a demander marks the upper limit of prices for natural resources or energy sources. Since nature provides stronger or weaker support for human labour, those to whom its forces belong can claim a rent. The same applies to specific inputs. If, e.g., a particular material reduces labour costs, the maximum price a buyer is willing to pay for it results from the cost savings compared to the process operated without the alternative raw material.

In this place, the general equilibrium theory fulfils its function. The missing integration of the reproduction of production means and the premise of exogenous initial endowments predestine it as a *supplement* to the labour theory of value. The general equilibrium theory is essentially a generalisation of the classical theory of non-reproducible resources.[14]

Rent phenomena occur within companies as well as in connection with natural resources. Individual work performance is also often distinguished by attributes that cannot be produced at will. In this analysis, as is standard practice, we mainly operated with homogeneous labour, even though the performance-related remuneration for

[14] See also Huth, Th., op. cit., p. 238.

working capacity was discussed in the context of the theory of comparative cost advantages (cf. p. 145 ff.). In reality, numerous different work qualities and pay rates can be observed. However, the reduction to simple labour is complicated by the fact that higher productivity or more comprehensive training is by no means always suitable as a weighting scheme. Therefore, such approaches fail to explain, e.g., gender-specific income discrimination.[15] For this reason, arguments were often based on labour costs rather than quantities. Nevertheless, the relatively constant wage *structure* over the longer term is striking. The main findings of the analysis presented are therefore retained, although they were derived under the assumption of a uniform remuneration.

14.3 Wage Rate, Choice of Technique and Employment

Because of the above results, the often-encountered belief that higher wages lead to substituting labour with "capital" and, *hence,* to less employment must be met with scepticism. The profit-maximising technique—irrespective of the wage rate—is the one that maximises labour productivity or, which amounts to the same thing, minimises the necessary work. From a microeconomic perspective, an old system, such as a waterwheel, is replaced by a new technique, e.g., a steam engine, if the total unit costs of the new system are lower than the average variable costs of the old one.

At best, a wage increase *accelerates* technical progress because the variable unit costs of the outdated method rise more substantially than the full average costs of the more progressive technique. However, process innovations will gain the upper hand sooner or later, even without higher pay. In any case, its effective direction can never be reversed: as soon as the time is ripe, the steam engine will replace the waterwheel. In the dispute that has repeatedly flared up since Ricardo as to what effect mechanisation has on employment[16], the following statement can be reasserted: "If the total quantity of the article produced by machinery, be equal to the total quantity of the article previously produced by a handicraft or by manufacture, and now made by machinery, then the total labour expended is diminished."[17]

---

[15] For an overview, see Lorenz, W., Wright, R., Die Messung geschlechtsspezifischer Einkommensdiskriminierung, in: Wirtschaftswissenschaftliches Studium (WiSt), vol. 19 (1990), pp. 573–577.

[16] Cf. Mettelsiefen, B., Technischer Wandel und Beschäftigung, Rekonstruktion der Freisetzungs- und Kompensationsdebatten, Frankfurt a. M. / New York 1981.

[17] Marx, K., Capital, vol. I, op. cit., p. 417. Yet, according to Marx, this "infallibe" law only applies to a limited extent in capitalism: "So far as capital is concerned, productiveness does not increase through a saving in living labour in general, but only through a saving in the *paid* portion of living labour, as compared to labour expended in the past ..." Marx, K., Capital, vol. III, op. cit., p. 262. According to Ricardo, too, the saving of labour constitutes the essence of machinery: "... these mute agents are always the produce of much less labour than that which they displace ..." Ricardo, D., On the Principles ..., op. cit., p. 42. See also Wicksell, K., Lectures ..., op. cit., p. 133 ff.

As mentioned, labour commanded prices of goods, their real prices, have, obeying this logic, fallen drastically in some cases during capitalistic development (cf. p. 105 n.). The dominant measurement of inflation using the purchasing power of money instead of the purchasing power of the wage per minute obscures this empirical fact. Once again, the capitalistic view dominated by monetary categories displaces reasoning based on the performance of employees and entrepreneurs.

The "wage unit" is much more than an alternative method for estimating inflation. In modern economic life, wealth and its increment are rarely judged by the possession of use values but mainly by the ownership of exchange values, i.e. purchasing power. However, the value of money is ultimately based on the quantity of the original form of the commodity—labour—that *might* be acquired for a currency unit.[18] It, therefore, makes sense, as has sometimes been done before, to express prices in terms of remuneration, i.e., to elevate the wage rate to the unit of account. But today, money is no longer a product of labour.[19] Liquidity merely embodies a *potential* mobilisation of labour power; its *realised* utilisation governs employment. This consideration can be incorporated into macroeconomic analysis.

In the first approach, wages in a closed economy without a public sector may be entirely spent. Hence, the accumulation of monetary wealth is fed exclusively by profits. Thus, the "luxury production", i.e., demand financed from unearned incomes, determines total employment.[20] That is to say, the labour input in the "basic sector", where goods bought out of wages are manufactured, will just level off in such a way that with a given surplus product of a person employed there, the wage goods for the needed staff in the luxury industry can be provided.[21]

In this light, an employment policy that relies mainly on incentives to increase capacity loses its attraction. The decisive factor for employing labour is final demand, especially its autonomous components: sooner or later, consumption must "confirm" expansions in the production potential. The investment follows a growing turnover of consumer goods; a stimulation deprived of this prerequisite fizzles out.

A successful fight against involuntary unemployment on the part of the state—if it is wanted indeed—should first and foremost strengthen the discretionary components of expenses, i.e., outlays independent from current income or government

[18] The idea of interpreting wealth as the ability to *command* the labour of others stems from Adam Smith. Cf. Rosner, P., Arbeit und Reichtum, Ein Beitrag zur Geschichte ökonomischer Theorie, Frankfurt a. M. / New York 1982, p. 87 ff.

[19] Cf. Helmedag, F., Geld: Einführung und Überblick, in: Knapps Enzyklopädisches Lexikon des Geld-, Bank- und Börsenwesens, article no. 4390, Frankfurt am Main 2007 and Helmedag, F., Monetäre (Un-)Ordnung …, op. cit., p. 187 ff.

[20] The affinity between this approach and the physiocratic class model is apparent. There, the work of the sterile class creates income without generating surplus product. Cf. Quesnay, F., Tableau économique [1759], ed. by Kuczynski, M., Berlin 1965. Sombart emphasises the importance of the consumption of the classes freed from compulsion to work, namely, the lifestyle of the nobility, for the capitalistic development. Cf. Sombart, W., Liebe, Luxus und Kapitalismus, Über die Entstehung der modernen Welt aus dem Geist der Verschwendung [1922], Berlin (no date given).

[21] Helmedag, F., Principles …, op. cit. and Helmedag, F., Principles of capitalistic commodity production: a rejoinder, in: European Journal of Economics and Economic Policies: Intervention, vol. 10 (2013), pp. 282–285.

spending for public goods. If necessary, these measures should be supplemented by fewer individual working hours to compensate for the employment-reducing effect of process innovations.[22] In fact, theoretical and empirical evidence suggests that blanket subsidy of tangible assets promotes the opposite of the proclaimed intention: rationalisation reduces socially necessary labour. Irrespective of this, investment subsidies may be beneficial for *other* reasons.

As much as the labour theory of value has proven itself as a theory of the conditions of the social division of labour and as much as it is suitable as the foundation of a theory of employment, it is inappropriate for specific purposes traditionally associated with it. The concept of economic exchange means that "exploitation" is of little avail as an *analytical* concept in economic theory. Economic exchange is voluntary; as a result, at least one participant is better off, and no one is put in a worse position. This property also applies to the dependent employee who offers his labour power on the market. The "initial endowment", which includes being embedded in a more or less tightly woven social network, influences the lower limit of the willingness to exchange.

Another question is how the welfare gain is apportioned between the partners.[23] According to the insights gained here, however, the prospects of the working people increasing their real wages for a *given* level of labour productivity are bleak. Unions and management bargain on nominal payment.[24] If the wage markup is passed on in full—and there is at first no reason why not—then rising money wages will entail higher absolute prices. In the end, labour commanded prices remain unchanged. However, the purchasing power of money is reduced by the increase in the price level. From this angle, there is a conflict of interest between asset-owning capitalists on the one hand and employees and employers on the other.

The possible applications of the labour theory of value outlined in this section still have some blank spots. A scrutiny of the macroeconomic coherences, in particular the role of the state, requires a separate investigation. The previously mentioned compatibility of the labour value theory with the "true" Keynesian doctrine (see p. 95 n.) plays a key role in the concept. It is worth recalling this link to the *magnum opus* of the great economist:

> "I sympathise, therefore, with the ... doctrine that everything is *produced* by *labour*, aided by what used to be called art and is now called technique, by natural resources which are free or cost a rent according to their scarcity or abundance, and by the results of past labour, embodied in assets, which also command a price according to their scarcity or abundance."[25]

---

[22] Cf. Helmedag, F., Nur mehr Stundenlohn …, op. cit.

[23] A proposal for 'fair' pay propounds Helmedag, F., Fair Wages and Social Welfare, in: Journal of Income Distribution, vol. 19 (2010), pp. 3–8.

[24] The basic sector, which supplies the wage basket of the entire economy, determines the real unit labour costs. See Helmedag, F., Möglichkeiten und Grenzen einer beschäftigungsfördernden Lohnpolitik, in: Kromphardt, J. (ed.), Zur aktuellen Finanz-, Wirtschafts- und Schuldenkrise, Schriften der Keynes-Gesellschaft, vol. 6, Marburg 2013, pp. 145–158. The mentioned determination of remuneration in the wage goods industry will subsequently be explained explicitly.

[25] Keynes, J. M., The General Theory …, op. cit., p. 213. Cf. also Helmedag, F., Die Beschäftigungstheorie …, op. cit.

After all, the presented exposition indicates that an economic theory entitled to rely on the law of value faces further perspectives. On this basis, practically relevant recommendations for action ensue, which we will now turn to.

Chapter 15
Law of Value and Economic Policy

This concluding chapter shows that, based on the findings of this enquiry, the possibilities for shaping economic conditions already hinted at in various places above can be elaborated. As the previous analysis has brought to light, the social division of labour in an ideal–typical world of free competition requires the rate of profit to match the rate of surplus value. According to the insights gained in the last section of the chapter on Karl Marx, an optimal profit rate of 100% balances the diverging interests in the entrepreneurial camp (cf. p. 193 ff.). The assumptions made there are now generalised to present a simple as possible "canonical" two-sector model, which nevertheless seems eminently suitable as the foundation of a functional, i.e., target-oriented economic policy.[1] Based on the labour theory of value, welfare-enhancing guidelines for promoting national income by fiscal and monetary policies emerge.

[1] In the first edition of Samuelson's internationally best-selling textbook mentioned at the outset (see p. 8), the author also presents a division of the economy into two parts that many others have adopted: a society operating on the 'production possibility curve' or 'transformation frontier' must choose between opposing production levels of butter or cannons. Cf. Samuelson, P. A., Economics, New York 1948, p. 18 f. In later editions, the butter depicted on the abscissa in the added diagram represents not merely a wage good but consumption itself. The ordinate measures the number of cannons, which, due to the absence of rivalry in and the impossibility of exclusion from consumption, do not reflect surplus items but symbolise public goods. The movement along the curve, concave to the origin, implies, in addition to full utilisation of production potential, increasing opportunity costs with the continued substitution of one good for another. The correspondence to the rising supply curves prevalent in microeconomics is evident. Still, in the case of goods that can be produced without limit, these represent the exception rather than the rule (cf. p. 87 n.). Incidentally, in Germany, "… by the fall of 1936 at the latest, the formula 'guns instead of butter' was firmly established everywhere." Schanetzky, T., Kanonen statt Butter, Wirtschaft und Konsum im Dritten Reich, München 2015, p. 9. [F. H.]

F. Helmedag, *Production of Commodities by Means of Labour*, Springer Studies in Alternative Economics, https://doi.org/10.1007/978-3-032-01457-3_15

15.1 Optimal Unit Labour Costs

At the start, total demand is dichotomised in the already familiar manner. A (primary) wage goods or basic industry differs from a (secondary) luxury or surplus product industry. It is not the physical form of the commodities manufactured or the types of services that are important, but rather the source of financing the particular expenditure: all goods bought with the employee's remuneration constitute the wage goods sector, and the rest of total sales establish the surplus production.[2]

According to the labour theory of value, the gross profit in the basic industry (P_B) results from the wage bill of this branch (W_B) times the profit rate (r). This profit equates to the difference between the revenues—i.e., domestic consumption out of disposable wages—and the costs of vertically integrated production, corresponding to the virtual industry's personnel expenditures. W_X symbolises remuneration in the luxury industry, c and t represent the domestic propensity to consume and the tax rate, respectively.[3] The profit in the basic department thus amounts to:

$$P_B = rW_B = c(1 - t)(W_B + W_X) - W_B \text{ with } 0 < c, t < 1 \qquad (15.1)$$

In macroeconomic equilibrium, the expansionary and contractionary forces balance each other. On the one hand, autonomous expenditure (A), which consists of non-income-dependent investments by private individuals and exports, expands the circular flow. On the other hand, the state's primary balance must be considered. A deficit (surplus) exists if the public expenditure (G) accruing to the secondary sector is greater (less) than the tax revenue (T).[4] The positive or negative amount corresponds to the current change in government debt (ΔD) less debt service, the product of a uniform interest rate, including repayment rate (i) on the debt level (D). According to the assumption, the total expansionary effect of autonomous demand (GA) is positive:

$$GA \equiv A + G - T = A + \Delta D - iD > 0 \qquad (15.2)$$

Taxes on gross national income ($t(1 + r)(W_B + W_X)$), as well as imports and the accumulation of financial assets from disposable wages and profits, narrow the circular flow. At the same time, autonomous expenditure causes it to swell. In equilibrium, the following condition holds:

$$GA = (1 - t)(1 - c)(1 + r)(W_B + W_X) \qquad (15.3)$$

---

[2] In his discussion of Arthur Cecil Pigou's unemployment theory, Keynes also approved of such a parting, but did not differentiate it from the demand side: "... we can identify Professor Pigou's wage-goods with my consumption-goods, and his 'other goods' with my investment-goods ..." Keynes, J. M., The General Theory ..., op. cit., p. 273.

[3] Insofar as contributions on wages and salaries finance the social security systems, they circulate in the basic industry. Taxes are payed to the surplus division.

[4] For now, public expenditures that flow abroad are not included. This aspect will be addressed later.

Rearranging Eq. (15.3) yields the aggregate wage bill:

$$W_B + W_X = \frac{GA}{(1-t)(1-c)(1+r)} \tag{15.4}$$

Inserting expression (15.4) in Eq. (15.1) gives:

$$\begin{aligned} P_B = rW_B &= c(1-t)\frac{GA}{(1-t)(1-c)(1+r)} - W_B = \\ &= c\frac{GA}{(1-c)(1+r)} - W_B \end{aligned} \tag{15.5}$$

From Eq. (15.5), the wage bill in the basic sector is ascertained:

$$W_B = \frac{c}{1-c}\left(\frac{GA}{(1+r)^2}\right) \tag{15.6}$$

Therefore, the profit in the wage goods segment comes to:

$$P_B = rW_B = \frac{cGA}{(1-c)}\left(\frac{r}{(1+r)^2}\right) \tag{15.7}$$

Incomes in the basic sector rise with the domestic propensity to consume c and the autonomous total expenditure GA. However, the tax rate t does not affect earnings in this sector. A look at Eq. (15.1) reveals that a varying tax rate must cause an exact compensating change in the wage bill of the luxury branch to ensure constant wages in the primary sector. The necessary condition for profit maximisation in this industry reads:

$$\frac{\partial P_B}{\partial r} = \frac{cGA}{(1-c)}\left(\frac{(1+r)^2 - 2r(1+r)}{(1+r)^4}\right) \overset{!}{=} 0 \Rightarrow 1 + r - 2r \overset{!}{=} 0 \tag{15.8}$$

As optimum profit rate ($r*$)[5] results:

$$r* = 1 \mathrel{\hat{=}} 100\% \tag{15.9}$$

An earlier result (cf. p. 197 f.) is thus confirmed within a broader framework: the wage goods sector strives for one hundred per cent exploitation of remuneration. If this is successful, half of the output serves to maintain the social labour force, and the other half comprises surplus production.[6]

---

[5] Because of the negative second partial derivative of the basic profit with respect to the profit rate, the sufficient condition for a maximum is fulfilled.

[6] Adam Smith's surplus rate of 100% (cf. p. 115 n.) thus finds a theoretical underpinning. As a reminder: ".. when … the labour of one family can provide food for two, the labour of half

What can be said about the secondary sector? Inserting the wage bill of the basic industry (15.6) into the equation for total compensation (15.4) finally provides the payment in the luxury sector:

$$W_X = \frac{1 + r - c(1 - t)}{(1 + r)^2} \left(\frac{GA}{(1 - c)(1 - t)} \right) \tag{15.10}$$

The profit in the secondary division (P_X) amounts to:

$$P_X = rW_X = \frac{r(1 + r - c(1 - t))}{(1 + r)^2} \left(\frac{GA}{(1 - c)(1 - t)} \right) \tag{15.11}$$

As already noted, in contrast to the basic division, the wage bill and, by the same token, the profits of the luxury sector rise with an increasing tax ratio t since the fraction's numerator on the right-hand side of the expression (15.11) grows, whereas the denominator shrinks. An increasing domestic propensity to consume c and a higher autonomous total expenditure GA have the same effect. The profit in the secondary sector is also positively correlated to the profit rate:

$$\frac{\partial P_X}{\partial r} = \frac{1 - c + r + cr(1 - t) + ct}{(1 + r)^3} \left(\frac{GA}{(1 - c)(1 - t)} \right) > 0 \tag{15.12}$$

Yet, in equilibrium, the luxury sector has adopted the profit rate $r^* = 1$ set by the basic industry. This branch determines the real unit labour costs (h) as the ratio between the nominal wage bill and the total income in the sector:

$$h = \frac{W_B}{(1 + r)W_B} = \frac{1}{1 + r} \tag{15.13}$$

The profit rate $r^* = 100\%$ fixed in the wage-goods sector generates real unit labour costs of $h^* = 50\%$. This industry thus also decides on the production price level in equilibrium (π^*) as the reciprocal of the real unit labour costs or the value of labour power (cf. p. 195):

$$\pi* = 1 + r* = \frac{1}{h*} = 2 \triangleq 200\% \tag{15.14}$$

The ratios mentioned are by no means a figment of the imagination but can be confronted with the national accounts, which provide the statistical material for the practical test of the theoretical derivations.

---

the society becomes sufficient to provide food for the whole. The other half, therefore ... can be employed in providing other things ..." Smith, A., An Inquiry ..., op. cit., p. 180.

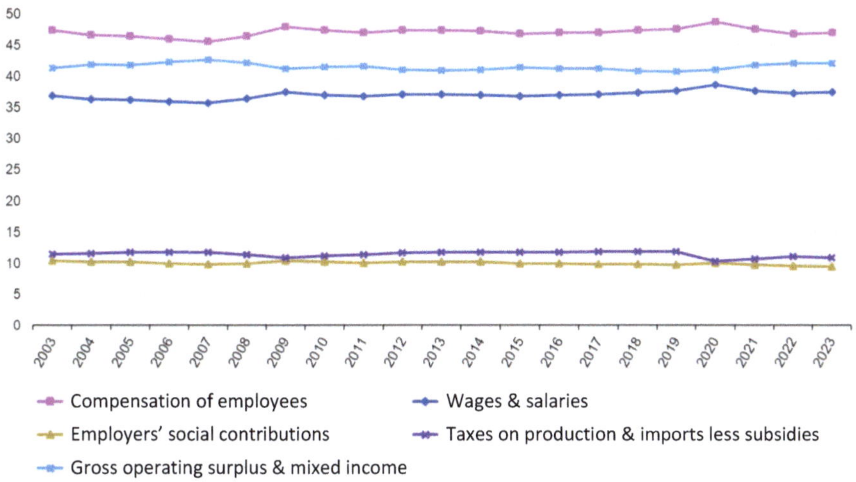

Fig. 15.1 Evolution of the main income components (% of GDP, 2003–2023). *Source* Eurostat (as of 14 March 2025, data for 2024 is also available, cf. https://ec. europa.eu/eurostat/statistics-explained/index.php?title = Annual natio-nal_accounts_-_evolution_of_the_income_components_of_GDP&oldid = 627,188)

15.2 Empirical Evidence

Even a cursory glance at reality shows that the determination of the 100 per cent profit rate in the wage-goods sector as the key variable of the system is entirely compatible with the facts. Let us first look at the conditions in the European Union, as shown in Fig. 15.1.

As the upper purple graph displays, the average compensation of employees, including social security contributions, has amounted to nearly half of the gross domestic product over 20 years in the 27 member states. Despite all the economic ups and downs, macroeconomic real unit labour costs have remained almost stable at this level across countries for decades. This finding strikingly confirms the "law of the constant wage share" named after Arthur L. Bowley.[7] Alongside other variables, the stability of the functional distribution is one of Kaldor's famous "stylized facts".[8]

[7] Cf. Bowley, A. L., Wages and Income in the United Kingdom since 1860, Cambridge 1937. Cf. on the naming Krämer, H., Bowley's Law: The Diffusion of an Empirical Supposition into Economic Theory, in: Papers in Political Economy, vol. 61 (2011), pp. 19–49, p. 24 ff.

[8] Kaldor identifies six empirical regularities, none of which "... can be plausibly 'explained' by the theoretical constructions of neo-classical theory." However, the stable rate of profit he refers to contradicts the decline over time assumed by classical economists: "... Adam Smith, Ricardo, Marx, alongside Böhm-Bawerk and Wicksell, predicted a steady fall in the rate of profit with economic progress." Kaldor, N., Capital Accumulation and Economic Growth, in: Lutz, F. A., Hague, D. C. (eds.), The Theory of Capital, London 1961, pp. 177–222, p. 179.

Notwithstanding minor national differences, two "developed" countries with established institutions, such as collective bargaining and competition authorities, confirm the derived real unit labour costs of almost 50%. Figure 15.2 shows Germany's wage share trend, representing a relatively industrialised economy. From 2010 to 2022, workers receive virtually 50% of gross domestic product directly or indirectly.

Figure 15.3 approves the same outcome for the United Kingdom, which is more strongly characterised by services. For over twenty years, even in this economy with a large tertiary sector, the gross domestic product was divided almost equally between labour and capital.

All empirical evidence is consistent with the theoretically derived macroeconomic real unit labour costs, corresponding to the optimal profit rate $r^* = 1$. Apparently, Keynes' dictum still applies:

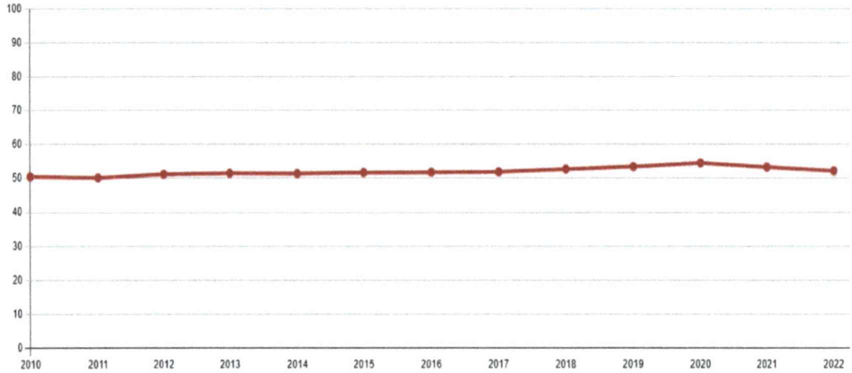

Fig. 15.2 Percentage share of employee's compensation in gross domestic product in Germany 2010–2022. *Source* Destatis, https://sdg-indikatoren.de/en/10-4-1/

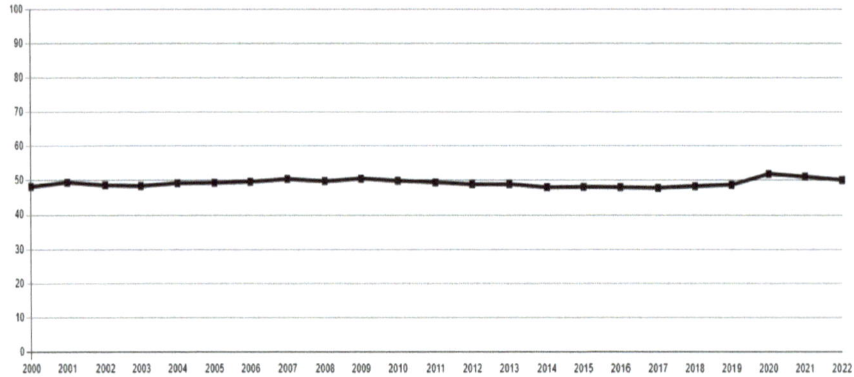

Fig. 15.3 Percentage share of employee's compensation in gross domestic product in the United Kingdom 2000–2022. *Source* Office for National Statistics (ONS), https://sdgdata.gov.uk/10-4-1/

> "... the stability of the proportion of the national dividend accruing to labour, irrespective apparently of the level of output as a whole and the phase of the trade cycle.. is one of the most surprising, yet best-established facts in the whole range of economic statistics..."[9]

However, Keynes admits, "... the result remains a bit of a miracle."[10] The miracle, however, is not due to the influence of supernatural forces but is the result of the decision-making behaviour of those entrepreneurs who strive to maximise profits from selling their products to workers. The optimal markup on the labour costs of vertically integrated production in the basic industry is 100%. Therefore, gross profits—the total income from entrepreneurial activity and assets—have been effectively almost precisely half of the gross domestic in developed economies for decades.[11]

The nearly constant functional distribution of gross domestic product across space and time provides a sound data basis that does not need to shy away from comparison with the empirical support for other theorems in economics—quite the contrary. Moreover, since the 50% splitting of gross domestic product is based on decision theory, an economic law exists that fulfils the conditions for tenets formulated at the outset. As mentioned several times, such "statements of principle" or "model predictions" must always be logically true and not fail in reality (cf. p. 33).[12] Thus armed, we turn finally to the design of practice.

15.3 Recommended Actions

The previous outcomes are qualified to serve as a foundation for a welfare-promoting fiscal policy. From Eq. (15.4) (cf. p. 308), the gross domestic product (*GDP*) is calculated after reversing the definition (15.2):

$$GDP = (1 + r)(W_B + W_X) = \frac{GA}{(1 - t)(1 - c)} = \frac{A + \Delta D - iD}{(1 - t)(1 - c)} \tag{15.15}$$

---

[9] Keynes, J. M., Relative Movements of Real Wages and Output [1939], reprinted in: The Collected Writings of John Maynard Keynes, vol. VII, Cambridge 1978, pp. 394–412, p. 408 f.

[10] Ibid., p. 409.

[11] In the literature, efforts have been made to refute the "law of the constant wage share" by including the (more or less fictitious) earned income of the (fluctuating number of) self-employed or rather their contributory family members in the numerator of the fraction. The denominator is usually the net national income, which leads to systematically higher percentage values than the 50% derived here. Cf., e.g., Krämer, H., Bowley's Law ..., op. cit., p. 21 ff.

[12] Differences in the actual profit rate to 100% can be explained by assuming specific tax rates (t_W) and (t_P) for wages or income from entrepreneurial activity and wealth, as well as distinct propensities to domestic consume (c_W) and (c_P). However, even then the profit rate is exactly r^* = 100% if $(1 - t_W)(1 - c_W) = (1 - t_P)(1 - c_P)$ applies. See Helmedag, F., Marx and Keynes: from exploitation to employment, in: European Journal of Economics and Economic Policies: Intervention, vol. 16 (2019), pp. 260–271, p. 265. In reality, the above condition is often valid with practically no deviations; it is also weaker than the condition of identical tax rates and propensities to domestic consume, i.e., $t_W = t_P$ and $c_W = c_P$.

As the right-hand side of the equation chain (15.15) shows, the profit rate r or the real unit labour costs h do not influence the size of the gross domestic product. Still, the exploitation factor rules the functional distribution: for the optimal profit rate r^* = 100, the total product goes, as per (15.9) (cf. p. 308), half and half to wage earners and capitalists. According to expression 15.14, the profit factor $(1 + r^*)$ corresponds to the production price level in equilibrium. Therefore, the total wage bill $(W_B + W_X)$ corresponds to the *real* gross domestic product, which thus accounts for half of the nominal gross domestic product.[13]

Furthermore, Eq. (15.15) shows that, contrary to popular belief, taxation does not diminish total disposable income $((1—t)GDP)$:

$$(1 - t)GDP = (1 - t)\frac{A + \Delta D - iD}{(1 - t)(1 - c)} = \frac{A + \Delta D - iD}{(1 - c)} \tag{15.16}$$

On the other hand, it has been hinted at a positive correlation between the tax rate and gross domestic product because wages and profits in the luxury department are rising. At the same time, incomes are constant in the wage goods sector. A look behind the scenes reveals precisely how the process works: tax revenues first accrue to the secondary sector, where they increase the wage bill (W_X) to such an extent that the profit in the basic industry (P_B) remains the same despite the higher tax rate (cf. the profit calculation (15.1), p. 307). The increasing tax burden in the surplus industry is compensated for by the growing demand from the tax authorities: the state takes with its right hand what it gives back with its left. The total disposable income of private individuals, therefore, stays the same.

However, not all taxpayers derive a corresponding benefit from public goods or transfers in return. For those who miss out, these are expenses *à fonds perdu*. Increasing regular government revenue is also accompanied by a structural change, as the larger administered part of economic activity grows relative to the production of goods for private use.

How many working hours are included in the national wage bill? To answer this question, we resort to the analysis in Sect. 2.4.3. There, it was demonstrated in Fig. 10.3 (cf. p. 197) that the 50%-level of the value of labour power—the multiplication of the labour value of a basic commodity v_B with the real wage w—distributes the total profit equally among the sectors and corresponds to the profit rate $r^* = 1$. In modern terminology, this share conforms to the real unit labour costs according to Eq. (15.14) (cf. p. 310):

$$h* = \frac{1}{1 + r*} = \frac{1}{\pi *} = \frac{1}{2} = wv_B \Rightarrow w = \frac{1}{2v_B} \tag{15.17}$$

[13] There are substantial reasons for approximating the real interest rate with the rate of change of the nominal domestic or national product. Cf. Helmedag, F., Grundsätzliches zur Geldkapitalverwertung in der Realwirtschaft und im Finanzsektor, in: Gesmann-Nuissl, D., Korte, S. (eds.), Kapital in Recht und Wirtschaft, Festschrift der Fakultät für Wirtschaftswissenschaften der TU Chemnitz für Ludwig Gramlich zum 70. Geburtstag, Göttingen 2021, pp. 127–140.

On the other hand, the real wage per hour (w) results from the division of the nominal wage (w_{nom}) by the production price level at $r^* = 1$ (π^*):

$$w = \frac{w_{nom}}{\pi *} = \frac{1}{2v_B} \quad (15.18)$$

Thus, Eq. (15.18) gives the remuneration expressed in a monetary unit:

$$w_{nom} = \frac{\pi *}{2v_B} = \frac{1 + r*}{2v_B} = \frac{1}{v_B} \quad (15.19)$$

The nominal wage w_{nom} is twice as high as the real wage w and, under the prevailing circumstances, matches the productivity in the basic industry, which is reciprocal to the labour value of the wage good. Consequently, wages are linked to the development of labour productivity in the primary sector through the pursuit of profit maximisation, a nexus corresponding to the actual process. The subsistence wage assumed by the classics and Ferdinand Lassalle's "iron law of wages" is based on outdated perceptions about the working of competition in the labour market.

Against the background of the empirically supported and theoretically derived stability of the functional distribution—with the result of an ideally paid productivity-adapted remuneration in the basic industry—the appropriate trade union strategy in the presence of unemployment requires a battle on two fronts. On the one hand, in addition to pay issues, the collective bargaining dispute is, in particular, about reducing "normal" full-time working hours.[14] On the other hand, the representatives of employees' interests in the political arena should urge the government to give more (of course, environmentally friendly) support for growth. What measures are advisable for this?

The macroeconomic volume of work (N) is ascertained by dividing the total wage bill of a particular period by the money wage per hour w_{nom}:

$$N = \frac{W_B + W_X}{w_{nom}} = v_B(W_B + W_X) = \frac{v_B GDP}{2} \quad (15.20)$$

In addition to the level of gross domestic product, employment depends solely on productivity in the basic sector; process innovations in the primary industry systematically lead to a declining labour value of the standardised wage good v_B. In contrast, the state of the art in the surplus department does not affect the volume of work for a given revenue in this sector; a reduction in the price of the luxury good in the course of process innovations is compensated *ceteris paribus* by increased sales. The total differential of the employment formula (15.20) is:

$$dN = \frac{\partial N}{\partial v_B} dv_B + \frac{\partial N}{\partial GDP} dGDP = \frac{GDP}{2} dv_B + \frac{v_B}{2} dGDP \quad (15.21)$$

[14] Cf. Helmedag, F., Von der Sozialen Marktwirtschaft ..., op. cit., p. 130 ff.

This results in a rate of change in the volume of work:

$$\frac{dN}{N} = \frac{dv_B}{v_B} + \frac{dGDP}{GDP} \tag{15.22}$$

Apparently, the "scissors theory" applies: changes in employment stem from different developments in labour productivity and gross domestic product.[15] Suppose the labour value of the basic good v_B decreases by a certain percentage (which may vary over time). Then, the gross domestic product must rise at a corresponding rate to maintain employment. The assertion of the so-called golden wage rule that hourly wages growing with productivity are job-neutral turns out to be false: although both the real and nominal wage reflect changes in productivity, neither of these wage rates appears in the employment formula (15.20) and the expression for the gross domestic product (15.15) (cf. p. 313).[16]

Even more substantial growth, which more than compensates for the labour-saving technical progress in the basic industry, is required to reduce existing unemployment. Fiscal policy can turn two screws to achieve this: the tax rate t and new debt ΔD.

Equation (15.15) immediately reveals the multiplier (m) of a change in autonomous total expenditure due to additional borrowing by the public sector:

$$m = \frac{1}{(1-t)(1-c)} > 1 \tag{15.23}$$

The multiplier increases with the behaviourally determined domestic propensity to consume c and the politically adjustable (average) tax rate t. However, the calculation of the wage bill in the basic and luxury sectors has shown that taxes do not influence wages and profits in the primary industry (see Eqs. (15.6) and (15.7), p. 308). In contrast, earnings in the secondary sector are positively correlated with the tax rate (see Eqs. (15.10) and (15.11), p. 309). The overall effect of a variation in taxation on the gross domestic product stems solely from the altered remuneration in the surplus sector, which, however, as demonstrated in Eq. (15.16) (cf. p. 314), does not affect the disposable total income.

Against this backdrop, the question arises as to whether and under what conditions self-financing of treasury borrowing is possible.[17] To this end, the additional tax revenue (ΔT) must exceed the increase in government debt (ΔD) as a result of the multiplier process:

---

[15] Cf. Helmedag, F., Industrial Revolution(s)..., op. cit., p. 213 ff.

[16] Cf. Helmedag, F., Nur mehr Stundenlohn ..., op. cit. and Helmedag, F., Kein Streit um des Kaisers Bart, Eine Replik zum schwelenden Diskurs über die Goldene Lohnregel, individuelle Arbeitszeit und Beschäftigtenzahl, in: Makroskop, (22.12.2017), https://www.tu-chemnitz.de/wirtschaft/vwl2/downloads/paper/helmedag/Kein_Streit_um_des_Kaisers_Bart_makroskop.pdf.

[17] Cf. on the following Helmedag, F., Schulden dulden, Kredit genießen: Zur Beständigkeit und Bedeutung von Budgetdefiziten, in: Wirtschaftsdienst, vol. 95 (2015), pp. 347–349 and Helmedag, F., Steuern und Budgetdefizite als Determinanten des Sozialprodukts, in: Wirtschaftsdienst, vol. 102 (2022), p. 229–235, p. 233 ff.

$$\Delta T = tm\Delta D > \Delta D \tag{15.24}$$

The condition is satisfied for:

$$tm = \frac{t}{(1-t)(1-c)} > 1 \tag{15.25}$$

From the expression (15.25) one gets:

$$t \geq t_{SF} = \frac{1-c}{2-c} \text{ with } 0 < t_{SF} < \frac{1}{2} \tag{15.26}$$

The tax authorities can finance loans with an average tax rate t_{SF} of less than 50%. However, it is questionable whether new debt should be covered entirely by regular revenues, not only because of the cumulative resistance of those taxpayers who, in return, benefit little or not at all from additional public services (see p. 45).

In principle, an appropriate debt policy improves the welfare of citizens because their total disposable income grows and, indeed, does not shrink individually. Regardless of the direction, tax rate variations do not affect the aggregate of disposable wages and profits. Still, tax increases can, as already mentioned, make individual taxpayers worse off if they receive too little as a "perceived return" in the form of additional public goods, higher transfers or jobs created.

With this in mind, it makes sense for the tax authorities to strive for a sustainable permanent primary deficit, particularly in the case of unemployment, i.e., the population receives more monetary benefits from the state than the taxpayers pay to it.[18] It must be ensured that at least the payments made by the state to foreign countries—for example, as a member of international organisations or in the context of development and military aid—are balanced out to direct, at any rate, the regular state revenue into the domestic circular flow. Definition (15.2) (cf. p. 307) must, therefore, be made stricter, with government expenditure (G) now also including payments to foreign countries:

$$G - T = \Delta D - iD = \frac{\Delta D}{D} D - iD = (g_D - i)D > 0 \tag{15.27}$$

When the growth rate of public debt (g_D) exceeds the interest rate on the stock of old loans, a primary deficit arises, stimulating the circular flow. With this hint, an additional instrument of the state moves into focus. The task of an "accommodative" monetary policy ought, if necessary, to provide the treasury with financing conditions for the provision of public goods and to combat crises, which allow inequality (15.27) to be fulfilled. Furthermore, if the initiated multiplier processes generate a corresponding percentage increase in the domestic product, the debt ratio will remain constant or may even fall.

---

[18] Cf. Helmedag, F., Staatsschulden als permanente Einnahmequelle, in: Wirtschaftsdienst, vol. 90 (2010), pp. 611–615.

Without going into further details of economic policy management here, the central finding of this treatise is that the law of value has stood up to all challenges. The labour theory of value provides a solid foundation for microeconomic and macroeconomic analysis and points to welfare-enhancing design options. Lastly, this insight constitutes the scientific progress that the discipline has urgently needed for quite some time.

References

Albert, H., Ökonomische Ideologie und politische Theorie, Göttingen 1954

Albin, P. S., Reswitching: An Empirical Observation, a Theoretical Note, and an Environmental Conjecture, in: Kyklos, vol. 28 (1975), pp. 149–153

Andreae, W., Geld und Geldschöpfung, Stuttgart/Wien 1953

Arni, J.-L., Die Kontroverse um die Realitätsnähe der Annahmen in der Oekonomie, Grüsch 1989

Aristotle, Politics I, Indianapolis/Cambridge 1998

Backhouse, R., A History of Modern Economic Analysis, Oxford/New York 1985

Bairoch, P., Die Landwirtschaft und die Industrielle Revolution 1700–1914, in: Cipolla, C. M., Borchardt, K. (eds.), Europäische Wirtschaftsgeschichte, vol. III, Die Industrielle Revolution, Stuttgart/New York 1985, pp. 297–332

Baisch, H., Wert, Preis und Allokation, Eine Verallgemeinerung des Marxschen Reproduktionsmodells, Meisenheim am Glan 1976

Balassa, B. A., Karl Marx and John Stuart Mill, in: Weltwirtschaftliches Archiv, vol. 83 (1959), pp. 147–165

Baldone, S., Fixed Capital in Sraffa's Theoretical Scheme, in: Pasinetti, L. (ed.), Essays on the Theory of Joint Production, London/Basingstoke 1980, pp. 88–137

Bartels, H. G., Was ist dran am Rationalprinzip?, in: das wirtschaftsstudium (wisu), vol. 17 (1988), pp. 135–137

Baudin, L., Der sozialistische Staat der Inka, Reinbek bei Hamburg 1956

Baumol, W. J., The Transformation of Values: What Marx "Really" Meant (An Interpretation), in: Journal of Economic Literature, vol. 12 (1974), pp. 51–62

Belshaw, C. S., Traditional Exchange and Modern Markets, Englewood Cliffs 1965

Bharadwaj, K., Classical Political Economy and Rise to Dominance of Supply and Demand Theories, 2nd ed., London 1986

Bharadwaj, K.,On the Maximum Numbers of Switches Between Two Production Systems, in: Schweizerische Zeitschrift für Volkswirtschaft und Statistik, vol. 106 (1970), pp. 409–429

Blaich, F., Die Epoche des Merkantilismus, Wiesbaden 1973

Blaug, M., Economic Theory in Retrospect, 5th ed., Cambridge 1997

Bliss, C. J., Capital Theory and the Distribution of Income, Amsterdam/Oxford/New York 1975

Böhm-Bawerk, E. v., Karl Marx and the Close of his System [1896], ed. by Sweezy, P. M., New York 1949, https://mises.org/library/book/karl-marx-and-close-his-system

Boos, M., Die Wissenschaftstheorie Carl Mengers, Graz/Wien 1986

Bowley, A. L., Wages and Income in the United Kingdom since 1860, Cambridge 1937

F. Helmedag, *Production of Commodities by Means of Labour*, Springer Studies in Alternative Economics, https://doi.org/10.1007/978-3-032-01457-3

Bortis, H., Structure and Change Within the Circular Theory of Production, in: Baranzini, M., Scazzieri, R. (eds.), The Economic Theory of Structure and Change, Cambridge et al. 1990, pp. 64–92

Bortkiewicz, L. v., Wertrechnung und Preisrechnung im Marxschen System, in: Archiv für Sozialwissenschaft und Sozialpolitik, vol. 23 [1906], pp. 1–50 (First Article); vol. 24 [1907], pp. 10–51 (Second Article) and pp. 445–488 (Third Article). An English translation of the second and third articles is available under the title "Value and Price in the Marxian System", http://gesd.free.fr/bortk7b.pdf

Bortkiewicz, L. v., Zur Berichtigung der grundlegenden theoretischen Konstruktion von Marx im dritten Band des „Kapital", in: Jahrbücher für Nationalökonomie und Statistik, vol. 34 (1907), pp. 319–335, English translation: "On the Correction of Marx's Fundamental Theoretical Construction in the Third Volume of *Capital*", in: Böhm-Bawerk, E. v., Karl Marx and the Close of his System [1896], ed. by Sweezy, P. M., New York 1949, pp.199–221, https://mises.org/library/book/karl-marx-and-close-his-system

Brems, H., An Attempt at a Rigorous Restatement of Ricardo's Long-Run Equilibrium, in: The Canadian Journal of Economics and Political Science, vol. 26 (1960), pp. 74–86

Bronstein, I. N., Semendjajew, K. A., Taschenbuch der Mathematik, 20th ed., Leipzig 1981

Brunner, O., Die alteuropäische „Ökonomik", in: Zeitschrift für Nationalökonomie, vol. 13 (1950), pp. 114–139

Brunner, O., Hausväterliteratur, in: Handwörterbuch der Staatswissenschaften, vol. V, Stuttgart/Tübingen/Göttingen 1956, p. 92 f.

Buchanan, J. M., The Limits of Liberty, Between Anarchy and Leviathan, Chicago 1975

Burmeister, E., Synthesizing the Neo-Austrian and Alternative Approaches to Capital Theory: A Survey, in: Journal of Economic Literature, vol. 12 (1974), pp. 413–456

Burmeister, E., On the Social Significance of the Reswitching Controversy, in: Revue d'Economie Politique, vol. 87 (1977), pp. 335–350

Burmeister, E., Capital Theory and Dynamics, Cambridge 1980

Burmeister, E., Kuga, K., The Factor-Price Frontier, Duality and Joint Production, in: Review of Economic Studies, vol. 37 (1970), pp. 11–19

Caravale, G. A. (ed.), The Legacy of Ricardo, Oxford 1985

Casarosa, C., A New Formulation of the Ricardian System, in: Oxford Economic Papers, vol. 30 (1978), pp. 38–63

Cassel, G., Theoretische Sozialökonomie [1918], 5th ed., Leipzig 1932

Champernowne, D. G., A Note on J. v. Neumann's Article on "A Model of Economic Equilibrium", in: The Review of Economic Studies, vol. 13 (1945), pp. 10–18, https://competitionandappropriation.econ.ucla.edu/wp-content/uploads/sites/95/2017/08/ChampernowneOnVonNeumann.pdf

Cipolla, C. M., Borchardt, K. (eds.), Europäische Wirtschaftsgeschichte, vol. III, Die Industrielle Revolution, Stuttgart/New York 1985

Coase, R., The Nature of the Firm, in: Economica, vol. 4 (1937), pp. 386–405

Coase, R., The Problem of Social Cost, in: The Journal of Law and Economics, vol. 3 (1960), pp. 1–44

Coddington, A., Keynesian Economics: The Search for First Principles, in: Journal of Economic Literature, vol. 14 (1976), pp. 1258–1273

Codere, H., Verteilungsmodus und Gesellschaftsform, in: Schlicht, E. (ed.), Einführung in die Verteilungstheorie, Reinbek bei Hamburg 1976, pp. 73–84

Cogoy, M., Wertstruktur und Preisstruktur, Die Bedeutung der linearen Produktionstheorie für die Kritik der politischen Ökonomie, Frankfurt a. M. 1977

Cogoy, M., Traditionelle und neue Arbeitswerttheorie, in: Gesellschaft, Beiträge zur Marxschen Theorie 13, Frankfurt a. M. 1979, pp. 115–139

Cogoy, M., Produktion, Markt und technischer Fortschritt, in: Analyse und Kritik, vol. 4 (1982), pp. 39–70

Cournot, A., Recherches sur les principes mathématiques de la théorie des richesses, Paris 1838

Dantzig, G. B., linear programming, in: The New Palgrave, vol. III, London/New York/Tokyo 1987, pp. 203–206
De Quincey, Th., Dialogues of Three Templars on Political Economy [1824], in: De Quincey's Collected Writings, vol. IX, London 1897, pp. 37–112
De Vivo, G., Robert Torrens and Ricardo's 'corn-ratio' theory of profits, in: The Cambridge Journal of Economics, vol. 9 (1985), pp. 89–92
De Vivo, G., Ricardo, David, in: The New Palgrave, vol. IV, London/New York/Tokyo 1987, pp. 183–198
Dmitriev, V. K., Economic Essays on Value, Competition and Utility [1904], ed. by Nuti, M. D., Cambridge 1974
Dobb, M., Value and Distribution Theories since Adam Smith, Cambridge 1973
Dorfman, R., Samuelson, P. A., Solow, R. M., Linear Programming and Economic Analysis, New York/Toronto/London 1958
Duden, Deutsches Universalwörterbuch, 5th ed., Mannheim/Leipzig/Wien/Zürich 2003
Duménil, G., Lévy, D., The dynamics of competition: a restoration of the classical analysis, in: Cambridge Journal of Economics, vol. 11 (1987), pp. 133–164
Eatwell, J., own rates of interest, in: The New Palgrave, vol. III, London/New York/Tokyo 1987, p. 786 f.
Eberle, F., Methodisches zur Wert-Preis-Transformation, in: Gesellschaft, Beiträge zur Marxschen Theorie 13, Frankfurt a. M. 1979, pp. 140–173
Eckstein, G., Die vierfache Wurzel des Satzes vom unzureichenden Grunde der Grenznutzentheorie. Eine Robinsonade, in: Die neue Zeit, vol. 20 (1902), pp. 810–816, https://www.marxists.org/deutsch/archiv/eckstein/1902/xx/wurzel.html
Einzig, P., Primitive Money, Its Ethnological, Historical and Economic Aspects, 2nd ed., Oxford et al. 1966
Engels, F., Review of Volume One of *Capital* for the *Düsseldorfer Zeitung*, in: Marx & Engels, Collected Works, vol. 20, pp. 216–218, Electric Book, https://aaap.be/Pdf/Nachschlagewerke/MECW20.pdf
Engels, F., Preface to Marx, K., Capital, vol. II., The Process of Circulation of Capital [1885], ed. by Engels, F., Moscow 1956, pp. 1–20, https://archive.org/details/capitalvol2/page/376/mode/2up
Erlei, M., Leschke, M., Sauerland, D., Institutionenökonomik, 3rd ed., Stuttgart 2016
Eucken, W., Die Grundlagen der Nationalökonomie, 5th ed., Godesberg 1947
Faber, M., Manstetten, R., Der Ursprung der Volkswirtschaftslehre als Bestimmung und Begrenzung ihrer Erkenntnisperspektive, in: Schweizerische Zeitschrift für Volkswirtschaft und Statistik, vol. 124 (1988), pp. 97–121
Farmer, K., Kubin, I., Marktpreise und natürliche Preise: Adam Smiths Konzeption und ihre gegenwärtige Bedeutung aus neoricardianischer und neowalrasianischer Sicht, in: Kurz, H. D. (ed.), Adam Smith (1723–1790), Marburg 1990, pp. 203–236
Fees-Dörr, E., Die Redundanz der Mehrwerttheorie, Ein Beitrag zur Kontroverse zwischen Marxisten und Neoricardianern, Marburg 1989
Flaschel, P., Sraffa's Standard Commodity: No Fulfillment of Ricardo's Dream of an "Invariable Measure of Value", in: Journal of Theoretical and Institutional Economics, vol. 142 (1986), pp. 588–602
Flaschel, P., The Standard Commodity as a Tool of Economic Analysis: A Reply to Schefold, in: Journal of Theoretical and Institutional Economics, vol. 142 (1986), pp. 623–625
Forstmann, A., Geld und Kredit, I. Teil, Göttingen 1952
Fourastie, J., Schneider, J., Warum die Preise sinken, Produktivität und Kaufkraft seit dem Mittelalter, Frankfurt a. M. 1989
Frey, B. S., Stroebe, W., Ist das Modell des Homo Oeconomicus „unpsychologisch"?, in: Zeitschrift für die gesamte Staatswissenschaft, vol. 136 (1980), pp. 82–97
Frey, B. S., Stroebe, W., Der Homo Oeconomicus ist entwicklungsfähig, in: Zeitschrift für die ge samte Staatswissenschaft, vol. 137 (1981), pp. 293–294

Fröhlich, N., Die Aktualität der Arbeitswertlehre, Theoretische und empirische Aspekte, Marburg 2009
Fujimori, Y., Modern Analysis of Value Theory, Berlin/Heidelberg/New York 1982
Fujimoto, T., Duality and the Uniqueness of Growth Equilibrium, in: International Economic Review, vol. 16 (1975), pp. 781–791
Furness, W. H., The Island of Stone Money: Uap of the Carolines, Philadelphia/London 1910
Galbraith, J. K., Economics, Peace, and Laughter, ed. by Williams, A. D., Boston 1971
Gale, D., The Theory of Linear Economic Models, New York/Toronto/London 1960
Galtung, J., Violence, Peace and Peace Research, in: Journal of Peace Research, vol. 6 (1969), pp. 167–191
Garegnani, P., Heterogeneous Capital, the Production Function and the Theory of Distribution, in: The Review of Economic Studies, vol. 37 (1970), pp. 407–436
Garegnani, P., On a Change in the Notion of Equilibrium in Recent Work on Value and Distribution, in: Brown, M., Sato, K., Zarembka, P. (eds.), Essays in Modern Capital Theory, Amsterdam/New York/Oxford 1976, pp. 25–45
Garegnani, P., Value and Distribution in the Classical Economists and Marx, in: Oxford Economic Papers, vol. 36 (1984), pp. 291–325
Garegnani, P., surplus approach to value and distribution, in: The New Palgrave, vol. IV, London/New York/Tokyo 1987, pp. 560–574
Georgescu-Roegen, N., The Aggregate Linear Production Function and Its Applications to von Neumann's Economic Model, in: Koopmans, T. C. (ed.), Activity Analysis of Production and Allocation, New York/London /Sydney 1951, pp. 98–115
Gerloff, W., Die Entstehung des Geldes und die Anfänge des Geldwesens, 3rd ed., Frankfurt a. M. 1947
Gerloff, W., Geld und Gesellschaft, Frankfurt a. M. 1952
Gossen, H., Entwicklung der Gesetze des menschlichen Verkehrs und der daraus fließenden Regeln für menschliches Handeln, Braunschweig 1854
Graf, H. G., „Muster-Voraussagen" und „Erklärungen des Prinzips" bei F. A. von Hayek, Tübingen 1978
Grözinger, G., Konkurrenzpreise und Arbeitswerte, Ein Input-Output-Modell für die Bundesrepublik Deutschland 1960–1984, Marburg 1989
Haberler, G., Der internationale Handel, Berlin 1933
Hagemann, H., Kurz, H. D., Schäfer, W. (eds.), Die Neue Makroökonomik, Marktungleichgewicht, Rationierung und Beschäftigung, Frankfurt a. M./New York 1981
Hahn, F., Revival of Political Economy: The Wrong Issues and the Wrong Argument, in: Economic Record, vol. 51 (1975), pp. 360-364
Hahn, F., The neo-Ricardians, in: Cambridge Journal of Economics, vol. 6 (1982), pp. 353–374
Harcourt, G. C., The Rate of Profits in Equilibrium Growth Models: A Review Article, in: Journal of Political Economy, vol. 81 (1973), pp. 1261–1277
Hart, K., barter, in: The New Palgrave, vol. I, London/New York/Tokyo 1987, pp. 196–198
Hartfield, G., Wissenschaftliche und soziale Rationalität, Stuttgart 1968
Hax, H., Rentabilitätsmaximierung als unternehmerische Zielsetzung, in: Zeitschrift für handelswissenschaftliche Forschung, vol. 13 (1963), pp. 337–344
Hayek, F. A. v., The Pure Theory of Capital (1941), 2nd ed., London 1950 [88].
Hayek, F. A. v., Three Elucidations of the Ricardo Effect [1969], reprinted in: Hayek, F. A. v., New Studies in Philosophy, Politics, Economics and the History of Ideas, Chicago 1978, pp. 165–178
Hayek, F. A. v., The Fatal Conceit, The Errors of Socialism, in: Bartley III, W. W. (ed.), The Collected Works of F. A. Hayek, vol. I, London 1988
Heckscher, E. F., Der Merkantilismus, vol. II, Jena 1932
Heilbronner, R. L., Die Entstehung von Märkten und Produktionsfaktoren, in: Schlicht, E. (ed.), Einführung in die Verteilungstheorie, Reinbek bei Hamburg 1976, pp. 85–99
Helmedag, F., Die Technikwahl bei linearer Einzelproduktion oder Die dritte Krise der Profitrate, Frankfurt a. M./Bern/New York 1986

Helmedag, F., Technikwahl, Profitstruktur und Arbeitsproduktivität, in: Jahrbücher für Nationalökonomie und Statistik, vol. 203 (1987), pp. 408–421[1]
Helmedag, F., (Review of) Postkeynesianismus, Ökonomische Theorie in der Tradition von Keynes, Kalecki und Sraffa, Marburg 1987, in: Zeitschrift für Wirtschafts- und Sozialwissenschaften, vol. 109 (1989), S. 148-154
Helmedag, F., Profit-Raten mittels Profitraten, in: Jahrbücher für Nationalökonomie und Statistik, vol. 207 (1990), pp. 67–83
Helmedag, F., Lohn- und Profitkurven, in: Wirtschaftswissenschaftliches Studium (WiSt), vol. 20 (1991), pp. 408–412
Helmedag, F., Zur Berechtigung der grundlegenden theoretischen Konstruktion von Marx im ersten Band des "Kapital", in: Jahrbücher für Nationalökonomie und Statistik, vol. 212 (1993), pp. 442–450
Helmedag, F., Ohne Fleiß kein Preis: Nochmals zur Erklärungskraft der Arbeitswertlehre, in: Jahrbücher für Nationalökonomie und Statistik, vol. 214 (1995), pp. 470–482
Helmedag, F., Geldfunktionen, in: das wirtschaftsstudium (wisu), vol. 24 (1995), pp. 711–717 and p. 729
Helmedag, F., Die arbeitsteilungskompatible Kalkulation von Produktionspreisen, in: das wirtschaftsstudium (wisu), vol. 26 (1997), pp. 573–582
Helmedag, F., Kapitale Böcke in der Kapitaltheorie: Der Test zum Protest, in: Jahrbücher für Nationalökonomie und Statistik, vol. 216 (1997), pp. 744–760
Helmedag, F., Die verteilungsinvariante Messung von Produktionspreisen, in: das wirtschaftsstudium (wisu), vol. 27 (1998), pp. 266–274, 284 f.
Helmedag, F., Ohne Werte und kreislaufschwach: Zum Status der Allgemeinen Gleichgewichtstheorie, in: Helmedag, F., Reuter, N. (eds.), Der Wohlstand der Personen, Festschrift zum 60. Geburtstag von Karl Georg Zinn, Marburg 1999, pp. 43–68
Helmedag, F., Zur Vermarktung des Rechts: Anmerkungen zum Coase-Theorem, in: Wolf, D., Reiner, S., Eicker-Wolf, K. (eds.), Auf der Suche nach dem Kompaß, Politische Ökonomie als Bahnsteigkarte fürs 21. Jahrhundert, Köln 1999, pp. 53–71
Helmedag, F., Möglichkeiten und Grenzen eines Beschäftigungspakts, in: Jahrbücher für Nationalökonomie und Statistik, vol. 205 (2005), pp. 151–162
Helmedag, F., Indikatoren erwerbswirtschaftlichen Erfolgs, in: das wirtschaftsstudium (wisu), vol. 35 (2006), pp. 1294–1299, pp. 1318, 1320
Helmedag, F., Geld: Einführung und Überblick, in: Knapps Enzyklopädisches Lexikon des Geld-, Bank- und Börsenwesens, Article No. 4390, Frankfurt a. M. 2007
Helmedag, F., Getrennt marschieren, vereint schlagen: Nationale Geldpolitik im Euro-Raum, in: Ohr, R. (ed.), Internationalisierung der Wirtschaftspolitik, Berlin 2009, pp. 39–51
Helmedag, F., Europäische Geldpolitik in der Krise, in: Chaloupek, G., Kromphardt, J. (eds.), Finanzkrise und Divergenzen in der Wirtschaftsentwicklung als Herausforderungen für die Europäische Währungsunion, Schriften der Keynes-Gesellschaft, vol. 3, Marburg 2009, pp. 108–121
Helmedag, F., Staatsschulden als permanente Einnahmequelle, in: Wirtschaftsdienst, vol. 90 (2010), pp. 611–615
Helmedag, F., Fair Wages and Social Welfare, in: Journal of Income Distribution, vol. 19 (2010), pp. 3–8
Helmedag, F., Fortschrittsillusionen in der Ökonomik: Die Neue Handelstheorie, in: Enke, H., Wagner, A. (eds.), Zur Zukunft des Wettbewerbs, In memoriam Karl Brandt (1923–2010) und Alfred E. Ott (1929–1994), Marburg 2012, pp. 39–55
Helmedag, F., Principles of capitalistic commodity production, in: European Journal of Economics and Economic Policies: Intervention, vol. 9 (2012), pp. 23–34

[1] Almost all of the author's papers are available as PDF files via the following link: https://www.tu-chemnitz.de/wirtschaft/vwl2/personal/helmedagold.php.

Helmedag, F., Kapitalistischer Kommunismus, in: Ökonomie und Gesellschaft, Jahrbuch 24: Entfremdung – Ausbeutung – Revolte, Karl Marx neu verhandelt, Mar-burg 2012, pp. 111–126

Helmedag, F., Die Beschäftigungstheorie von Keynes: Dichtung und Wahrheit, in: Busch, U. (ed.), Jenseits der Orthodoxie, Ansätze für einen Paradigmenwechsel in der Wirtschaftstheorie, Berliner Debatte Initial, vol. 23 (2012), pp. 63–76

Helmedag, F., Individuelle und kollektive Gewinnmaximierung auf homogenen Märkten, in: Oberender, P. (ed.), Private und öffentliche Kartellrechtsdurchsetzung, Berlin 2012, pp. 9–38

Helmedag, F., Möglichkeiten und Grenzen einer beschäftigungsfördernden Lohnpolitik, in: Kromphardt, J. (ed.), Zur aktuellen Finanz-, Wirtschafts- und Schuldenkrise, Schriften der Keynes-Gesellschaft, vol. 6, Marburg 2013, pp. 145–158

Helmedag, F., Principles of capitalistic commodity production: a rejoinder, in: European Journal of Economics and Economic Policies: Intervention, vol. 10 (2013), pp. 282–285

Helmedag, F., Monetäre (Un-)Ordnung als Ursache von Finanzmarktkrisen, in: Busch, U., Krause, G. (eds.), Theorieentwicklung im Kontext der Krise, Abhandlungen der Leibniz-Sozietät der Wissenschaften, vol. 35, Berlin 2013, pp. 179–193

Helmedag, F., Mit der Schuldenbremse zum Systemcrash, in: Perspektiven der Wirtschaftswissenschaften, ed. by Gesmann-Nuissl, D., Hartz, R., Dittrich, M., Wies-baden 2014, pp. 123–137

Helmedag, F., Über Kapital im „Kapital“: Einige elementare Überlegungen, in: Wirtschaft und Gesellschaft, vol. 40 (2014), pp. 405–415

Helmedag, F., Schulden dulden, Kredit genießen: Zur Beständigkeit und Bedeutung von Budgetdefiziten, in: Wirtschaftsdienst, vol. 95 (2015), pp. 347–349

Helmedag, F., Nur mehr Stundenlohn oder auch weniger Arbeitsstunden? Gewerkschaftsforderungen im Widerstreit, in: Hagemann, H., Kromphardt, J. (eds.), Keynes, Schumpeter und die Zukunft der entwickelten kapitalistischen Volkswirtschaften, Schriften der Keynes-Gesellschaft, vol. 9, Marburg 2016, pp. 273–287

Helmedag, F., Komparative Kostenvorteile, fairer Handel und Beschäftigung, in: Hagemann, H., Kromphardt, J. (eds.), Die Krise der europäischen Integration aus keynesianischer Sicht, Schriften der Keynes-Gesellschaft, vol. 10, Marburg 2017, pp. 167–183

Helmedag, F., Kein Streit um des Kaisers Bart, Eine Replik zum schwelenden Diskurs über die Goldene Lohnregel, individuelle Arbeitszeit und Beschäftigtenzahl, in: Makroskop, 22.12.2017

Helmedag, F., Barter, efficiency, and money prices: dissecting Nash's bargaining example, in: International Journal of Pluralism and Economics Education, vol. 9 (2018), pp. 292–299

Helmedag, F., Marx and Keynes: from exploitation to employment, in: European Journal of Economics and Economic Policies: Intervention, vol. 16 (2019), pp. 260–271

Helmedag, F., Industrielle Revolution(en): Transformationsprozesse des Kapitalismus, in: Wirtschaftsdienst, vol. 99 (2019), pp. 210–215

Helmedag, F., Von der Sozialen Marktwirtschaft zum globalen Kapitalismus, Fehlentwicklungen und tarifpolitische Konsequenzen, in: Mythos Soziale Markt-wirtschaft, Arbeit, Soziales und Kapital, Festschrift für Heinz-J. Bontrup, ed. by Marquardt, R.-M., Pulte, P., Köln 2019, pp. 123–140

Helmedag, F., Wissenschaftstheoretische Aspekte der Ökonomik: Überblick und Positionsbestimmung, in: Chemnitz Economic Papers, No. 037, May 2020

Helmedag, F., Böhm-Bawers Kapitaltheorie im Licht des Waldproblems: Eine Neubewertung, in: Trautwein, H.-M. (ed.), Studien zur Entwicklung der ökonomischen Theorie XXXV, Berlin 2020, pp. 41–55

Helmedag, F., Profitrate, Zinssatz, Gewinn: Irrungen und Wirrungen, in: Caspari, V. (ed.), Einkommens- und Vermögensverteilung in historischer Sicht, Studien zur Entwicklung der ökonomischen Theorie XXXVII, Berlin 2020, pp. 65–84

Helmedag, F., Grundsätzliches zur Geldkapitalverwertung in der Realwirtschaft und im Finanzsektor, in: Kapital in Recht und Wirtschaft, Festschrift der Fakultät für Wirtschaftswissenschaften der TU Chemnitz für Ludwig Gramlich zum 70. Geburtstag, ed. by Gemann-Nuissl, D., Korte, S., Göttingen 2021, pp. 127–140

Helmedag, F., Ultra posse nemo obligatur: Grenzen und Möglichkeiten der Geldpolitik, in: Berliner Debatte Initial, 33 Jg. (2022), pp. 48–65

Helmedag, F., Zum Theorem komparativer Kostenvorteile: Praktische Probleme der reinen Lehre, in: Wirtschaft und Gesellschaft, 48. Jg. (2022), pp. 267–279

Helmedag, F., Steuern und Budgetdefizite als Determinanten des Sozialsprodukts, in: Wirtschaftsdienst, vol. 102 (2022), pp. 229–235

Helmedag, F., Weber, U., Die Zig-Zag-Darstellung des Tableau Économique, in: das wirtschaftsstudium (wisu), vol. 31 (2002), pp. 115–121, 135 f.

Helmedag, F., Weber, U.,Die Kreislaufdarstellung des Tableau Économique, in: das wirtschaftsstudium (wisu), vol. 31 (2002), pp. 1128–1133, 1155

Helmedag, F., Weber, U.,Entwicklungslinien und Schwankungen des Sozialprodukts im Überblick, in: Wirtschaftswissenschaftliches Studium (WiSt), vol. 33 (2004), pp. 80–87

Helmreich, Th., Das Geldwesen in den deutschen Schutzgebieten, 1. Teil, Neu-Guinea, Fürth 1912

Helmreich, Th., Das Geldwesen in den deutschen Schutzgebieten, 2. Teil, Mikronesien, Fürth 1913

Hennings, K. H., The Exchange Paradigm and the Theory of Production and Distribution, in: Baranzini, M., Scazzieri, R. (eds.), Foundations of Economics, Oxford 1986, pp. 221–243

Herskovits, M. J., Economic Anthropology – A Study in Comparative Economics, New York 1952

Hicks, J. R., Value and Capital [1939], 2nd ed., Oxford 1946

Hicks, J. R., Linear Theory [1960], reprinted in: Surveys of Economic Theory, vol. III (Resource Allocation), London et al. 1966, pp. 75–113

Hildenbrand, K., Hildenbrand, W., Lineare ökonomische Modelle, Berlin/Hei delberg/New York 1975

Hödl, E., Müller, G. (eds.), Die Neoklassik und ihre Kritik, Frankfurt a. M. 1986

Hofmann, W. (ed.), Wert- und Preislehre, 2nd edition, Berlin 1971

Homans, G. C., Social Behavior as Exchange, in: Homans, G. C., Sentiments and Activities, London 1962, pp. 278–293

Homans, G. C., Elementarformen sozialen Handelns, Köln/Opladen 1968

Huth, Th., Kapital und Gleichgewicht, Zur Kontroverse zwischen neoklassischer und neoricardianischer Theorie des allgemeinen Gleichgewichts, Marburg 1989

Hüther, M., Die „Sattelzeitgerechte" Entstehung der Nationalökonomie. Ein Beitrag zur Dogmengeschichte, in: Jahrbücher für Nationalökonomie und Statistik, vol. 205 (1988), pp. 150–162

Hymer, S., Robinson Crusoe and the secret of primitive accumulation, in: Monthly Review, vol. 23 (1971), pp. 11–36 [40]

Immler, H., Natur in der ökonomischen Theorie, Teil 1: Vorklassik – Klassik – Marx, Opladen 1985

Issing, O., Einführung in die Geldtheorie, 7th ed., München 1990

Jevons, W. St., The Theory of Political Economy, 2nd ed., London 1879

Kaldor, N., Alternative Theories of Distribution, in: The Review of Economic Studies, vol. 23 (1955/56), pp. 83–100

Kaldor, N., Capital Accumulation and Economic Growth, in: Lutz, F. A., Hague, D. C. (eds.), The Theory of Capital, London 1961, pp. 177–222

Kant, I., Prolegomena to Any Future Metaphysics [1873], ed. by Carus, P., 3rd ed., Chicago 1912, Project Gutenberg 2016, https://dn721802.ca.archive.org/0/items/rmcg0004/Kant-Prolegomena-a1.pdf

Kaufmann, F.-X., Wirtschaftssoziologie I: Allgemeine, in: Handwörterbuch der Wirtschaftswissenschaft, vol. IX, Stuttgart/Tübingen/Göttingen 1982, pp. 239-267

Kesting, H., Produktionspreise, Wachstum und Verteilung, Marburg 1990

Keynes, J. M., The General Theory of Employment, Interest and Money [1936], in: The Collected Writings of John Maynard Keynes, vol. VII, Cambridge 1978

Keynes, J. M., Relative Movements of Real Wages and Output [1939], reprinted in: The Collected Writings of John Maynard Keynes, vol. VII, Cambridge 1978, pp. 394–412

King, J. E., David Ricardo, Houndmills/New York 2013

Kirsch, G., Zwang, Tausch und Geschenk, in: das wirtschaftsstudium (wisu), vol. 17 (1988), pp. 221–226

Knapp, G. F., Staatliche Theorie des Geldes (1905), 3rd ed., München/Leipzig 1921

Knie, A., Das Konservative des technischen Fortschritts – Zur Bedeutung von Konstruktionstraditionen, Forschungs- und Konstruktionsstilen in der Technikgenese, Wissenschaftszentrum Berlin 1989 (FS II 89–101)

Knight, F. H., The Ricardian Theory of Production and Distribution, in: The Canadian Journal of Economics and Political Science, vol. 1 (1935), pp. 171–196

Koch, H., Das Wirtschaftlichkeitsprinzip als betriebswirtschaftliche Maxime, in: Zeitschrift für handelswirtschaftliche Forschung, vol. 3 (1951), pp. 160–170

Köhler, M., Akkulturation in der Südsee, Die Kolonialgeschichte der Karolinen-Inseln im pazifischen Ozean und der Wandel ihrer sozialen Organisation, Frankfurt a. M./Bern 1982

Koopmans, J. G., Zum Problem des „neutralen" Geldes, in: Hayek, F. A. v. (ed.), Beiträge zur Geldtheorie, Wien 1933, pp. 211–359

Koopmans, T. C. (ed.), Activity Analysis of Production and Allocation, New York/London/Sydney 1951

Kratena, K., Produktion, Umweltpolitik und Einkommensverteilung, in: Jahrbücher für Nationalökonomie und Statistik, vol. 207 (1990), pp. 417–431

Krause, U., Geld und abstrakte Arbeit, Über die analytischen Grundlagen der Politischen Ökonomie, Frankfurt a. M./New York 1979

Krause, U., Elemente einer multisektoralen Analyse der Arbeit, in: Gesellschaft, Beiträge zur Marxschen Theorie 13, Frankfurt a. M. 1979, pp. 15–53

Krelle, W., Die kapitaltheoretische Kontroverse, Test zum Reswitching-Problem, in: Zeitschrift für Wirtschafts- und Sozialwissenschaften, vol. 98 (1978), pp. 1–31

Krämer, H., Bowley's Law: The Diffusion of an Empirical Supposition into Economic Theory, in: Papers in Political Economy, vol. 61 (2011), pp. 19–49

Kromphardt, J., Wirtschaftswissenschaft II: Methoden und Theoriebildung in der Volkswirtschaftslehre, in: Handwörterbuch der Wirtschaftswissenschaft, vol. IX, Stuttgart/Tübingen/Göttingen 1982, pp. 904–936

Kromphardt, J., Analysen und Leitbilder des Kapitalismus von Adam Smith bis zum Finanzmarktkapitalismus, Marburg 2015

Kubin, J., Neoricardianische Gleichgewichtsmodelle und Änderungen in der Zusammensetzung der Nachfrage, Marburg 1989

Kurz, H. D., Adam Smiths Komponententheorie der relativen Preise und ihre Kritik, in: Zeitschrift für die gesamte Staatswissenschaft, vol. 132 (1976), pp. 691–709

Kurz, H. D., Zur neoricardianischen Theorie des Allgemeinen Gleichgewichts der Pro-duktion und Zirkulation, Berlin 1977

Kurz, H. D., Rent Theory in a Multisectoral Model, in: Oxford Economic Papers, vol. 36 (1978), pp. 16–37

Kurz, H. D., Sraffa After Marx, in: Australian Economic Papers, vol. 18 (1979), pp. 52–70

Kurz, H. D., Zum Problem der Rente in der Wert- und Produktionspreistheorie, in: Gesellschaft, Beiträge zur Marxschen Theorie 13, Frankfurt a. M. 1979, pp. 174–200

Kurz, H. D., Classical and Early Neoclassical Economists on Joint Production, in: Metroeconomica, vol. 36 (1986), pp. 1–37

Kurz, H. D., Capital theory: debates, in: The New Palgrave, vol. I, London/New York/Tokyo 1987, pp. 357–363

Kurz, H. D., Adam Smith, die Regel der freien Güter und die >vent for surplus<-Begründung des Außenhandels, in: Kurz, H. D. (ed.), Adam Smith (1723–1790), Marburg 1990, pp. 237–260

Kurz, H. D., Ökonomisches Denken in drei Jahrhunderten, Band 1: Bedeutende Ökonomen, Band 2: Ausgewählte Felder und Themen, Marburg 2021

Kurz, H. D., Kalmbach, P., Elemente einer neuklassischen Analyse von Verteilung, Wert, Akkumulation und Beschäftigung: eine Skizze, in: Wirtschafts-theorie und Wirtschaftspolitik, Gedenkschrift für Erich Preiser, ed. by Mückl, W. J., Ott, A. E., Passau 1981, pp. 283–311

Lancaster, K., Mathematical Economics, New York 1968
Landshut, S., Historische Analyse des Begriffs des „Ökonomischen" (1969), in: Wehler, H.-U. (ed.), Geschichte und Ökonomie, Köln 1973, pp. 40–53
Laum, B., Heiliges Geld, Eine historische Untersuchung über den sakralen Ursprung des Geldes, Tübingen 1924
Leach, J. W., Leach, E. (eds.), The Kula, New Perspectives on Massim Exchange, Cambridge et al. 1983
Lehner, H., Meran, G., Möller, J., De Statu Corruptionis, Entscheidungslogische Einübungen in die Höhere Amoralität, Konstanz/Litzelstetten 1980
Leontief, W., The Structure of the American Economy 1919–1935, An Empirical Application of Equilibrium Analysis, 2nd ed., New York 1960
Levhari, D., A Nonsubstitution Theorem and Switching of Techniques, in: The Quarterly Journal of Economics, vol. 79 (1965), pp. 98–105
Levhari, D., Samuelson, P. A., The Nonswitching Theorem is False, in: The Quarterly Journal of Economics, vol. 80 (1966), pp. 518–519
Lilley, S., Technischer Fortschritt und die Industrielle Revolution 1700–1914, in: Cipolla, C. M., Borchardt, K. (eds.), Europäische Wirtschaftsgeschichte, vol. III, Die Industrielle Revolution, Stuttgart/New York 1985, pp. 119–163
Lorenz, W., Wright, R., Die Messung geschlechtsspezifischer Einkommensdiskriminierung, in: Wirtschaftswissenschaftliches Studium (WiSt), vol. 19 (1990), pp. 573–577
Luhmann, N., Knappheit, Geld und die bürgerliche Gesellschaft, in: Jahrbuch für Sozialwissenschaft, vol. 23 (1972), pp. 186–210
Mainwaring, L., Value and Distribution in Capitalist Economies, Cambridge 1984
Malinowski, B., Argonauts of the Western Pacific, An Account of Native Enterprise and Adventure in the Archipelagoes of Melanesian New Guinea, London 1922
Malthus, Th. R., Letter to Ricardo, August 5, 1814, in: The Works and Correspondence of David Ricardo, ed. by Sraffa, P., vol. VI, Cambridge 1973, pp. 115–118
Malthus, Th. R., Letter to Ricardo, March 10, 1815, in: The Works and Correspondence of David Ricardo, ed. by Sraffa, P., vol. VI, Cambridge 1973, pp. 181–183
Malthus, Th. R., Letter to Ricardo, March 12, 1815, in: The Works and Correspondence of David Ricardo, ed. by Sraffa, P., vol. VI, Cambridge 1973, p. 185 f.
Malthus, Th. R., Letter to Horner, March 14, 1815, in: The Works and Correspondence of David Ricardo, ed. by Sraffa, P., vol. VI, Cambridge 1973, pp. 186–188
Manara, C. F., Sraffa's Model for the Joint Production of Commodities by Means of Commodities [1968], in: Pasinetti, L. (ed.), Essays on the Theory of Joint Production, London/Basingstoke 1980, pp. 1–15
Maneschi, A., Ricardo's Four Magic Numbers, in: The Elgar Companion to David Ricardo, ed. by Kurz, H. D., Salvadori, N., Cheltenham/Northampton 2015, pp. 482–489
Marglin, S., Was tun die Vorgesetzten? Ursprünge und Funktionen der Hierarchie in der kapitalistischen Produktion, in: Duve, F. (ed.), Technologie und Politik, vol. 8, Die Zukunft der Arbeit 1, Reinbeck bei Hamburg 1977, pp. 148–203
Marshall, A., Principles of Economics [1890], 8th ed., London 1952
Marshall, A., Handbuch der Volkswirtschaftslehre, Stuttgart/Berlin 1905
Marx, K., Letter to Engels, 30. April 1868, in: Marx and Engels, Collected Works, vol. 43, Letters 1868–1870, Electric Book, pp. 20–25, p. 23, https://www.koorosh-modaresi.com/MarxEngels/V43.pdf
Marx, K., The Poverty of Philosophy [1847], 3rd ed., Beijing 1977, https://foreignlanguages.press/wp-content/uploads/2021/11/C30-The-Poverty-of-Philosophy-1st-Printing.pdf
Marx, K., A Contribution to the Critique of Political Economy [1859], ed. by Dobb, M., Progress Publishers Moscow, https://archive.org/details/marxcontributioncritpolecon/page/2/mode/2up
Marx, K., Capital, vol. I, A Critical Analysis of Capitalist Production, [1867], Progress Publishers Moscow, https://archive.org/details/capitalvol1

Marx, K., Capital, vol. II, The Process of Circulation of Capital [1885], Engels, F. (ed.) Moscow 1956, https://archive.org/details/capitalvol2/page/376/mode/2up

Marx, K., Capital, vol. III, The Process of Capitalist Production as a Whole [1894], ed. by Engels, F., Moscow 1959, https://archive.org/details/capital-vol.-3/page/205/mode/2up

Marx, K., Das Kapital, vol. I, Der Produktionsprozess des Kapitals [1867], in: Marx Engels Werke, vol. 23, Berlin 1977

Marx, K., Das Kapital, vol. III, Der Gesamtprozeß der kapitalistischen Produktion [1894], ed. by Engels, F., in: Marx Engels Werke, vol. 25, Berlin 1976

Marx, K., Theories of Surplus Value, Part I, Moscow 1963, https://archive.org/details/marxtsvpart1

Marx, K., Theories of Surplus Value, Part II, London 1969, https://archive.org/details/marxtsvpart2

Marx, K., Theories of Surplus Value, Part III, Moscow 1971, http://www.marx2mao.com/PDFs/TSV-Part%203.pdf

Mathes, M. (ed.), Geschichte der Technik, Düsseldorf 1983

Mathias, P., Wer entfesselte Prometheus? Naturwissenschaft und technischer Wandel von 1600–1800, in: Braun, R. et al. (eds.), Industrielle Revolution, Köln 1972, pp. 121–138

Matschoss, C., Die Entwicklung der Dampfmaschine, 2 vols, Berlin 1908

Mauss, M., Die Gabe [1923/24], 2nd ed., Frankfurt a. M. 1984

McKenzie, R. B., Tullock, G., The New World of Economics – Explorations Into Human Experience, 2nd ed., Homewood 1978

Menger, C., Geld, in: Handwörterbuch der Staatswissenschaften, vol. IV, 3rd ed., Jena 1909, pp. 555–610, reprinted in: Collected Works (in German), vol. IV, London/Bradford 1936, p. 1–116, https://mises.org/library/book/collected-works-carl-menger-german-four-volumes

Menger, C., Principles of Economics [1871], Ludwig von Mises Institute, Auburn 2007, https://cdn.mises.org/principles_of_economics.pdf

Menger, C., Investigations into the Method of the Social Sciences with Special Reference to Economics [1883], ed. by Schneider, L., New York University Press 1985, https://mises.org/library/book/investigations-method-social-sciences

Mettelsiefen, B., Technischer Wandel und Beschäftigung, Rekonstruktion der Freisetzungs- und Kompensationsdebatten, Frankfurt a. M./New York 1981

Mill, J., Letter to Ricardo, August 23, 1815, in: The Works and Correspondence of David Ricardo, ed. by Sraffa, P., vol. VI, Cambridge 1973, pp. 250–254

Mill, J., Letter to Ricardo, December 22, 1815, in: The Works and Correspondence of David Ricardo, ed. by Sraffa, P., vol. VI, Cambridge 1973, pp. 337–341

Mill, J., Elements of Political Economy, London 1821

Mill, J. St., Essays on Some Unsettled Questions of Political Economy, London 1844, https://archive.org/details/in.ernet.dli.2015.275463

Mill, J. St., On the Definition of Political Economy; and on the Method of Investigation proper to it, in: Mill, J. St., Essays on Some Unsettled Questions of Political Economy, London 1844, pp. 120–164

Minsky, H. P., Minsky, H. P., John Maynard Keynes, London/Basingstoke 1975, http://digamo.free.fr/minsky75.pdf

Mirrlees, J. A., The Dynamic Nonsubstitution Theorem, in: The Review of Economic Studies, Vol. 36 (1969), pp. 67–76

Morel, J. et al, Soziologische Theorie, Abriß der Ansätze ihrer Hauptvertreter, München/Wien 1989

Morishima, M., Refutation of the Nonswitching Theorem, in: The Quarterly Journal of Economics, vol. 80 (1966), pp. 520–525

Morishima, M., Marx's Economics: A Dual Theory of Value and Growth, Cambridge 1973

Morishima, M., Marx in the Light of Modern Economic Theory, in: Econometrica, vol. 42 (1974), pp. 611–632

Morishima, M., Positive Profits With Negative Surplus Value – A Comment, in: The Economic Journal, vol. 86 (1976), pp. 599–603

Morishima, M., Catephores, G., Value, Exploitation and Growth, London 1978

Morishima, M., Seton, F., Aggregation in Leontief Matrices and the Labour Theory of Value, in: Econometrica, vol. 29 (1961), pp. 203–220
Napoleoni, C., Ricardo und Marx, ed. by Pennavaja, C., Frankfurt a. M. 1974
Nash, J., The bargaining problem, in: Econometrica, vol. 18 (1950), pp. 155–162
Needham, J., Science and Civilization in China, 7 vols, Cambridge 1954 ff. (reprint 1972 ff.)
Neumann, J. v., A Model of General Economic Equilibrium, in: The Review of Economic Studies, vol. 13 (1945/6), pp. 1–9, http://piketty.pse.ens.fr/files /VonNeumann1945.pdf
Neumann, J. v., Morgenstern, O., Theory of Games and Economic Behavior [1943], 2nd ed., London/Oxford 1953, https://archive.org/details/in.ernet. dli.2015.215284
Neumann, M., Theoretische Volkswirtschaftslehre II, Produktion, Nachfrage und Allokation, München 1982
Newman, P., Production of Commodities by Means of Commodities, in: Schwei-zerische Zeitschrift für Volkswirtschaft und Statistik, vol. 98 (1962), pp. 58–75
Newman, P., Letter to Sraffa, June 8, 1962, reprinted in: Bharadwaj, K., On the Maximum Numbers of Switches Between Two Production Systems, in: Schweizerische Zeitschrift für Volkswirtschaft und Statistik, vol. 106 (1970), pp. 409–429, pp. 426 f.
Nikaido, H., Introduction to Sets and Mappings in Modern Economics, Amsterdam/London 1970
Nobel, K., Außenhandelseffekte in linearen Wachstumsmodellen, Berlin 1982
North, D. C., Structure and Change in Economic History, New York/London 1981
Nowoshilow, W., Arbeitswerttheorie und Mathematik, in: Sowjetwissenschaften, 1965, pp. 1029–1047
Nutzinger, H. G., Concepts of Value in Linear Economic Models, in: Operations Research Verfahren, vol. 26 (1977), pp. 717–724
Nutzinger, H. G., Wolfstetter, E. (eds.), Die Marxsche Theorie und ihre Kritik, vol. I, Frankfurt a. M./New York 1974
Okishio, N., A Mathematical Note on Marxian Theorems, in: Weltwirtschaftliches Archiv, vol. 91 (1963) pp. 287–299
Ott, A. E., Wirtschaftstheorie, Eine erste Einführung, Göttingen 1989
Pareto, V., Manual of Political Economy [1927], London/Basingstoke 1971
Pasinetti, L., A Mathematical Formulation of the Ricardian System, in: The Review of Economic Studies, vol. 27 (1960), pp. 78–98
Pasinetti, L., On "non-substitution" in production models, in: Cambridge Journal of Economics, vol. 1 (1977), pp. 389–394
Pasinetti, L., The Unpalatability of the Reswitching of Techniques, in: Revue d'Economie Politique, vol. 89 (1979), pp. 637–642
Pasinetti, L., The Notion of Vertical Integration in Economic Analysis [1973], reprinted in: Pasinetti, L. (ed.), Essays on the Theory of Joint Production, London/Basingstoke 1980, pp. 16–43
Pasinetti, L., Introductory Note: Joint Production, in: Pasinetti, L. (ed.), Essays on the Theory of Joint Production, London/Basingstoke 1980, pp. xii–xvii
Pasinetti, L., Structural Change and Economic Growth, A theoretical essay on the dynamics of the wealth of nations, Cambridge et al. 1981
Pasinetti, L., Lectures on the Theory of Production, New York 1977
Patinkin, D., Money, Interest and Prices, 2nd ed., New York et al. 1965
Paulinyi, A., Die industrielle Revolution, in: Troitzsch, U., Weber, W. (eds.), Die Technik, Stuttgart 1987, pp. 232–281
Peter, H., Einführung in die politische Ökonomie, Stuttgart/Köln 1950
Petrovic, P., The deviation of production prices from labour values: some methodology and empirical evidence, in: Cambridge Journal of Economics, vol. 11 (1987), pp. 197–210
Petry, F., Der soziale Gehalt der Marxschen Werttheorie, Jena 1916. Partially reprinted in: Nutzinger, H. G., Wolfstetter, E. (eds.), Die Marxsche Theorie und ihre Kritik, vol. I, Frankfurt a. M./New York 1974, pp. 197–228
Pichler, E., Vollautomatische Güterproduktion, Marburg 1990
Pigou, A. C., The Economics of Welfare [1920], 4th ed., London 1952

Polanyi, K., The Great Transformation, New York/Toronto 1944
Polanyi, K., The Economy as Instituted Process, in: Polanyi, K., Arensberg, C. M., Pearson, H. W. (eds.), Trade and Market in the Early Empires, Glencoe 1957, pp. 243–270, https://archive.org/details/in.gov.ignca.36501/page/n5/mode/2up
Polanyi, K., Ökonomie und Gesellschaft, Frankfurt a. M. 1979 [15, 36, 50, 55, 63]
Polanyi, K., Arensberg, L. M., Pearson, H. W. (eds.), Trade and Market in the Early Empires, Glencoe 1957
Preiser, E., Wachstum und Einkommensverteilung, 3rd ed., Heidelberg 1970
Quesnay, F., Tableau économique [1759], ed. by Kuczynski, M., Berlin 1965 [303]
Quiggin, A. H., A Survey of Primitive Money, The Beginning of Currency [1949], New York/London 1970
Radwitzky, G., Bernholz, P. (eds.), Economic Imperialism, The Economic Approach Applied Outside the Field of Economics, New York 1987
Recktenwald, H. C., Würdigung des Werkes, in: Smith, A., Der Wohlstand der Nationen, Eine Untersuchung seiner Natur und seiner Ursachen, translated by Recktenwald, H. C., München 1978, pp. XV–LXXIX
Ricardo, D., Letter to Malthus, August 17, 1813, in: The Works and Correspondence of David Ricardo, ed. by Sraffa, P., vol. VI, Cambridge 1973, pp. 94–95
Ricardo, D., Letter to Trower, March 8, 1814, in: The Works and Correspondence of David Ricardo, ed. by Sraffa, P., vol. VI, Cambridge 1973, pp. 103–105
Ricardo, D., An Essay on the Influence of a low Price of Corn on the Profits of Stock [1815], in: The Works and Correspondence of David Ricardo, ed. by Sraffa, P., vol. IV, Cambridge 1951, pp. 9–41
Ricardo, D., Letter to Malthus, March 14, 1815, in: The Works and Correspondence of David Ricardo, ed. by Sraffa, P., vol. VI, Cambridge 1973, pp. 188–190
Ricardo, D., Letter to Malthus, March 17, 1815, in: The Works and Correspondence of David Ricardo, ed. by Sraffa, P., vol. VI, Cambridge 1973, pp. 192–194
Ricardo, D., Letter to Mill, August 30, 1815, in: The Works and Correspondence of David Ricardo, ed. by Sraffa, P., vol. VI, Cambridge 1973, pp. 261–265
Ricardo, D., Letter to Trower, October 29, 1815, in: The Works and Correspondence of David Ricardo, ed. by Sraffa, P., vol. VI, Cambridge 1973, pp. 314–317
Ricardo, D., Letter to Mill, December 30, 1815, in: The Works and Correspondence of David Ricardo, ed. by Sraffa, P., vol. VI, Cambridge 1973, pp. 347–349
Ricardo, D., Letter to Malthus, February 7, 1816, in: The Works and Correspondence of David Ricardo, ed. by Sraffa, P., vol. VII, Cambridge 1973, pp. 18–20
Ricardo, D., Letter to Mill, October 14, 1816, in: The Works and Correspondence of David Ricardo, ed. by Sraffa, P., vol. VII, Cambridge 1973, pp. 82–84
Ricardo, D., On the Principles of Political Economy and Taxation [1817], in: The Works and Correspondence of David Ricardo, ed. by Sraffa, P., vol. I, Cambridge 1970
Ricardo, D., Grundsätze der politischen Ökonomie und der Besteuerung, ed. by Neumark, F., Frankfurt a. M. 1972
Ricardo, D., Letter to Mill, December 28, 1818, in: The Works and Correspondence of David Ricardo, ed. by Sraffa, P., vol. VII, Cambridge 1973, pp. 376–383
Ricardo, D., Letter to McCulloch, May 2, 1820, in: The Works and Correspondence of David Ricardo, ed. by Sraffa, P., vol. VIII, Cambridge 1973, pp. 178–183
Ricardo, D., Letter to McCulloch, June 13, 1820, in: The Works and Correspondence of David Ricardo, ed. by Sraffa, P., vol. VIII, Cambridge 1973, pp. 191–197
Ricardo, D., Letter to Malthus, October 9, 1820, in: The Works and Correspondence of David Ricardo, ed. by Sraffa, P., vol. VIII, Cambridge 1973, pp. 276–280
Ricardo, D., Absolute Value and Exchangeable Value, in: The Works and Correspondence of David Ricardo, ed. by Sraffa, P., vol. IV, Cambridge 1951, pp. 361–412
Richter, R., Sichtweise und Fragestellung der Neuen Institutionenökonomik, in: Zeitschrift für Wirtschafts- und Sozialwissenschaften, vol. 110 (1990), pp. 571–591

Robbins, L., An Essay on the Nature and Significance of Economic Science (1932), 2nd ed., London 1952
Robertson, D. H., Money, London/Cambridge 1922, https://archive.org/details/cu31924013818145/page/n7/mode/2up?q=Uap
Robinson, J., The Production Function and the Theory of Capital, in: The Review of Economic Studies, vol. 21 (1953/54), pp. 81–106
Robinson, J., Ideology and Analysis, again in: The Subtle Anatomy of Capitalism, ed. by Schwartz, J., Santa Monica 1977, pp. 364–370
Robinson, J., Introduction, in: Walsh, V., Gram, H., Classical and Neoclassical Theories of General Equilibrium New York/Oxford 1980, pp. xi–xvi
Roemer, J. E., Analytical Foundations of Marxian Economic Theory, Cambridge 1981
Roemer, J. E., Value, Exploitation and Class, Chur et al. 1986
Roncaglia, A., Sraffa and the Theory of Prices, Chichester et al. 1978
Rosner, P., Arbeit und Reichtum, Ein Beitrag zur Geschichte ökonomischer Theorie, Frankfurt a. M./New York 1982
Rothschild, K. W., Wie nützlich ist der Homo Oeconomicus? Bemerkungen zu einem Aufsatz von Bruno S. Frey und Wolfgang Stroebe, in: Zeitschrift für die gesamte Staatswissenschaft, vol. 137 (1981), pp. 289–292
Salvadori, N., Existence of Cost-Minimizing Systems within the Sraffa Framework, in: Zeitschrift für Nationalökonomie, vol. 42 (1982), pp. 281–298
Salvadori, N., Switching in Methods of Production and Joint Production, in: The Manchester School, vol. 53 (1985), pp. 156–178
Salvadori, N., Signorino, R., From stationery state to endogenous growth: international trade in the mathematical formulation of the Ricardian system, in: Cambridge Journal of Economics, vol. 40 (2016), pp. 895–912
Samuelson, P. A., Economics, New York 1948
Samuelson, P. A., Abstract of a Theorem Concerning Substitutability in Open Leontief Models, in: Koopmans, T. C. (ed.), Activity Analysis of Production and Allocation, New York/London/Sydney 1951, pp. 142–146
Samuelson, P. A., A New Theorem on Nonsubstitution, in: Hegeland, H. (ed.), Money, Growth and Methodology and Other Essays in Economics in Honor of Johan Åkerman, Lund 1961, pp. 407–423
Samuelson, P. A., The Way of an Economist [1969], reprinted in: Merton, R. C. (ed.), The Collected Scientific Papers of Paul A. Samuelson, vol. III, Cambridge (USA)/London 1991, pp. 675–685
Samuelson, P. A., Understanding the Marxian Notion of Exploitation: A Summary of the So-Called Transformation Problem Between Marxian Values and Competitive Prices, in: Journal of Economic Literature, vol. 9 (1971), pp. 399–431
Samuelson, P. A., Maximum Principles in Analytical Economics, in: The American Economic Review, vol 62 (1972), pp. 249–262
Samuelson, P. A., The Canonical Classical Model of Political Economy, in: Journal of Economic Literature, vol. 16 (1978), pp. 1415–1434
Samuelson, P. A., Foundations of Economic Analysis [1947], Cambridge (Mass.)/London 1983
Samuelson, P. A., Volkswirtschaftslehre, vol. I, 7th ed., Köln 1981
Sato, K., The Neoclassical Postulates and the Technology Frontier in Capital Theory, in: The Quarterly Journal of Economics, vol. 88 (1974), pp. 353–384
Schaaff, H., Kritik der eindimensionalen Wirtschaftstheorie: Zur Begründung einer ökologischen Glücksökonomie, Thun/Frankfurt a. M. 1991
Schanetzky, T., Kanonen statt Butter, Wirtschaft und Konsum im Dritten Reich, München 2015
Schefold, B., Different Forms of Technical Progress, in: The Economic Journal, vol. 86 (1976), pp. 806–819
Schefold, B., Capital, Growth, and Definitions of Technical Progress, in: Kyklos, vol. 32 (1979), pp. 236–250

Schefold, B., Fixed Capital as a Joint Product and the Analysis of Accumulation with Different Forms of Technical Progress, in: Pasinetti, L. (ed.), Essays on the Theory of Joint Production, London/Basingstoke 1980, pp. 138–217

Schefold, B., Von Neumann and Sraffa: Mathematical Equivalence and Conceptual Difference, in: The Economic Journal, vol. 90 (1980), pp. 140–156

Schefold, B., Nachfrage und Zufuhr in der klassischen Ökonomie, in: Neumark, F. (ed.), Studien zur Entwicklung der ökonomischen Theorie I, Berlin 1981, pp. 53–91

Schefold, B., Sraffas Theorie der Kuppelproduktion, in: Zeitschrift für Wirtschafts- und Sozialwissenschaften, vol. 103 (1983), pp. 315–340

Schefold, B., Cambridge Price Theory: Special Model or General Theory of Value?, in: The American Economic Review, Vol. 75 (1985), pp. 140–145

Schefold, B., Sraffa and Applied Economics: Joint Production, in: Political Economy, vol. 1 (1985), pp. 17–40

Schefold, B., The Standard Commodity as a Tool of Economic Analysis: A Comment on Flaschel, in: Journal of Institutional and Theoretical Economics, vol. 142 (1986), pp. 603–622

Schefold, B., Über Änderungen in der Zusammensetzung des Endprodukts, in: Postkeynesianismus, Ökonomische Theorie in der Tradition von Keynes, Kalecki und Sraffa, Marburg 1987, pp. 119–164

Schefold, B., (with the colaboration of Weihrauch, P.), Ricardo – Marshall – Sraffa, Ökonomische Theorie als Geschichte der Ricardo-Interpretation, in: das wirtschaftsstudium (wisu), vol. 16. (1987), pp. 383–387 and pp. 462–467

Schefold, B., The dominant technique in joint production systems, in: Cambridge Journal of Economics, vol. 12 (1988), pp. 97–123

Schefold, B., Mr Sraffa on Joint Production and Other Essays, London 1989

Schilcher, R., Geldfunktionen und Buchgeldschöpfung, 2nd ed., Berlin 1973

Schlicht, E., Einleitung, in: Schlicht, E. (ed.), Einführung in die Verteilungstheorie, Reinbek bei Hamburg 1976, pp. 12–64

Schmölders, G., Geldpolitik, 2nd ed., Tübingen/Zürich 1968

Schneider, D., Geschichte betriebswirtschaftlicher Theorie, München/Wien 1981

Schneider, D., Allgemeine Betriebswirtschaftslehre, München/Wien 1985

Schneider, E., Einführung in die Wirtschaftstheorie, I. Teil, Theorie des Wirtschaftskreislaufs, 14th ed., Tübingen 1969

Schneider, E., Einführung in die Wirtschaftstheorie, II. Teil, Wirtschaftspläne und wirtschaftliches Gleichgewicht in der Verkehrswirtschaft, 13th ed., Tübingen 1972

Schneider, E., Einführung in die Wirtschaftstheorie, IV. Teil, Ausgewählte Kapitel der Geschichte der Wirtschaftstheorie, vol. I, Tübingen 1962

Schneider, J., Der Beitrag der Arbeitswertlehre zur Theorie der kapitalistischen Warenproduktion, Frankfurt a. M./New York 1980

Schneider, J., Die Fortsetzung eines Irrwegs, Replik, in: Arbeit für alle ist möglich, ed. by Matzner, E., Kregel, J., Roncaglia, A., Berlin 1987, pp. 35–38

Schneider, O., Muschelgeld-Studien, Dresden 1905

Schopenhauer, A., Parerga and Paralipomena [1851], Short Philosophical Essays, vol. II, Oxford 1974

Schumpeter, J. A., Wesen und Hauptinhalt der theoretischen Nationalökonomie [1908], reprint Berlin 1970

Schumpeter, J. A., Theorie der wirtschaftlichen Entwicklung [1912], 6th ed., Berlin 1964

Schumpeter, J. A., The Theory of Economic Development, Cambridge (Mass.) 1949, https://archive.org/details/theoryofeconomic0000schu/page/n7/mode/2up

Schumpeter, J. A., History of Economic Analysis, ed. by Schumpeter, E. B., London 1954, https://archive.org/details/dli.ernet.505700/page/n3/mode/2up

Schütte, F., Die ökonomischen Studien von V. K. Dmitriev, https://nbn-resolving.org/urn:nbn:de:swb:ch1-200600220 (2002)

Shaikh, A., Neo-Ricardian Economics, A Wealth of Algebra, A Poverty of Theory, in: Review of Radical Political Economics, vol. 14 (1982), pp. 67–83
Siegenthaler, H., Industrielle Revolution, in: Handwörterbuch der Wirtschaftswissenschaft, vol. IV, Stuttgart/Tübingen/Göttigen 1978, pp. 142–159
Simmel, G., Philosophie des Geldes [1907], 5th ed., München/Leipzig 1930
Singer, K., Oikonomia: An Inquiry into Beginnings of Economic Thought and Language, in: Kyklos, vol. 11 (1958), pp. 29–57
Skourtos, M., „Der Neoricardianismus", V. K. Dmitriev und die Kontinuität in der klassischen Tradition, Pfaffenweiler 1985
Smith, A., An Inquiry into the Nature and Causes of the Wealth of Nations [1776], vol. I, Indianapolis 1981
Solow, R. M., Review of "Capital and Time" by J. Hicks, in: The Economic Journal, vol. 84 (1974), pp. 189–192
Sombart, W., Der moderne Kapitalismus [1902], vol. I, 2nd ed., München/Leipzig 1916
Sombart, W., Liebe, Luxus und Kapitalismus, Über die Entstehung der modernen Welt aus dem Geist der Verschwendung [1922], Berlin (no date given)
Sraffa, P., An Alleged Correction of Ricardo, in: The Quarterly Journal of Economics, vol. 44 (1930), pp. 539–544
Sraffa, P., Introduction, in: The Works and Correspondence of David Ricardo, ed. by Sraffa, P., vol. I, Cambridge 1951, pp. xiii–lxii
Sraffa, P., Note on 'Essay on Profits', in: The Works and Correspondence of David Ricardo, ed. by Sraffa, P., vol. IV, Cambridge 1951, pp. 1–8
Sraffa, P., Note on Fragments on Torrens, in: The Works and Correspondence of David Ricardo, ed. by Sraffa, P., vol. IV, Cambridge 1951, pp. 305–308
Sraffa, P., Notes on "looms", in: Papers of Piero Sraffa, Trinity College, Cambridge, SRAF/D/3/12/5, https://archives.trin.cam.ac.uk/index.php/notes-on-looms
Sraffa, P., Production of Commodities by Means of Commodities, Prelude to a Critique of Economic Theory, Cambridge 1960, http://pombo.free.fr/sraffa60.pdf
Sraffa, P., Letter to Newman, June 4, 1962, reprinted in: Bharadwaj, K., On the Maximum Numbers of Switches Between Two Production Systems, in: Schweizerische Zeitschrift für Volkswirtschaft und Statistik, vol. 106 (1970), pp. 409–429, pp. 425 f.
Sraffa, P., Letter to Newman, June 19, 1962, reprinted in: Bharadwaj, K., On the Maximum Numbers of Switches Between Two Production Systems, in: Schweizerische Zeitschrift für Volkswirtschaft und Statistik, vol. 106 (1970), pp. 409–429, pp. 427 f.
Sraffa, P., Warenproduktion mittels Waren, Frankfurt a. M., 1976
Stamatis, G., Zur Entmythologisierung Sraffas, in: Staatsgrenzen, Argument-Sonderband AS 89, Berlin 1982, pp. 168–182
Stamatis, G., Sraffa und sein Verhältnis zu Ricardo und Marx, Göttingen 1984
Stanger, M., Krisentendenzen der Kapitalakkumulation, Berlin 1988
Starbatty, J., Die englischen Klassiker der Nationalökonomie, Lehre und Wirkung, Darmstadt 1985
Steedman, I., Positive Profits With Negative Surplus Value, in: The Economic Journal, Vol. 85 (1975), pp. 114–123
Steedman, I., Positive Profits With Negative Surplus Value: A Reply, in: The Economic Journal, Vol. 86 (1976), pp. 604–608
Steedman, I., Positive Profits With Negative Surplus Value: A Reply to Wolfstetter, in: The Economic Journal, Vol. 86 (1976), pp. 873–876
Steedman, I., Marx after Sraffa, London 1977
Steedman, I., Joint Production and the Wage-Rent Frontier, in: The Economic Journal, vol. 92 (1982), pp. 377–385
Steedman, I., Joint Production and Technical Progress, in: Political Economy, vol. 1 (1985), pp. 41–52
Steedman, I., Introduction, in: Steedman, I. (ed.), Sraffian Economics II, Aldershot 1988, pp. 1–7

Stigler, G. J., Ricardo and the 93 % Labour Theory of Value, in: The American Economic Review, vol. 48 (1958), p. 357–367
Stiglitz, J. E., Non-Substitution Theorems With Durable Capital Goods, in: The Review of Economic Studies, vol. 37 (1970), pp. 543–553
Stobbe, A., Volkswirtschaftslehre II, Mikroökonomik, Berlin u. a. 1983
Stollberg, G., Zur Geschichte des Begriffs „Politische Ökonomie", in: Jahrbücher für Nationalökonomie und Statistik, vol. 192 (1977/78), pp. 1–35
Stoltenberg, H. L., Zur Geschichte des Wortes Wirtschaft, in: Jahrbücher für Nationalökonomie und Statistik, vol. 148 (1938), pp. 555–561
Streißler, E., Adam Smith – Der Adam oder nur Wachstum? Paradoxien einer wissenschaftlichen Revolution, in: Neumark, F. (ed.), Studien zur Entwicklung der ökonomischen Theorie I, Berlin 1980, pp. 9–52
Takayama, A., Mathematical Economics, 2nd ed., Cambridge et al. 1985
Thünen, J. H. v., Der isolierte Staat in Beziehung auf Landwirtschaft und Nationalökonomie [1842], 3rd ed., Berlin 1875, ed. by Breuer, W., Gerhardt, E., Darmstadt 1966
Troitzsch, U., Ansätze technologischen Denkens bei den Kameralisten des 17. und 18. Jahrhunderts, Berlin 1966
Trower, H., Letter to Ricardo, September 21, 1815, in: The Works and Correspondence of David Ricardo, ed. by Sraffa, P., vol. VI, Cambridge 1973, pp. 278–281
Tucker, G. S. L., The Origin of Ricardo's Theory of Profits, in: Economica, vol. 21 (1954), pp. 320–331
Varri, P., Prices, Rate of Profit and Life of Machines in Sraffa's Fixed-Capital Model, in: Pasinetti, L. (ed.), Essays on the Theory of Joint Production, London/Basingstoke 1980, pp. 55–87
Veblen, Th., The Theory of the Leisure Class, New York/London 1899, http: //files.libertyfund.org/files/1657/1291_Bk.pdf
Veit, O., Reale Theorie des Geldes, Tübingen 1966
Vogel, G., Die Ökonomik des Xenophon, eine Vorarbeit für die Geschichte der griechischen Ökonomik, Erlangen 1895
Vogt, W., Die Angst des kritischen Ökonomen vor der Neoklassik, in: Hickel, R. (ed.), Radikale Neoklassik, Opladen 1986, pp. 103–113
Wagner, A., Mikroökonomik, 5th ed., Marburg 2009
Walras, L., Elements of Pure Economics, [1926], ed. by Jaffé, W., 2nd ed., Homewood 1965
Webb, S., Webb, B., The History of Trade Unionism, London 1920, https://www.gutenberg.org/ebooks/66887
Weber, M., The Protestant Ethic and the Spirit of Capitalism [1904/05], New York/London 1930, https://archive.org/details/protestantethics00webe/page/n17/mode/2up
Weber, M., Wirtschaftsgeschichte, München/Leipzig 1923
Weber, M., Critical Studies in the Logic of the Cultural Sciences, A Critique of Eduard Meyer's Methodological View [1906], in: Weber, M., On the Methodology of the Social Sciences, ed. by Shils, E. A., Finch, H. A., Illinois 1949, pp. 113–188, https://archive.org/details/maxweberonmethod00webe
Weitzman, M., On Choosing an Optimal Technology, in: Management Science, vol. 19 (1967), pp. 413-428
Weitzmann, M. L., Increasing Returns and the Foundations of Unemployment Theory: Rejoinder, in: The Economic Journal, vol. 98 (1988), pp. 172–174
Weizsäcker, C. C. v., Steady State Capital Theory, Berlin/Heidelberg/New York 1971
Weizsäcker, C. C. v., On Ricardo and Marx, in: Paul Samuelson and Modern Economic Theory, ed. by Brown, E. C., Solow, R. M., New York et al. 1983, pp. 203–210
Whately, R., Introductory Lectures on Political Economy, London 1831
Wicksell, K., Lectures on Political Economy [1913], vol. I, London 1935, https://cdn.mises.org/Lectures%20on%20Political%20Economy%20-%20Volume%20I%20General%20Theory_2.pdf
Wiese, L. v., Mill, John Stuart, in: Handwörterbuch der Staatswissenschaften, vol. VII, Stuttgart/Tübingen/Göttingen 1961, pp. 343–346

Wieser, F. v., Geld (Theorie des Geldes), in: Handwörterbuch der Staatswissenschaften, vol. IV, 4th ed., Jena 1927, pp. 681–717
Wilken, F., Die Phänomenologie des Geldwertbewußtseins, in: Archiv für Sozial wissenschaft und Sozialpolitik, vol. 56 (1926), pp. 417–469
Williamson, O. E., The Economic Institutions of Capitalism, New York/London 1985
Winch, D., Das Aufkommen der Volkswirtschaftslehre als Wissenschaft 1750–1870, in: Cipolla, C. M., Borchardt, K. (eds.), Europäische Wirtschaftsgeschichte, vol. III, Die Industrielle Revolution, Stuttgart/New York 1985, pp. 333–377
Winternitz, J., Values and Prices: A Solution of the So-Called Transformation Problem, in: The Economic Journal, vol. 58 (1948), pp. 276–280
Wöhe, G., Einführung in die Allgemeine Betriebswirtschaftslehre, 21st ed., München 2002
Wolfstetter, E., Wert, Mehrwert und Produktionspreis, in: Jahrbuch für Sozialwissenschaft, vol. 24 (1973), pp. 117–144
Wolfstetter, E., Positive Profits With Negative Surplus Value: A Comment, in: The Economic Journal, vol. 86 (1976), pp. 864–872
Wolfstetter, E., Wert, Profitrate und Beschäftigung, Frankfurt a. M. 1977
Woll, A., Volkswirtschaftslehre, 15th ed., München 2007
World Trade Organization, The case for open trade, https://www.wto.org/english/thewto_e/whatis_e/tif_e/fact3_e.htm
Xenophon, Die sokratischen Schriften, Stuttgart 1956
Xenophon, Ökonomische Schriften, Berlin 1992
Zaghini, E., On Non-Basic Commodities, in: Schweizerische Zeitschrift für Volkswirtschaft und Statistik, vol. 103 (1967), pp. 257–266
Zinn, K. G., Wirtschaft und Wissenschaftstheorie, Herne/Berlin 1976
Zinn, K. G., Politische Ökonomie, Apologien und Kritiken des Kapitalismus, Opladen 1987
Zinn, K. G., Kanonen und Pest, Über die Ursprünge der Neuzeit im 14. und 15. Jahrhundert, Opladen 1989
Zorn, W., Wirtschaftsgeschichte, in: Handwörterbuch der Wirtschaftswissenschaft, vol. IX, Stuttgart/Tübingen/Göttingen 1980, pp. 55–82

Index

F. Helmedag, *Production of Commodities by Means of Labour*, Springer Studies in Alternative Economics, https://doi.org/10.1007/978-3-032-01457-3

MIX
Papier aus verantwortungsvollen Quellen
Paper from responsible sources
FSC® C105338

If you have any concerns about our products,
you can contact us on
ProductSafety@springernature.com

In case Publisher is established outside the EU,
the EU authorized representative is:
Springer Nature Customer Service Center GmbH
Europaplatz 3, 69115 Heidelberg, Germany

Printed by Libri Plureos GmbH
in Hamburg, Germany